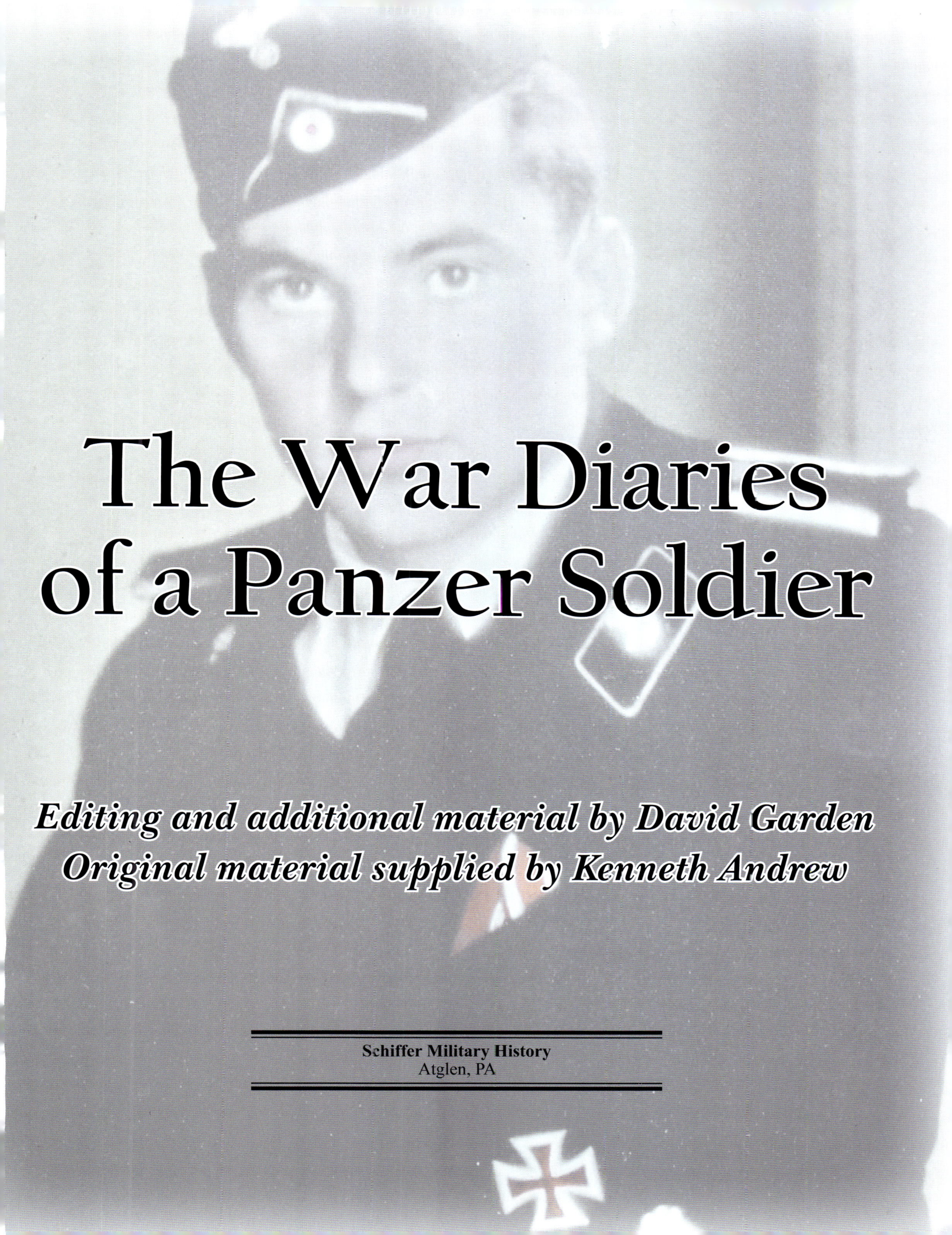

The War Diaries of a Panzer Soldier

Editing and additional material by David Garden
Original material supplied by Kenneth Andrew

Schiffer Military History
Atglen, PA

Many thanks to Steffi Schindler, Rosemary Laird, and Eileen for translation. Steffi recognised the first four diaries were written in Sutterlin. Rosemary did the almost impossible and read the Sutterlin handwriting. Eileen carried out the bulk of the translation, including what was written on photographs.

This book is dedicated to all young men who have to go to war to further their nations' aims.

Erich in Panzer uniform with rank of *Unterofficier.* Awards are the Iron Cross 1st class, Iron Cross 2nd Class, Panzer Assault Badge, Black Wounds Badge, and Winter Medal 1941.

Title Page:
Formal colourised portrait of Erich in black Panzer uniform with rank of *Unterofficier*. Awards are the Iron Cross 1st class, Iron Cross 2nd Class ribbon, Panzer Assault Badge, Black Wounds Badge, and Winter Medal 1941 ribbon.

Book Design by Mark David Bowyer

Library of Congress Control Number: 2010926874

Printed in China
ISBN: 978-0-7643-3514-3

We are interested in hearing from authors with book ideas on related topics.

Published by Schiffer Publishing Ltd.
4880 Lower Valley Road
Atglen, PA 19310
Phone: (610) 593-1777
FAX: (610) 593-2002
E-mail: Info@schifferbooks.com.
Visit our web site at: www.schifferbooks.com
Please write for a free catalog.
This book may be purchased from the publisher.
Please include $5.00 postage.
Try your bookstore first.

In Europe, Schiffer books are distributed by:
Bushwood Books
6 Marksbury Avenue
Kew Gardens
Surrey TW9 4JF, England
Phone: 44 (0) 20 8392-8585
FAX: 44 (0) 20 8392-9876
E-mail: Info@bushwoodbooks.co.uk.
Visit our website at: www.bushwoodbooks.co.uk
Free postage in the UK. Europe: air mail at cost.
Try your bookstore first.

Contents

Introduction

Erich Totsauer (later Hager) was born in Graz, Styria, in Austria, on 27 July 1922. It seems he changed his name as Totsauer in German means "sour death," and the woman he wanted to marry did not approve of changing her surname to such a morbid sounding one! As he changed his name mid-war it is possible that, being a member of a tank crew, the other crewmen thought this name could be unlucky. However, his daughter states that his parents only married later in the war.

Erich was not a Nazi, but after Austria was annexed in the *Anschluss* he joined the Hitler Youth (HJ) at age 15, serving in Schar Number 5 in St Georgen and rising to the rank of *Scharführer*. However he was arrested and charged with the crime of attending meetings of societies banned by the Nazis. This had consequences to his career in the Hitler Youth.

Before the war Erich learned the trade of a butcher, probably from his father, who was also a butcher and had his own business in St. Georgen, near Linz. Erich's main hobby was river trout fishing, and he later claimed he could catch trout by hand.

Erich had two brothers, Helmut and Hermann, who were born after the war because his father had also been in war service. This made them much younger than Erich!

When war broke out Erich joined the Army. He trained with 7. *Kompanie II Batailon Infantrie-Ersatz Batallion* 462 (7th Company, second battalion, infantry replacement battalion 462). This was the replacement training division of the 187th Division that provided basic training for new recruits. It was based in Linz, Austria. Erich's identity disc was marked -759-7./II. I. E. B. 462. His first service was in the 27th Infantry Division. He then transferred to the *Panzerwaffe* (tank troops), training with 6.*Kompanie Panzer-Ersatz-Abteilung* 4 (6th Company tank replacement unit 4), and his identity disc was marked -59-6. Pz. Ers. Abt. 4. Erich joined Panzer Regiment 39 of the 17th Panzer Division and fought with it throughout the war.

Erich's speciality was that of a radio operator, and as such he formed part of the crew of the Company command tank. Most of his service was in the sixth company of Panzer Regiment 39, but Erich later served in the *VersorgungsKompanie* II. Pz.Regt.39 (supply company of second battalion Panzer Regiment 39.

Erich reached the rank of *Unteroffizier* and was awarded:

The *Medaille Winterschlacht im Osten* 1941/42 (Ostmedaille) - Winter War medal,
Panzerkampfabzeichen (Panzerassault badge in silver),
Eiserne Kreuz 2 Klasse EK II (Iron cross second class),
Eiserne Kreuz 1 Klasse EK1 (Iron Cross 1st Class),
Verwundetenabzeichen in *Schwarz* (Wound Badge in black)
Panzerkampfabzeichen in *Silber* an 50 *Einsatztagen* (the very rare level three Panzer Assault badge for 50 armoured attacks)

Erich served with 17.Panzer Division throughout the war on the Eastern Front from 22 July 1941 - the start of operation "Barbarossa" - up to his capture by the Russians in early 1945.Throughout this time Erich kept a written record of his day to day experiences in a series of 11 handwritten diaries. These were a mixture of German pocket diaries, notebooks, and Russian school notebooks. In addition, Erich was a keen photographer and backed up his notes with many photos of the men and machines he served with.

There are gaps in Erich's diaries, and we assume that he lost some notebooks in combat, perhaps left in a knocked out tank. The first four notebooks are written in Sutterlin script. Erich dropped this in 1942 when, like the rest of Germany, he changed to the modern German alphabet. Some of the text is very small and/or faint. This made reading difficult.

Amazingly, he managed to save most of these with other notes and his award certificates, and they survived until his death in 2003. To go along with his award certificates Erich's *Ostmedaille* and EKII survived. It is extremely rare for the certificates to survive with the medal that was awarded with them. Erich's other awards, which were worn on his tunic, were taken by the Russians at the time of his capture.

The written diaries provide an amazing record of a German tank soldier on the Eastern Front who was involved at the "sharp end" in the bitter fighting and some of the major battles of World War II. Erich wrote an account of what he experienced every day, even when he was on leave. Very few days have been left blank.

Spelling of the town and people names are his. Erich gives routes of march as lists of place names, and this is the same format as Divisional or Company orders. German ranks and titles have been kept in the text to give a period flavour to the diaries.

We have left the diary entries as Erich wrote them. Occasionally we have tidied up the language only to improve the sense of what was written. Remember, they would often be made under difficult conditions and after combat, which would have left Erich in an emotionally charged state. Place names were always entered in capital letters and we have retained this in our text. We have only added small notes in the diaries to provide explanation. These we have put in brackets to show they are not Erich's writings.

Erich often refers to an individual whom he calls "Gef." We believe this to be his Company commander due to the respect he gives him and the command function of the individual. We therefore do not believe it refers to the non-commissioned rank of *Gefreiter*. To distinguish between the *Gefreiter* ranks and the term "Gef" we have added an "r" to the abbreviation of *Gefreiter*, ie "Gefr." in the text. Erich changed his abbreviations as he wrote the diaries, eg T34 became T-34, and PAK became PaK or Fak. We have kept these as written.

All the photographs are Erich's own. We realise that many have been damaged by storage and some are not of great technical quality. However, they are important historical artefacts, as few photos were taken of 17.Panzer Division and operations such as "Winter Storm," the attempted relief of Stalingrad. In that they are pretty unique. The photographs illustrate Erich's story.

German Ranks

Enlisted men

Schütze, Panzerschütze	Private
Oberschütze	Senior Private
Gefreiter (Gef.)	Lance-corporal
Obergefreiter (OberGef.)	Corporal
Stabsgefreiter (StabsGef.)	Senior staff Corporal

Non-commissioned officers

Unteroffizer (Uffz.)	Lance-sergeant
UnterFeldwebel (Unterfeld.)	Sergeant
Feldwebel (Feld.)	Company sergeant-major
OberFeldwebel (Oberfeld.)	Battalion sergeant-major
HauptFeldwebel (Hauptfeld.)	Regimental sergeant-major
StabsFeldwebel (Stabsfeld.)	Staff sergeant-major

Officers

Leutnant (Ltn.)	Second Lieutenant
Oberleutnant (OberLtn.)	First Lieutenant
Hauptmann (Hauptn.)	Captain
Major	Major
Oberstleutnant (ObsLtn.)	Lieutenant Colonel
Oberst	*Colonel*

Generals

Generalmajor	Major General
Generalleutnant	Lieutenant-general
General der Panzertruppen	General
Generaloberst	Colonel-general
Generalfeldmarschall	General field-marshal

Chapter 1

Pre-war Civilian and *Reichsarbeitsdienst*, RAD (State Labour Service.)

Erich left no diary of this but we have these photographs.

A young Erich.

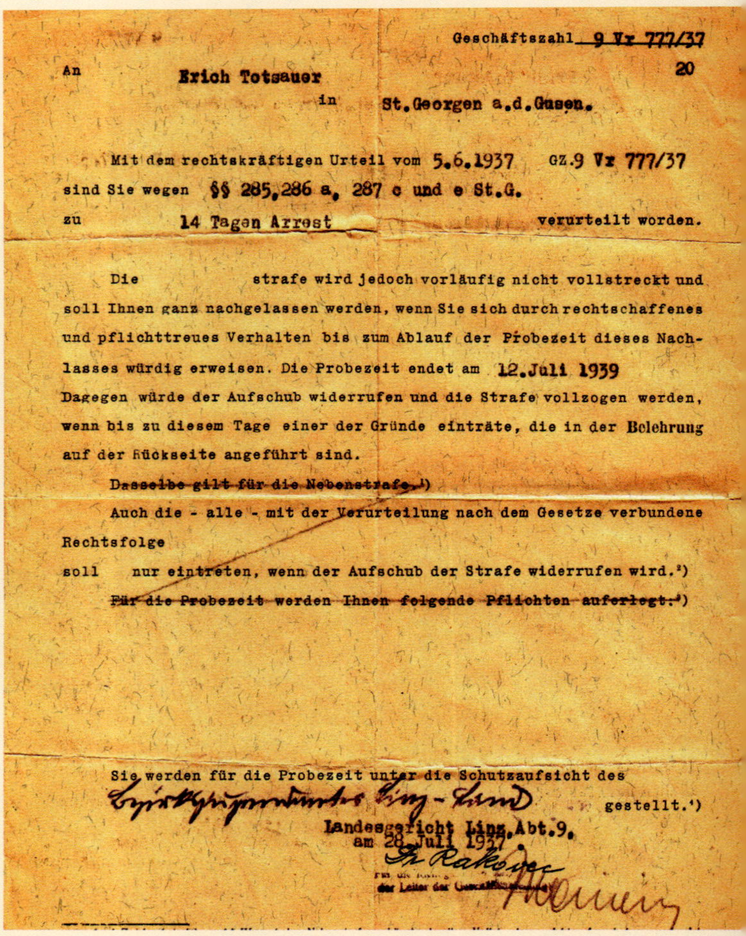

Geschäftszahl 9 Vr 777/37 20

An Erich Totsauer in St.Georgen a.d.Gusen.

Mit dem rechtskräftigen Urteil vom 5.6.1937 GZ.9 Vr 777/37 sind Sie wegen §§ 285,286 a, 287 c und e St.G. zu 14 Tagen Arrest verurteilt worden.

Die strafe wird jedoch vorläufig nicht vollstreckt und soll Ihnen ganz nachgelassen werden, wenn Sie sich durch rechtschaffenes und pflichttreues Verhalten bis zum Ablauf der Probezeit dieses Nachlasses würdig erweisen. Die Probezeit endet am 12.Juli 1939 Dagegen würde der Aufschub widerrufen und die Strafe vollzogen werden, wenn bis zu diesem Tage einer der Gründe einträte, die in der Belehrung auf der Rückseite angeführt sind.

~~Dasselbe gilt für die Nebenstrafe.~~[1])

Auch die - alle - mit der Verurteilung nach dem Gesetze verbundene Rechtsfolge soll nur eintreten, wenn der Aufschub der Strafe widerrufen wird.[1])

~~Für die Probezeit werden Ihnen folgende Pflichten auferlegt:~~[1])

Sie werden für die Probezeit unter die Schutzaufsicht des Bezirksjugendamtes Linz-Land gestellt.[1])

Landesgericht Linz,Abt.9, am 28.Juli 1937.

Letter sentencing Erich to 14 days arrest for attending meetings of an organisation not considered legal by the authorities. Erich at this time was 15, a member of the Hitler Youth (HJ), and at middle school. The Nazis wanted the HJ to be the only youth organisation. Many German young people continued to have meetings of other organisations in secret. Erich was bound over and did not need to serve his sentence.

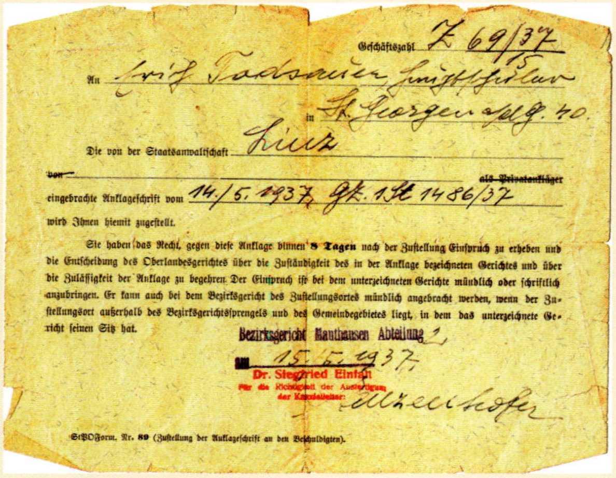

Geschäftszahl Z 69/37

An Erich Todsauer

in St. Georgen a/G. 40.

Die von der Staatsanwaltschaft Linz ~~von~~ ~~als Privatankläger~~ eingebrachte Anklageschrift vom 14./5.1937, Gz. 1 St 1486/37 wird Ihnen hiemit zugestellt.

Sie haben das Recht, gegen diese Anklage binnen **8 Tagen** nach der Zustellung Einspruch zu erheben und die Entscheidung des Oberlandesgerichtes über die Zuständigkeit des in der Anklage bezeichneten Gerichtes und über die Zulässigkeit der Anklage zu begehren. Der Einspruch ist bei dem unterzeichneten Gerichte mündlich oder schriftlich anzubringen. Er kann auch bei dem Bezirksgericht des Zustellungsortes mündlich angebracht werden, wenn der Zustellungsort außerhalb des Bezirksgerichtssprengels und des Gemeindegebietes liegt, in dem das unterzeichnete Gericht seinen Sitz hat.

Bezirksgericht Mauthausen Abteilung 1, am 15.5.1937.

Dr. Siegfried Einfalt

StPOForm. Nr. 89 (Zustellung der Anklageschrift an den Beschuldigten).

Mauthausen district summons letter.

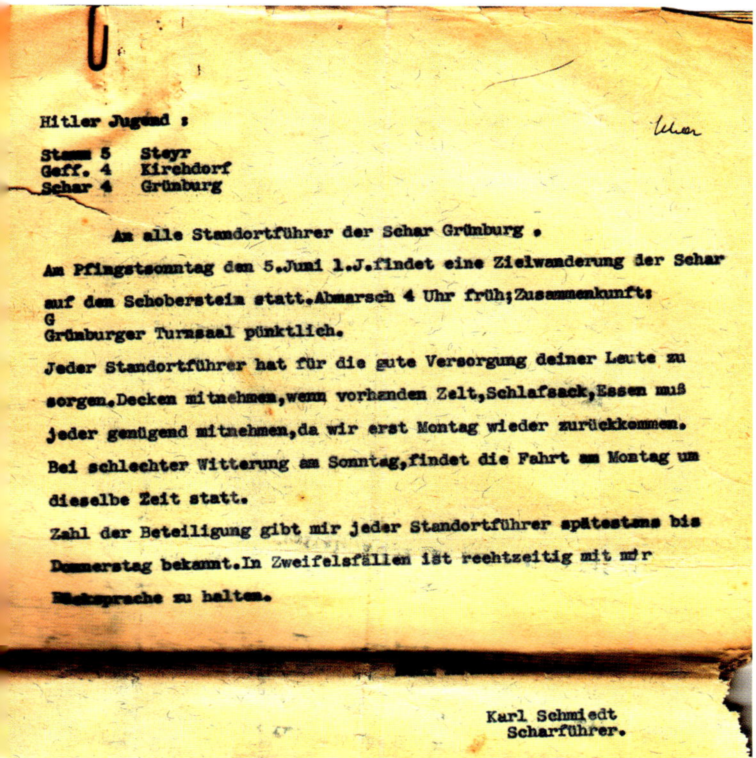

Hitler Jugend :

Stamm 5 Steyr
Geff. 4 Kirchdorf
Schar 4 Grünburg

An alle Standortführer der Schar Grünburg .

Am Pfingstsonntag den 5.Juni l.J.findet eine Zielwanderung der Schar auf den Schoberstein statt.Abmarsch 4 Uhr früh;Zusammenkunft: G Grünburger Turnsaal pünktlich.

Jeder Standortführer hat für die gute Versorgung deiner Leute zu sorgen.Decken mitnehmen,wenn vorhanden Zelt,Schlafsack,Essen muß jeder genügend mitnehmen,da wir erst Montag wieder zurückkommen.

Bei schlechter Witterung am Sonntag,findet die Fahrt am Montag um dieselbe Zeit statt.

Zahl der Beteiligung gibt mir jeder Standortführer spätestens bis Donnerstag bekannt.In Zweifelsfällen ist rechtzeitig mit mir Rücksprache zu halten.

Karl Schmiedt
Scharführer.

Hitler Jugend letter. Call up and instructions for camp.

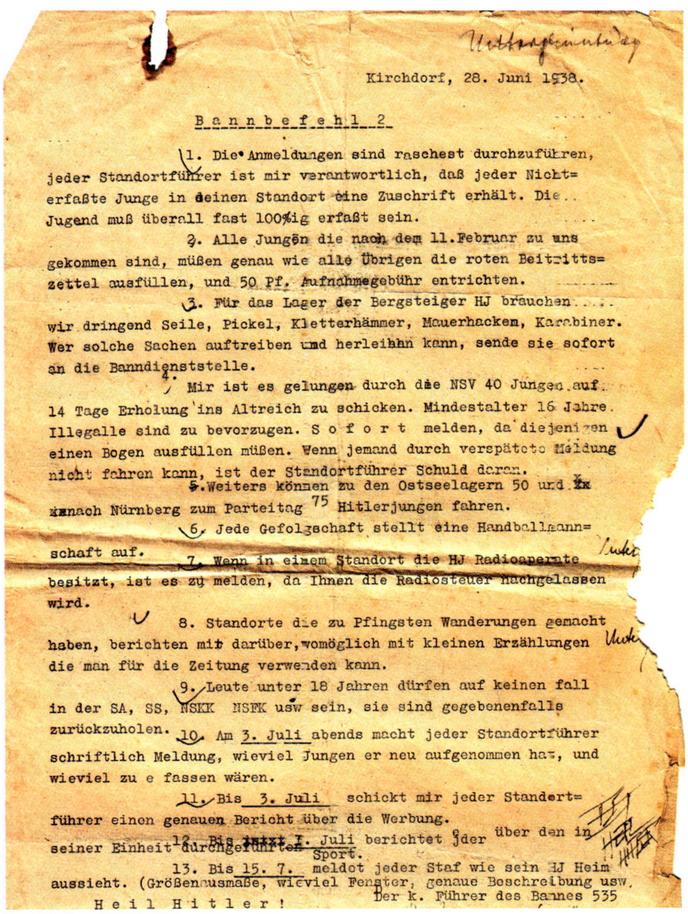

Kirchdorf, 28. Juni 1938.

B a n n b e f e h l 2

1. Die Anmeldungen sind raschest durchzuführen, jeder Standortführer ist mir verantwortlich, daß jeder Nicht=erfaßte Junge in deinen Standort eine Zuschrift erhält. Die Jugend muß überall fast 100%ig erfaßt sein.

2. Alle Jungen die nach dem 11.Februar zu uns gekommen sind, müßen genau wie alle Übrigen die roten Beitritts=zettel ausfüllen, und 50 Pf. Aufnahmegebühr entrichten.

3. Für das Lager der Bergsteiger HJ brauchen wir dringend Seile, Pickel, Kletterhämmer, Mauerhacken, Karabiner. Wer solche Sachen auftreiben und herleihen kann, sende sie sofort an die Banndienststelle.

4. Mir ist es gelungen durch die NSV 40 Jungen auf 14 Tage Erholung ins Altreich zu schicken. Mindestalter 16 Jahre. Illegalle sind zu bevorzugen. S o f o r t melden, da diejenigen einen Bogen ausfüllen müßen. Wenn jemand durch verspätete Meldung nicht fahren kann, ist der Standortführer Schuld daran.

5. Weiters können zu den Ostseelagern 50 und nach Nürnberg zum Parteitag 75 Hitlerjungen fahren.

6. Jede Gefolgschaft stellt eine Handballmann=schaft auf.

7. Wenn in einem Standort die HJ Radioaperate besitzt, ist es zu melden, da Ihnen die Radiosteuer nachgelassen wird.

8. Standorte die zu Pfingsten Wanderungen gemacht haben, berichten mir darüber, womöglich mit kleinen Erzählungen die man für die Zeitung verwenden kann.

9. Leute unter 18 Jahren dürfen auf keinen fall in der SA, SS, NSKK NSFK usw sein, sie sind gegebenenfalls zurückzuholen.

10. Am 3. Juli abends macht jeder Standortführer schriftlich Meldung, wieviel Jungen er neu aufgenommen hat, und wieviel zu e fassen wären.

11. Bis 3. Juli schickt mir jeder Standort=führer einen genauen Bericht über die Werbung.

12. Bis 1. Juli berichtet jeder über den in seiner Einheit durchgeführten Sport.

13. Bis 15. 7. meldet jeder Staf wie sein HJ Heim aussieht. (Größenausmaße, wieviel Fenster, genaue Beschreibung usw.

H e i l H i t l e r !

Der k. Führer des Bannes 535

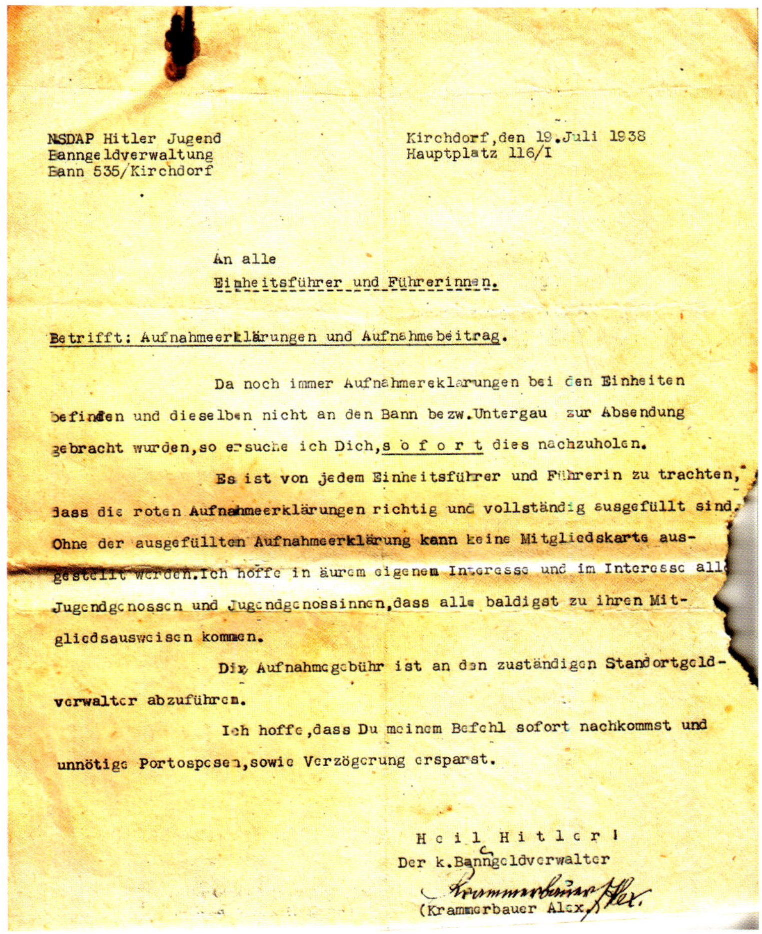

NSDAP Hitler Jugend
Bannge ldverwaltung
Bann 535/Kirchdorf

Kirchdorf,den 19.Juli 1938
Hauptplatz 116/I

An alle
Einheitsführer und Führerinnen.

Betrifft: Aufnahmeerklärungen und Aufnahmebeitrag.

Da noch immer Aufnahmereklarungen bei den Einheiten befinden und dieselben nicht an den Bann bezw.Untergau zur Absendung gebracht wurden,so ersuche ich Dich, s o f o r t dies nachzuholen.

Es ist von jedem Einheitsführer und Führerin zu trachten, dass die roten Aufnahmeerklärungen richtig und vollständig ausgefüllt sind. Ohne der ausgefüllten Aufnahmeerklärung kann keine Mitgliedskarte aus-gestellt werden.Ich hoffe in äurem eigenem Interesse und im Interesse aller Jugendgenossen und Jugendgenossinnen,dass alle baldigst zu ihren Mit-gliedsausweisen kommen.

Die Aufnahmegebühr ist an den zuständigen Standortgeld-verwalter abzuführen.

Ich hoffe,dass Du meinem Befehl sofort nachkommst und unnötige Portospesen,sowie Verzögerung ersparst.

H e i l H i t l e r !
Der k.Banngeldverwalter
Krammerbauer Alex.
(Krammerbauer Alex.)

NSDAP *Hitler Jugend* letter giving detailed instructions for camp.

Orders for HJ camp.

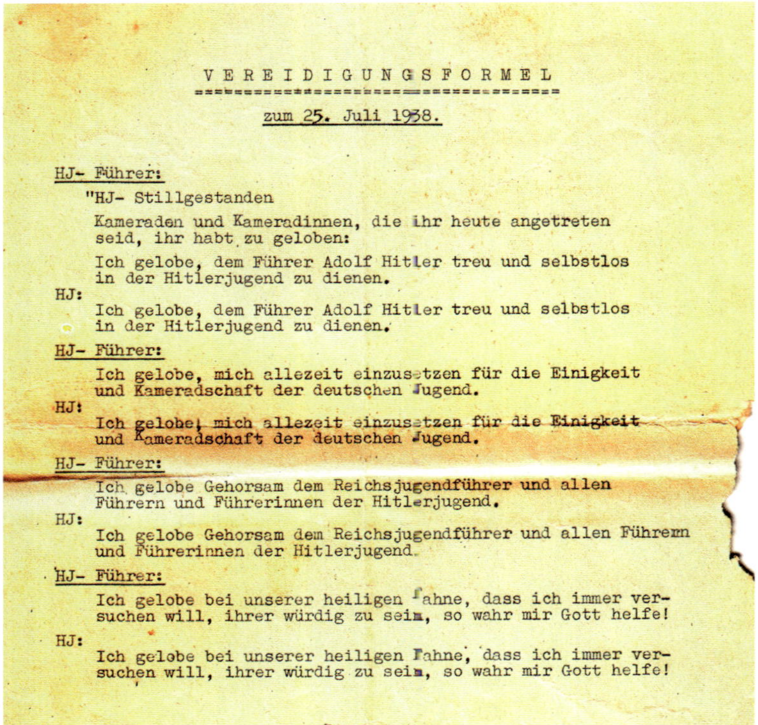

VEREIDIGUNGSFORMEL

zum 25. Juli 1938.

HJ- Führer:

"HJ- Stillgestanden

Kameraden und Kameradinnen, die ihr heute angetreten seid, ihr habt zu geloben:

Ich gelobe, dem Führer Adolf Hitler treu und selbstlos in der Hitlerjugend zu dienen.

HJ:

Ich gelobe, dem Führer Adolf Hitler treu und selbstlos in der Hitlerjugend zu dienen.

HJ- Führer:

Ich gelobe, mich allezeit einzusetzen für die Einigkeit und Kameradschaft der deutschen Jugend.

HJ:

Ich gelobe, mich allezeit einzusetzen für die Einigkeit und Kameradschaft der deutschen Jugend.

HJ- Führer:

Ich gelobe Gehorsam dem Reichsjugendführer und allen Führern und Führerinnen der Hitlerjugend.

HJ:

Ich gelobe Gehorsam dem Reichsjugendführer und allen Führern und Führerinnen der Hitlerjugend.

HJ- Führer:

Ich gelobe bei unserer heiligen Fahne, dass ich immer versuchen will, ihrer würdig zu seim, so wahr mir Gott helfe!

HJ:

Ich gelobe bei unserer heiligen Fahne, dass ich immer versuchen will, ihrer würdig zu seim, so wahr mir Gott helfe!

Hitler Jugend oaths swearing loyalty to Hitler.

Hiking trip.

Erich's parents.

"On the trip to the Salzkammergut (Austria). 1 week from 28 Aug. – 5 Sept. at the farmer's house. I'm on the extreme right."

"Climbing up to the mountain pasture hut. Down below, the hut where we spent the 1st night. Got lost before that."

"In the mountains at the alpine hut on an outing."

Erich in RAD uniform.

"In memory of your apprenticeship 1938 with Karl Zellinger SS Man."

RAD group.

Relaxing during a break.

Male and female RAD uniforms.

RAD group marching.

RAD on transport.

RAD group with local child.

This shows the way the RAD laid out their uniforms and spades. In the Army rifles were stacked as the spades are here.

Mixed RAD group.

Another view of the uniform and spade arrangements.

RAD women sow while the men relax.

RAD work project.

RAD at work.

The work creates a thirst.

RAD work drill uniform.

After hot, hard work the dress ended up like this.

A RAD comrade.

Sharing a joke.

In the truck.

During a work break.

Leaving the work site.

End of working day.

After work boot cleaning.

Relaxing after work.

In RAD track suit.

On the meadows.

With female spectator.

The RAD mixed sport with Nazi indoctrination.

Sports parade. Note musical accompaniment.

March to sports field with music.

Going swimming. Note duty man in uniform.

RAD training included military skills like shooting, as it was intended to be an introduction to military life.

"Reminder of SS comrade."

Chapter 2

Army Service Pre-Barbarossa

Again, Erich left no diary, but we have the following photographs which illustrate his training and the build up to the invasion of the Soviet Union.

Infantry soldiers. Erich is on the back row, third from the right.

Erich in Infantry field grey uniform of the 27th Infantry Division. The tunic is interesting, as the pockets show it is a converted Austrian tunic and not the standard German M36 or M40. Many sources claim these are converted Czech tunics, but by looking at photographs the authors are sure these were from Austrian stocks. As Infantry Ersatz Battalion 462 was based in Linz, Austria, this makes it more likely that the tunic was Austrian.

Full field grey uniform. Note use of short boots and puttees. Again, another part of Austrian uniform?

Guard duty. Note single ammunition pouch and WWI full length 98 rifle.

Walking out in the smart Panzer uniform.

Erich in black Panzer uniform of Panzer Regiment 39. The tunic has the early pink *Waffenfabre* piping round the collar.

Parade at the Kaserne.

Guard duty in black Panzer uniform and wearing the early padded Panzer berets.

Relaxing at the Kaserne.

"Our driving school on ground near Brück at the Neusiedlersee. December 1940."

"1st Christmas celebrations. Enzersdorf near Mödling, Vienna. December 1940."

"Live firing in Brück at the Neusiedlersee. December 1940.

Food eaten outside the mess hall. December 1940.

"Spiess Hauptfldw. January 1941." Note position of notebook tucked into the jacket as carried by "Spiess."

"Enzersdorf. Uffz. Kor. January 1941."

"Full kit inspection. Enzersdorf. Our company. Feb. 1941."

Full kit inspection in Enzersdorf before departure. Feb. 1941.

"March off. Station at Oldenburg.'

"Rail transport to Putbos. March 1941."

"Oldenburg – departure station. March 1941."

Erich's postcard of the Futbos area. Putbos is to the west of Oldenburg.

"Transport to Putbos. March 1941." Putbus is a small town on the Baltic island of Rügen, North Germany.

"Putbos. March 1941." Panzer II Ausf b in foreground. Three Panzer IVs in the background.

"Putbus – vehicle hall. One 5cm vehicle. Panzer III Ausf J."

"Idyllic time in camp. Putbus. March 1941."

"Vehicle hall Putbus. March 1941." Panzer III Ausf Js.

"Putbus March 1941." Panzer II Ausf b. Spiess on right.

"Break in shooting. Putbus. March 1941."

"Transport from Putbus to Grafenwöhr." Grafenwöhr is a town in the Neustadt district of the Oberpfalz, eastern Bavaria, Germany.

"Grafenwöhr 1941." Vehicles are Panzer IIIs.

Gef and Obltn. Graulitz at the railway from Putbus to Grafenwöhr. March 1941.

"Grafenwöhr April 1941." Erich is on the right.

"At a place in Thüringen. Putbus to Grafenwöhr. March 1941." Panzer IV Ausf C.

"Our W and G Fldw. Fromm August 1941." Weapons NCO.

Tanks at the vehicle hall. Panzer II Ausf b, Panzer III Ausf E, and Panzer IV Ausf C.

Panzer III Ausf A climbs slope.

Panzer III Ausf A with Panzermen. Most wear early berets and one at front has a traffic control baton.

Panzer III Ausf E. Crews in greatcoats and Panzer berets.

Panzer IVs on the range.

Panzer III Ausf A on training ground.

Panzer IV Ausf C at rest.

Panzer III Ausf A on road. Soldier on right has traffic control baton.

One of Erich's Panzer comrades.

Panzer IV Ausf E and Protze Kfz. 69 truck.

"2.2.1941"

Panzer IV Ausf E *Tauchpanzer*.

"In memory of your old friend."

Eastern Front Middle and South.

Chapter 3

The Sütterlin Diary: 5 June to 18 July 1941

Written in a grey covered Russian school notebook.

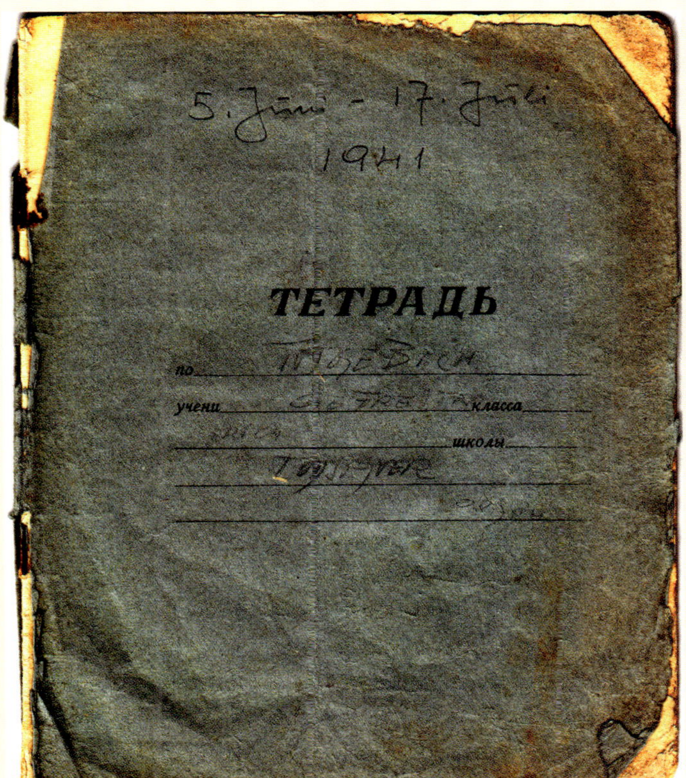

Front cover of Erich's first Sutterlin Diary. He calls it his *Tage Buch* and has written his rank, *Gefreiter*, and his name, Erich Totsauer, on the front. Perhaps he meant it as a war diary of Panzer Regiment 39.

From my memory, written on the day of 28 June 1941 near MINSK. In the gorge at OLESINO, 7km from MINSK.

Wearing black Panzer uniform in the Kaserne.

Just before the advance to Russia.

Erich wearing the steel helmet in front of a Panzer IV E *Tauchpanzer*.

Crews relax on top of a Panzer IV E *Tauchpanzer*.

Two of Erich's comrades in steel helmets. Note unusual marking on the front mudguard. This could possibly be a command tank of 6 *Kompanie*.

5 June. Finally away. But where to? Everyone is excited already. Went swimming for the last time. Wakened at 2 AM. Accommodation hurriedly tidied up. To Grufenwihr (Training area)?

An officer with a Panzer IV C outside the vehicle hall.

6 June. Up at 2 AM. 3 AM to the vehicles. March off to Grufenwihr? 170 km to travel. On the autobahn to LAGENFELDT to private billet. Met women. Great night.

"On the Reichsautobahn on the way to the embarkation station at FORST. 6 June 1941."

"Travelling on the Autobahn. My tank and my comrades. 6 June 1941."

7 June. 7 AM move on. Autobahn. 160km to Sinsdorf. Private billet. Met Liesbeth. On guard duty. Liesbeth collects me round about 2 AM. Came back for fall-in parade. Great night.

8 June. 6 AM. Move on. Have to pack. To private billet again. Stay here for 2 days. Great food.

9 June. Have technical duty. Met Hilde. Came with us. Went round Mariendorf with her. All sorts of things going on. Came back at 3 AM.

10 June. Fall in. Travelled on to FORST, where we were loaded up. This time destination unknown. Everywhere we are greeted enthusiastically by the people. Most decent time here.

11 June. Crossed the border. 12.00 arrival in PROSCAR, in Poland. Unloaded. Travelled on through UNNANJE to WARSAW in light rain. 70 km to the positions in Poland via a small village, WITHY.

12 June. Because of war the vehicles have to be sheltered. We drive into the village. Sleep in a barn.

Camouflaging the tank.

13 June. Now come some quiet days. Technical duty. Received weapons. Instruction in immersion into water and preparation for immersion. (17.Panzer Division was equipped with *Tauchpanzer*, ie tanks that could be driven under water by sealing hatches and allowing in air with a snorkel.) Mount guard.

14 June. Have guard duty. 10 to 3 (time) the barn burns down. Through enemy sympathisers. *Feldwebel* Pietsch. Great excitement. Got money in Zloty (Polish currency).

15 June. Saturday. Did washing. Quiet day.

Washing in the forest. Panzer II tank in the background.

16 June. Drumhead service. It's gradually getting serious. We can feel it.

17 June. Technical duty.

18/19 June. Russian language duty. Instruction about Russia.

20 June. March off via SIELDDE, OPOLN KOMARNO, KONSTANTINOF to the assembly area in a large forest 12km from the Russian border. The whole Division is here. There is only one fountain available for us. Washing a luxury.

Panzer IV E *Tauchpanzer*. By the mudflap marking this is the same tank that Erich stood by when wearing the steel helmet. On the original print the divisional marking is just visible below the rhomboid.

In the woods before the invasion.

21 June. Technical duty. We listen to the unit commanding officer and the order of the *Führer*. So tomorrow it's starting against Russia. War. Received money and exchange into *Reichskredite*. (Erich stands on the verge of "Operation Barbarossa," the invasion of the Soviet Union. 4.5 million Axis troops attacked along a front of 2,900 km. Planning and preparations had started in December 1940.)

"Our luggage vehicle."

22 June. 0.00 Met the Russians. 03.10 our artillery fire begins. A mighty display of firepower. We are standing ready for attack. However, the Russians skedaddle. At midday we come to the Bug (river), stand for an hour at the bridge, which has been built.
See my first air battle. 8 bombers were shot down by our aircraft. Awful to watch. Crossed the Bug. We come to the first of our dead. Snipers were the culprits? Wounded Russians are still lying here. Password is drive and keep driving. All through the day and night. Firing catches us at the back. 5 tanks kaput. We travel on alone. We had to arrive on time. Our first attack is ahead of us. 200 Russian tanks are against us.

"Advance at the beginning of the campaign. Still in Russian part of Poland." Panzer IV number 622, the second tank of the second platoon of sixth company. The vehicle lacks its exhaust, which would have been fitted where the white "G" is on the rear plate. Note water Jerrycan on the smoke discharger rack with white cross. Faster LKWs pass on the better part of the road on the right.

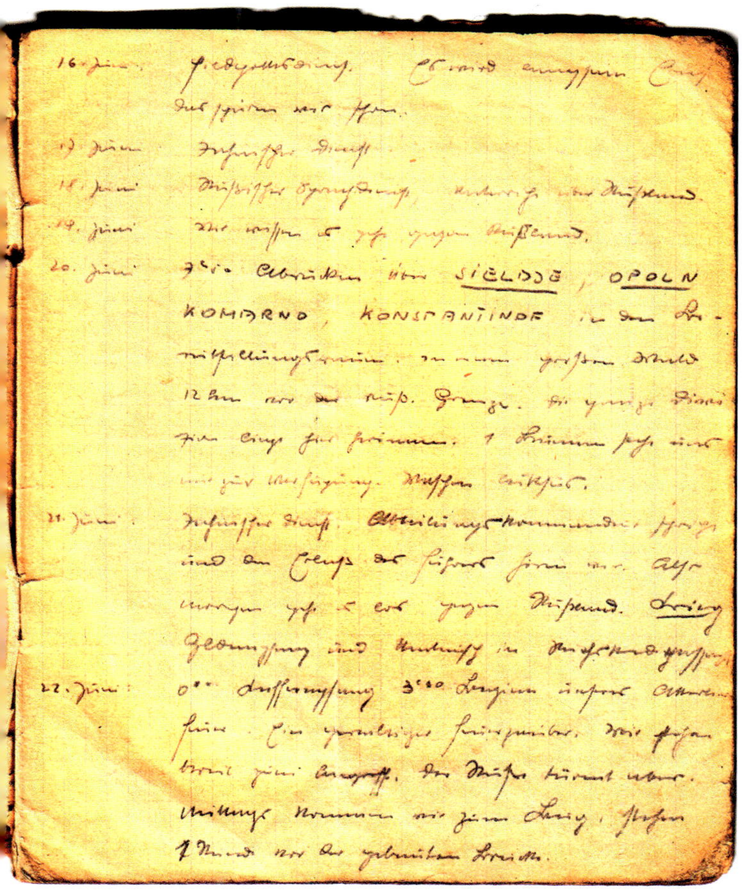

Diary page of 22 June 1941, the opening of *Operation Barbarossa*.

Advance into Russia.
Panzer IV E *Tauchpanzer*.

23 June. 03.50 we arrive at the Company. 4 AM, march off for the first battle. Tank versus tank. A long forest, they must be there. Great gunfight. Our tank on fire. All 5 of us flew out and extinguished the fire. A 2cm shot lands near me and the tank track in to the ground. Like lightning we are back in our crate and drive on. Right and left of the road there are burning tanks. Our unit commander, Major Sassinger, dead. Had his foot torn off - direct hit. The only death in the attack. Heavy loss. Hptm. Krüger takes over the unit. Our battle initiation was in BIAKISDORFER FORS, near PRUZANA. The Russians were beaten.
We drove on all through the night. Take control of 2 aerodromes. PRUZANA. All the aircraft are still standing here. We find a whole load of things. Lard, butter, everything your heart desires. We cut up the parachutes and make scarves out of them. Lovely silk.

"Before SLONIM. Tank repairs, restoring tanks to working order. June 1941." Panzer IV E.

"All dead bodies (Soviet) near SLONIM. June 1941."

24 June. We arrive in SLONIM and are surrounded. Behind us Russians, in front of us Russians, to the left and to the right. An unpleasant feeling. Meantime, set up next to the road and do technical duty. All of a sudden we are attacked from behind. Tanks. Tanks come and a load of vehicles. We shot all of them. Everything was burning. We were shot at from the corn fields all around. The wounded Russians were even firing at us. We are surrounded. Anything that came into view was shot. 12 Russians and one of our Uffz. were shot. Kottendorf and Mertel shot. These were our first wounded. Russians using special bullets, Uffz. Feder hit by a special bullet. Fldw. Kummistan a shot in the backside.

"Near SLONIM our I troop (maintenance)."

25 June. Firing all night. There's no peace. I watch the front, it looks horrible. Most Russians are burned. There's a lot of booty though. I've taken a lot of photos. At 4 AM we go on through SLONIM to the road to STOLPJE. A tank of 3 Platoon knocked out making bridgehead. Burning, no one seriously injured.

"Travelling through the burning town of STOLPJE. June 1941."

"Travelling through the burning town of STOLPJE before MINSK. June 1941."

26 June. We drive on, keep going, almost no more fuel. And we feel alone in enemy territory. Quite scary. Further firing. It's such a strange feeling. Nothing happens to us, however. At 3 AM tanks come and give us 40 litres fuel. We go on the outer part of our convoy and learn that the General has been hit.

"Near SLONIM on 26 June 1941. Advance. Russian tank 4.7 K.W.K."

"Near SLONIM the Russians are digging graves for their dead. 26 June 1941."

27 June. The Gef, ObLtn. Graulitz, and our vehicle will drive with the leaders and 5 light tanks. Bring out the General and drive all through the night.

"Obltn. Graulitz, platoon commander of our company, then Gef of 4 *Kompanie*."

"Our tank before the attack against MINSK, where we were knocked out. 27 June 1941." Again no exhaust is fitted.

28 June. Everything keeps moving. I think it is KÖDANON, near west MINSK. We get 60 litres of fuel from the half tracks and drive on through the line of bunkers. Receive fire and transmit okay. Get stuck in the mud, also ObLtn. Zinschütz. The Gef pulls us out. We get in, get the shells, and get to the rendezvous point. Drive through the burning town which has been destroyed by Stukas. Outside the bunker there is Pak (anti-tank) artillery. We fire at

everything and drive on. Firing from the left and the right again. The Russians are hiding themselves and firing from an ambush. In any war there has never been such a sniper war, also by civilians. When we found the first objective it was midnight. It was near SLONIM. The Soviets had naked women with them. We have such pride.

We drive on at the head and come to a village. Heavy firing here. We come to a corner and it happened there. 3 shots from not more than 20-30 metres away went into our tank. Driver Uffz. Wedde dead. Driver of the commanding officer quite seriously wounded. We bale out as the tank already on fire. We have only with what we have on us. It was so quick. Fritz disappeared. Albert, me, Fuchs, and Uffz. Kirsch were the 4 who lay in the ditch. Fuchs and I creep along the ditch. Come to an underpass and huddle into the mud with our only weapon, a pistol. Albert lost his getting out of the tank. We lay in the mud for ¾ of an hour. The Russians were continuing to fire. The enemy all around, we can't get away. We see our last hour coming. But it turns out differently. At the last minute comes a patrol of infantry. They take us with them and we go back. 2 crews come but Fritz is not with them. 5 wounded are here. Albert and I are the only healthy ones. The 2 drivers are dead. Fritz is missing. Our tanks come back, can't get any further forward. It was close. I just can't believe that we got away. We went back with 2 MTW (troop carrying vehicles).

Shots went directly into the driver and next to me (in the tank). I can only speak of luck that I didn't get hurt. I'm so sorry about Wedde. He didn't give out a sound. He must have been killed outright. Often the wounded lose a foot. The wounded are looked after but what do we do? The infantry take us with them. 76km, we do the same journey again! We stop and settle down for sleep. Half of our vehicles have to leave the village and look for security. There are burnt-out vehicles. Who are they??? Where is the crew? Hopefully, not one of us. It's LEUTNANT ERNSTIN's tank.

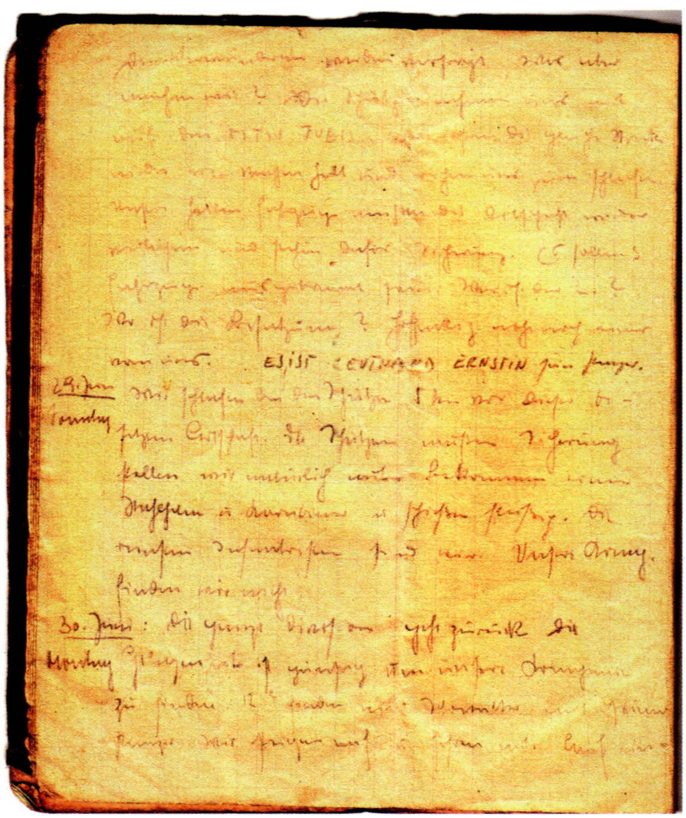

Diary page, "It's *LEUTNANT* ERNSTIN'S tank."

Bunkers.

On the bunkers.

"Our first prisoners near MINSK from the encirclement. June 1941."

29 June. Sunday. We're sleeping with the infantry 1km outside of an occupied village. The infantry have to stand security. Of course we have to join them. Get an infantry helmet and rifles and get on with firing. We are fighting with the infantrymen. We can't find our Company.

30 June. Monday. The whole Division is retreating. We take the opportunity to find our Company. At 12.00 we find Sch... (illegible) with his tank. We get on top and ride with him. All of a sudden behind us comes snow-white, Uffz. Hertlein with 3 pals. No one believes we are still alive. The whole Company gathers together. We had been reported as dead and signed off by the boss. There is great joy. Fritz is also here. He had confirmed in writing that we were dead. I learn more exact facts. Fritz ran crying as the first shot was fired and jumped on to the boss's tank. That was really good of him! But now everything is okay. Shame that Wedde is no longer.
At 4 AM Inspektor Wallender comes and takes me to his office. Livestock has to be collected for the *Abteilung* (unit). I went with him as an expert. Collected a cow and a pig. Pinched a pair of Russian boots for myself. This day also came to an end. I confirmed to the master radio operator that 2 radio sets had been lost. The boss signed everything off. The boss asked me if I wanted rest time. So from today I am on light duties. Fritz had to go to St Polsten today.

1 July. Tuesday. Light duties. Fetch water. We take 2 calves with us and slaughter them. The officers and Fldw. went up front to the tanks (those that had been knocked out). It's simply horrible. Nothing whole remained in the tank. They found one good body part of Wedde. They were buried. 10km from MINSK is where I spent the greatest hours. The bogies (parts of the tank's suspension and running gear) are lying around the area. If you look up into the turret you see the ground again. The tank armour had been blown away. That's what had happened to many tanks. I can go up there tomorrow. Will also take some photos. Have to roast 40 chickens. Work for the Spiess. Gef H (illegible) and I will then do the chickens. Don't find any time to eat.
Got 2 letters today. Liesbeth and Ruth.

"My tank knocked out in the gorge at OLESINO on 28 June 1941."

"My tank with the grave of Uffz. Wedde near Minsk on 28 June 1941."

"Our first fatality. Uffz. Wedde. I am here in the gorge of OLESINO, knocked out for the first time. 7 km. from MINSK on 28 June 1941. Uffz. Wedde was driver in my tank."

2 July. Wednesday. We're still sitting in the same place. Everything has retreated. We are surrounded again. The first prisoner of war convoys arrive. Deserters. No more can be shot. On the hill the Russians are still high-tailing back. Artillery has been firing all day. We lost 3 tanks here again by direct hit of enemy artillery.

Russians are retreating. Infantry is on our right. We can't go back any more. What's going to happen now? When will we get back to MINSK out of necessity? I haven't even got a uniform. Everything has been burnt. The day before yesterday we wanted to drive to our tank with a cross for Wedde. Can't get there because of artillery fire and the Russians are there. Have to go back.

In the afternoon more promotions. Me again, *Gefreiter*. Fritz Bergen got his *Verwundetenabzeichen* (wound badge), everything was given out today. Here F is Uffz. Uffz. Bergen again Fldw.

We have 1 bridge and I hope for the command to march off soon. We go back 3km to secure area. The Russians try to break out. 2 armies are encircled here. Things are going on all day. Several deserters arrive. It's already 12 midnight, so much work. Wakened at 2 AM. Going to MINSK.

"Advance on Minsk. 1941."

"Advance – start of the convoy 1941.
Also the medics on the way to Minsk."

"Street battle in a town near Minsk."

3 July. Thursday. Wakened at 2 AM. I prepare beef and then we set off for MINSK. Drive north about 5km to my tank. Really horrible. Nothing left in one piece. As already mentioned cleared out and torn apart. It's 5 AM. I took photos here and hopefully the pictures will come out. The 2.5cm (pictures) look better but not much. The journey continues through MINSK. 7 AM. This house here is in one piece, the town is in ruins, I've never seen anything like that. Here the Russian road made of asphalt begins. Quite a good road. Left and right of the road lie lots of shot up LKWs (lorries). Lots of Russian tanks are lying around. We stop in large buildings, 100km to MINSK, where lots of commissars lived.

"Minsk."

4 July. Friday. I search through these buildings. I've never seen such a mess, everything cut to pieces. These were elegant apartments. Every commissar had his women. Bathrooms. Every comfort available. We saw photos here, everything easy. The civilians plundered all the apartments. Quite right too. A lovely Russian tankard. Freyer? Such an opportunity. Something Russian. For the first time Russian bombers come. Flak (anti-aircraft guns) shoot one down. Martin and I slaughter a chicken. We chased the chicken round the meadow with a pistol. Was a great hunt

5 July. Saturday. Got up at 2 AM. Prepare the meat for lunch. Russian aircraft come again. 12 o'clock march off, on the road. 100km then we turn off on to a side road. Whole batteries of artillery and tanks lie here. 17 Div (17.Panzer Division) must be away from the road. I've never seen a road like this. I'll always remember this road. Can't really say road, when you drive 100km over fields and arable land. The tow trucks have to pull every vehicle forward. We assemble every few kilometers. Can't always see our tanks up ahead. Goodness knows how many are ahead of us. I see another neat air battle. Our pilots play a real cat and mouse game. Wherever our pilots are in action, the Russians don't come back.

6 July. Sunday. We stop again in a large village. Eggs are pinched. The people make us aware of the commissar's house. Lehmann and I break in and we are the first. I take the microphone with the portable record player, but give it away to a pretty girl. Shame that we had to leave again so quickly. The people here are very grim. But these villages. Afterwards I saw a house made of bricks. Like in a town. I haven't seen a bucket well since we were in Germany. You have to have experienced something like this. We slaughtered another bull and an ox. Gave some away to the villagers. Can't get to our tanks so quickly. In the evening we fry liver.
On it with Lehmann, he's to work first. Stabs Fldw. F (illegible) puts him on guard duty. He's not so lucky.

7 July. Monday. 4.30 up. Boiled 600 eggs which were pinched from a Commissar! All the meat cut up. The march goes on. 3km then everything stuck again. Slowly goes on. Lois on guard duty. Sleep on the way.

8 July. Tuesday. Lots of work, it continues. Reach our post. 1 tank knocked out. Direct artillery hit. Ltn. Wolkendorf's tank turret completely destroyed. Broke through on the bridge. One of the 5 tanks a dead loss. We are on the front line. Terrible amount of artillery. All day aircraft above us. Lots of Russian infantry. Tank knocked out. Mühlbauer injured. Shot in the thigh. We were surrounded. Behind us Russians, on all sides. The Russians behind us are also surrounded. They are trying to get out. Slaughter 2 cows.

9 July. Wednesday. Sit here all day. More aerial combat. The Russian pilots shoot down one of our Stukas. Our own Stukas bombed us. Shocking that.
Gefr. Wollander and his tank are being pulled out. It can move. The turret is broken. The *Befehlspanzer* (command tank) has been knocked out. No one injured. Everything cleared out. Today there is roast veal, cooked on an open fire, of course. In the evening the *Kompaniestaffel* (company

detachment) not yet back. 7 Div drives up with Skodas. (7.Panzer Division was equipped with Czech tanks, the Pz.Kpfw. 38t. These were not made by the firm of Skoda but by ČKD.)

Column of Panzer 38t tanks.

10 July. Thursday. Finally going on. We still have to go 30km. We see lots of destroyed Russian tanks. We drive on 'til 2 AM and come to the DNEPR, the big river. This is our stopping point. Great resistance from the Russians.

"Bridge over the DNEPR."

11 July. Friday. 2.00 asleep on tank. 4.30 calf has to be slaughtered. We already going on but this time not yet. We're still at the river. Still firing from Russian tanks but this time quiet over by us. Wrote 2 letters home to Mother. Otherwise not much happening all day. The Commander gets a rocket from the Spiess. (senior NCO); I make sure I get away. It's nothing to do with me. Everything is half as bad. Slaughter all sorts of things as we are self-sufficient.

12 July 41. Saturday. Today all sorts of things were going on. Fall in. Roll-call for clothing items if anything needs to be renewed. I get everything new. We fall in for delivery roll-call. Suddenly a low level attack by Russian fighter-bombers. 30m above us. Something quite fantastic with the 2cm and MG (anti-aircraft fire.) Houses are burning down. Ammunition explodes, several wounded. Such a surprise. That was at the river DNEPR, at OSCRIDO ORSCHA.
The second surprise we got from the Russians - heavy mortars. Always landing 50 - 100 metres behind us. The shrapnel flew around. Thank God the Russians can't see us. I think they are firing at the trig point above us and next to that on to the road. When a mortar comes it roars and we lie down on the ground. That goes by and we move to another place.
Met a nice girl when fetching water. All sorts going on. But hard to come to an understanding. 2km from us an airstrip. The Russians are still firing at it. Lots of our aircraft landing.

13 July. Sunday. In the night an alert. The Russians tried to attack. Nothing came of it. Lots of fog. Lots of deserters (Soviets). The lads don't want to know. They've (the Soviets) been so much fooled into thinking that we're going to cut off their hands and feet and all sorts. That's why they are so scared. A lot try to flee. They do not know that nothing will happen to them! They are cut down by our pilots.
In the village where we collect water we cleared out 3 military camps. The people fight over the things. Never seen anything like it. Great girls after collecting the water. Nino, Tania, Freya, Lobia, Marusca. Uffz. Hertlein took our photo. Curious to see what the picture looks like.
ORSCHA is on fire. SMOLENSK is occupied by the Russians. When will it ever go away. All day troops go by.

14 July. Monday. Making a roast today. 2 pigs, lots of work. 4 o'clock move off. Finally we are going forward. But came to nothing. The 20th Russian army has pushed through from SMOLENSK. Destination is still unknown. However, we are remaining here on the other side of the DNEPR at ORSCHA, which is burning furiously. Guns here all afternoon. Got 4 letters, write 4 back. Not much happening for us. 1 Russian aircraft attacked. Didn't hit anything.

"Behind SMOLENSK at the DELNA bend."

15 July. Tuesday. Still at ORSHA all day. When are we going on? 3 times we have gone on and 3 times we've had to come back again. ORSHA is under artillery fire, in ORSHA everything is burning.

"After the air attack near ORSCHA by Russian fighter bombers." The LKW has been liberally painted with the G, denoting the troops under the command of Guderian.

"Before the tank battle at SDENNO near ORSCHA. July 1941." In common with the other Panzer IVs, Erich's photograph at this time shows the exhaust seems to have been removed. This is shown by the position of the G on the rear plate, which would have been covered by the exhaust. The small exhaust for the turret traversing motor is also missing. This would have made the tank very noisy.

"ORSCHA near SMOLENSK."

16 July. Wednesday. 11.30 at night we gone on. The DNEPR. Russian aircraft attack. Flak is firing. Floodlights flicker back like fire. Unprecedented artillery is firing at us. Everyone runs for cover. It's 4 AM. Then we go on. I'm driving with Karl and at 1 PM we come to a town. The bridge blown up DNEPR. We have to drive on. Then comes an artillery attack. Every strike a crater of 50-100m. They are firing so much that we get out as quickly as possible. We're shot at again and again.

At the DNEPR river.

17 July. Thursday. On the road to SMOLENSK. 12 midday we drove past General Field Marshall von Kluge, also took a photo of him. Drive through a small town, get terrible artillery fire, strikes left and right on the streets. All sorts going on.

17 July. Friday. We move on to LOADY. Now we can have a good bathe. Unexpected artillery fire before the village. Doesn't bother us. Find tank ditches. Monstrous. They must have worked at them for a long time. 2 Russian tanks are lying in them. How did they manage to get them in? Beside us is lying a Russian tank. Examine it in minute detail. There's a cloudburst. We are flooded out. Have to dig our way out. But did little here.

18 July. We go on to DNEPR. KRASSNY. That says something.

Notes for 5 June to 18 July 1941 Diary

This is the first of Erich's diaries and is handwritten in Sutterlin script. The use of a Russian school notebook and the first entry show that Erich made the decision to keep a journal after the invasion of the Soviet Union. It is amazing that he kept his efforts up for the next three and a half years.

The diary starts with preparations and uncertainty about the Division's mission. Erich refers to the "diving tanks" (*Tauchpanzer*) that 17.Panzer Division and 18.Panzer Division used. These could be driven underwater up to 15 metres deep and were designed for the invasion of Great Britain, the cancelled operation "Sealion." *Tauchpanzers* could be used to assault from the sea or cross deep rivers. This was two years in front of the British, who designed DD (Duplex Drive) tanks that could be made to float with the use of waterproof canvas screens on a frame.

The troops could have had some idea of their future enemy by the Russian language lessons and briefing on Russia on the 18 June. However, the Third Reich had a nonaggression pact with the Soviet Union and they had carved up Poland together. All doubt was dispelled on the 21st when the commanding officer's briefing and Hitler's edict was given to the troops. Erich records this entry in large letters in his diary. The Polish money was exchanged into the German military currency.

The first few days of "Operation Barbarossa" see Erich involved in some heavy fighting. He witnesses air combat, as well as the armoured battles in which he is involved. There are the sights of the Soviet casualties and the first German fatalities and wounded. Many German soldiers found the initial stages of the invasion involved fierce fighting before the fanatical Soviet resistance could be broken. After crossing the River Bug, Erich would have been in the Panzer *Abteilung*, which was the second unit in the order of march behind the Panzer Regiment Headquarters. Shortly after this the tanks took over as the spearhead of the Division and captured the airfield at Pruzana.

The Panzer Divisions' mission was to keep going to provide the momentum of the assault. Enemy prisoners and wounded were bypassed. Often they outran the supply lines, as Erich reports on 26 June when they were running out of fuel. The Division had to request a halt to replenish fuel and ammunition at this time. Erich reports the wounding of the Divisional Commander, *Generalleutnant* von Arnim, who was replaced by *Generalmajor* Karl Ritter von Webber. Erich seems to have had a part in evacuating von Arnim.

Erich's unit, like many others, took the chance to resupply with captured stocks, particularly food and drink. Captured parachute silk was popular to make articles of clothing, such as Erich's scarf. The soft but tough material stopped the chaffing of the troops' necks on their uniforms. The parachutes were probably obtained from the captured airfield at Pruzana.

The order of march towards Slonim put the First Panzer Battalion ahead of Erich's Second Battalion. Erich reports seeing a tank from the third platoon (First Battalion) knocked out. During this period 17.Panzer Division was involved in heavy tank versus tank fighting, which is reflected in Erich's diary entries.

June 28th sees an action from which Erich is lucky to escape with his life. The driver Wedde, sitting beside him in the tank, was killed outright, something that obviously affected Erich deeply. Erich has lost everything with the tank and has to be equipped by and fight alongside the infantry. Later Erich takes photos of the destroyed tanks and is shocked by the way the armour protection was stripped off by the impacts. The remains of his dead comrades are buried.

Erich also mentions the Soviet prisoners, many of whom were deserters. A lot of Soviet citizens did not like the harsh Communist regime, and in the early part of the war took every opportunity to be captured. However, when the cruel reality of the Nazi's intentions became clear through atrocities against civilians this soon changed, with many joining the highly effective Partisan forces.

On 2 July Erich refers to the Soviet prisoners and deserters with the phrase "no more can be shot." It's not clear whether he means they cannot be shot as they are prisoners, or that it was not physically possible to shoot any more and they had to be processed as prisoners of war. As we cannot be certain it is up to the reader to judge.

The next day Erich remarks on one of the few good Soviet asphalt roads and the amount of destroyed Soviet equipment. The Soviets took huge losses in men and materials at this time, which were commented on and photographed by many German soldiers. Erich again refers to it later in the diary. Many Germans considered the Soviets had been beaten due to the heavy losses. They did not realize the huge military reserves, industrial power, and manpower of the Soviet Union.

Next Erich comes across the dwellings of the Commissars. These were luxurious affairs compared to the simple dwellings of the ordinary people. Commissars, as party officials, enjoyed vast privileges and took every opportunity to increase their comfort. Little was passed on to others. Erich reports that the villagers took the chance to loot these houses on the demise of the party officials; a scene which was repeated in Iraq after the downfall of Sadam Hussein's regime. Erich settles for a tankard, which would probably be useful for drinking with his comrades. Later he shares the Commissar's spoils with the local population.

On 5 July Erich experiences the terrible state of the majority of the Soviet roads. These were little better than dust tracks. The German forces were just beginning to realize the difficulty of their logistic task on these roads. These would later turn into mud baths in the heavy rains and freeze solid in the winter.

An incident of friendly fire is reported on 9 July when German Stukas (Junkers 87 dive bombers) attack Erich's unit by mistake. As we now know this is a common incident in war, even up to the present day.

A lot of the latter part of the diary is taken up by Erich procuring and cooking all types of meat. His pre-war training as a butcher gave him skills that would be in constant demand by his comrades. There are a few references to girls, both local and back at home. This is an interest that Erich will show throughout the diaries.

The Germans had captured Smolensk on 16 July under the command of General von Kluge. Erich took the chance to take his picture.

The diary ends with Erich on the Dnieper river. He is clearly impressed with the scale and speed of the German advance, as many German troops were in this early period.

"Graves of our comrades."

Chapter 4

The Sütterlin Diary: 18 July 1941 to 18 December 1941

Diary written in a Russian school notebook that has a picture of a composer or literary figure on the front.

Diary 18 July 1941 to 18 December 1941 cover.

18 July Friday. Journey goes further on through KRASSNY towards SMOLENSK, that was taken on Tuesday. We stop temporarily before SMOLENSK as there is fighting there in which our tanks are involved. The Russians wanted to recapture SMOLENSK. Bloody battle. On the road here I see the dead comrades from 29 MOT Infantry Div. (29th Motorised Infantry Division. This division fought with distinction in Poland and was later wiped out in Stalingrad.) Quite a lot of officers. There was a terrible battle here. Ltn. KEITEL, SON of the Gef of the O.K. (Army High Command) fell here. Took a photograph of his grave. I've never seen so many graves. But I wonder how many Russians have perished. Russian tanks lie in huge numbers here. In the night we continue through SMOLENSK on a lovely tarred road. Spend the night below SMOLENSK. We arrive here at 4 AM. German tanks are still fighting. W….'s (illegible) tank a casualty. Clutch broken, tracks torn off. Often have this problem.

(Ltn. Keitel was the younger son of General Wilhelm Keitel, who was Chief of the Armed Forces Command. Keitel was a primary planner of the *Wehrmacht* campaigns, but advised Hitler against invading France and later Russia. After that Keitel became subservient to Hitler and Himmler, particularly over racial and war crime matters. He signed many orders regarding the killing of prisoners, including the notorious Commissar Order. For this he was sentenced to death and hanged as a war criminal at the Nuremberg trials.)

"*Hauptman* Kaiser's tank knocked out before SMOLENSK. July 1941."
Panzer IV Ausf.E

"Hptm. Kaiser's destroyed tank near SMOLENSK. July 1941."

Soviet dead.

19 July Saturday. It's 4 o'clock in the afternoon and we are still sitting here. Tanks still in battle. Receive Russian artillery fire behind us. Have to go back 1km and away from the road. We're sitting here now. Artillery fire all day. Beside us is an airfield with numerous aircraft which has been shot to pieces.
Write 7 letters.
All afternoon we take artillery fire in which there is all sorts. The heaviest fragments fly about. One guy from the Lehr (instruction unit) took a direct hit. We all take cover. In the evening I have guard duty. 2 Russian aircraft come. MG (Machine gun) given special munitions, all sorts going on, great to watch. 2 tanks knocked out. Clutch, track knocked off. Fldw. Grosse's tank has gears broken.

20 July Sunday. Half past three again artillery fire from above. They are firing continuously into SMOLENSK. Ours are attacking. Then it is quiet. Gef's tank took a direct hit from artillery fire. Everyone gets out quickly. Uffz. Fritz wounded, Wendel, Meyer wounded. Gef and radio operator unhurt. A piece of luck. Wollende filled me in. One Panzer 4 is still going. It's Heuer's with the Spiess as commander. What will happen to us now? 17 Div? Spiess' tank takes a direct hit on the right track cover, 5 road wheels broken. turret MG broken. Crew bail out. We cross over to the left on the main road in peace. For how long? Probably for a while. We drink our first Sekt. At the moment one vehicle is ready to go.

SMOLENSK July 1941.

21 July Monday. Four weeks of war. Now a period of rain is beginning. It's freezing cold. We set off again at 4 o'clock in the afternoon. We have to take over security. SS Div. Reich is ahead of us. High time, our Div is done for. Our infantry is supposed to be 40-60 km ahead of us. Still fighting before SMOLENSK. The Russians want to retake SMOLENSK at all costs, as 300 Russian tanks are sitting ready at the station. They haven't got many more tanks. You can see that. Russian artillery is very stretched from here. Artillery fire all day. But a bit away from us. It's been raining all day.

(The *Das Reich* Division was formed from three SS regiments: "Deutschland," "Der Führer," and "Germania." It fought in Poland as *SS-Verfügungstruppe*, or special purpose troops. After losing "Germania" to form 5 *SS Panzergrenadier* Division "Wiking" it was expanded to become the 2 SS Division "Das Reich" and fought in the Low Countries, France, Yugoslavia, and Greece. In the invasion of the Soviet Union "Das Reich" was in Army Group Centre and part of the spearhead to take Moscow.)

"On an advance-destroyed town."

"Russian artillery gun near SMOLENSK."

22 July Tuesday. During the night the Russians attacked SMOLENSK and were beaten back in a bloody battle. Günter is still great. Bodies lie around here, dead horses. There was a bloody battle here. Russian prisoners have to bury them. Not a nice feeling. Cleaned 2 MG (machine guns). Otherwise not much happening. 1 Div (1.Panzer Division) was relieved and gives its tanks to 3 Abt. (*Abteilung*). What will they do with us? We're waiting here for tanks. Will we get any? The Russian MOT (motorised) armies must have been cut to pieces already because from here everything is horse-drawn. Where the Gef's tank took the direct hit are standing 56 guns, all long-barrelled, horse-drawn.

Eventually there was mail again today. Unfortunately not for me. Russian bombers flew over without noticing us. Flak did not fire. There was a newspaper from the 8/7 (8 July). We don't know any news.

23 July Wednesday. Gef says we'll sit here 'til round about the 1st. We can rest. The vehicles are being washed down. Am with Karl doing the cleaning. Otherwise not much happening. General Arthur von Weber (17.Panzer Division commander) fell on the 17/7 (17 July). Pflaum Typ also died, in the field hospital. One comrade less.

Still sitting here.

Tanks after cleaning.

24 July Thursday. Wash my outfit. 4 Russian bombers come over us as cool as you please. Don't see us though. No Flak fired. Pity! Today roll call in our company etc.

25 July Friday. The new battle groups. We are not included. Just lads from the VB (Supply Battery). Today 4 Pz 2s (Panzer 2 tanks) arrived and 2 Pz 4s (Panzer 4 tanks). Have in total 4 Pz 4s and 5 Pz 2s.
Got mail. L. writes some letters. To be ready for march off again at 17.00. That's our peace come to an end.

26 July Saturday. The black day for the Company. March off at 2 AM. Travel 75 km towards MOSCOW, via STRINOJEDNE. It's about 250 km to MOSCOW. 2 Pz 4 are casualties and one Pz 2. Our track broken. We stay with the tank. Stubig also a casualty, has to be collected. Lots of aircraft activity. Lots of Russian aircraft spot us. Flak doesn't bring any of them down. Pity! We reach the Company at 12 o'clock. For the first time today we were overtaken by horse-drawn troops. Yesterday ObLtn. Koosen from 4 Kp came to us. He goes to the *Feuerpanzer* (flame throwing tank) with a driver. I wrote a letter to Berg (illegible) in the field hospital. Great aerial battle above us at 17.00. One Russian was shot down, came down a thousand metres from us burnt to pieces. The company ahead of us has a hard battle. Can't get forward. To our left 10 Divisions are surrounded. That's something for the troops who are following on! Stuben's son must have been overrun by an army.

Broken track. Panzer IV Ausf. E

Good view of the mudflap insignia.

27 July Sunday. Today is my birthday. Out of hospitality I open a tin of meat. Sunbathe. 3 o'clock mighty thunderstorm with heavy hailstones and pouring rain. Otherwise nothing happening all day. *Grossdeutschland* regiment pushing forward. Mount guard.
In the morning had an examination by doctor. Important clarification. One Russian aircraft was shot down by us. Dismantled Henschel engine (Tank engine). Towards evening an intense battle. Troops arriving now from everywhere. We are closing in on Moscow. Mount guard duty.
(The Infantry Regiment "Großdeutschland" (Greater Germany) had been formed from the *Wachtregiment* in Berlin. From the outset it was intended as an elite force and recruited from all over Germany. Members were entitled to wear a *Großdeutschland* cuff title on the right cuff and "GD" in metal thread on their epaulettes.
The regiment took part in the battle of France in 1940. Attached to Panzer Group 2, it fought in Barbarossa from the beginning. In the battles outside of Moscow in late 1941 the regiment was decimated and reduced to a single battalion. This was expanded to a new *Großdeutschland* regiment in February 1942 and later given armour and designated as a *Panzergrenadier-Division*. Finally, in November 1944 further units were added to form *Panzerkorps Großdeutschland*.)

28 July Monday. Sitting peacefully. Russian bombers are bombing the forest in front of us. 2 were shot down. Lie about all day and sunbathe. Write a few letters. Otherwise nothing happening. Fall in, examined by doctor, all morning.

29 July Tuesday. In the afternoon we are going foraging. Ltn. Schipfer, Obfldw. Heidrich, Uffz. Brückner, Gustenberg, and I. We drive back about 50km and finally arrive as the first Germans in a village. There's not much here. I take a pig with me. It was a good hunt. We shot it with rifles. In the evening football was played.

"Oberfldw. Heidrich's tank before an attack."

30 July Wednesday. After roll call we're going foraging. The same ones, back to where we were. Today there is a bigger hunt. We got 30 chickens and 10 ducks, worked out well with guns and rifles. Played football in the evening. The Russians attacked at night but didn't manage to succeed. They bombed the airfield heavily. Heavy Flak was fired.

31 July Thursday. There were promotions on 29 July. Mayer Rudi became Uffz, Schneider became Obgfr., Trauner became Gefr., and Sch (illegible) became Gefr. Went foraging again. I already belong to the squad.

1 August Friday. Arms inspection. Go foraging. We slaughter a fine bull. In the evening we make roast liver. Otherwise nothing happening. 3 ABT (third *Abteilung*) fast unit has been disbanded and is going home. We're taking over the vehicles.

2 August Saturday. Drumhead service in the morning. Went swimming 'til midday. Otherwise nothing. Got one Pz 3 (Panzer 3 tank). Uffz. Scheungrub came to the Company and two new Ltn. (Lieutenants). Supposedly we are getting nine Pz 4 (Panzer 4 tanks). Russian aircraft appear and bomb a bit behind us. Mount guard.

3 August Sunday. Artillery fire all night. I think the offensive has begun. Without us? Today early sport with the Gef. Otherwise nothing happening.

4 August Monday. Leather equipment inspection. We got quite a lot of mail. Go foraging. Slaughter a bull. 500kg, great.

5 August Tuesday. Have efficiency inspection. Got new Pz 3s (Panzer 3 tanks), now have ten Pz 3 and Pz 4 and six Pz 2 (Panzer 2 tanks). Quite good now. Today we go out for a walk. I get possession of a motorbike, the Russian 250cm, goes rather well. Russian aircraft come without bothering us.

Motorbike. "Lehrmann."

6 August Wednesday. Battle Group goes forward for an attack, nothing comes of it. 7,000 prisoners are taken ahead and next to us. The encirclement (of Soviet troops) must be complete now and for the greatest part destroyed.

"Kossack stragglers still fighting here. August 1941."

7 August Thursday. Go by car to the workshop 30km back. The dust would have driven you mad! All day foot soldiers go forward, lots of them. In the workshop we have four Pz 4 which will be ready in a few days. Russian planes visit us again. 2 of them were driven away by our fighter pilots. Grün is back from Warsaw, brought a lot of things with him. Today there are fried potatoes.
In the afternoon I go foraging. Get a calf. Also go swimming, drive on my own with an Opel (make of vehicle, probably the Opel "Blitz" 4x2 cargo truck). There's mail again today, also for me. Thank God the battle for SMOLENSK is over. Some pals were attacked by armed civilians when they went to fetch water.

8 August Friday. No roll call today. In the afternoon weapons inspection by a weapons guy. Yesterday General THOMA visited us, I almost forgot. Battle group goes up for attack. Russian aircraft come, but have no success.

Cleaning weapons. Panzer IV E *Tauchpanzer*.

"Our Gef with General Thoma at the divisional command post." Gef here is *Hauptman* Kaiser.

9 August Saturday. Am ill. Infection in the chest. Constantly at the doctor. Can hardly move. Can't get my breath. It rained all night and early morning. Bitter cold. We go round with our coats on. Fall in, then there is drill for the Assault as the battle group is not here. Ferdinand's tank broken down.
Write 4 letters. At 19.00 9 Russian bombers come and are all shot down by our fighter pilots in front of our eyes. It was as if they all crashed down like in a ball of fire. Also one fighter bomber away. Today we cook plain Schnitzel as every evening, only for the 6 of us. Quite delicious of course. We go to bed late in a haze of Schnaps.

"Tank repairs on the advance route."

10 August Sunday. Wakened at 1.45. We're going forward. Where to?
Today going on our bike. 7 o'clock I'm out of action. Damage to the chain. I don't have Russian chains. So I have to leave it lying. Go on by car. There is terrible firing, everything south of LOGUREBUSCH. There is a big Kessel (cauldron battle, an attempt to encircle and eliminate an enemy force) here, they have to be destroyed. Ended at 9 o'clock. We put camouflage on the tank. Stay 'til midday. Then we go back to our old position. That was a nonsense, what was it for?

"Battle stations near SMOLENSK, as we had to attack further south at the Kessel in KIEW. August 1941." Panzer III J. Swastika flag on the turret roof for air recognition.

11 August Monday. Lie around all day. 3 Russian dive-bombers fire at us, but fired into the field. We now have nine Pz 4 and six Pz 3. Four Pz 4 still to come. Dividing up today, mostly of VW vehicles. (Volkswagen Type 82 *Kübelwagen* light two wheel drive field car. This had superb cross country performance and could carry four fully equipped soldiers.) Everything has to be taken from the other PKW (personnel carrying vehicle) and put on the VW car. Today we made omelettes. Great!

12 August Tuesday. Wakened at 2.00. 2.30 march off in the direction of ROSLAWI, southwards therefore. Our goal is the industrial area south of MOSCOW. We travel 70km. Then stop 10km before ROSLAWI. Have to drive 80km to the Front. Information about partisans. A group that has caused losses at our backs, quite dangerous people. Have to be crushed at all costs. Mount guard here.

13 August Wednesday. Have to stand guard again today. Cleaned Spiess' (senior NCO) car 'til 12 o'clock. Go into the nearest village to collect water. Wash myself. Obgfr. Heidrich got EK1 (Iron Cross first class). A huge Russian bomber made an emergency landing 5 km from here. 40m wing span, 4 engines, 40 bombs. Such a giant. Never seen anything as big as it. Took photos.

(No entry for 14 August.)

15 August Friday. Go to the next village and bathe. Lie around all day. Nothing happening. Moving further left. There were tanks and towing vehicles.

16 August Saturday. Today we go further south. We have to surround 40 divisions. Our goal is to target the back of the enemy, not to go forward. We travel 120 km today, then rest. The Russians skedaddle in front of us. We follow the Russians without any fighting. The bridges are all kaput. There are a lot of mines. Stand guard.

17 August Sunday. Lie here all day. Going swimming in the river. The area is much nicer. There's lots of butter to eat, all day. Otherwise nothing happening. Troops are advancing. Stand guard.

18 August Monday. Supposed to march off at 3 o'clock. Nothing comes of it again. Swimming in the morning. Prepared geese and deer. Lie around all day in peace. On stand-by. All day divisions advance. We are standing security.

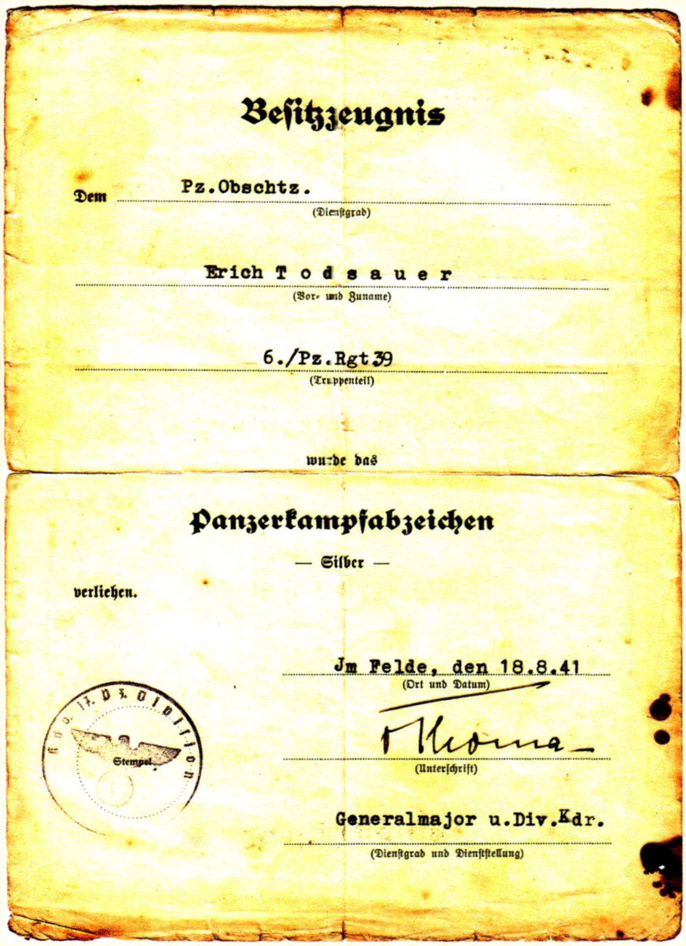

Besitzzeugnis

Dem Pz.Obschtz.
(Dienstgrad)

Erich T o d s a u e r
(Vor- und Zuname)

6./Pz.Rgt 39
(Truppenteil)

wurde das

Panzerkampfabzeichen

— Silber —

verliehen.

Im Felde, den 18.8.41
(Ort und Datum)

(Unterschrift)

Generalmajor u.Div.Kdr.
(Dienstgrad und Dienststellung)

Erich's award document for the *Panzerkampfabzeichen im silber*, the Panzer Assault badge. Note it is in his first name of Todsauer and signed by von Thoma.

19 August Tuesday. Battle Group has to advance again, 6km to the side of us. Russians with 2 tanks, cars, and 2,000 civilians who have been called up but could not yet be evacuated, as we were unexpectedly called to attack. Prisoners were taken. Obflw. Gruscholz was shot. No one else dead or injured except one man from 3 Kp (third Company) was shot by a Russian. He was from the Fast troop.

20 August Wednesday. Lön is Unit and regimental dispatch rider. Stand-by for march off. Troops are still moving forward. 35 Pz Rt of 4 Div (35 Panzer Regiment of 4.Panzer Division, the armoured regiment of 4th Panzer Division), etc. Otherwise nothing happening. Very bad thunderstorm and rain. The first here in Russia.

21 August Thursday. 5 o'clock departure. What a road! Half dust. Just Awful these roads! 'til before BOSLAP 70km. A low-level attack by 2 Russian fighter-bombers. Dropped bombs 100 m away from us. We've never moved out of our vehicles so quickly. Good that they are so cowardly and don't attack a second time. Our good luck! Battle detachment forward for attack against BOSLAP. Today got cigarettes and booze.
Got 7 parcels from M (illegible). It is now 4.30. When we set off we had 8 Pz 4, 3 Pz 3, 6 Pz 2. When we arrived we had 2 Pz 4, 1 Pz 3, 4 Pz 2. There are higher wages, so we were told. It is 5.10, another Russian air attack on us. Nothing serious happens to us. No one injured. At 5.30 PM 7 Russian aircraft attack us again. Two more Russian air attacks, then peace.

22 August Friday. 7 o'clock departure. Forward 40km. Lots of Russian aircraft here which keep attacking us. Pz 3 direct hit, engine completely broken. Rest is a village.
Went back the same way again, to starting point. What nonsense, forward and back! We've been here an hour already. Departure. Forward again, a bit further into a village. This is where we finally stop. We've gone 50km.

23 August Saturday. Day off. Have guard duty then radio duty. 9 o'clock in the evening night-time departure. 3 LKW (lorries) overturned on this road. Kuscher injured. Cows knocked down. What a road! Early on we come into a village and stay there.

24 August Sunday. Are dead tired as we couldn't sleep. Sch... (illegible) and I seek out Kuscher. 6 o'clock fall in. Great SURPRISE, there are *Panzersturmabzeichen* (Panzer Assault Badges, awarded for three attacks on three different days.). Straight afterwards red wine. Company is now together. Drinking and singing! Great mood! In a stupor Schross and I pitch a tent.

"Presentation of the *Sturmabzeichen* with drinking session. August 1941. Beyond ROSLAWL."

"At the presentation of the *Sturmabzeichen*. August 1941."

"1941," drinking and singing.

25 August Monday. Day off. Pay day. More money. Another 5RM (Reich Marks) increase. Today 40 RM for 20 August. In the evening departure forwards. During the day an air attack. Halting place, spending the night in huge cornfields.

26 August Tuesday. Nothing happening in the morning. Played cards 17.00. Won 20 RM. 4 o'clock departure. 'til 9 o'clock, then stayed overnight near BOLEP. BOLEP not shot to pieces. Lots of prisoners. Have guard duty. Lots of graves for our soldiers.

27 August Wednesday. Go by BMW (motorbike) with Sch.... (illegible). Back to the town of BOLEP. Had to go. Sch.... and I all sorts going on!
At BOLEP. NARE, a woman, all sorts going on. Really taken to task. Are farmers living off their own produce here. What a life!
1 Abt (First *Abteilung*) leads off again and loses 4 tanks. The 1 Abt still has 5 tanks. All 3 of us go into the town in the afternoon. Suddenly in the middle of the town an artillery direct hit, then one after the other. The Russians are attacking. Break through the town, everything abandoned, infantry on foot. Everyone is running around in confusion. Get out of the town in an LKW (lorry). Our Abt (*Abteilung*) and the advancing infantry are beaten back. The enemy came from the flanks to the station. Our infantry has to retreat. All sorts going on. Attack after attack of Stukas followed. Highest state of alert for us. Now we are stuck. Because our vehicles won't move, we can't even get away.

"The tank battle in ROMANOWKA in the DESNA valley in August 1941. Ltn. Schupfer's tank. Ltn. Schupfer fell in the battle."

29 August Friday. Russian bombers bomb the town. Let's get going! Now much quieter again. The Russians can't take the town.
We're astonished. Lots of people speak German. You can understand them well. An aircraft battle unequalled. Stuka after Stuka. Russian aircraft are attacking us. Nothing happens to us though. One bomb falls in the town into the prisoner of war camp. 130 Russians killed. Am curious to know what's happening with us. The workshop is not coming here. We have a great life here. Living off the land!

30 August Saturday. Russian bombing attack. 12 of them. Low-level attack over us. 1 shot down. Not much happens. Air attacks all day. One air attack after another and no fighter pilots are here. A piece of luck that nothing happens. Smoke bombs also fell.

31 August Sunday. More air attacks. That's really getting on our nerves! In the evening there are huge amounts of dust. 6 bombs fell near us, so that everything is covered in dust. No one was hurt. Of course go into town. Lovely girls here.

1 September Monday. Started again at 3.30. Air attack after air attack. Our flak moves into position near us. All of a sudden an artillery attack. Strike after strike. 1 dead, 9 wounded. But skedaddle! Guns stay put. They are firing from 15 km away and make direct hits. Another air attack, dropping more bombs on us. 5 houses burn down because incendiary bombs are falling, but all round about us. That was a black day! We went into town in the evening. Girls good, great.

2 September Tuesday. Go to the messing office and fetch things. Today it's finally peaceful. Go to the field hospital. Lots of our wounded are returning. Uffz. Meyer wounded. Leninghofer Arthus lost both arms. At the Front there was all sorts going on! 7 of our tanks were knocked out. Ltn. Schüpfer fell. Everything lumped together in one unit. They are 75km ahead. The supply line was attacked by 40 Russian tanks. Here the Russians had thrown into the scrap every last tank apart from 52T (Erich is referring to the massive KV2 tank armed with a 15.2 cm howitzer) and also dug in 74 tanks. Stukas had to take strong action.

3 September Wednesday. Rainy day today. Heavy rain and thunderstorm. Lying in bed in the morning. Today we are having roast turkey leg with rice. Quite quiet. Not from us, as usual! Artillery fire. Quite peaceful! Go into town. Meet Seichter Willi who comes from the Kp. (Company). Leninghofer Erwin has lost his arm. Brunner Willi came here - POSTCHEP - to the field hospital.

"During the advance in 1941 our 1st *Zugmachine* with Obgefr. Neubold Friedl."

4 September Thursday. Leninghofer was General Schüpfer's radio operator. Last night Russian aircraft bombed POSTCHEP. The bombs fell down in the town. No expense spared! To the left of POSTCHEP the Russians attacked with armoured cars but were beaten back. We are sitting here

Russians ↓ ↓ ↓
* we are here

*POSTCHEP

Went to the field hospital in the morning. How much longer will we sit here? In the afternoon collected supplies. 9 Russian bombers attacked. The bombs exploded 100m to our right. We are waiting. 20.00 we continue. 3 low-level Russian attacks. Bombs explode again 100m behind us. We remain by the 5.N17 (map reference or roadway). We go away. About 300m six more bombs, I see that they are coming directly for us. We run for our lives. I've never run like that! Hear the bombs roaring, throw myself down. The shrapnel whistles round our eyes and incendiary bombs fall round about us. You can't see a metre in front of you. The house next to me bursts into flames and I run on. I was exhausted so much so that I couldn't write down my "silent thoughts." I'll never forget that. 20 minutes later a huge mine explodes. All hell breaks loose!
At 7 o'clock I stand guard. Brukofsky and Heuser are not here yet. Where on earth could they be? At 9 o'clock I am going to meet Mariz, lovely girl. All sorts going on! *Hauptmann* Truger, our ART (artillery) commander, has also fallen. Everything gone into open order. *Hauptmann* Grudt leads the *Abteilung*. Regiment consists of 1 *Abteilung*.

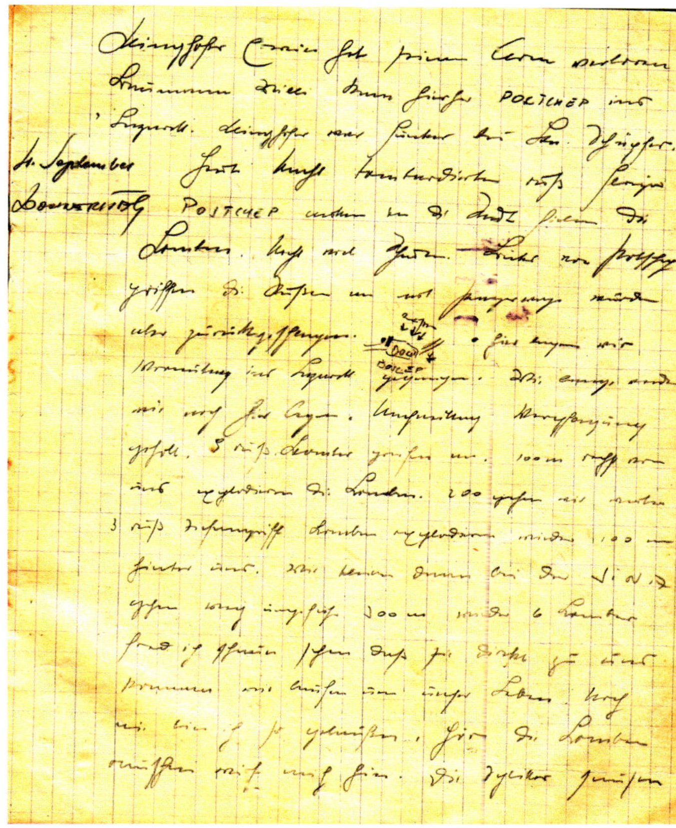

Diary page "we are here.'

5 September Friday. Look for our 2. Scour the whole town. We can't find them. Yesterday the bombs fell on the stand-in company. 1 dead, 7 wounded. Russian artillery is firing. Wet day. After bloody Russian air attacks nothing happens. What's happened to our two? Missing presumed dead. Bad luck! My radio bag is filled with 2kg of sugar, 11 loaves of bread. With the girl 'til 12.00.

6 September Saturday. Brukofsky and Heuser are still not here. Something must definitely have happened to them. Russian fighters are circling above us and firing. Yesterday 2 aeroplanes landed, unloaded fuel for us. Washday in

the morning. Air attack following air attack. 30 Russians bombing again, 20m from us. The bombs fell on the road. No flak and no fighters are here. They kept on hitting us. We've been here for 11 days. It's already bitter cold. Wearing coats. It's very cold in the tent.

7 September Sunday. Lovely morning greeting! 29 Russian bombers dropped their eggs. We got out of our tent and went for cover. Played Skat. More attacks. First of all? Fighters, Russian, then bombers again. The bombs fall ahead of us again. The Russians have broken through again beyond POSTCHEP. There is fire. 7 bombers and 4 fighters are attacking us. Bombs fall ahead of us again. Not even any peace at lunch. 7 bombers come, chased away by our fighters. They hardly notice our fighters, they drop their bombs and skedaddle. Low-level attack by Russians continue on us. Bomb attack again. Fall in the middle of the town, immediately afterwards a low-level attack by the Russians. *Feldwebel* goes to the Kfz.5 (light transport vehicle) makes a note of the chassis. We have to hand it over. The tanks are going into the army repair shop. Our regiment is heading south. We can see that we are going to follow on. Have guard duty. A lonely experience. I saw a Russian funeral. The coffin open on a lorry. The family accompanies it in the already muddy ground. There's no cemetery anywhere. They are covered with earth like dogs at home.

"This is what the Russians look like."

"A Russian PAN, local clergyman."

8 September. Monday. Early morning greeting! Russian bomb attacks. 8.8 Flak is also finally here (8.8 cm Flak 36 anti aircraft gun). Bombers attack us. Then 10 more bombs, all on to the road. It's a terrible mess! 2 bombers and 1 fighter plane attack us. Bombs land near us. Great surprise. The town has to be cleared by 6 PM. What will we do then? It's already 5 o'clock. We can pack our things and retreat. In any case, the PzII (Panzer II tank) crews, 15 of them, are here. 7 Motorbikes, all broken. Left lying, I think. 18 Div (18th Panzer Division) comes back and follows on after 17 Div (17th Panzer Division). What does that mean? POTSCHEP is to be the main battle line. A nice state of affairs! In the evening the prime mover (recovery vehicle) arrives, comes and gets us and 1 PKW (troop carrying vehicle) with 5 infantry. Go along to unload. The town is completely abandoned. Infantry assault detachment goes through the town. The wheels for the Kfz.5 (small troop carrying vehicle) arrive at the workshop. There are 100 wheels here. However we are remaining here overnight.

9 September Tuesday. Leave here at 4 AM. Me with my bike attached. Hand over Division Kfz.5. Continue by recovery half track to the workshop. Russian attack on the town is already starting. We get stuck 10km from the town. Recovery half track has to go back to POTSCHEP and tow the tanks back. Stop the next LKW (truck) and go to the workshop. 4 of our tanks are standing here, 610 Nebel (smoke shell), 600 *Panzergranate* (Anti-tank shell), 612 *Sprenggranate* (Explosive shell). We stay overnight.

10 September Wednesday. 612 ready (Erich's tank number 612. This signifies 6th Company, 1st Platoon, 2nd tank.). Midday we go to the Company by tank. Go as far as MGLIN, stay there overnight. All the tanks are assembling here for the army workshop.

11 September Thursday. 7 AM we move on, 5 Pz II (Panzer II tanks). 3 don't come with us, we drop out again. We change vehicles and move on with the others, through UNETSCHA to STAROGDVP on route 2. What traffic! Nothing but infantry. 4 Div, 5 Div. Pz 35 (panzer regiment 35 of 4 Panzer Division), everything here. Our 5 Comp is here. Other Panzer Companies, who have no more tanks, are being firmly drilled. In rank and file, marching and singing. Troop reserves are also here. We travel with them to our workshop and stay there overnight. Meet Guggenberger, who's to get the EK2 (Iron Cross second class). Stesih, Artlegy, and Wagenknecht are going to the Company. Company is 120km ahead. Ltn. Razer also wounded but not seriously.

12 September Friday. Keep on going 'til KOROSTDUP. On the way are lying two 2cm guns. Write to Jesberger and Weidmann. We stay overnight in KOROSTDUP in a house. Many RAD units are in action here. 312, 311, 313, 314, and 316. (The numbers of RAD Battalions.)
(The *Reichsarbeitsdienst* - Reich Labour Service, RAD - was set up by the Nazis to combat unemployment. Its members, both male and female, carried out construction projects and farming. During the war it was classed as an Armed Forces' Auxiliary formation. Although not officially members of the armed forces, they had protection under the Geneva Convention. RAD units supplied front line troops with food and ammunition, repaired damaged roads and bridges, built and repaired airstrips, constructed fortifications, laid mine fields, and guarded vital locations and prisoners. Later in the war RAD personnel manned anti-aircraft guns and even took part in combat as infantry.)

13 September Saturday. Early, 6,000 - 7,000 prisoners march past. You should have seen how they fight over each mouthful! Today we have to get as far as NONGOROD. The road is smashed up. There is light rain. Before we got to NONGOROD attacked by 5 Russian aircraft. Bombs landed in the town. 4 dead and some injured. Met a man from Linz, Nusko from the *Leichte* Panzer 12 (Light tank) Abt. (unit). Radio operator. 3 bombers. We spend the night in the supply office in billet of 3.Panzer Division. (Erich gives the symbol of this Division as an inverted Y with two bars.) Great house.

14 September Sunday. Wakened during the night by air raid alarm. I didn't get up! Moved on, very bad roads to SCHOSKA. A wonderful town. The first real town I've seen in Russia. Also very pretty girls. Not one house destroyed here. A rarity in Russia. Great sleeping accommodations. On sofas. Our Comp. (Company) is supposed to be a bit further on! Today we met Fldw. Trauter, Uffz. Inderbich, Mertens, Herzberg, and Wagenknecht from the convoy. Played Skat 'til 12 o'clock, then to bed.

15 September Monday. Up at 8 o'clock. Wanted to go to the public baths. Closed, doesn't open 'til 11 o'clock. Went on to GLUGNAW. Very pretty town. Everything here seems prettier. We get off at GLUGNAW. This is the Front. I am dumbfounded! Local commander is our Abt. commander. Our Comp is now assigned as security for 63 Infantry Unit. (Panzer Grenadier Regiment 63, part of 17.Panzer Division.) The turning point: we are infantry! Everything is already divided up. Grab rifles, hand over vehicles. We're in a village. 2km to the security area. One platoon is relieving the other. 1 o'clock duty, at 7 o'clock we get to the Comp. We sleep in the school. Uffz Friese got EK1. (Iron Cross First Class.)

16 September Tuesday. Wakened at 7. Fall in, mail distribution. 9 letters, 1 parcel. Get to the 2nd platoon. Received pay, 51 RM, bought cigarettes, 80 of them. 2 o'clock inspection of mess tins and water bottles. 1 o'clock 3 platoon goes for security. Write a few letters. In the evening huge din because of captured partisans. 20 have been caught. Had to let them go again. They were harmless. 1st platoon had to join in.

17 September Wednesday. In the morning fell in with complete equipment. Huge fuss. 1 o'clock we go to security. MG (machine Guns) go into position. We sit in the station master's office. Lots going on at nighttime! 29 MOT attack (29 Motorised Division), east of us. Security goes on 'til 1 o'clock in the morning.

18 September Thursday. In the morning more security. Relieved at 1 o'clock. Mail distribution. 8 letters. Otherwise not much happening.

19 September Friday. Parade in gas masks. Radio inspection. Have guard duty. Relieved at 1 o'clock. Go as guard. 5 men til 6 o'clock. Got eggs. Lovely girls.

20 September Saturday. In the morning back to company. As guard 'til 1 o'clock. Bomb attack ahead of us. Lots of pamphlets. Huge palaver! Fldw. Seifert shot down a horse.

21 September Sunday. Got a bull and slaughtered it. In the morning my work. Parade. Us, too. Got tanks, none for us. No winter clothing either. As a consequence we have to go home. Russian infantry has attacked us. Increased alert. Relieved at 12 o'clock. Today we have to go on security. Write 8 letters here. Mail comes. M (illegible) got married on 29 August. Of course I am very surprised. Out to the beech tree road. We are assigned here. 10 PM, have to go on a patrol, Lechner, Baumgarten, and I. 12 o'clock patrol and report in. Took 2 prisoners.

22 September Monday. The gruesome day is over. We did not get to sleep. The Russian attack started early. We were firing with all barrels. Walter Schers gets a shoulder wound. Seriously wounded. Poor guy! Now all hell is breaking loose. We've really got to keep our heads down. Russian Infantry firing mortars, firing like mad at us. We change position with our MG (Machine Gun). Traumann Sepp and I. Have to do all sorts of tasks. Including kit. All of a sudden they fire at us, a muddle, a mortar shell lands 3 metres behind us. I'm deaf in my left ear for a long time. At night we get back into our position. On the right of us 3 platoon and 1 platoon have to skedaddle, as the Russians have reached the beech wood road. 5 men fell here and 5

seriously wounded. Fldw. Pusch, Krethner Max are dead. Shot in the back. Grossmann shot in the lung, Mäusl Fritz shot in the stomach, seriously wounded. Flamethrowers attack. All sorts happening! 1,000 prisoners taken. They had to attack 3 times. We haven't had anything to eat for a long time. Now we've had it! There is no one left on our right. Flamethrowers are coming from our right. Dare not raise our heads. We can go to the left where Obfw. Heidrich is. The MG *Schützen* (Infantry) are taking to their heels here. Getting direct hits from flamethrowers, run to the left again. Now there is a gap 1km wide where there are no Germans. We go back again, our old position. The flamethrowers come again, more prisoners. All of a sudden a 52 tonne (KV2) tank attacks. Comes from the edge of the woods with a Russian assault gun. Our flamethrowers clear off. What do we do? The Russians are firing so much that the mud is flying! We run for our lives as never before. Right, left, behind us, in front of us MG strikes. Up down, that's how it went, always on open ground. Sweat runs down us, we run for our lives. Everyone runs. The Gef Ltn. Meyer, the whole second platoon. Further and further, just get away from here. The tank behind us. We get out. In our village SLOUT there are 8 of us. Uffz. Welker, Obgefr. Amort, Träumer, Karser, Bongars, Kircher, Spielwergel, and I. Our Company is not yet here. What will we do? An armoured car and off! Then we walk again. Stay in a wood overnight.

23 Sept Tuesday. We're still shocked to our bones. We march on early on. Come to the village of SILO. Here we get milk, bread, eggs. Have a good feed. A cart and horse and on we go. I'm writing this up on the move. That was the Russian *Wehrmacht* (Armed Forces)! We rest for a bit. An armoured car is snapped up and we go on in the direction of SCHOSKA. LKWs (Trucks) are going towards GLUCNOW. A marching infantry section meets us and we hand over some of our hand grenades to them. LKWs are coming back because they have been shot up. Bringing wounded from the marching infantry. We get into one of the LKWs and go to SCHOSKA. Command post, we get food and a room. Go to the baths. 15 Rpf. (unknown reference). Bed at 6 o'clock.

"Our destroyed *Zugmaschine*."

24 September Wednesday. Wakened by a Russian bombing attack. Boil eggs. Now I am writing very long letters. Just heard news. Zimmer Kurt dead, Willi Schreiber also seriously wounded. Otherwise nothing happening. Went swimming, great swimming baths available.

25 September Thursday. Went to the telephone exchange twice, can't get through, though, everything ruined. Otherwise nothing happening. Got vodka. Can do anything now. 96% proof.

26 September Friday. Examined our building. Must have been some kind of headquarters. Telephones, transmitters, everything here. Cellar is kitted out up-to-date. Must also have been a torture chamber. Water, lighting, modern toilets, everything available. Steel doors. Large maps are lying around. Before tonight GLUCNOW has to be cleared. Inspector Gerf arrives with the food supply depot. We have to go with him to WORONESCH. No one knows anything about our Company. Where on earth can they be! We go back to our billets. Another scoundrel here today, from the *Schützen* 40 (*Panzer Grenadier* Regiment 40).

27 September Saturday. Today 5 bombers visited us, but soon turned away. Otherwise nothing happening. It's extremely cold already. New orders, GUDERIAN has to go towards MOSCOW again. Fine with me! The last night here. Tomorrow we're off to WORONESCH.

28 September Sunday. At the commissars' building we meet LKWs and we go with them to WORONESCH. 2km on foot to the Company. All kinds of surprises at the station. Zimmer Kurt is dead. Grossmann is dead. Busch, Waldi Schros have got the EK1. Today there are cigarettes on sale. Mail given out.

29 September Monday. The exact story: the battle for GLUCNOW. The 8 of us went to SCHOSKIZ, while Ltn. Meyer went with the others to BERISA. Uffz. Aug on the same road til evening. He escaped in the darkness. However, BERISA was attacked and the company had to go to GLUCNOW. There were more large scale battles. Horpf was run over by a tank. They lay for two more days in the mud. Gef Aulekie had the whole defence of the north-eastern area. GUDERIAN was with us in BERISA. We were outnumbered by 50 to 1. All sorts of Russian tanks attacked here. Now it is all over. Nothing much happening today. We have to get ammunition. It looks like we might get more tanks. I'd be pleased! We're heading for MOSCOW again. 2 new divisions have been assigned to GUDERIAN. That must be enough! 6 Kp were praised by all HQ for their bravery at GLUCNOW. Raining today. Uffz. Schilling, Stubfelder, Feske have all to come to the Abt. Gef Zimmer died on the way to the field hospital and Grossmann died in the field hospital on the 22nd. Lux, Rupp were shot dead by the Russians. They took off Rupp's boots and stole his ring.

30 September Tuesday. Therss, Schilling, Ltn. Wube, StabsGefr. (HQ Corporal) awarded the EK2. Wash my

clothes. Inspection in leather equipment (load bearing shoulder straps). This evening all sorts going on. Gef tore a strip off the conscripts. Made them roll around in the mud. 10 o'clock parade.

1 October Wednesday. The Company has been together now for one year. 10.00 fall in. 3 days of attacks. Sprenger 5 days detention because of yesterday. In the evening because they came to his attention during guard duty, the Gef hassles the conscripts again. Kasche becomes Obergefr., Feder becomes Feldw. Crews are re-assigned for 5 Pz IV, (Panzer IV tank) 3 Pz 2. (Panzer II tank). I am not included. Yesterday I got 8 letters and 8 parcels. All kinds of things!

2 October Thursday. Today 5 Pz IV arrived. Newest equipment. Uffz. Heuer and Obgfr. also arrive with a Pz IV. Spiess (Senior Non Commissioned Officer) is the commander. Today we have to give out all the ammunition. Was a load of work.

3 October Friday. Technical duty. Assigning of replacement vehicle. Inspection of the IRON CROSS recipients. 5 o'clock the *Führer's* speech. All sorts, we were really enthused. Many were drunk.

4 October Saturday. Tank test drive. I was assigned to the crew of Fldw. Gross, Obgfr. Zehntnas, Gfr. Link, Obgfr. Rerungen. Am happy that I am getting into a vehicle. In the afternoon instruction for the battle detachment. Our tank arrives in the evening. We work unashamedly.

Sunday5 October. 5.00 departure. 80km to SERIDINA-BUDA. All sorts were going on here! All kinds of Russian assault guns. Loads.

6 October Monday. 88km, driving all day, driving! 20 Russian tanks are lying here, 52 tonners and 64 tonners, alongside one another. Something was going on here. 1 Abt attacked.

7 October Tuesday. The first snow and bitter cold. Don't get out of the turret all day. Moving forward, moving forward. The Russians are fleeing everywhere.

Panzer IV E *Tauchpanzer.*

8 October Wednesday. 5 o'clock, onwards, the whole day. During the night we drove on and on. Where is the road! One of our aircraft was shot down by our people. Bad luck! Today, guard duty, radio watch.

9 October Thursday. 05.00 awake. Drive on and on. We just about can't go any more. Today we have to get to BRYANSK. We come to a huge, long forest. A shot-up tank is lying here. German convoys of ours shot to pieces. 2 Russian tanks 52 tonner and 64 tonner. One is still lying upside down. The crew still inside. The driver is hanging in the tank. Noticed 3 German assault guns. 8.8 Flak also there. They let all hell loose on the tanks. This forest has been burned down by the Russians. One camp after another built into the ground. In the evening we get to BRYANSK. Pull up and sleep. It's snowing heavily. So cold!

10 October Friday. 10cm snow lying. Stay here all day. *Hauptmann* Grudl from 1 Abt has taken BRYANSK. The Russians were surprised by our forces and surrendered immediately. *Hauptmann* Grudl will be awarded the *Ritterkreuz* (Knight's cross of the Iron Cross, the highest level of this famous award.). At 9 o'clock our tank will be handed over. Damnation! I'm furious! Have to go to BRYANSK again. 3 Company will be there to get it.

11 October Saturday. Still here. It froze in the night. The snow is still lying. Bitter cold! Unprecedented aircraft activity. Only get 8km further to the left. Fuel LKWs arrive. At midday we drive on again. Autobahn to KARATSGEF. Infantry and even more infantry on the march here. 7 Russian bombers attack us. *Sturmpioniere* (Assault pioneers, one of the elite branches of the army) have dead and wounded. One had his head torn off. Horrible! All good looking guys. The march goes on. KARATSGEF. This beats everything! We have to go back. 17 Div (17.Infantry Division) and 5 Pz Div (5. Panzer Division) are already through here. They don't need us any more. Turn round in the night. 1 vehicle breaks down.

12 October Sunday. Stop and midnight and sleep. Tomorrow we are going on to BUTRI. Battle group is ahead, engaged in a battle involving 29, 18, 15 Infantry Div. (29th, 18th, and 15th Infantry Divisions). We have to establish contact. Have guard duty. Vehicles are warm, running very well.

13 October Monday. Nothing happening. No rest. No food supply vehicle. Such bad luck! Still sitting here. Icy cold and it's snowing. We've had it if we have to spend a winter here. Otherwise nothing happening. All day only excruciating cold.

14 October Tuesday. Nothing happening. The cold doesn't loosen its grip. Damn this cold! Today security behind the village. Such nonsense! Can only happen to us! Lots of prisoners taken. They all give themselves up. The cold and hunger has got to them.

15 October Wednesday. Food supply vehicle came today. There is food for 3 days. Excellent! Also there is calm. Otherwise not much happening. I play a lot of skat. What else are we supposed to do! **Today I've been with the tanks for a year.** Our billets are lousy. In such a dump! Lice, bugs, fleas. Armies of them!

16 October Thursday. Go to get fuel today. Towards KARATSGEF. BRYANSK, DUBOFSKA, to ROSLAWL, 15km. Get back to the billet in the evening and sleep. There's been a snowstorm all day and it's so cold. Huge crowds of prisoners are marching backwards.

17 October Saturday. Lick and I go foraging. Bread. Set off at midday. Drop out, radio fails. Then we go on. So damned cold! BRYANSK. Then to supply line 2. Arrived here at 12 o'clock. Slept.

18 October Sunday. Our Company about 60km ahead. We have to come afterwards, leave at 1.30 and go to the Company. Mud everywhere. No vehicle can move. We are back at the place where our own aeroplane was shot down. We've driven in a circle.

19 October Monday. Up at 05.00. Ready to march off. 10.00 march off. Tanks pull us through the mud. We drive at the front with the VW (*Kubelwagen*) car, have to keep pushing it. We've got to get to KARATSGEF. That's going backwards again. We are massing there. We arrive at 8 o'clock. It's dark already. Gef is not there yet. Neither is Ltn. Kruger. When will the Gef arrive? Billets and bed.

20 October Tuesday. Gef coming on Thursday. All those in Tross 1 (Unit Supply and Logistics Train) have to go to Tross 2. Me too. Tross 1 are now only 2 vehicles, 2 men. No more people there. Drive to Tross 2 with Brandstüber, Uffz. Fromm, Guckenberg and I collect rations for 10 days. There is also a loaf of bread. This is what happened to us! Thomas shot himself in the leg. The left leg, with a Russian rifle. Stanninger Hans replaces him as radio operator for the Spiess.

21 October Wednesday. Wakened at 8.45. Fall in with webbing and polished shoes. A mad house! Drill cancelled because of heavy rain. Thursday technical duty. Weapon cleaning. Everything bug-ridden. An awful state of affairs.

22 October Thursday. 6.15 awake. 8 - 10.30 drill. Go to KARATSGEF with Lehmer, get 2 loaves of bread. 2 o'clock roll-call in shirt, trousers, and socks. Distribute the supplies. When will we get mail. It's a month today since we got mail. When can we get to the delousing station?

23 October Friday. Go off to the delousing station in KARATSGEF. In the afternoon the Gef comes to the Tross. Ltn. Wibke is to be demoted. So Pfeifer said. Drill is no good. Excellent! Mail, 1 letter.

25 October Saturday. Today I am going to Tross 1. Our vehicle goes through KARATSGEF to OREL. Lovely town. Stay overnight. There were all sorts of heavy battles here. 3 and 4 Div (3.Panzer Division and 4.Panzer Division) attacked.

26 October Sunday. Drive on to EMENZ, in the direction of TULA. There was quite heavy fighting here. Night time, you can see 4 Russian tanks here: 52 tonners. One bomb crater after another. The dead are still lying around. You can also see our tanks lying here shot to pieces. Can't be any other way. Russian tanks are lying here in their masses. 8.8 Flak (used as anti-tank guns) wreaked terrible havoc here. Stay overnight. Can't go forward to the Company. Such traffic. 2 armies are marching here to TULA. 47 and 48 AK. (47 and 48 Army Korps). Great deal of Russian resistance here.

27 October Monday. Today we go on. One convoy beside the next and Russian tanks on the left and right shot to pieces. LKWs too. Everything lying around here. When will we find our Company? A wonderful day begins. A rarity, this. 'til now it has just rained. Can't describe the road. We were bombed twice. 2 Russian bombers are shot down. Huge amount of aircraft activity. It's bitter cold. We've been travelling since 6 AM and have only gone 5km. Damnation. 3 bridges destroyed. A standing convoy of 50km. We turn off to MZENSK. Look for accommodation. The Henschel (tank engine) given up the ghost. Track rod and front axle broken. Sit here today. We make up our own little club. 3 vehicles from Pomerania. No grub to eat. We're furious! In the evening we brazenly roast potatoes. Otherwise we've got nothing.

28 October Tuesday. Stay in our billet for the time being. Snowed heavily during the night. The convoys are still stuck. Guderian drives past us. We go foraging. We stay all day in this town. No vehicle can move forward. We have to sit here without any supplies. Look at the town. Jonnap shoots a Russian. We left it at that. The Russians have set up rocket launchers here. LKWs with the tyres facing upwards. Strange things. We were also bombed. TULA has fallen.

29 October Wednesday. We set off early. Unfortunately in vain. Only V and III vehicles allowed ahead. Go back to our accommodation. We can't go across open countryside as there are mine fields to left and right, as well as anti-tank ditches and bombs. It seems the Russians don't have many more pilots as they are half-burying the bombers. Tanks, 52 tonners are lying here. In one there were 3 officers and a driver inside. That's how it is with the Russians. All four were shot on the spot. Probably setting off at midday. We look for a diversion and only go for 3km and then come to the convoy. We turn round and go back to MZENSK to our billet. Nothing to eat. That's how it is for us. No vehicle allowed in or out of the town. Officers stand at the street exits. From KARATSCHE. Everything is stuck here. Such bad roads.

30 October Thursday. Get up late. Look for something to eat. No vehicle can leave here. In one day 25 vehicles are towed forward by recovery half track. Such bad roads. We stay put. Mines are blown up all day. In the evening we play skat. No supplies We make potato pancakes. Play skat 'til late evening in billet.

31 October Friday. Stay here in the village. No vehicle in or out anyway, just this dump. There is firing here all day. Otherwise nothing happening all day. I do my washing. Nothing to eat. That's the way of it for us.

1 November Saturday. Today is All Saints' Day. We're hungry and do nothing. Our misfortune! Go foraging. I fry a piece of meat. Play skat. That's all for today. We can't get away from here.

2 November Saturday. Stay in our billet in the morning. Apart from bread we've got nothing to eat. Nothing going on all day. Today we get rations from A.V.L. (*Aufklärungs*, or reconnaissance supply troop). Thank God. Now things are easier for us. Play skat 'til late evening. There's a bit of excitement during the night. A radio operator gets drunk. He tries to bump off a woman, her husband arrives, he shoots the husband. Runs out into another house, shoots another man out of hand. In the early hours he hands himself in.

3 November Monday. We stand guard to catch any vehicle from our Regiment. Otherwise nothing happening. When will we reach the Company? Hopefully soon. We don't know any news.

4 November Tuesday. One day goes by like any other. Today Kurkins and Kuher are back from OREL and bring ½ a sack of mail. One letter for me, that's all! Got 100 cigarettes. It's becoming damned cold, freezing during the day.

5 November Wednesday. Another boring day. A Russian bomber unsuccessfully fires at us with his guns. Otherwise nothing all day. Freezing all day.

6 November Thursday. That was some night! 12.45 it started. A moonlit night. Bitter cold! One bombing attack after another. At least 10, 'til daybreak. Our house rocked and vibrated. The window panes burst. Everything ahead of us on the bridge, which they attacked. But missed the field hospital. A sawmill burned down. No peace. We stay up because today we are going forward to the Company. Out of MZENSK, behind us more bombs are already falling. It goes on all morning. All of a sudden we were bombed on the advance road. Get to TSCHERM. On to MLAFSK, further on to the Company, which is lying 30km before TULA. On the exit roads we are sitting in a village. Big news. Deisch Willi and Mäusl Fritz have been killed. My best friends. 2 radio operators. I just can't believe it. That's a heavy blow for me. Ltn. Bever bullet in the stomach, wounded. All 5 tanks destroyed. That's what it looked like when we arrived. Battle group on security, 15km ahead.

Constant air attacks. On the right 6 Div are deploying in the countryside. Non-stop firing. Scarcely have we fired then we have to start defending. No calm in sight!

7 November Friday. Cleared everything up in the morning. Received winter clothing. Last night was dreadful. Real Russian winter. A snowstorm like I've never seen before, and a dry cold. If it goes on like this it will be bad for us. News from the Company. Our troops were in TULA a week ago. As there were no reinforcements our men had to leave. The Russians put up a big fight in TULA. Heavy street battles. One Russian LKW and Russian DMW were captured by us and taken away. There was mail yesterday. 13 parcels and 11 letters. All sorts of things! 3 o'clock roll call with cooking utensils, water bottle, and pistol. More for me. I am pillion rider for *Wagenknecht*. Go straight away to get fuel from MZENSK. We stay overnight in MZENSK. Meet Uffz. Fengen and Etzlinger with a Russian LKW. Write 6 letters.

"Workshop with Schirmeister in picture."

8 November Saturday. Drive to PLAFSK. We're staying here. Thuss and Benterwertz in the billet. Have to wait for fuel to arrive. Coming with Ju (Junkers 52/3m aircraft) or supply drop. One bombing attack after another follows. Low level attack and blizzard. 6 bombs in the pond next to us. This is highly unpleasant! Play skat.

9 November Sunday. *Schirmeister* (Supply NCO) arrives, flying by Ju to ROSLAWL. Hiller brings news from the Company. 1 Abt has been disbanded. We are getting 2 Pz III (Panzer 3 tanks). Lothar Kress fell while piling up hay this morning, broke his knee-cap. Another radio operator less. With the winter coming it looks bad. Word has it that some are going back to Germany to buy Christmas presents. Still haven't got any fuel.

"Ju – advance towards OREL. November 1941."

10 November Monday. A low level attack by 5 Russian aircraft. One vehicle explodes. News from the Company: 10 days ago Feldw. Burger EK1, Ltn. Berger EK1, Hubinger, Zehntner, Naster Tauner, Weber, and Welker got EK2. ObLtn. Gruschlitz, ObLtn. Mummen, and 2 Obffz, 15 Uffz. from the U.K. (billets) were wounded by hand grenades in an attack. Uffz. Welker is going to OREL to get a change of crew. I have to go forward immediately to the battle group. Kress as radio operator for the Spiess. Great, go with Hüller to Tross 1. Spend the night there.

"Destroyed Russian infantry carrier - American type – in the battles for the defence of OREL."

11 November Tuesday. Today Uffz. Bruckner to battle detachment, Gef is away to the attack. The Comp tanks are still here. Our Company has got 2 Officers and 1 Feldw. Gunther is great. No duty. There are 3 coal mines here. We are lying on the right, a bit further south. Also lovely girls.

"Driving through the burning town of OREL. November 1941."

Wearing greatcoats in front of the tank.

12 November Wednesday. Have guard duty. Nothing to do all day. Am curious to know when Frickling will come. Battle group is in action. Russian aircraft attack. Low level attack nearby a division was cut to pieces. We had just left our vehicles. Otherwise nothing happening.

13 November Thursday. We were bombed at 4 AM. Otherwise nothing happening. Played a bit with Sina. The cold is beyond endurance. -20 degrees. That's quite something! If I go out, then I run. How will things go on? In this cold? Battle group still in action. 1 LKW full of ammunition blew up. All night long it burned and exploded. The girls Sina and Escuvra came to us. E. can speak a little German. We finished them off. Loi and I. I have described the bitter cold. Today winter clothing arrived. 50 earmuffs and 10 greatcoats. By these calculations we will probably not be here over the winter. That can only suit me fine.

14 November Friday. Spiess wakens me and L. He's going to the Battle Group. Am curious to know what's going on. It's still so cold that you don't want to go outside. Today canteen goods arrived. Cigarettes. Feldw. Feder, my driver, Jak and Huggenberger and Ernst came back. Feldw. Bruger drove over a mine. Feder a casualty. They led 2 attacks against Russian cavalry. Also brought sabres with them. Regiment drove further south. Gef the only one from our Company. Every day artillery fire on TULA, all kinds of calibre, 7.5cm to 28cm. That was something! Guggenberger, injured finger from the mine. He sat on it. There are now 5 of us in our building. All of them are missing.

Getting cold, donned greatcoats. Panzer IV E *Tauchpanzer*. Good view of mudflap insignia.

"Our artillery at DELINOWO before the attack on Moscow in November 1941."

15 November Saturday. Gef appears on the scene. Big row. He wants to bring Mertel before a court-martial, because his tank is wrecked We take off 2 road wheels and change them, quite a lot of work. There was mail. 16 parcels and 16 letters for me. Troops are pushing forward. Tross 1 arrived. Artillery hammering TULA without interruption.

"Junkers after emergency landing on the road MZENSK, PLAWSK near TULA. November 1941."

16 November Sunday. Spiess drives to Feldw. Burger to get a pinion for our tank, more action for us. I hope we will be in it. Work on the tank all day. Greasing it, cleaning it. Checking weapons. Touching up the boneshaker with newspaper. Spiess not yet back with the pinion. Got a new pair of trousers. Not as good as the old ones.

17 November Monday. Up at 4.30. Try to fit the pinion. Gef puts it in. Doesn't go in. Such hard luck! 5.30 in the evening we get it in with a spanner. We can't go to the big offensive. In the evening Heuer Franzl arrives with his tank. Spiess goes with him when he has finished. Write 8 letters.

18 November Tuesday. The offensive begins. 60 batteries fire. 5 Div attack: 17, 18, 3, 4 Divisions on the outer flank and one infantry on the inner. (Encircling movement). At 1 o'clock the battle detachments march off. They have to go 70km. The beginning was bigger than at the Bug. Quite powerful. I wasn't there. Pity! Gunnersberger became Uffz. Schirmeister arrived from MAGDEBURG, brought 3 pinions with him. Got to work. We've got to get finished. Roasted 4 chickens. Worked 'til 5.30.

19 November Wednesday. This was the start of our worst time for the Company.
8 o'clock it kicked off. Set off. Fell into a ravine. We were lucky. Everyone could have been killed. Spiess as the commander injured his foot. At midday went to the *Oberst* for a special mission. Unit is surrounded. Tanks have no fuel. We as the only tank pushed through with the infantry. Great attack. In the evening went to the Abt. Four 52 tonners (Soviet KV2 tanks) 200m from the village, fired over our heads. Flak goes into position (to engage the soviet heavy tanks). All night long terrible firing. During the night ammunition and fuel arrived.

20 November Thursday. Now the fun starts. Flak begins. Fires with 5 shots. The Obgefr. comes to us as tank commander. 52-tonner on fire. Great to watch. A bit further on another 2 down. We attack 13 tanks. One tank destroyed. LKWs set on fire. Lots of Russian infantry destroyed. Run over by the tanks. Then the best bit. We attack two 52-tonners and start a real hare hunt. He couldn't turn his turret after the first direct hit and took off. We were after him with force, 20 metres behind him. ½ an hour the hunt went on for until he lost a track and fell into a ditch. We fired 30 shots into him. Nothing got through. There weren't 10cm without a direct hit. We'd never experienced anything like it. Will never forget. Then we went back. Regrouped. Infantry, flak, artillery fire came at us. Attack again. Destroyed LKWs, destroyed infantry. Great battle. Villages burnt to the ground. Finally calm. That day our vehicle fired 110 rounds. Reported in for the Abt in KUKUI. Have no more rounds. About 65 Russian tanks destroyed, loads of LKWs and infantry.

21 November Friday. Into attack again early. Build a bridgehead. Ltn. Schunberger and us. Spiess is with us again. Great attack with 63 Infantry (63. *Panzergrenadier* Regiment), captured lots of LKWs and prisoners. A radio station also. One village set on fire. All sorts going on. 5th attack into the evening.

22 November Saturday. It starts again early. Attack with 63 Infantry. Captured all sorts of things. Lots of prisoners and then leading on. Heuer Franz drove over a mine. Drive shaft broken. Wait behind the lead. Attack in the dark. Houses set on fire. Anti-tank rifles fired beyond us. The attack lasted 'til late. The whole village was on fire. Tanks were destroyed. Plenty happening here again. Then there was silence. Lots destroyed. 2 Russian aircraft attacked us, with bombs. Flak shot down 1. Flak 8.8 has destroyed several tanks.

23 November Sunday. Filled up with fuel during the night. Cheer myself up. Radio watch. 07.15 the attack with 63 Infantry increases. 2 vehicles go in. Ltn. T (Illegible) our platoon commander. All the others attack. For the moment we are right in the middle of the battle. 3 tanks destroyed just now. Flak and us. I also fired (the hull machine gun). Fired like mad at the infantry. There were lots of dead and prisoners. But when the tanks arrived all hell broke loose! A Russian Flak is still standing to our right behind the house. Can't move very well. But we have to get to WENNEF today? That's our target. From there the Russians are loading up their soldiers and tanks. A Stuka attacked us just now. At night we reached WENNEF and dig in. Wonderful *Feuerpanzer*. (Flamethrower tank). Action until 3.15. Then 2 hours' sleep.

"Russian flak gun."

24 November Monday. The dark day for the Company. Early attack on WENNEF, we are the Panzer Regiment. I am with the N.O. (Signals Officer). Panzer regiment 35 (4.Panzer Division) attack from the south, Panzer Regiment 6 (3.Panzer Division) go forward in a wave ahead of us, can see the town already. Flak guns shot a lot of our tanks to pieces. PKWs and LKWs set on fire. Then the fun starts. Into the town. Then the fun starts. (Erich repeats this). Unprecedented street fighting. The Russians are just stumbling around. Our infantry come and mop up, that was a hard battle. We are standing at the monument. 52 tonners arrive (KV 2 tanks). Obfldw. Heidrich fires at it for all he is worth. Us too. Nothing gets it. Heidrich pulls out, then comes back. Again he moves forward and fires. We advanced 10m and went through. Nothing to be done. The Russian fired at us, went close by me. I could see myself getting out. Fire again and Obfldw. Heidrich fires into it. The Russians fire back and their tank goes on fire and they jump out. Obfldw. Heidrich 's legs have been blown off. Träumer Seppl killed outright, Zehnter Franzl fairly seriously wounded, foot and head. Hinterberger Fritz burnt on the hands and head, and Ortlupp, the driver, slightly burned and Spieker on the head. I just can't believe it, Seppl has gone! It's all fate! We stop, get out. They drag Obfldw. Heidrich out. He's still alive, is still conscious. The 52 tonner is now on fire. We take him (Heidrich) into the vehicle and drive to the nearest first aid post. He dies in the radio car. The battle goes on, run, more tanks coming. The journey goes on. Pz IV leads on into the next village. Despatched one 52 tonner and one 32 tonner (T-34 tank). Then we are leading again. We've been leading for 6 days. All sorts going on. Then something moves. Let's go. About 20km still. Destroyed another 52-tonner, caught another one in the next god-forsaken place. What they must have! We've been quite disheartened today. What a day! 'til 9 o'clock we are in pursuit of the Russians. Then the unit reports.

25 November Tuesday. The whole regiment consists of 13 vehicles, amongst them is our company. Still 5 Pz IV. Ahead of us is an airfield, we saw the Russians landing. That was yesterday during the day, we've just realised it today though. Just now Pz 35 (Panzer Regiment 35) has gone past us and I think it's going to attack the airfield. Then *we* are in the lead again. Feldw. Trauter is going to the field hospital. Concussion as he jumped out of the tank in HENNEF as we tried to save Obfldw. Heidrich. Shame about our Lois! 15.30 march off, about 35km. Pulled ourselves together. We went into 7 attacks recently. We go on 'til 10.00. Then we dig in at a school with our infantry. Schmieder took one prisoner. Now ready to load up. Now surprise. The Spiess is coming along the road with his loaded weapon over his shoulder. He could hardly believe that we were here already. Spiess fired a shot then he realized it was us. In the school there are all sorts of things to take. (Possibly the source of Erich's school notebooks). One of the tank's suspensions broke, the outer road wheels gave way. Drive out without suspension. Heidrich got the EK1.

26 November Wednesday. 9 AM we retreat. Only 2 villages back, battle stations. Constant low level attacks by Russians. We tell fleeing prisoners to get back. Curious to see what's going to happen here. Can't work it out yet. Attack on MONONET with infantry after the tanks, but no tanks around. Take prisoners and occupy the station. There is still vodka here. Dispatch riders bring us mail. Parcel for me from F. Hinum. Great news. A mean low level aircraft attack on us, all day it seems. Damned cold, as usual. We continue on early. Have taken MONONET. Turn round and go back to the village. Stukas attack us in a low level attack. A trail of smoke. Fill up with fuel and on we go. All night long as advance unit. There are rather few of us. 1 tank has collided with a bridge. The 6 of us pull him out. Then we go on. 2 Russian LKWs drive past us cool as you please. At the bridge, which was our goal, they drove over our mine. The bridgehead is secured at 3 AM.

27 November Thursday. 3 AM. We go back, attack the village, and go into a billet. No time for sleep. Guard duty. 4.30 awake and go off on attack. Right of the bridge. There was a real firework display. 7 assault guns knocked out, which had all fired at the same time. That went badly for us! The attack continues. 2 tanks shot down, 42 tonner (KV 1), 1 22 tonner (T-34). It's 4 AM, still dark. Bitter cold. On defence duty tonight. Rubbish! Russian low level aircraft attack. Ltn. Meyer returned with his tank. 15 of us again. All day round about the bridge. But it's in our hands. This is the main road to TULA. Lies south of us. Food. Today there were 3 bottles of Sekt (sparkling wine) and 2 bottles of wine per crew. Guard duty, defence 'til 12 o'clock and then a drink. 00.20 return. Manage to get some sleep during the night. Our lips are chapped with the cold. Filled up with fuel. 2 o'clock to bed. Tanks captured from the Russians.

28 November Friday. A firework display. All sorts going on. They've re-taken the bridge. The heaviest lumps (shells and shrapnel) are flying around. In action again here. Our tank a casualty, suspension. Yesterday Schwerkurkt took a direct hit in the turret from 5m. Turret kaput, this time seriously injured. 2 Pz IV drive up to the bridge again. Take heavy artillery fire. 3 Russian tanks were knocked out, which had been reported, were already behind the bridge. Hubert shot down one of them. Ours then moved back. That was a whole km before KASCHIRA, we were so far away from the battle group. KINO attacked.

29 November Saturday. Marched off at midday, retreated a bit. Only two villages back. Here at KASCHIRA is the outer defence point south of Moscow. We few men can't achieve anything here. Have a nice billet with neat and tidy people. In the evening we open 3 bottles of Sekt and 1 bottle of wine. All 5 of us including Spiess a bit tipsy. You can sleep better. A battle-free day. Apart from being shot at by tanks and bombed.

30 November Sunday. Today another Sunday. Gef talks to us. We remember Obfeldw. Heidrich and Sepp Träumer. We come to terms with the fact that we will celebrate Christmas here in Russia. Can't do anything about it! That's why we're soldiers. Sort out the tank, write our Christmas mail in the tank. Otherwise nothing happening. Have to make a beef stew, great meal. In amongst our peace and quiet comes march off, for tomorrow at 03.30. We had felt so good.

1 December Monday. Awake at 03.15. Now the fun starts. There's a snowstorm, never seen one like it. I don't want to put my head outside the tank. The current situation. 63 Infantry (63. Panzer Grenadier Regiment) are on defence with Artillery, *want* to attack the Russians. We've got to go as well! Because otherwise everything goes to pot. 1/:100,000 (map size). Am curious to see what happens. Writing this while we're moving. Black day again. Attack with infantry on the village. A mighty firework display. 6 tanks destroyed by our Flak. Village set alight. Attacked village on the right. Flak knocks out a tank. One 5cm (Panzer III tank) lost. Schilling Adi looks out of the hatch, took a shot in the head, dead. I just can't believe it. Adi, a good comrade and friend. The battle goes on. Ours have contributed so well. In the evening peace, which we have deserved.

2 December Tuesday. Drive back to MOHADEP, Mo5 IBS (Map reference). Just got there when we were sent back to the front. 30 Russian tanks reported. Bombed and shot at all the time on the way. Driving, then twice as many attacks into the village. Can't go over, a ravine over there. The Russians, who are firing at us from a distance of 5.6 km! We can't do anything about it. You can already hear the Russian tanks. So it gets dark and we have to stand defence for all tanks. There's supposed to be a re-grouping of troops. Fill up with fuel during the defence. An indescribable cold. Then we go back. The front suspension bolts on our vehicle break. 12 o'clock into our billet and now there is no more room. We creep in anyway.

Erich's original Iron Cross second class certificate and the original medal. Only the ribbon was worn on the soldier's tunic. Note Erich's name at this time was Totsauer.

3 December Wednesday. It looks as if we have a day off. No march off for the time being. Nothing happening today. It's snowing very heavily. Tank repair company working here. Otherwise nothing happening. The ring round TULA has been closed.

4 December Thursday. Still staying here. Our infantry involved in lots of firing in the night. The Russians attacked twice. Infantry made a run for it, lost all vehicles. Officers all dead. Infantry could get back into the village, but not much point in that, the vehicles are all gone. 8. Comp. 63 Regiment (8th Company of 63 Panzergrenadier Regiment). They've had enough. Last night -36°. Such cold is awful. One Flak 8.8 went to pot. But 3 tanks are waiting on the road.

5 December Friday. The cold is dreadful. -36°. All tanks are frozen solid. We work 'til 2.00 then gave up. You dare not go

out the hatch. The place where we buried Adi has been taken by the Russians again. Zehntner Franzl and Waldi Thors get the EK1 for their injuries. Some new ones have arrived now. The tank is ready. Thank God! Great excitement tonight. 2 houses next to us burning down. 1 house from Flak. Fire watch, so that our house does not catch fire.

6 December Saturday. So cold! -46°. Dreadful! Unless it's necessary, no one leaves the house. 5 AM ready for march off. Spiess is leaving us today, we are getting Feldw. Pechmann. We stand defence in front of the village. Russians are out. Infantry go back, drive 'til 11 o'clock, mines laid everywhere. 4 tanks gotten hold of, 4 LKWs, half track recovery vehicle and two 15 cm. howitzers. We gave up 50km of open country. What does that really mean? 11 o'clock we go back towards WENNEF. Travel all through the night in the bitter cold, more than -40°.Yesterday a large scale attack on TULA began.

7 December Sunday. Finally arrive at 12.00 completely frozen through. 8km south of WENNEF. In a small village, we dig in here. What on earth will happen to us now? In this cold? Almost beyond endurance. Yesterday a parcel arrived from home. Chocolate. Regiment has 8 tanks, less and less. Jesberger was at the court martial yesterday. Tomorrow we'll find out the verdict. Shame for him. The Division is keeping moving here, I think. Gef arrives. 24-hour ready to march off state to DELILOBA. Am just in Delousing 1 and you can't do anything about it, it's like having a pet, lovely and warm. Got undressed and looked for lice! Sad, but there's no other way for it! Today we can get a proper sleep again.

8 December Monday. Surprise: America has declared war on Japan. What will happen there? Today, when I got up and tried to go out, I was thrown back in. An unprecedented snowstorm. The wind blows you away, dreadful. Behind us the blowing up of damaged tanks and bridges. WENNEF is also being opened up. Why? 150km is being opened up. Why?

So the Japanese are giving it all they've got. 2 battle ships sunk, 4 destroyers sunk, 20 aircraft. Attack on the Philippines. Britain has also declared war.

(Erich is talking about the Japanese surprise attack on the U.S. Naval Base at Pearl Harbour in Hawaii on the morning of Sunday, 7 December. This was carried out without a declaration of war. Actually four U.S. battleships were sunk and four damaged. In addition three cruisers, three destroyers, and one minesweeper were either sunk or damaged. 2,402 U.S. personnel were killed and 1,282 wounded.

Japanese losses were light, with 29 aircraft and four midget submarines lost. 65 Japanese were killed or wounded. However, the USA had entered the war with its massive manpower and industrial might. Hitler declared war on the USA as an ally of Japan, as he thought the Japanese would invade the USSR from the east. They never did, being overstretched in the far east and remembering their defeats in Eastern Mongolia in 1938 and '39.)

9 December Tuesday. Up at 5.00, set off at 6.00. Go to DELILOBA, 1 km back. Snow storm has eased up, it's only snowing lightly. -40°. We were scarcely out of the village when we were shot at quite unexpectedly, 30m from us the impact. Tross (unit supply and logistics) to go forward straight away, we stay behind. The infantry go racing by us with the pioneers. We also take some wounded with us, who can walk. You have to have joined in with such a withdrawal. Vehicles come from left and right.
Everything which is left is being blown up so that nothing falls into Russian hands. 3 tanks from our Regiment blown up. There are 8 of us now. We retreat on the old stretch of road which we had captured, 100km. In WENNEF today the Russians took prisoner the commander of the infantry. The journey continues without food 'til 9.30. In the evening we get to DELILOBA, where we spend the night. Bombing attack 5.00 - 8.15.

10 December Wednesday. Early on we go further *back*. Big building round about the railway, we dig in here. We have to keep going 'til KARATSLNEF. We would have thought we were going home. Delousing for us again. That's something else! Tross closed.
The Japanese up to all sorts of things. 2 British battleships sunk, 32,000 and 3[illegible],000 tons. U.S. submarine and 2 freighters. We are delighted about that. The houses are shaking with the bombs being dropped by the Russians, nothing happens. There is all sorts of news. A drastic change for the company.
(Erich has heard of the sinking of the British battleships *Prince of Wales* and *Repulse* by Japanese aircraft off the coast of Malaya.)

11 December Thursday. 2 *Abteilung* disbanded. Our Gef is taking over all the tanks, 13 of them, eight 5cm (Panzer III tanks), four 7.5 cm (Panzer IV tanks), 1 *Befehlspanzer* (Command tank). Regrouping of the men. I'm going to Stabsfeldw. Habel and getting the Gef's vehicle. Feder is tank driver, Guckenlange, Köth, Rakler, and Werreman are also tank drivers of Panzer III. Ltn. Meyer, 1st platoon of Pz IV, Habel, Panzer IV. Ltn. Scheunberger, and Feldw. Pechmann a platoon each 5cm (Panzer III tanks). At 3 o'clock the *Führer* speaks in the *Reichstag*. Today unit parade, *Hauptman* (Captain) speaks to us. It's also our turning point. Division is coming back to the area round PLAFSK. We don't know what might happen to us there. We are protecting the Division, and if the Russians smash through, then we have to go up to the front. We are waiting to be relieved by ObLtn. Frank; when he comes, he's taking over the tanks. 7 o'clock departure. Commanding Officer, Stabsfeldw. Habel, Seifert, Widemann, and I.

12 December Friday. Go back through GOIJEISCHKIND, to PLAFSK and left. Spend the night in a little village. 29 Mot.Div comes back, we advance to there.

13 December Saturday. Journey goes on. Casualty. Bomb damage. Stay behind with the I troops (Maintainance) and do repairs. Tomorrow we'll catch up with the Company. Slaughter a sheep. Company has already reached its position. 3 sacks of mail arrive.

14 December Sunday. Another dark day. We set off early and went down a ravine. Track comes off, we can't get out. We work in bitter cold, but a waste of time. So we were stuck. Scharwoler goes to fetch a recovery half track. When will it get here? Such bad luck! 3 of us are here and we can't get out. That was some Sunday!

15 December Monday. An unprecedented snowstorm. Stand for hours beside the tank. When will the recovery half track get here? The big bridge is being blown up at 12 o'clock today. How will we get to the Company? The half track comes alone. No use! Wait for the second one. Nothing to eat. That's what happens when you are a casualty.

16 December Tuesday. Wagner's tank makes a detour. The second half track appears. 18 Div (18.Panzer Division) blow up 4 tanks next to us. LKWs and PKWs are blown up. In the afternoon the recovery half track comes and we still can't get the tank out. It's already dark and we have to clear out the tank. Finished, on to the half track and go back. Try to tow another tank, but no use, is blown up instead.

17 December Wednesday. Look for and find Herzberg with his LKW, but radiator is burst. Load up our things. Am curious to know whether Habel will send us an LKW. Find ourselves something to eat. Spend the whole day in PLAFSK.

18 December Thursday. Leave at 8 o'clock and go to TSCHERN. Awful journey. 16 hours needed to drive the 30 - 40 km. Arrived in TSCHERN at 12.30.

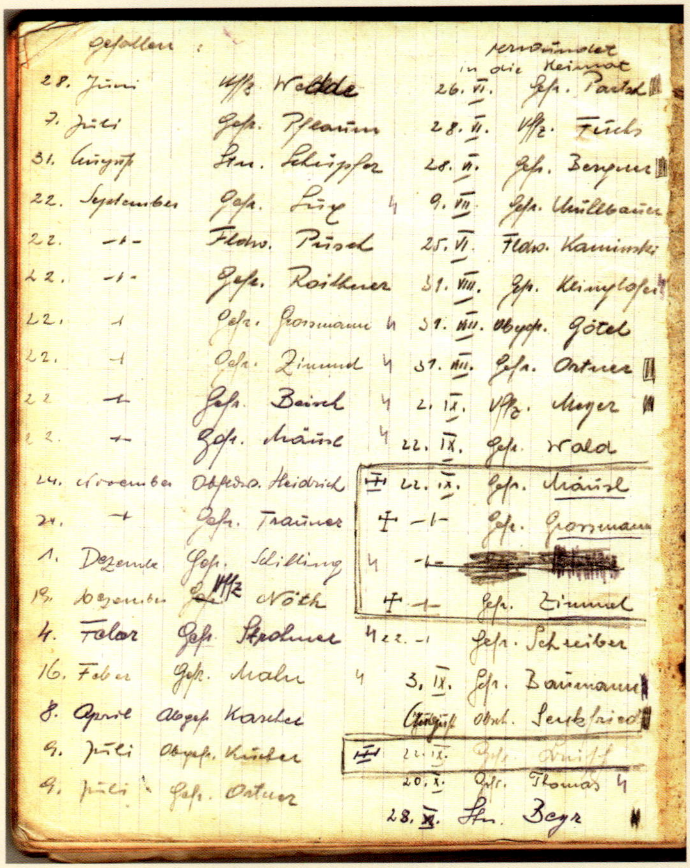

Diary record of "Gefellen," fallen comrades. Many are radio operators as shown by the "Blitz" symbol.

Fallen comrade.

Notes for 18 July to 18 December 1941 Diary

The diary starts with Erich witnessing the bitter fighting around Smolensk. He views the large number of soviet casualties, as well as the German dead and graves of the German fallen, including a son of General Keitel.

Throughout the diary Erich notes the ferocity and intensity of Soviet artillery and aircraft attacks. Many German veterans remember these unpleasant experiences on the Eastern Front.

On 22 July the extent of Soviet vehicle losses are shown by their use of horse-drawn transport. This was before the U.S. supplied trucks as war aid.

The next day, the loss of comrades starts to affect Erich, as it did many other German soldiers. On the 29th Erich reports his foraging activites. Many soldiers had to forage for food, taking it from the civilian population, the enemy, or even other units of their side. Food, or the lack of it, was always on soldiers' minds.

Erich regrets that 17.Panzer Division was left out of the action on 3 August, and on the 7th there is his first mention of attacks on German troops by civilians. This is a harbinger of the Partisan attacks of the future. The early German successes meant they could not take all the encircled Soviet troops prisoner, and many slipped away with weapons to attack the German units in the rear. Reports of brutal treatment of prisoners, including execution, reduced the willingness of Soviet troops to surrender. The brutalities carried out against the civil population and the Nazis' enemies, such as Jews and Commissars, alienated many and encouraged them to take up arms in revenge for the loss of relatives or friends. On 12 August Erich starts to call these Soviet fighters "Partisans." This is the term we now refer to them with, but the Nazis thought this was too heroic. They preferred to call them "Bandits."

The Partisan attacks would plague the German forces on the Eastern Front. The Soviet command would send elite troops to fight alongside the Partisans.

On the 16th Erich reports on the large encirclement battles, and on the 21st puts in an entry about higher wages. We do not know if this was a promotion or something given to all the troops. He is less happy about the contradicting orders his unit receives on the next day. Soldiers often complain of this in wartime, as they are moved from place to place and back again. He manages to lift his spirits on the 31st by meeting girls for the first time in this diary.

Mounting German casualties are noted on 2 September. How many German soldiers could have predicted the scale of the losses on the Eastern Front? The losses force Panzer Regiment 39 to be reduced from a regiment to an *Abteilung*, roughly the size of a Battalion, on the 4th. The same day two of Erich's comrades go missing and are never found. Most probably they were murdered by partisans. They could have deserted.

Due to the long supply lines and shortage of transport elite units the Panzers were resupplied by aircraft. Erich reports this on the 6th. These would probably be the three-engined Junkers 52/3m (Ju 52/3m). This was the maid of all work air transport plane the German troops referred to as the "Antie Ju" (Tante Ju). On the same day Erich gets a foretaste of the severe winter ahead when it is so cold that they have to don their greatcoats.

Erich's experience of other people is expanded by watching a Russian funeral. After the usual air attacks, of course!

Early September brings a lot of combat, with other Panzer units, such as 18.Panzer Division, 3.Panzer Division, and 4.Panzer Division. Erich sees the contribution made by the Auxiliary service or RAD (Reich Labour Service). They helped the troops by carrying out engineering and supply work. On 16 September there is mention of Partisans being released. These lucky souls were probably recognized as civilians caught up in the fighting. Later such distinctions were not always observed.

In the action on 22 September, Erich refers to the lumbering KV series of Soviet heavy tanks. These were named after Kliment Voroshilov, the Soviet Defence Minister. The thick armour (maximum 110 mm) came as a great shock to the Germans, as their tank and anti-tank guns could not penetrate the Soviet tanks. The Flak 8.8cm guns and howitzers had to be brought up to deal with these tanks.

Despite all the fighting and air attacks Erich is still preoccupied with food, comfortable billets, and girls. In this he is a typical soldier of all countries. Mention is made of the famous Panzer General Guderian.

October 3rd brings an EK1, or Iron Cross First class award. This, the *Führer's* speech, and a good booze up raises morale. Ominously, on 10 October Erich notes the first snow of the dreadful 1941/42 winter, which was to cripple the German armed forces and greatly help to stem their advances. Despite the hope of a unit Knight's Cross award Erich is angry over the loss of his tank, which forced him to serve as an infantryman for a while.

Around this time 17.Panzer.Division, in Bryansk, was coming under attack from Soviet units desperately trying to flee east. Erich records the fighting of his Division, which was acting as the Northeast corner of a pocket that forced the enemy to surrender.

Due to the increasing cold Erich is concerned over spending a winter in Russia. His soldierly instincts would prove right. Erich's pride as a tank man is obvious by his highlighting the first year as a tank soldier. The soldier longs for mail, and Erich complains over the lack of contact with home on 22 October.

The great losses on both sides are noted, as are the massive forces involved in the fighting. Even as an enlisted man Erich is aware of the involvement of two German Army Corps, the 47th and 48th.

Erich notes that one Soviet tank had three officers in the crew. The Soviets did not trust the Army and kept a lot of officers loyal to the party close to the front. These and the enlisted men captured were shot. This would indicate that they were Commisars. The notorious "Commisar Order" instructed that all Commissars were to be shot when captured. This order was signed by General Keitel under pressure from Hitler and Himmler.

After reporting a shortage of food Erich hears that a fellow soldier has shot and killed two civilians while drunk. This would be typical of the atrocities and loss of life on the Eastern Front. Erich feels this loss when, on 6 November, two of his best radio operator friends are killed. However, he is cheered up by meeting girls on the 11th.

The temperature continues to drop, and by 13 November it reaches -20 degrees centigrade. In the bitter cold Erich runs everywhere to keep warm. Those that had to keep still, such as sentries, suffered from frostbite and even froze to death. Winter clothing arrived on the 13th, and Erich was lucky to get this, as many did not. As this was designed for continental Europe it was to prove totally inadequate for the extreme cold in Russia. Erich hopes not to be in Russia over the winter. Many German troops no doubt made this wish.

Around the middle of November Erich records the major part that 17.Panzer Division played in encircling and capturing the major town of Tula. However, Erich regrets he missed the big encircling battle carried out by five Divisions on 18 November. The next two days see more problems with the Soviet heavy tanks. However, the Soviets take further heavy losses. The following period, from 19 to 28 November, brings fierce fighting, and there are large numbers of Soviet casualties and German losses. Erich loses more friends.

Erich does take comfort from the initial Japanese successes at Pearl Harbour and against the British at Malaya. However, these would be as deadly as the Russian winter when the USA entered the war. Hitler declared war against the United States, unleashing its manpower and industrial might against him. Erich would later experience the U.S. supplied tanks, trucks, and supplies the Soviets would receive in plenty in the following years.

Erich resigns himself to having to spend Christmas in Russia away from loved ones at home. Again, this was on the thoughts of most German servicemen. From 2 December to the 6th the temperature plummets to -36 degrees and then to -40 degrees centigrade. Erich cannot describe the cold. Most would have experienced nothing like it. Tanks froze solid, as did weapons and other vehicles. Men died from the cold and the German advance ground to a halt.

Erich was witness in this diary to the dreadful winter fighting of 1941/42. The Germans had invaded the USSR in the summer when the conditions were hot and dry. This was followed by rains and the thick "Rasputitza" mud. In Russia the spring and autumn are very short; the year consists mainly of summer and winter. Both are quite extreme. The first snow falls in October and winter lasts seven months. Temperatures are commonly -40 degrees and can fall as low as -60 degrees centigrade. The wind chill can make any temperature feel even lower.

The Russian winter affected all aspects of military operations from the highest command echelons to the soldiers' everyday living. Tactics and doctrines had to be adjusted and new ones implemented. Logistics, transport, communications, use of weapons, and medical treatment were all affected.

Weapons failed to operate properly in the extreme cold. Components such as firing pins broke. Bolts, breech blocks, and actions froze. Optical sights fogged up. Primers failed to detonate and propellant charges malfunctioned. The effects of artillery, mortars, and grenades were muffled by the snow. Soldiers learned the quick way to unfreeze weapons was to urinate on the working parts. Later lubricants based on sunflower oil and/or containing gasoline were used that improved the situation.

Vehicle and aircraft engines' oil and coolants froze. The various metals expanded and contracted at different rates, which lead to malfunctions. Tins and pans of petrol were burned to thaw out frozen engines. Vehicle tires and tracks froze solid to the ground. Insulating materials, such as layers of canvas and thick reed mats, were lashed over engine hoods to retain heat and stop freezing on halts. Horse-drawn sledges replaced motor vehicles, as they could move in the extreme conditions.

Wounded froze to death; hands froze to weapons and the tops of ears to steel helmets. More soldiers succumbed to frostbite and hypothermia than battle wounds. Any wounds could easily turn septic. Open wounds could freeze and kill from shock. Due to the lack of opportunities for washing clothes and bodies lice were rife. Straw and newspapers were stuffed in boots and under clothing for warmth. Urinating and defecating had to be done very carefully to avoid frostbite. Central European winter uniforms were inadequate for Russian conditions. Padded winter clothing was issued later.

The first winter was so bad the troops were awarded the *Medaille Winterschlacht im Osten* 1941/42 (The Winter Battle Medal in the East 1941/42). One of the soldiers' more polite names for it was the *Gefrierfleischorden*, or the Order of the Frozen Meat. It was given for service on the Eastern Front between November 1941 and 15 April 1942. Combat troops had to have served at least 14 days and support troops at least 60 days on the Eastern Front. Erich certainly qualified for his.

Chapter 5

The Sütterlin Diary: 19 December 1941 to 29 January 1942

Written in a grey Russian school notebook.

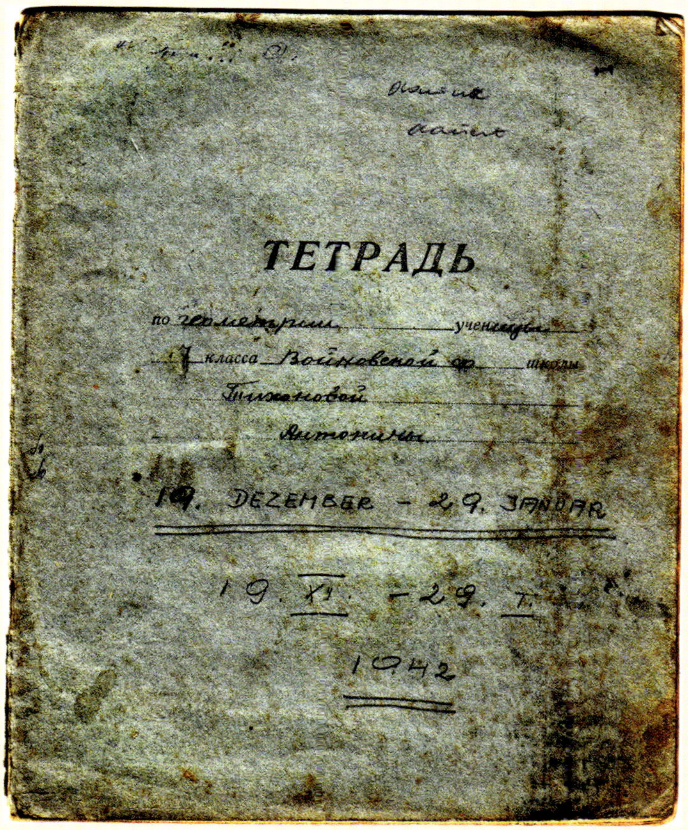

Diary cover.

19 December Friday. We spend the night in the former G.R.U. (soviet military intelligence) prison. We continue at midday, away from the Rollbahn (main route of advance and supply) and after the Division. Battle Group had an encounter. *Gefreiter* Christian Nuth was killed by an MG (Machine Gun) bullet while bailing out; we couldn't save him. He got his EK1 (Iron Cross First Class) in vain. Stay at the rendezvous point. Spend the night there.

"On the retreat from MOSCOW at WENNEF – own Junkers after emergency landing. December 1941."

20 December Saturday. Stop *Wagenknecht*, who takes us with him to the Company. Thank God we are here. Got 2 parcels and 4 letters. We have to stand defence, with MG (MG 34 Machine Gun from the tank). Damnation! Loaded MG. In the evening quite a musty billet. Scheunberger's tank also useless, same problem as happened with ours. We still have 7 tanks and 1 *Befehlspanzerspanzer*.

21 December Sunday. Set off, going back the same way. Quartered in a school. Herst has arrived. The infantry have suffered the most losses in this retreat. I don't want to write any more details about it. At one place ahead of us 8 partisans were hanged. The Russians had hanged 80 of our soldiers beside the partisans. That's what it's like in Russia. Heavy artillery fire over our heads. The Russians will be coming.

22 December Monday. The usual snowstorm. We have to move on at midday. Drive 10km back into our quarters. Snowstorm as before. The Russians are following after us.

"Grave of Obfldw. Heidrich and Gefr. Trauner. Fell in WENNEF. 22 January 1941."

23 December Tuesday. In the morning fall in. Gef speaks to us. Regiment 39 getting 60 tanks, and we have therefore to remain here in Russia. Such hard luck! Nothing will come of the reinforcements. The Tross (supply and logistics unit) is moving over to the Division command tank post as it is too dangerous here. LKWs are stuck. 10km back to the Div. Got mail with Christmas things. No one in the "Christmas schnaps mood," no one on hand! Tomorrow is Christmas Eve. What will it be like at home? If only I could celebrate at home for a moment!

"In memory of your friend Rudi Bischof. 23.12.41. Died 10.4.1945."

24 December Wednesday. Christmas today. Waken us. The march off order has come already. 30km back behind the line of defence. Arrive in a godforsaken place. It's even worse here. Can't upset us. There was wine and biscuits, 1 bar of chocolate. Tomorrow we move on again. There are passwords. We have to be loaded up on 18 January?? What is going to happen to us? We have our Christmas celebration. 10 men in our vehicle. Heussler Erich. Made a pot roast. Shot cows and thought of home. What else were we supposed to do? Start to stand guard 1 to 4. Have bad luck. Lost 120RM. Our thoughts were at home. That's how we spent Christmas Eve.

25 December Thursday. 1st day of the holiday. We make real coffee, ourselves, of course. Have mutton to eat, make stew for all us old meat lovers, but make it ourselves, of course. We have no cows. March off, retreating again. The place is 4km beyond the river, regrouping again. 4 vehicles go on ahead. Battle group, Tross 1 (Supply Train), and then all of us break through elsewhere. In the evening we arrive. Billets, perhaps our winter quarters. We have the best. Our crew has guard duty today.

26 December Friday. Another snowstorm and bitter cold again. We're used to it. What do we do? Play cards, won 17 to 4, won 230 RM, great! Won more again. Played Skat at night. Otherwise nothing happening. Wrote a few letters.

27 December Saturday. Busy myself with the cooking. Make beef for 10 men. Get a parcel from Gefre. Otherwise nothing happening. Villages ahead of us are on fire. The Russians have not to find any accommodation. Artillery gets into position beside us. There will be canteen goods tomorrow.

28 December Sunday. Awake and cards in my hands already. Now 17.00, then Skat. There are canteen goods. Cigarettes, up to 20 packets. Next to us in position, firing all morning, the house shakes. They are firing 3km at the Russians, who attack brazenly. They have heavy losses. Battle group was bombed. Feldw. Burger slightly wounded with shrapnel in the head. Roast beef. Got 3 letters. News from Arthur. What will it be, a boy or a girl? In the evening played Skat. Lots of noise because of Artillery. G (illegible) caught again, is already in the field hospital.

29 December Monday. Artillery firing like mad, our house shaking. Take ammunition up. Bitter cold. During the night Russian artillery fires at us, heavy shrapnel. Otherwise nothing happening.

30 December Tuesday. Wait for Uffz. Gross to drive to Orel for ammunition. Also took the opportunity to go to a cinema. Artillery firing like mad. You get used to it! So cold, as ever. Only went 20km. When we came back our Tross had moved out. One house on fire. Russian artillery is firing at our hill. Go to Tross 1. Unload there, then to our village, which is our winter quarters. A shed! We have to sort out everything ourselves.

31 December Wednesday. The *big surprise*, I have to report to the Gef. The entry was 1A. Here with the Gef, ask about whether they are going to relieve us. Gef, of course, says no. So we are staying. Our artillery firing so much that our house is shaking. Promotions have also been announced. Uffz. Fiese becomes Feldw., Obgfr. Ortlepp, Gefr. Guckenberger, Merkler, Bauernfeind, Wenmann, and W…. (Illegible) become Uffz. Seven made Obergefr: Hopf, Krapf, Schonwalten, Schneeweis, Seifert, Pflauge, and Wendel. There was one *Gefreiter* and several *Oberschützen*. Go to Gef. Wagenknecht and I were awarded EK2. Am extremely happy. At Tross 1 Obffz. Guckenberger. Celebrated New Year until 3 AM. Springer got hold of a radio. That's how the old year ended.

1942 Happy New Year

1 January Thursday. With Wagenknecht to Tross 2. The surprise: Walter, Manngold, and I are going to Feldw. Frist's tank. Driver is Pilshofer Karl. Slaughter another calf, then to battle group with the cooking.

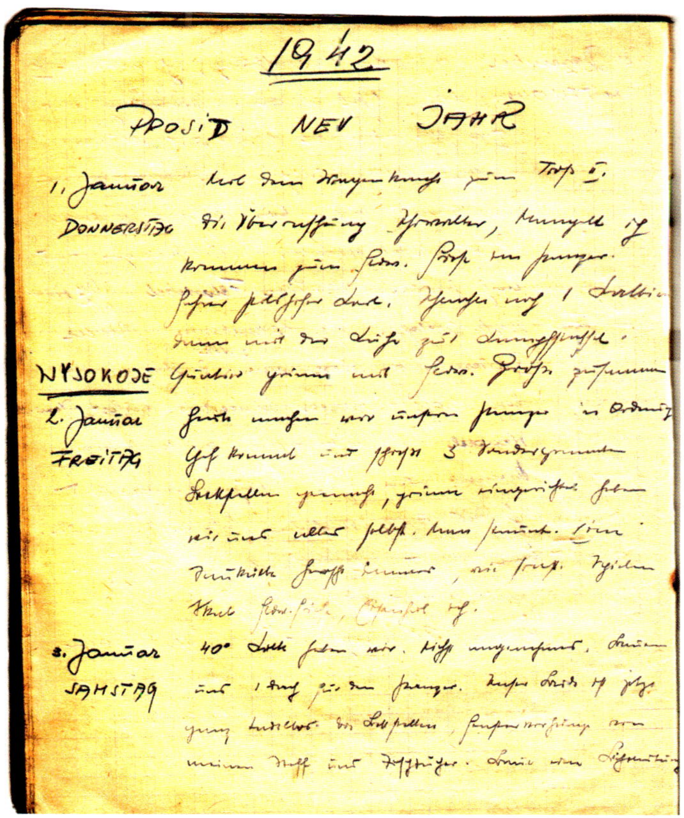

"Happy New Year"

2 January Friday. Great billet with Feldw Grosse Today we are sorting out our tank. Gef arrives and fires 3 special shells. Made bed spaces, have settled in well, done everything ourselves. They are astonished! Still bitter cold. Played skat, Feldw. Friese, Ersteinhart, and me.

3 January Saturday. It's -40 degrees. Very unpleasant. Built a shelter for the tank. Our space is quite exceptional. Bed sheets, curtains made of new table cloth material. Fix lighting. Slaughter a sheep, there's mutton stew again. Guderian sends us a farewell speech. When will we be relieved? A Gefr. is supposed to be on his way. Whether he's for us? Big surprise. Bergen Fritz, Ortner Hansl, Bartzl, Sackfried, K.. (Illegible), and others come from the reserve unit. Today -45 degrees, enjoy schnaps, a crying shame! Spiess visits us, stays 'til 1.30 AM.

"To remember your friend Hansl."

4 January Sunday. Continue building the shelter. Drove 3 hours with the tank because of freezing up. Infantry blowing holes in the frozen ground for foxholes next to us as 2nd line. Down to -45 degrees, not pleasant. Stemminger, Eisenfurth, Krupf, Krubak EK2, and Feldw. Feder get EK1 (Iron Cross First Class). In the evening I make a roast.

5 January Monday. Nothing happening. 1 Russian aircraft firing at our artillery. General Schmidt, our commander from 2 A.K. (Army Corps) visits. Nothing happens all day. It's a bit less cold. Make pastry for baking. Get 3 letters. One from Hilde.

6 January Tuesday. One day like the rest. Only bitter cold as ever. Pass the time as usual. Gef visits us.

7 January Wednesday. Bake 4 loaves of bread in the morning. I think we are going to get snow. There's a storm and a bit of snow. Bitter cold. Hear there's going to be mail. THE BIG SURPRISE. I have got a little cousin. Aunt Mitzl wrote me today, born on 27 November at 9 o'clock. I hear about it a bit late. It doesn't matter! Received a kilogram parcel.

Postcard from an unknown officer to Erich's aunt Mitzl on the occasion of her Saint's day. He hoped the war would soon be over and that the harvest had been good. He ends by sending kind regards to her and her family.

8 January Thursday. We radio operators from 2nd platoon have to build a new telephone line. Work all day. Great excitement. 2 Russian aircraft land 10 men. Fighting detachment detailed. Highest state of standby. We send out vehicles. I go too. The whole day aircraft activity from the Russians and not one single Flak (anti-aircraft gun). Where is it? Still no Flak here for the whole defensive day. It's starting to snow.

9 January Friday. Snowstorm again today. Is more snow on its way? Have to lay the telephone line again. Work 'til evening and bitter cold. More aircraft activity, only Russian guys. Got a parcel from Hilde.

10 January Saturday. One day goes by like the last. Russian aircraft activity. It's snowing quite heavily. Otherwise nothing happening.

Panzer I Ausf. A

11 January Sunday. It's snowing heavily. Have to take the snow plough out (ploughs could be attached to the front of trucks or even tanks). Have 24 hours of guard duty. Otherwise nothing happening.

Tauchpanzer commander.

12 January Monday. Have tank guard duty. Artillery firing as usual. Russians are attacking more often. They can't achieve anything though. Infantry have to hold out.

13 January Tuesday. We hear from Goresshart that the attack could be useful. On Saturday have to attack BOKD and destroy it.

14 January Wednesday. Supposed to leave in the evening. Ready for march off from 5 o'clock. We set off. Drive to the infantry. We spend the night there.

15 January Thursday. Awake at 2.00, everything starts. Engineers built the bridges for us. 1 Battalion goes with us. The Russians must have got wind of the event. We get to SMARADOKKO. The Russians, of course, are no longer there. We go over the bridges. We fire after the fleeing Russians. Engineers blow up the village. There are 3 prisoners. Then we retreat. Feldw. Grosse collides with the bridge. Uffz. Gertlein couldn't get across with us. Now we are standing in front of the bridge and can't get back. The engineers are still building. We stand there, all of a sudden air attack by 2 Russian dive-bombers. We creep round the tank. Run for it. They've just gone when 4 more arrive, furiously firing with all guns. At the last minute I got to the tank. And then it crashed. Too much! The tank is surrounded by a firework display. Hit after hit and I'm sitting inside. Nothing happens though. Burning embers fall on to our tank but none caused a fire. Finally we get back over the bridge and back to our quarters.

16 January Friday. Calm now. We get our food. I divide it up for the whole platoon Weapon cleaning. 10 o'clock cholera injections. Now we have to be self sufficient for a few days. It's snowing as usual and bitter cold.

17 January Saturday. Cooked all day. Everyone shows their cooking skills. Mostly meat. Aircraft over us, firing on occasions. 5 artillery shots land in the garden next to us. Nothing lands on the house.

18 January Sunday. Cooking and cooking again. Tyrolean dumplings are made and apple puree. Clean MG. I write 8 letters. Otherwise nothing happening. The whole time we play Skat.

19 January Monday. Have guard duty. We fell out to the Feldw. Tr (illegible) gets a punishment guard duty. In the evening the big surprise. Gef gets the order to be ready immediately for march off in the direction of OREL for the next piece of action. South of KALUGA 20 Russian divisions have broken through, so there is to be a battle there. 18 Div (18.Panzer Division) is already up there. I think we'll get there too late. Doesn't matter.

20 January Tuesday. Am relieved earlier for slaughter (animals for food). I slaughter 3 cows on my own. In freezing cold. In the evening we have liver. The battle should be over. 18 Div and others are doing that. *Oberst Kuno is getting the* Ritterkreuz. *Our Gef is getting the* Grosskreuz *in Gold.*

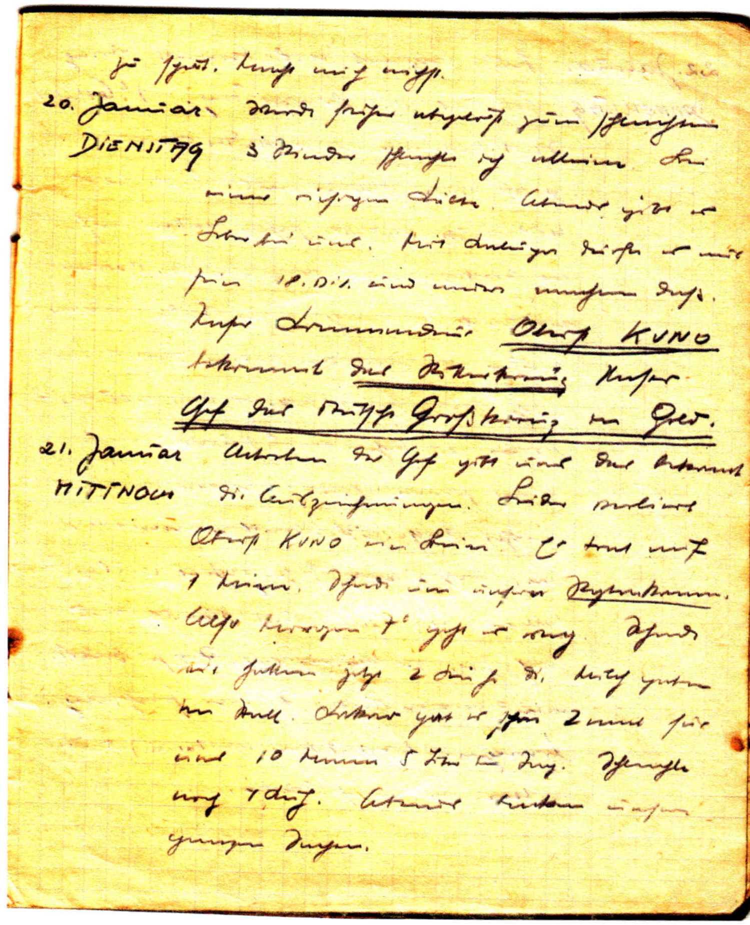

"*Oberst* Kuno is getting the *Ritterkreuz*. Our Gef is getting the *Grosskreuz* in Gold."

"Our regimental commander *Oberst* Kuno."

21 January Wednesday. Fall in. Gef tells us the awards. Unfortunately Oberst Kuno has lost a leg. He stepped on a mine. Shame for our regiment's commanding officer. So tomorrow at 7.00 he's leaving. Shame! We now had 2 cows

that were giving us milk in the byre. There was butter twice for the 10 of us, 5 litres per day. Slaughter another cow. In the evening we make roasts.

22 January Thursday. Today is the beginning of the 8th month of war for us! A dark day. 7 o'clock departure. We don't get far. The tank makes a clanking noise and we're out of action again. Today it's -45 degrees and we're standing in the middle of the road. Guard the tank. So cold, we run round and round the tank so that we don't freeze. My hands are soon frozen. So we stand for hours on an open plain. Finally we stumble into the nearest village. We arrive at 6.30 PM. Eichmann was out of action earlier here. Uffz. Schurre and Wendel are also here. We stay here. Thank God, a warm billet. Such an unlucky day! Company is lying 7km further on and still trying to get to OREL.

23 January Friday. Still here. Tank repair crew working at it. Will the stupid thing go today? Tank repairers work 'til midday. We set off at 1 o'clock. 100m and then the same thing. It clatters and then a piece of bad luck, the fan belt is on fire. Goes out quickly. We look and find the cable is broken. We are standing on the road in the bitter cold. Uffz. Gefrühner and his Pz IV (tank) are also here. We take out the cable. Hopf is with us. Then we go on, but noisier and noisier. By evening we've managed to do 7km. Billet in a village. Am curious to see when we will get to OREL.

24 January Saturday. Hopf works at the old crate (the tank); it's going but not yet. Bad luck! Finally he gets it going. Drive to OREL. However, our Company is outside of OREL. 1 hour's walk. Arrive. Tanks already left on the 21st for BOLCHOW, 60km and then 26km more. Tross is there.

"Defence and counter attack in winter. January. North of OREL round about BOLCHOW."

"Counter attack in winter towards BOLCHOW. January 1942."

25 January Sunday. Still staying here. Heuer, Uffz Hertlein, command tanks are in the workshop. Got 3 new ones therefore. We don't do much today. Play the gramophone. Great dance music, also Viennese waltzes.

26 January Monday. Hopf sorts our wreck out. I think he's going now. Sort out the tank. Track links changed etc. Tomorrow we'll catch up with the Company. Has already seen an attack with our aircraft. The road has to be cleared to TARATSCHEPP. I don't know any other details. Today I handed over my leather boots to our shoemaker so that he can make me fur boots. Looking forward to them already. Am curious to know when I'll get them.

27 January Tuesday. Up at 4.00, then leave for DOLCMON, beyond OREL, also further on a drive shaft breaks. Sort the tank, then we get on towards the battle group. Bitter cold, -45 degrees. That is on the Rollbahn to KARATJUE.

28 January Wednesday XVI DULBINO, village on the Rollbahn
10 o'clock departure for the attack with the 2nd Batl 63 (II./ Panzer Grenadier Regiment 63). Take the village, no great resistance. In a snowstorm the likes of which I have never seen. PK went with us taking photographs. Our tank and a few others. (Propaganda *Kompanie* – troops in the *Whermacht* or *Waffen* SS that acted as war correspondents. As serving soldiers they reported from the thick of the combat, taking photographs and film. Many were killed and wounded in the course of their duties.) Dead Russians are lying around the village. Then we go back into the old village. Make billets. Our soldiers were attacked by the Russians without warning here. All the regiment's supplies. Everything is lying around here. The bloody Russians have devoured all the Christmas presents. Infantrymen must have had to make a run for it. Some are just back. They also have dead. The Russians were Cossacks. The Battle Groups fought 3 battles without us here. The Russians were already on the Rollbahn. Could be bad for us.

ter Angriffe der Sowjets und des | sind dringend erforderlich, wenn die | Feind!

Foto: Kriegsberichter Lachmann von unserer PK

Auch Sturmgeschütze können in einer Schneewehe festsitzen. Aber dann hilft der gute Bruder, der Panzer

Erich kept this newspaper photo taken by *Kreigsberichter* Lachmann. *Sturmgeschütze* III Ausf. B and Panzer III Ausf. J.

29 January Thursday. Nothing happening today. No attack. A ski battalion of ours has attacked, 5km ahead of us. Sort the tank. Yesterday there came a new *Oberleutnant* Graf von Douglas, seems to be a great guy. Tomorrow we're off again. A snowstorm all day. Visibility is less than 50m. The road from DULCUOW to here is impassable, everything snowed in with snowdrifts. They bring us our fuel on sledges. We are completely snowed in. Russian tanks are ahead of us, 2 behind us also. The day before yesterday Ltn. Nager got a direct hit on the track. Nothing else happened. Tank is back in one piece again.

"At the counter attacks in KOSMINKA. January 1942." Panzer IV Ausf. E on right.

"Fuelling up in KOSMINKA. January 1942." Panzer III Js.

Notes on 19 December 1941 to 29 January 1942 diary

The Diary starts with the death of one of Erich's friends. Erich is struck by the fact that he had just won the Iron Cross First Class. Death and wounding never stopped on the Eastern Front. The quality of Billets was very important to the troops, particularly in that first severe winter.

On 27 December Erich hears of one of the many tit for tat killings that were designed to spread fear and were carried out by both sides. In reprisal for the hanging of eight partisans, eighty German prisoners had been hanged in the same spot. This brutality was typical of war in the East. The Germans often killed ten locals for the killing of one German. This would rise to the leveling of whole villages later in the war. Many Soviet troops saw the Germans as ruthless invaders and resorted to torture, mutilation, and execution of any prisoners.

The fact that Erich considered snowstorms common is an indication of the severity of that winter, which was the worst seen for many years. He has resigned himself to Christmas at the front, but thinks of and longs to be with his family. This was common to most of the troops. "No one was in the Christmas Schnaps mood." The unit does cheer itself up with Christmas treats in "a God forsaken place."

The amount and accuracy of the Soviet artillery and air attacks are noted throughout. Erich was no doubt still popular due to his training in food preparation, which he often mentions. On 31 December promotions and awards brighten up the troops' spirits. Just into the New Year Guderian takes his leave of the troops under his command as Erich notes on 3 January.

Probably just as he thought he had seen it all, Erich is amazed to find he has a new baby cousin. He didn't know anything about it but is clearly delighted.

Another indication of the variety and sophistication of Soviet tactics is shown by the landing of airborne troops on 8 January. These would probably be Special Forces inserted to train and fight with the Partisans. A problem for all fighting units was the availability of bridges and the problems of access if one could not be crossed. This was to plague the *Whermacht* throughout the war. Erich reports on an incident where his unit was cut off by a bridge being unavailable. He has to sit in his tank under artillery and air attack. It cannot have been a pleasant experience. The tank offered armour protection but was full of fuel and ammunition if hit.

On 20 January, Erich shows his pleasure by underlining the entry concerning Colonel Kuno being awarded the Knight's Cross, the highest level of the Iron Cross series, and the Company Commander's award of the second highest award, the German Cross in Gold. Actually Kuno had been awarded the German Cross in Gold on 14 January and the Knight's Cross on the 18th. Although these were awarded to individuals, they reflected on the performance of the whole unit and were a source of pride to all the troops involved. Unfortunately Colonel Kuno did not enjoy it for long, as he lost a leg to a mine soon after. He then served in the *Führer* reserve.

Early 1942 saw 17.Panzer Division in a holding area in "Winter Line" positions near Mtsensk.

The terrible cold temperatures are shown by Erich saying he has to run round the tank at halts to keep warm. Like many of the troops he has to improvise by getting the cobbler to make fur boots from his service ones. By this time collections in Germany for warm clothes for the troops at the front were getting through. Even women's furs were donated and used. These did not make up for the woeful lack of suitable clothing for the Russian winter. Furs could be sewn into troops' clothing or, as seen here, boots.

The diary ends with Erich observing the way the PK - troops serving as War Correspondents - took photographs in the thick of combat. Erich is annoyed at the Soviets looting the unit Christmas presents and concerned that they will cut the Rollbahn, the main route of supply, and threaten any withdrawal of his unit.

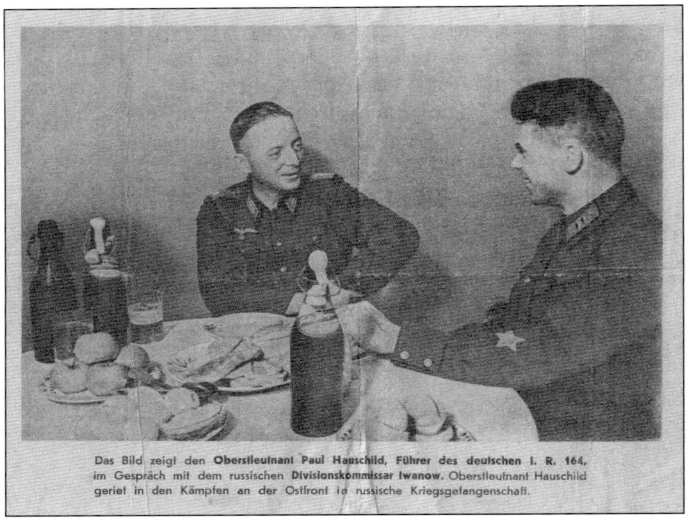
Das Bild zeigt den **Oberstleutnant Paul Hauschild, Führer des deutschen I. R. 164,** im Gespräch mit dem russischen **Divisionskommissar Iwanow.** Oberstleutnant Hauschild geriet in den Kämpfen an der Ostfront in russische Kriegsgefangenschaft.

Soviet leaflet enticing German troops to surrender by showing the supposedly good treatment of a German officer. The reality for German (and Soviet) POWs was quite different.

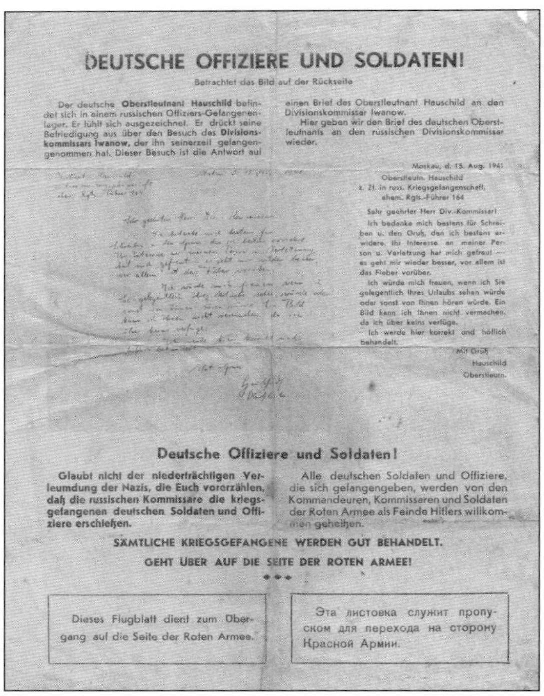
DEUTSCHE OFFIZIERE UND SOLDATEN!

Betrachtet das Bild auf der Rückseite

Der deutsche **Oberstleutnant Hauschild** befindet sich in einem russischen Offiziers-Gefangenenlager. Er fühlt sich ausgezeichnet. Er drückt seine Befriedigung aus über den Besuch des **Divisionskommissars Iwanow,** der ihn seinerzeit gefangengenommen hat. Dieser Besuch ist die Antwort auf einen Brief des Oberstleutnant Hauschild an den Divisionskommissar Iwanow.

Hier geben wir den Brief des deutschen Oberstleutnants an den russischen Divisionskommissar wieder.

Moskau, d. 15. Aug. 1941

Oberstleutn. Hauschild
z. Zt. in russ. Kriegsgefangenschaft,
ehem. Rgts.-Führer 164

Sehr geehrter Herr Div.-Kommissar!

Ich bedanke mich bestens für Schreiben u. den Gruß, den ich bestens erwidere. Ihr Interesse an meiner Person u. Verletzung hat mich gefreut — es geht mir wieder besser, vor allem ist das Fieber vorüber.

Ich würde mich freuen, wenn ich Sie gelegentlich Ihres Urlaubs sehen würde oder sonst von Ihnen hören würde. Ein Bild kann ich Ihnen nicht vermachen, da ich über keins verfüge.

Ich werde hier korrekt und höflich behandelt.

Mit Gruß
Hauschild
Oberstleutn.

Deutsche Offiziere und Soldaten!

Glaubt nicht der niederträchtigen Verleumdung der Nazis, die Euch vorerzählen, daß die russischen Kommissare die kriegsgefangenen deutschen Soldaten und Offiziere erschießen.

Alle deutschen Soldaten und Offiziere, die sich gefangengeben, werden von den Kommandeuren, Kommissaren und Soldaten der Roten Armee als Feinde Hitlers willkommen geheißen.

SÄMTLICHE KRIEGSGEFANGENE WERDEN GUT BEHANDELT.

GEHT ÜBER AUF DIE SEITE DER ROTEN ARMEE!

Dieses Flugblatt dient zum Übergang auf die Seite der Roten Armee.

Эта листовка служит пропуском для перехода на сторону Красной Армии.

The reverse of the same leaflet promising safe passage in German and Russian.

Another Soviet surrender leaflet trying to suggest that when German soldiers were dying on the battlefield their wives, girlfriends, and sisters were being ravished by the SS.

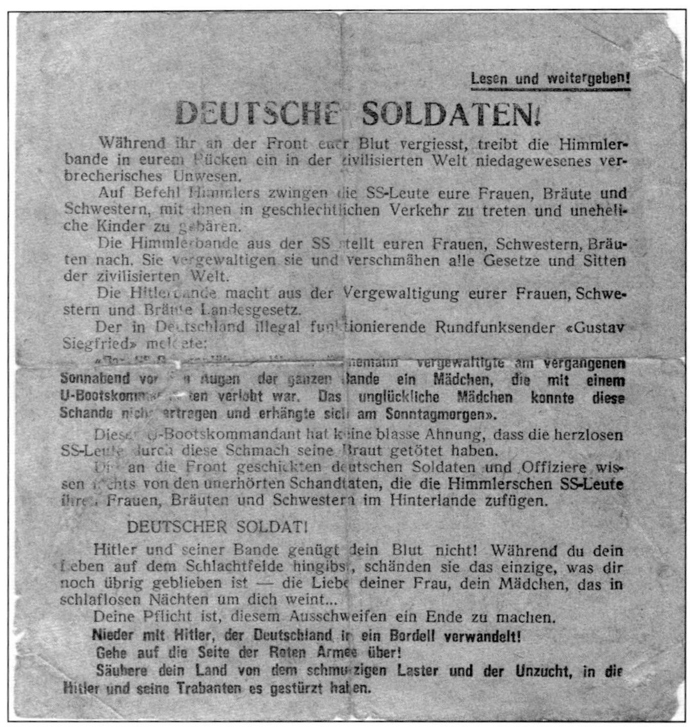
Lesen und weitergeben!

DEUTSCHE SOLDATEN!

Während ihr an der Front euer Blut vergiesst, treibt die Himmlerbande in eurem Rücken ein in der zivilisierten Welt niedagewesenes verbrecherisches Unwesen.

Auf Befehl Himmlers zwingen die SS-Leute eure Frauen, Bräute und Schwestern, mit ihnen in geschlechtlichen Verkehr zu treten und uneheliche Kinder zu gebären.

Die Himmlerbande aus der SS stellt euren Frauen, Schwestern, Bräuten nach. Sie vergewaltigen sie und verschmähen alle Gesetze und Sitten der zivilisierten Welt.

Die Hitlerbande macht aus der Vergewaltigung eurer Frauen, Schwestern und Bräute Landesgesetz.

Der in Deutschland illegal funktionierende Rundfunksender «Gustav Siegfried» meldete:

«[illegible] nemann vergewaltigte am vergangenen Sonnabend vor den Augen der ganzen Bande ein Mädchen, die mit einem U-Bootskommandanten verlobt war. Das unglückliche Mädchen konnte diese Schande nicht ertragen und erhängte sich am Sonntagmorgen».

Dieser U-Bootskommandant hat keine blasse Ahnung, dass die herzlosen SS-Leute durch diese Schmach seine Braut getötet haben.

Die an die Front geschickten deutschen Soldaten und Offiziere wissen nichts von den unerhörten Schandtaten, die die Himmlerschen SS-Leute ihren Frauen, Bräuten und Schwestern im Hinterlande zufügen.

DEUTSCHER SOLDAT!

Hitler und seiner Bande genügt dein Blut nicht! Während du dein Leben auf dem Schlachtfelde hingibst, schänden sie das einzige, was dir noch übrig geblieben ist — die Liebe deiner Frau, dein Mädchen, das in schlaflosen Nächten um dich weint...

Deine Pflicht ist, diesem Ausschweifen ein Ende zu machen.

Nieder mit Hitler, der Deutschland in ein Bordell verwandelt!

Gehe auf die Seite der Roten Armee über!

Säubere dein Land von dem schmutzigen Laster und der Unzucht, in die Hitler und seine Trabanten es gestürzt haben.

Reverse of the same leaflet.

Chapter 6

The Sütterlin Diary: 30 January 1942 to 16 March 1942

Written in a grey Russian School notebook.

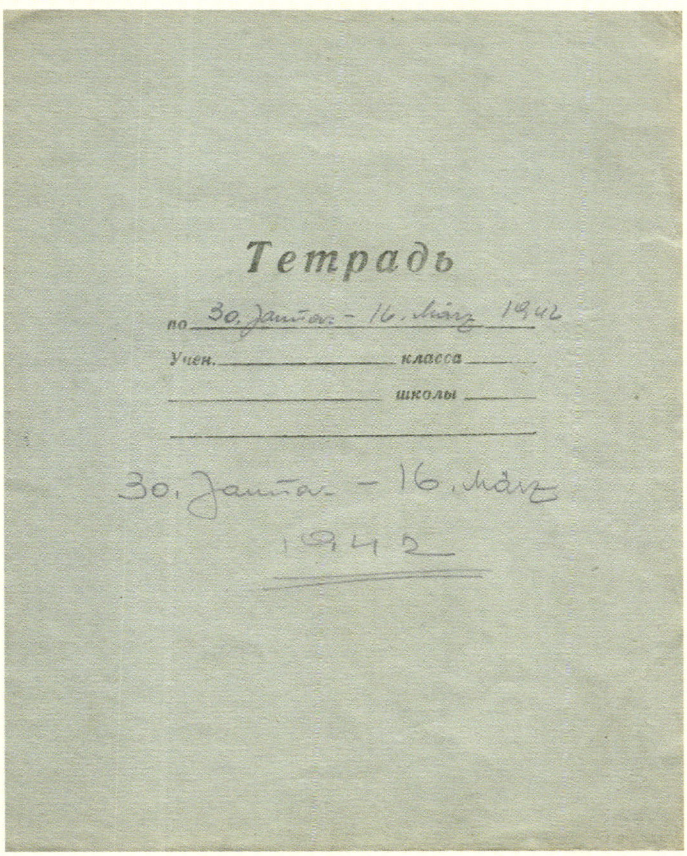

Diary cover.

30 January Friday. XVII 10 o'clock march off into battle. Have to attack a small town, KRASNIKONO, and take it with two batteries and a ski battalion, the 63 infantry (63. Panzer Grenadier Regiment). Battle lasts 'til 4 in the afternoon. I've never fired so much, the whole tank is empty. There were masses of cavalry and infantry. I fired like mad (the tank hull MG 34 7.92mm machine gun) and the guys just fell. The Russians had many dead. One of our infantry was killed. PK man was also there (War Correspondent). I came upon it alone with the tank. The hatch was open, I went past. Filled up with fuel in the evening. Prepared ammunition ourselves 'til late evening. Yet another day of battle. The Russians have about 250 dead. We captured 14 MG (machine guns) and 7 tanks. We have 1 dead, 6 wounded.

31 January Saturday. Day off today and nothing happening. Cook some lovely liver. We're almost snowed in. No vehicle can get to us. Only vehicles on sledges. Ammunition and fuel comes on sledges. Snowstorm as usual, hardly 50m visibility.

1 February Sunday. XVIII 8.15 departure for attack with 1 Batl. 40 (1st Battalion of Panzer Grenadier Regiment 40, ie 1./Pz.Gren.40) with skis to KOKTENO. Often get stuck in the snow. Robert crushed his finger. Thumb will be a bit shorter. Hard luck! Got caught in the track; we race after everyone and got to the battle. We fired 80 shells again, was great. Loads of cavalry and infantry. One assault gun was even destroyed. We got booty. Took 7 vehicles and 1 sledge. Stocked up with ammunition and fuel. On the way there a brake band burst. Hard luck!

2 February Monday. Alert again. Krupp with me working on the brake band, Schnauder on the old crate. But at KRASNIKONO 2 shells fired into the village. Direct hit on the police station. 2 infantry dead. We have reached the Division area. 15cm artillery also came here into position.

3 February Tuesday. 8 AM departure. To go to KOKTENO. Only our platoon. So that the infantry are kept busy. The Russians are wanting to attack. Can't get through the snow though, all 3 of us get stuck, so we go back. Act as cover. Ltn. Mayer also moves up with his platoon. He's unlucky. Standing out there, has no more fuel. Feldw. Bürger drives out with 1,000 litres. There are all sorts of supplies. 5 bars of chocolate and raisins. Everything that 5th platoon threw away yesterday. That was quite something. I also grabbed 5 bars. As no vehicles can get through, that's the way it is. There are drifts of 2 to 3 metres on the road. You can imagine how much snow there is here and it's bitter cold.

"Uffz. Mayer, (now Ltn.) Obgefr. Wurm our Gef driver, Kubel PKW." An earlier photo.

4 February Wednesday. Up at 6 AM. Attack on a small village, we get stuck in the snow, so the attack was a flop. Went back to KOSWENKA. Mayer gets in with us. We're standing and suddenly we are fired at by a 52 tonner (KV 2 Soviet heavy tank), also MG (machine gun) fire. We got into a house. Retreat. One had to be dragged, wounded. I think we are going back again tomorrow. Damnation! More than -40 degrees. 4.30 march off with ski platoon. Damnation! No rest. When driving this happened. Every 5m someone gets stuck; 6 set off, 2 out of action. When being pulled out Strohmer Seppl got crushed, his belly. I helped and carried him to the sledge. Spiess (Senior NCO) drives him to the nearest village. He's dead. One good pal less. We arrive at 11.30. Billets overcrowded.

5 February Thursday. XIX 4 AM march off. The Russians are attacking. We draw in to the edge of a village and wait. Then the sun starts. Knocked out a PAK. Today Uffz. Werrmann is *Richtschütze* (gunner), leave the village alone after giving it a good hammering. The attack continues. The big village higher up with the windmill, go round and fire for all we're worth. Attacked by Cavalry. Also take out an assault gun. The Russians just fall like flies. We shot entire convoys to pieces. Went back into the village. The 15.2 cm artillery fires at us. Hit after hit, everything sprays into the turrets. Go to the next village again. We wait for fuel there. 2 tanks had to go back for defence. We go home alone. The infantry had to clear out the village again. The wounded were left lying. On the way home we picked up Strohmer Seppl and brought him to the Regiment. We're completely exhausted. This cold! No Gef and nowhere to bed down.

6 February Friday. Slept 'til 9 AM today. Beschl coming. Our tank march off at 12.00. Have to fill up with fuel and ammunition. 130 shells. Thank God it (the attack) fell through. I think we're having a day off. Have such a temperature. Bitter cold as usual, despite sunshine. Beschl arrives in the evening. 7 o'clock march off.
(Erich stocked his tank with main gun ammunition well. The book ammunition load for the Panzer IV was 87 shells. Most tank crews going in to action stored ammunition anywhere they could in the vehicle, such as on the floor. Running out of ammunition was not a good option in the thick of combat.)

7 February Saturday. XX We set off in bitter cold. Advance. Feder's tank kaput. Herst's also. We set off. Ltn. Scheunberger and us go to LIPOFKA. Fire all our ammunition. Stand 'til 4 o'clock in front of this dump. Our infantry beaten back again by 2 Russian tanks. REVTONO lies 100m straight ahead. We get quarters here with 1 platoon of the infantry with 5 MG. 50 men in one room.

8 February Sunday. Today we are continually shot at by artillery, mortar fire, and MG. Otherwise nothing happening. Have quite a high temperature. Supplies are trash. Company torn apart. Mayer with 2 vehicles in KRASSNO. 134 Infantry Div combining with us soon. We can already hear them firing MG.

9 February Monday. XXI XXII
Attacks on LIBOFKA, which was taken. Go back. Slaughter 1 cow. Another attack. I'm writing this at 4.30 AM in LESIN under attack. Only 2 vehicles. Ltn. Scheunberger and us still together with Staunninger Hansl. The Russians are clearing off to the north. Am curious to know when we'll get back to the Company. Ammo and fuel come by sledge. Mail yesterday, 1 picture. Am curious to know where we'll sleep today. Will it be so crowded? Shame, I made liver today. What will happen to our cow? Go back into our old quarters. Nothing to drink, 5 days only melted snow. That's what it's like here.

"When we were snowed in Jan/Feb 1942 north of BOLCHOW near OREL. Our Tross had to bring our supplies by sledge. 1942."

"Were snowed in January 1942. Food dropped by Ju. Ammo and fuel brought by sledge. The comrade copied the Russians. KURMINKA, Feb '42."

10 February Tuesday. Day off. The infantry are moving out, now we've all got space. We cook. Otherwise nothing much happening. Yes, 2 crews brought us supplies. Orders for departure for tomorrow come. Then cancelled during the night.

11 February Wednesday. Both of our tanks have to go to KUTZI into the forest, only to set it on fire. Stannungen and I stay in our quarters and play Skat. Otherwise not much happening all day. It's snowing heavily.

12 February Thursday. 7.30 departure. Back to KOSNENKA. Taking a towing vehicle up with us. It's thawing today. Reach our old quarters and fill up with fuel. Tomorrow we're going off towards BULCHOW. Have a wash, first time for 6 days. Is that good! Now that we've a cow in the shed and we're off.

13 February Friday. 7 AM departure. There are 6 tanks. At midday we arrive in OSK, 4km from BULCHOW. Have my own billet. I saw Pietsch yesterday for the first time and spoke to him. How long will we be staying here? 3 Company is also here. Schowalter is our *Richtschütze* (gunner) again. Tanks are on the hill; we are waiting down in the village. Going on guard duty. I am radio operator for 2 platoon.

14 February Saturday. Schramm, Neuhold, Reisinger, and Weidmann get EK2 (Iron Cross second class). Ltn. Heuer and Spiess get the EK1 (Iron Cross first class).
Today 2 tanks are coming from the workshop with Guckenberger and Lehner. Have to go to the *Abteilung* as relief radio operator. Going with Feldw., will fetch fuel at the same time, also reach Tross 1 (Unit Supply and Logistics Train). There was winter clothing today from the army and fur clothes from home. Took a fur jacket, scarf, and socks.

15 February Sunday. Yesterday the Gef told us that we will probably be provided with new vehicles here in Russia and fight on in the spring. That finished us off! Today we are going to BULCHOW for a bath. 8km on foot, we were exhausted when we got back. There is schnaps today. This village is called OSK. Have to notify the radio operators with a view to a meeting.

16 February Monday. Meeting of radio operators in our billet. Otherwise nothing happening all day.

17 February Tuesday. Surprise today. We're going to BULCHOW to the front-line theatre organised by the Flak (anti-aircraft troops) with Russian girls. In the middle of the performance an alert for 6 Comp. Out and back to the billet and march off. The Russians have broken through in the OKA. Drive to just before a town and stay overnight. 6 tanks, we're to the right of BULCHOW.

18 February Wednesday. Moved off early, straight into action. We break down and infantry follow on. All hell has broken loose here. Move up, then assault guns. The Russians have got artillery here, never been like this before, hit after hit. We went back, got stuck. Gef with us. We walk. Gef and I back to the village. We lay down often. Fetch a rope and 2 hooks, then back on foot , pull us out. But hit after hit ahead of us right and left. Come back, straight ahead of us 2 T 34, 28 tonners. Anti-tank shells are firing. 4 prisoners. Have to guard them. Stay overnight in this village.

19 February Thursday. Today we (the tank) finally broke down. Towing half track towed us away. Being bombed. Company into battle, knocked out 16 tanks. Our tank slightly damaged because of anti-tank rifle. In total 92 enemy tanks were knocked out here. Russians attacking with 4 armoured brigades. Fresh troops sent for us. Also reinforcements for the infantry.

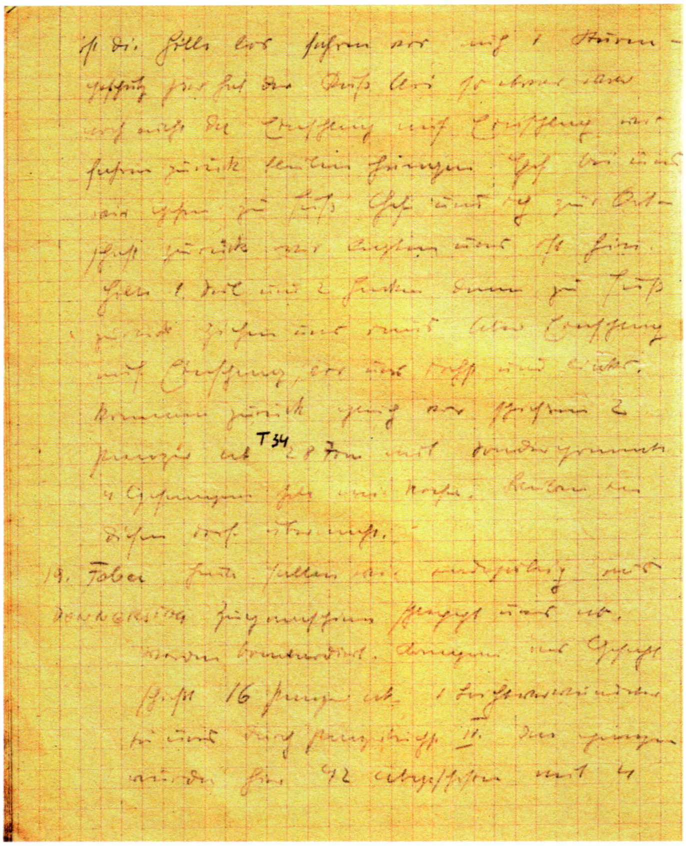

T-34

20 February Friday. Today we have 9 tanks. In the evening 4 KP (4th company) comes with 4 tanks. Kp (Erich's company) moving up. 1 tank knocked out, 28 tonner (Soviet T 34). Artillery firing like mad. What the Russians have got here is not very nice. Never experienced anything like this. Russians broke through 2km away. If that had not happened, we would have been loaded up for SMOLENZ. Hard luck! 17 (17.Panzer Division) is there. This is the area of 25 MOT Div. (25 Motorised Division).

Tank assembly point. Panzer II Ausf. b and Panzer III Ausf. G.

21 February Saturday. 6.30 alert. 12.00 departure, move up to the infantry. Artillery firing like mad. Set off. Got there in the evening, beside 8.8 (8.8cm Flak gun). Then back again. Our old crate is just not pulling. What on earth is wrong with it! Constant bombing attacks by the Russians.

22 February Sunday. 8 months of war. Dreadful artillery fire. Russians have got reinforcements, attacking constantly. Our old tank kaput. Tank repairers working on it. This is one of the worst times that we have experienced. Approximately 45 (enemy) tanks knocked out today.

23 February Monday. Russians attacking with mighty force, but get repelled again and again. Lots of tank attacks and ours (Erich's tank) nowhere in sight. The artillery fire is a bit lighter. Thank God! Lots of reinforcements for the infantry. No sleeping space left. Our old tank is still not going. This is a dreadful time here.
One tank was knocked out by Gefr. Wugler. The Russians attacked us with 2 tanks and infantry. All sorts of tank attacks. I also hid in the tank as bombs were falling.

24 February Tuesday. Feldw. Feder wounded with shrapnel in the head. 5 tanks move forward. G (illegible) took one through artillery fire, only the road wheel broken. Today we took out our battery and charged it up. Finally got time to write.

25 February Wednesday.
Schowalter, Seifert get EK1 (Iron Cross first class).
Mangold, Pilshofer, Hülze, and Brachowitz get EK2 (Iron Cross second class).
It's snowing heavily; there's more snow instead of less. It's snowing, we've got to march off. Worked on our tank all day. In the evening finally got it started. Not running right, though. Tanks move up every day. Bombers and dive-bombers let us have it. I hid in the tank. Artillery firing like mad. Russians attacked us with 8 tanks. Our Company knocked 3 of them out. Ltn. Mayer got 2, Ltn. Scheunberger got 1. Our 8.8 (8.8 cm flak, anti-aircraft gun here firing in the anti-tank role) took a direct hit. 2 dead, one of them a Ltn. Schowalter, who is Scheinberger's *Richtschütze* (gunner), knocked out a MARK III today. British tank with Russian crew. The Russians have many American weapons. We have to take over security of the village. If our tank gets going.
(The Valentine Infantry Tank III. A British tank armed with a 2 Pounder 40mm gun. Supplied as war aid to the Soviets.)

26 February Thursday. Up at 4.30. We have to go forward to our old post at the front line. Arrive in an old billet where we can not have any heating, or the place will go up in flames. Today our hearts just about came to a stop. The 15.2 cm Russian artillery fire landed 2m beside the tank, so much so that the windows and all the frames fell into the house. This firing continued all day. Houses nearby taking direct hits, everything's exploding. Mortars all round about. That gets on your nerves; it's almost evening, then retreat. *Richtschütze* is Bauernfeind Toni Uffz. Back in the evening, our tank gave up the ghost. Gearbox kaput. We have to leave it. We'll collect our things tomorrow.

28 February Friday. Early on Karl Pilshofer and I walk to the tank. We were just there when we had to answer the call of nature. In the middle of it 3 bombers and 6 dive-bombers came and caught us. With our trousers in our hands we ran round and round the tree; we couldn't get to the tank. Finally we got to the tank and lay underneath it. Tank also took a hit, incendiary. But nothing happened. Go back to the village and sit down in the house. Then the Russians fired 15.2 cm artillery. Very unpleasant. At midday the recovery half track came and towed us in the midst of artillery fire. Accompanied us to our old position, where they were also firing in 15.2 cm artillery. Spiess visited us. I want to go to Uffz. John. Then the sad part. Sledges with wounded come by, amongst them is one of us, Hermann. Artillery shrapnel in his stomach. He was also lying under his tank. Going back. His lung might be punctured, says the doctor. Aircraft visit us, so much so that the house shakes. Even more artillery fire.

1 March Sunday. Hermann injured. With shrapnel. Morning greeting by artillery fire. 15.2 cm artillery firing in front of us in the hollow, then 2 dive-bombers. Another Pz IV arrives. Uffz. Hertlein has taken it over. Uffz. Bauernfeind has to leave us to go to Scheunberger. Shame.

2 March Monday. *Gef has been awarded the* Ritterkreuz (Erich Kaiser on 26 February 1942). Up at 5.00 Going in Ltn. Mayer's tank. 12 hours in the tank. Houses are all destroyed. Bunker full, so we had to remain sitting in the vehicle. Artillery firing as ever and lots of mortars. Behind us our own mortars. 4 men dead. There's mail and money. Another day less to do. Gef says we will probably be relieved in about 8 days.

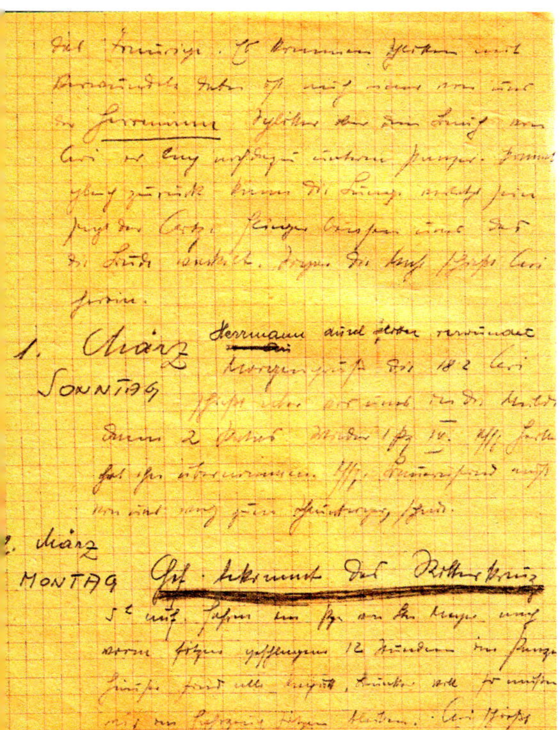

"Gef has been awarded the *Ritterkreuz*."

3 March Tuesday. Today I'm sending 500RM to my Post Office Savings account. It's snowing again. Today our aircraft are here for the first time. Me 109s (the *Luftwaffe* single seat fighter aircraft. Also used as a fighter-bomber). Day off for us. In the afternoon the Gef came to us. Special mission. To go to the infantry in the hollow, where we knocked out the 2 tanks. A platoon of Russians broke through here during the night. Drive there with the tank, Feldw. Burger, and fire 20 shells and MG and then back. Uffz. John is going to OREL about our replacements. *Gef has been promoted to* Hauptmann. All sorts of things going on recently for the Gef. In the end they destroyed a heavy battery that surrounded us.

4 March Wednesday. A day off for the time being for us, but not for long. In the afternoon a man came from 1 Kp (1st Company), *Hauptmann* Franke is also coming today. So we are being relieved. Robert has to go with Fldw. Trauter on a special mission. Staying away overnight with the *Kradschütze* (motorcycle infantry).

5 March Thursday. Away at 4.30. Move forward to KRIZOWA as usual. Damned quiet today. Artillery fire as usual. The heavy shells are firing over our heads. All over the place. Strange feeling. At least in the tank you are safe from shrapnel. Robert had to bale out. Got shrapnel from a shell in his right leg. Got stuck in the snow. Got hit by a 7.6 cm shell. Otherwise not much happening. The vehicles are being handed over tomorrow. Thank God.

6 March Friday. Day off. Stay in FATKEWO. Nothing happening. Relief has fallen through. We've to go at 12.00.

7 March Saturday. Move up to KRIZOWO with Ortner as *Richtschütze*. Robert Schowalter is coming back. Quite quiet today. Amazing. Russians attacking at 2 KP. (2nd Company). They left behind lots of dead. We weren't needed. 2 Kp had to go to WISKODE, where we were. The Russians have broken through there again.

8 March Sunday. We go early to delousing and can get washed again. Is that good! The sun is shining beautifully today. Gef and Scheunberger go forward. Artillery fire. With radio and V.B. (Supply unit). Heavy artillery fire.

9 March Monday. 1 Kp (1st Company) arrives with only 3 crews for the time being. We're now being relieved. We and our tank have to go to BOLCHOW so that it can be collected. Stay overnight at Tross 1 (Supply train).

10 March Tuesday. Leave for OREL. It's very windy today. The road is again almost impassable. But arrive in OREL in the evening. 6 crews are following on. 2 Pz. IV were handed over to the Company, which has been loaded up today to go to KURSK. There are serious things going on there. Pay 25 RM cold weather payment, one whole basic pay. Here we are put up in a former bank building. 10-12 men. Rooms quite nice. Only no washing facilities. Not too far to the baths, though.

"Bridge in OREL over the ORLOG. March 1942."

"Obergefr. Piffl now Fldw. Piffl.

11 March Wednesday. Sort out the room. Remove my washing. Otherwise nothing happening. It's snowing but it's thawing. It's evening; that's the crew arriving, Mayer and Scheunberger. Today all sorts of things were going on. The Russians attacked us with 8 tanks, and 6 were knocked out. 3 by us and 3 by the artillery. 4 of ours were knocked out. Uffz. Fromm, Obgfr. Krupf, and Gefr. Stosko Ernst were wounded. Ernst in field hospital. The others are here. One radio operator from 1 Kp fell. Ltn. Stöhl from 1 Kp was in charge. The radio operator was to be relieved. Such bad luck on the last day. 1 tank completely gone to pot. They got 3 others going again. Our Gef was not there. Otherwise I don't think it would have happened. Krupf was wounded in his tank, the others while bailing out, by this damned artillery which was firing like mad.

12 March Thursday. Sort out the room. 12.00 delousing. 6 o'clock to the cinema. The first time for 10 months. "The Sky-blue Eveningdress." Stanninger, Mertel into our room.

13 March Friday. Write a few letters. Otherwise nothing happening. We've sorted out our room. 11 men: Uffz. Mekler, Gefr. Imfanger, Gefr. Mertel, Obgfr. Pilshofer, Gefr. Stamminger, Obgfr. Mangold, Gfr. Ortner, Obergf. Fuchs, Gfr. Feinbringer, and Obgfr. Sch ... (illegible). We've got a gramophone, very nice here.

14 March Saturday. During the night all sorts going on. *Hauptmann* Franke from 1 Kp. fell today. Going bathing. Otherwise nothing happening. It's snowing and damned cold. Schmerold has jaundice.

15 March Sunday. As usual. 8.00 fall in. Weapons inspection. Otherwise nothing happening. It's snowing and bitter cold.

16 March Monday. 8.00 fall in, then delousing. *Abteilung* fell in. Major .. (illegible) spoke to us and praised us, especially 6 Kp. (6th Company). Awarded 3 EK1 and 7 EK2. Uffz. Heuer, Uffz. Bauernfeind, and Gef Wachter got the EK1. EK2 went to J.. (illegible), Patsch, Prediger, F (illegible), and Werner. Then fall in the billets. Gef spoke to us and awarded more EK2 and *Sturmabzeichen* (Panzer Assault Badges). Aust, (illegible), Hopf, (illegible), Wurm, Ortlap, Alexander, etc. EK2. In the afternoon "Bunte Bühne" variety show: all Russian girls and men. Sang through the hit song "Lili Marlene," great. Otherwise nothing happening. Read books. While I'm writing Russian air attack. Flak firing like mad. Obfeldw. Schmerold has jaundice, is already in the Reich.

Notes on the 30 January to 16 March Diary
We are not sure what the Roman numerals refer to or why Erich wrote them in bold letters.

For much of 1942 17.Panzer Division was stationed near Orel with Army Group Centre. These German forces were to stop any Soviet assaults aimed at preventing *Fall Blau*, the German conquest of the Caucasus and Stalingrad.

The Diary starts with action in battle and Erich manning the hull MG 34 7.92 mm machine gun. The heavy Soviet casualties show their determination to throw back the German invaders. The heavy and violent snowstorms hamper combat and the advance. These weather conditions had never been seen by the German planners and were not anticipated.

Throughout the diary there are mechanical problems with the Panzer IV tank. As this was not a particularly unreliable vehicle it must be assumed that a lot of this was due to the low temperatures. German vehicles were not designed to cope with the severe Russian weather. An accident due to breakdown kills another of Erich's friends. Soldiers found loss in combat difficult enough, but to lose friends and comrades due to accidents was particularly hard.

There are several references to the use of Soviet cavalry. This may seem archaic in 1942, but often only cavalry had mobility in the heavy snow and mud. Both sides used cavalry for scouting, but the Soviets had whole brigades which they would throw into the attack. In all the bitter combat, the only relief comes in the awards of the Iron Crosses first and second class. No doubt hard earned.

On 25 February Erich first experiences Lend Lease equipment to the Soviets. This is in the form of a British supplied Valentine tank. As with the earlier diaries, the Soviets deliver terrific barrages of artillery and air attacks. On 28 February Erich is caught literally with his trousers down while answering a call of nature. This was not an uncommon occurrence for soldiers of all nations. Performing bodily functions in the midst of combat was difficult and dangerous. Many soldiers, if they had the chance, trained or forced themselves to defecate first thing in the morning before enemy activity commenced.

Erich records Erich Kaiser's award of the Knight's Cross on 2 March, and shortly after his promotion to Captain (*Hauptmann*). It was common for officer Knight's Cross winners to be promoted. The award often reflected the performance of the unit under the Officer's command.

The diary ends with the appropriation of good billets and a chance wash and delouse. This could be a matter of survival in the Russian winter. Due to the extreme cold preventing washing of bodies and clothes lice were always present in large numbers. Erich and his comrades get the chance to visit a Russian theatre complete with pretty young women. No doubt welcome! The Nazis forbade the interaction of Germans and Slavs, but this does not seem to have stopped the troops.

Chapter 7

Diary 17 March 1942 to 9 June 1942

Written in a Russian notebook.

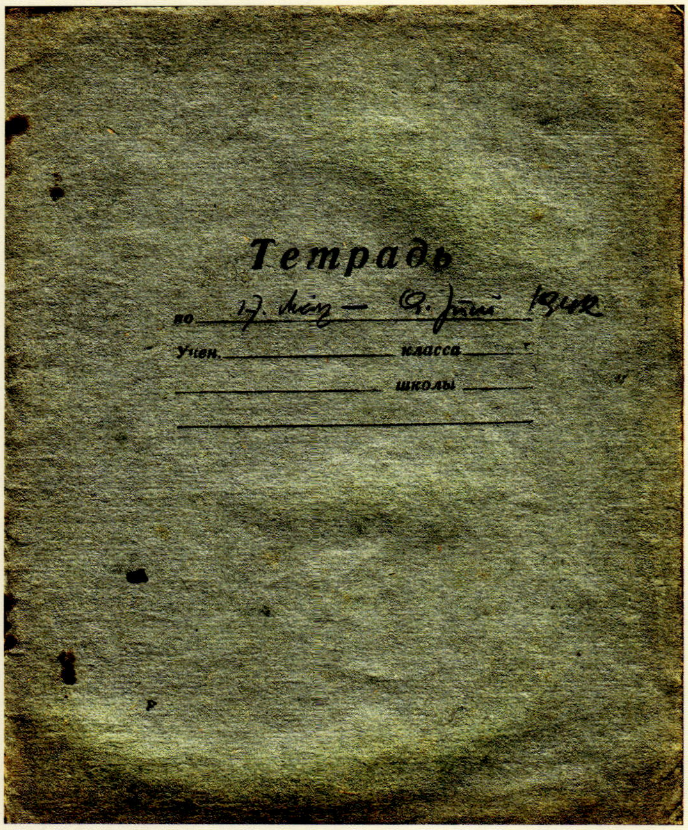

Diary cover.

Tuesday 17 March. Gasroom test (room filled with teargas to test the fit and function of gasmasks.)
Divided up for Guard Duty. We're guarding a Brewery. Six officers: Bauernfeind, Gef, Seifert, Stauber, Holst, Hofmeister, and Schaulandt. I arrive there, am received and what, we are being relieved already? It could well be, I think, and it's just too much.
We celebrate the departure of the old guard, of course, with beer, 'til 1200. It was great, everyone a bit drunk. Later we danced. We have private accommodations where there are two lovely girls. This is the right guard for us. I didn't sleep.

Wednesday 18 March. In the morning Gef came and Schlumberger inspected us. Gef in a great mood. It's the right guard for us and we should just drink enough, but within limits. That's what we're doing, of course! Today we got told we have to stay here for 8 straight days. Great! Couldn't be better.
Dancing in the evening. Connect up our radio to the loudspeaker. It's not a station that we want. We want a German station. We also collect our luggage.

Thursday 19 March. Our whole *Kompanie* has to be on guard duty. We've got the best guard. When I get to the *Kompanie* everything is empty. Only the sick. Tank guard and *Kompanie* guard are here. The rest are on Station guard, Bridge guard, Road guard, etc.
There's a gramophone here. We dance and the girls dance. Great!
Today the *Abteilung* is going to BRUDANSK and staying in the neighbourhood. I'm curious to know when we'll follow on.
This guard duty is really great.

Friday 20 March. The whole *Abteilung* is going towards BRUDANSK (SCHIZDRA?). What's happening there?
Lots of passwords going about. Also because of leave

Gef visited us out here. He said that one man from the *Kompanie* can go on leave. Drew lots. 48 men from the whole regiment are to get 20 days leave.
Great mood in the evening. Danced and had a good booze up. Karli Wurm, Karli Schuster, and Prediger visited us. I was as drunk as everyone else. Some airmen visited too.

Saturday 20 March. Went to the cinema in the morning, "Before he was a husband." Lots to laugh at. Dancing again at lunch time. Also supposed to be post.
Flak fire! Russian aircraft shot down at the station. Pumpler wounded by Flak splinters in the ear. There *was* mail.

Sunday 22 March. Gef visited us, had a drink with us. Still in good humour. Karli Schuster visited us. Great company. Had a good drink. Snowing again. Is Spring not going to come?

Monday 23 March. A great day today. Quite warm in the sun. Otherwise not much happening. Jesberger and Höller went home, transferred to KFZp (driver training command). Also lorry parked with driver for HQ.
Loads of visitors - half the *Kompanie* came to us. Went to the cinema in the afternoon, "Before he became a husband" for the second time. Dancing in the evening.

Tuesday 24 March. Went swimming. It's snowing again - all morning. Lousy weather. Does Spring not want to come? A bit of dancing.

Wednesday 25 March. Snowed again in the morning, then thawed. Streets are running with water. Otherwise nothing happening.
We're on guard duty as always. Saw another burial, quite strange.
Dancing in the evening. With Tatjana. A great kisser.

Thursday 26 March. Last night an unparalleled storm but we were warm. In the morning it snowed like it can. Such awful weather. When will Spring come?
One day passes like any other. Gef. and Odi Schnauder went on leave 'til 2 May. There was post - two parcels from Gusti.

Friday 27 March. At night it is freezing and in the morning it snows as hard as it can. Such awful weather. In the afternoon wonderful weather – lovely and warm.
Great dut (pop) music on the radio.
In the evening a snowstorm. Going to the *Bunte Bühne* (brightly coloured stage). "The Mad Hotel" – great, we killed ourselves laughing. Good rustic theatre.
Last night brazen flak fire. A few bombs also fell.
PK (Propaganda *Kompanie* – war correspondent) Lachmann is taking our photos.

Saturday 28 March. Slept late into the morning as usual, with great music on the radio.
Great day. At night it's freezing and snow fell.

Sunday 29 March. A snow storm all day. Snowdrifts, lots of snow. When will it become warm? Doesn't look like it will be yet.
Willi Eisenhut coming to us as postman. Seifert will be replacement. The pocket at SDRA going well. Our Division not involved.

Monday 30 March. *Soldatenheim* (German equivalent of NAAFI) has been opened.

Tuesday 31 March. Bitter cold, lots of snow, otherwise a day like all the rest. Gef and the other officers meet where we are and go to the front for reconnaissance.
OREL when the flooding begins.
Today all the Ukrainians were released. We are delighted and have a booze up.

Wednesday 1 April. Weather a bit warmer. Gef and also Oberfldw. visited us. Uffz. Gehlmann visited us at 0100 on the first day of April (played an April fool's joke). It was fun.
Got my boots from Schuster. Great! Going swimming.
Now you find lots of things going on. *Kompanie* has one RK (Knight's Cross), one German Cross in Gold, 23 EK1 (Iron Cross 1st class), and 99 EK2 (Iron Cross 2nd class).

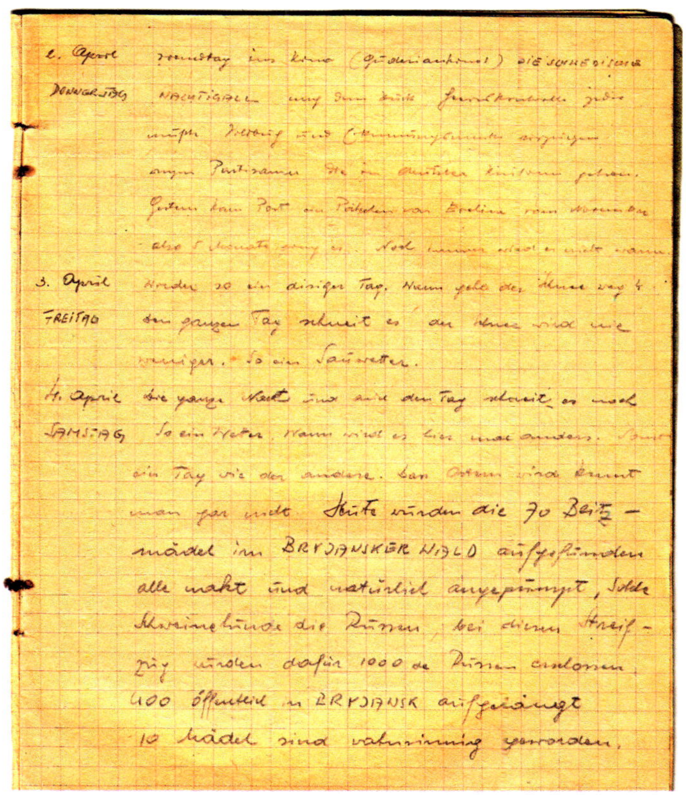

Rape in the Brydansk woods.

Thursday 2 April. Morning at the cinema to see "The Swedish Nightingale." Got mail yesterday – a parcel from Erdine.
It's still not warm.

Friday 3 April. Such a misty day again. When will the snow go away? Snowed all day. The snow will not get any less. Such awful weather.

Saturday 4 April. Snowed all night and all day. When will it be anything other than that here? Otherwise a day like any other.
Today over 70 girls were discovered in the BRVJANSKER wood all naked and of course raped. Such dirty dogs the Russians. In this raid 1000s of Russians were shot for it, 400 publicly hanged in BRVJANSK.
Ten girls have gone mad. These Russians should be exterminated.

Sunday 5 April. Easter Sunday. The Sun is shining, but it's quite cold, everything frozen. The snow has not got any less. Nothing makes you think of Easter here.

Monday 6 April. All sorts of Flak fire in the night. Lovely weather today. Sunshine. Lots of visitors again. Lovely and warm in the daytime. Great music on the radio.

Tuesday 7 April. Lovely day again. Guard duty as usual. Flak firing at night. There was mail, two letters. Wrote a few as well.

Wednesday 8 April. Went to the cinema, Zeutrale Rio (HQ Rio), great film.
Early today Gefreiter Kaschee had a fatal accident. He was on station guard and knocked down by a lorry. Shame. Great guy, from Berlin, married. There was mail. Ten parcels for me.
Special announcement from VROOTE towards AMERIKA.
Everyone working madly for the defense of OREL, even the captured Russian tanks are being dug in for defense. Kaschee was knocked down yesterday in the evening. It was on the way to the guard room. To get there quicker he tried to jump up, slipped and fell underneath a supply wagon. He died at 0800 in the field hospital. Two draymen caught who were responsible were locked up.

Thursday 9 April. Snowed all day - lousy weather. Hofmeister had to take the two Russians (draymen) to the local HQ. There's mail again.

"The 8-wheeled *Spähwagen*," Armoured car.

Friday 10 April. Nothing happening. Snowed all day. Melted again though. Lousy weather. Otherwise we're on guard duty as usual.

Saturday 11 April. Mail again – two parcels. We have three tanks – a good thing.
New passwords. 17 PD is to be relieved. 39 Panzer Regiment to go to GERMANY! Wouldn't be bad. Spiess, Stabs *Feldwebel*, Habel, Friese visited us.

Sunday 12 April. After guard duty went to Nina's. 1400-1600 guard duty again and bad luck with that. Oso came and we sat in the boiler house. Am curious to see what happens (caught neglecting guard duty).
Great hit music today. Wrote a few letters. Otherwise nothing happening.

Monday 13 April. It's snowing again. Snow also lying. Miserable weather. The first bollocking from Ltn. Mayer. Am curious to see what will happen because of the guard duty.
Otherwise nothing happening. Mail – nine parcels.

Tuesday 14 April. We're being relieved tomorrow by 5 *Kompanie*. In the evening it's snowing again. Went swimming.
New passwords.
2 *Abteilung* to be re-formed. Each *Kompanie* to another Division.
Today we're having our last booze up. A little drinking session.

Had a good booze up.

Wednesday 15 April. At mid-day we are being relieved by 5 *Kompanie*. Will meet a few pals. Now life in the *Kompanie* will be tolerable again. We have five tanks. Clear up the room.

Thursday 16 April. Instruction from Gef about the situation. It is planned that only one *Abteilung* stays here. That is what the Gef said so today.
Stabs. *Feldwebel* putting a radio into his tank.
Went to the cinema – "Stories from Vienna" – great film. Then to the hairdresser. In the newsreel our *Kompanie* was practising fire control.

Friday 17 April. Technical Duty. 0900 instruction then labour service. Newsreel filming our tanks. I'm not on it. There is flooding everywhere. Up to 6.5 metres.
Want to go to the cinema. No electricity there. Had a little adventure. In the evening the hairdresser. Lola here, lovely girl.

Saturday 18 April. Clearing ice from *Kompanie* building 'til 1730, then off to the girls. 2200 home – all sorts of things going on.

Sunday 19 April. Wonderful day. Everything decorated for the *Fuhrer's* birthday. We were with the girl who's going home to the Reich tomorrow.
Hungarians arrived. Quite a few marched through here. (Hungary was an ally of Germany. Their forces fought on the Eastern front. Lack of heavy weapons, particularly tanks and artillery, limited their effectiveness against the Soviets. The Red Army forces concentrated their attacks against the points in the line held by Germany's allies where they knew they had the best chance of breaking through and outflanking the German forces.)

Monday 20 April. Parade (Adolf Hitler's birthday). Gef spoke. *Feldwebel* Trauter, Uffz. Hartlein were awarded the EK 1 (Iron cross first class) and Pflauger, Seemann awarded the EK 2 (Iron cross second class).

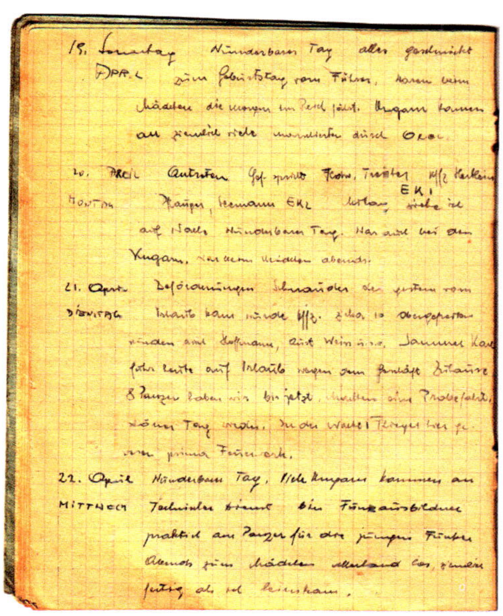

Hitler's birthday. EK1 and EK2 awards.

At midday I went on sentry duty. Wonderful day. Was also with the Hungarians. Was with the girl in the evening.

Tuesday 21 April. Promotions – Schnauder, who just came back from leave, became *Unterofficier*. About ten Gefreiters also – Hoffmann, Aust, Weiss, etc. Karl Jammer went on leave today because of the business at home. We've got eight tanks up 'til now. Had a test drive.
Lovely day again. In the night aircraft were here. Great fireworks.

Wednesday 22 April. Wonderful day. Lots of Hungarians arriving. Technical duty. I am radio trainer – practice on the tank for the young radio operators. In the evening to the girls. All sorts going on, quite exhausted when I got home.

Thursday 23 April. Lovely day again. Hardly any more Hungarians arriving. Radio training for the young ones. We old ones are showing everything to the young ones.
At midday, special job – all radio operators – there are ten of us – here to unload the mail – eight carriages. Ate a lovely Goulash with the Hungarians. One of them played old Hungarian music on the violin. Just great, I felt right at home.
Cleaned up the square 'til about 1800.

Friday 24 April. Regimental parade. Discharge of 1 *Abteilung* who are going to 29 Mot. Div. We're staying here. In the afternoon Technical Duty.

Saturday 25 April. We're doing Radio Operator training on the vehicles for the young ones. Three new ones arrived. Gefreiter from St. Polten as officer candidate.
Yesterday Uffz. Bruckner and I made liver sausage for the *Kompanie*. It was quite good. There was mail too. Four letters for me.
Uffz. Gukenberger went to the Reich (Germany) to Officer training school. He was given a bollocking from Gef as he left.

Sunday 26 April. Went to the baths – great. Wrote a few letters. Big surprise, Karl Schuster brought the war newspaper. There are eight pictures of the *Kompanie* – Graf with Schuster, me and Mangold cleaning the guns of a Pz IV at KOSWINKA. Merks, Koubek, Weinhold, and Hopf are on it. PK Lachmann (Propaganda *Kompanie*, presumably the unit was visited by a war correspondent called Lachmann).
The *Führer* spoke in the *Reichstag*.
Had a joint reception. Hungarians and ours played music in the square.

Monday 27 April. Technical duty. We have 12 tanks.
At midday suddenly "Alarm." Got the vehicles ready immediately. We can leave at any time.
For the first time Stuka planes again from MZENSK, where the Russians came to the HKL (*Hauptkampflinie*, the main line of resistance). They could break through 29 Mot. Div. All sorts of flak fire as the Russians are trying to attack OREL.

(29th Motorised Infantry division was later destroyed at Stalingrad in January 1943.)

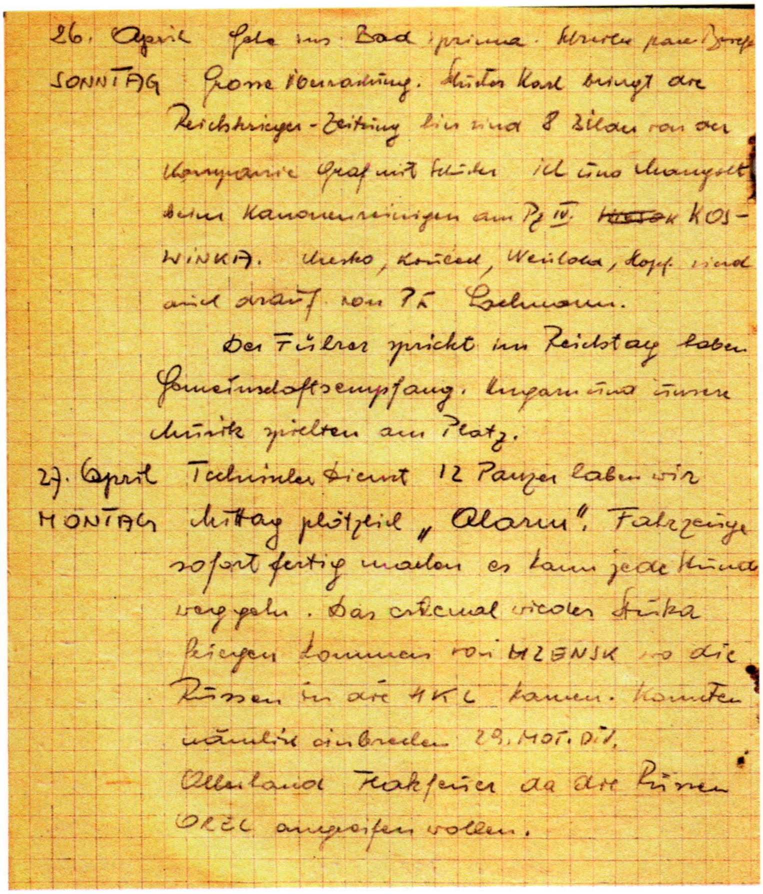

26. April ... Bad prima ...
SONNTAG ...
... KOS-
WINKA. ...
Der Führer spricht im Reichstag ...
Gemeinschaftsempfang. ...
Musik spielten am Platz.
27. April Technischer Dienst 12 Panzer haben wir
MONTAG Mittag plötzlich „Alarm“. Fahrzeuge
sofort fertig machen es kann jede Minute
weggehen. Das erstemal wieder Stuka
fliegen kommen von MZENSK wo die
Russen in die 4K ... kamen. Konnten
nämlich einbrechen 29. MOT. DIV.
Überall Flakfeuer da die Russen
OREL angreifen wollen.

"Alarm"

Ready to move off.

Tuesday 28 April. It snowed all day and it's bitter cold. Am with the Spiess in the car as Ltn. Schlumberger has gone away. Great. Schnauder and Höllinger have gone with Schlumberger.
The situation is calming down. Am getting a new tank – has to come yet. Our crew – Ltn. Schlumberger, Schnauder, Reisinger, and Schäneberger. Instruction from Gef – 2 *Abteilung* – we're the education unit, funny.
Cinema – "Pedro should hang." Quite good.

Wednesday 29 April. Still on standby for marching off. We're giving up two Pz IV and Uffz. Winzig. Getting more tanks. We've got 13. Still working for the chief radio operator. Was in the bath.
Radio, receiver, exercise. Shit!
In the evening and night ridiculous Flak fire. All sorts going on.

Thursday 30 April. Mayer's platoon has to be ready for march off at any time. Vehicles are ready for action. Curious to know when it will all get going. Setting up the radios.

Friday 1 May. Still ready for march off. Otherwise day off. Not much happening. We went for a walk and in the evening to Toni's, great girl. Just as good a kisser.

Saturday 2 May. Technical duty. Still ready for march off, therefore not away from *Kompanie* for more than two hours.
We have 13 tanks. Rainy day. Lots of flak fire.
Went out in the evening, always in twos (protection from Partisan murder). Got into a Buff (possibly slang term currently unknown). Am speechless. Did an immediate about turn. I can't be doing with anything like that.
Yesterday there was mail. – 12 letters.

Sunday 3 May. Day off but ready for march off.
Write all my letters. In the afternoon we're going out to Toni, then we listened to the gramophone. In the evening a walk. Everything OK.
Have to give up a Pz IV to 4 *Kompanie*. It has to be Koubele. He's going to MZENSK to 4 *Kompanie*. Shame.
Very loud flak.
Lots of Hungarians here. More and more.

Monday 4 May. Radio instruction. In the afternoon cinema – "The Granfather who was sold" – Great.
In the evening – girls.

Tuesday 5 May. Radio instruction. Snowed in the afternoon. Miserable weather. Parade. Now things are going.
Went dancing in the evening.

Wednesday 6 May. Went with three tanks towards MSZENSK and had radio practice with the young ones at the same time. Back in the afternoon.
Parade in the evening. Tomorrow parade again. Schwartz etc (black tank uniforms).

Thursday 7 May. Rainy day. Radio instruction. In the afternoon radio practice at the *Abteilung*. Went with 5 tanks until 1700. No parade for us. Went out with Donia, then with Maria went dancing – home at 2200. Today Ltn. Beyer came to the *Kompanie*.
Fighter pilots came to our HQ.

Friday 8 May. Rainy day. Instruction. *Stabsgefreiter* Habel and Uffz. Hicht have gone on leave. In the evening with Wally to the dancing. Great.

Saturday 9 May. New detail. Ltn. Beyer to 1st platoon. Ltn. Schlumberger to 2nd platoon. Me radio operator. Schnauder, Ltn. Meyer to 2nd platoon. But still no vehicles.
Mail two pieces. Wrote a few letters. Went to Toni – was just great. My Pfr. given for getting ready (unknown term).
(Soviets launch counter-offensive to retake Kharkov.)

Sunday 10 May. Lovely day. Our guard duty – hard luck.
Special announcement from U-boats, 118,000 BRT (tonnage sunk).
There was mail. Another of those letters from home. What could be going on? Time I got home.
Lutz Gaus is in PUTHOS, he wrote. They've got new tanks there.
Flak firing like every day. A firework display.

Monday 11 May. Lovely day. Guard duty going well. In the evening to Toni – was just great.

Tuesday 12 May. Lovely day. Technical duty. Labour service levelling our square.
Played football.
Am in the employ of the signals sergeant major. Must learn thoroughly.
In the evening to Toni – came home happy.

Wednesday 13 May. Lovely day again. Am with the signals sergeant major. The brakes have to be removed from our tank.
Duty in the afternoon, still going quite well, then football.
In the evening to Toni – just great.

Thursday 14 May. Technical duty. Radio exercise in the afternoon, RMRSENSK, lovely day – was great and went well. In the evening to Toni – walk to OVA, was great.

Friday 15 May. Technical duty. Today one hour drill with Gef – the first time – went well. Radio exercise RKROMNY.
Food is now always damned scarce.

Saturday 16 May. Technical duty. Rain in our tank. Leaving early, got stuck in a bog – RKUNSK – stuck for 9 hours. Got out at 2000. Home at 2100.

Stuck in a bog.

Sunday 17 May. Went swimming – damned hot already.
The Hungarians came to RKUNSK.
Gef gone on leave today. Football match.
Alarm – got the vehicles ready. Have to go to 4 *Kompanie* at MZENJK (German counter-offensive towards Kharkov).

Monday 18 May . Everything's calmed down again. We're not going.
Today is my name day (Saint's Day).
Cleaned out the vehicles again. Labour service – clean the car park.

Tuesday 19 May. Technical duty. Labour service.
Gefreiter Omort promoted to Uffz. Our car park is lovely.

Wednesday 20 May. Guard duty – noticed because I went to the bath. Punishment guard duty and labour service. In the evening to Toni.
From 1 *Abteilung*, 30 men from each company went to Madgeburg to collect tanks – 12 days leave as well.

Thursday 21 May. Tank Regiment 4 drove through OREL to KURSK with the new tanks – Pz III with the long 5cm guns and Pz IV with the long 7.5 cm guns.

"Our cobbler, Obgefr. Schindeler, meets up with his 3 brothers here in OREL. 2 brothers are in our Company. May 1942."

"Obgefr. Selm, Obgefr. Wach, Gefr. Saur, Uffz. Koubeck, Obgefr. Kautschitz, Obgefr Murrich – killed in a tank accident March 1944 - and Obgefr. Schindeler our cobbler."

Friday 22 May. Labour service – delousing. Then sport. Yesterday 10 recruits came to the *Kompanie* – from St Polten – real Austrians. Swimming in the OKA.

Saturday 23 May. Up at 0500. 0600 – 0800 drill on the sports ground then technical and labour service. In the afternoon cleaned up the sickbay. In the evening to Toni.

Sunday 24 May. Have a guard duty. 1st *Abteilung* of Tank Regiment 35 came to OREL and belongs to us, the 39 Tank Regiment. Also with old vehicles.

Monday 25 May. Whit Monday – quite a lot of mail.
Big surprise! There are 5 leave passes for those who have been in Russia since 22 June '41. Lots will be drawn. *Gefreiter* Grosse, *Feldwebel* Volk, *Gefreiter* Schramm, and *Gefreiter* Franz Kaiser drew the lots. Such luck.
In the evening to Toni and Helene.

Tuesday 26 May. Spiess to the field hospital – jaundice. Shame. Uffz. Hertlein leads as Spiess.
On the 30th those who won the draw are going on leave.
1st *Abteilung* already has the new tanks with the long gun barrel.
In the evening parade. Then to the girl's.

Wednesday 27 May. Got ready for exercise. Firing with live ammunition using five Pz IV. 1200 away then night exercise. What an exercise. Night firing with tracer warheads. After the exercise played football and gramophone outside.
Home at 2400. Lots of mail here.

Thursday 28 May. Technical Duty went to the workshop. Afternoon off. Looked at the new tanks. Long gun barrels of the 1st *Abteilung* (New upgunned Panzer IV tanks). That's the limit.
Toni in the evening.

Friday 29 May. *Soldatenheim* goods – lots of cigarettes. Labour service. Looked at the 7.5 cm gun barrels. Too much. In the afternoon roll call by Schwarz.
Straffing by five fighter bombers – Russian at the station.
To Toni again.

The long gun barrels of the First *Abteilung*. Tank is a Panzer IV Ausf. G here finished in factory fresh *Dunkelgelb*, or dark yellow.

Saturday 30 May. Labour service. Two Russians came. Flak firing alongside. Cleaned the medical centre.
Seven leave passes. No more lots to be drawn.
At 1000 four Russian fighter-bombers attacked the airfield. Three of ours dead. Two Russians shot down. In the afternoon a thunderstorm and downpour. New infantry division came through.
Went swimming. In the evening Toni.

Sunday 31 May. Went to the leave centre.
Ltn. Von Schlumberger got the German Cross in Gold. My tank commander.
Went to the cinema – "The one who comes off best."
Ltn. Schlumberger went to the Reich to get spare parts. Also Friedl, Neuhold, and Grun. They will also be going on leave.

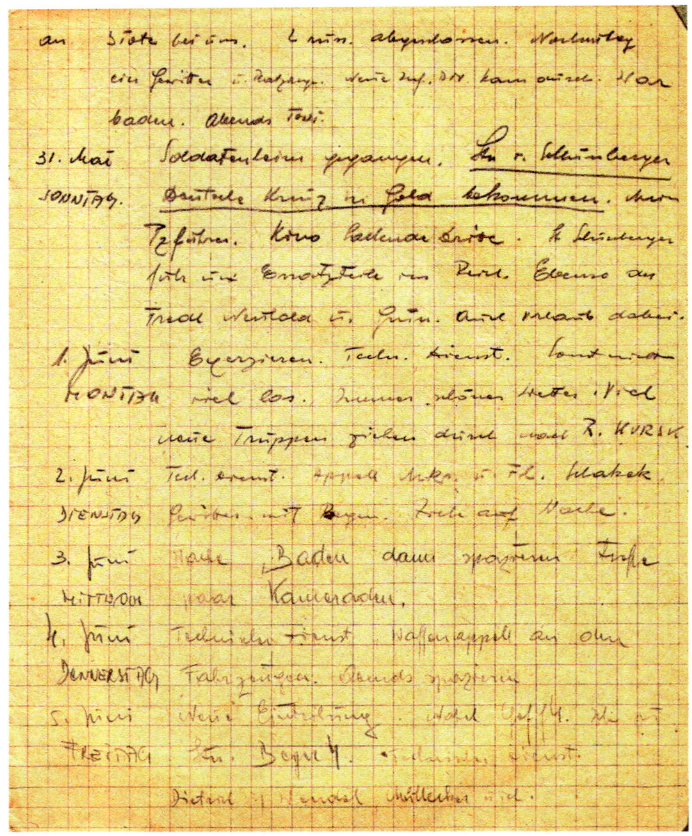

"Ltn. Von Schlumberger got the German Cross in gold. My tank commander.'

Monday 1 June. Drill. Technical duty. Otherwise nothing much happening. Still lovely weather. Lots of new troops going through to Kursk.

Tuesday 2 June. Technical duty. Parade. *StabsFeldwebel* and *Feldwebel* Schatzek.
Thunderstorm with rain. Mount guard.

Wednesday 3 June. Guard. Swimming then a walk. Met a few friends.

Thursday 4 June. Technical duty. Arms inspection at the vehicles.
In the evening a walk.

Friday 5 June. New detail. Me to Ltn. Berger as radio operator. (Erich indicates this with a Signals "blitz" symbol.) Others Dietrich, Wendel, Mullecker, Tank crew.
Technical duty.

Saturday 6 June. Cleaned out the vehicles. Drill.
We are conspicuous in the room with *Feldwebel* Trauter. (Erich probably means that their room has come to the Sergeant's attention for the wrong reasons.) Every half hour roll-call. That's madness.
Having a masked ball in the evening.

Sunday 7 June. Leave centre. Cinema – operetta. Rained all day.
Was with the girls.
Tomorrow *Feldwebel* Trauter, Uffz. Gfrorer, Uffz. Gellmann, and *Gefreiter* Koublek going on leave.

Monday 8 June. Gas room test. Injections against dysentery.
Mount guard. Flak fire as every day – ridiculous.
I go into town. Otherwise nothing happening.

Tuesday 9 June. Technical duty. We have 10 Pz IV tanks and 2 Pz III tanks.
Otherwise not much happening.
Lots of new divisions. 10th, 11th, and GD with new tanks. (10. Panzer Division, 11.Panzer Division, and *Grossdeutschland*) Krauser has a Volkswagen (*Kubelwagen* or *Schwimmwagen*). New reconnaissance cars – all sorts going south (to defend against Russian attacks to retake Kharkov.)
(10th Panzer Division was formed in April 1939 in Prague. The division fought in the western campaign and on the eastern front until May 1942, when it was refitted in France. 10. Panzer Divison acted as a reserve to counter the Dieppe landings. Sent to Tunisia, the division was destroyed 12 May 1943.
11th Panzer Division was formed in August 1940. It fought in the Balkan campaign, then South and Central Russia, retuning to the South in June 1942.
11. Pz. Div. fought at Kursk, Krivig Rog, and took serious losses when encircled south of Kiev. Transferred back to France, it opposed the Allied landings in the south before withdrawing to Germany.
The division fought in the Ardennes and Remagen.
GD, the *Grossdeutschland* Division "Greater Germany." Formed from the "*Wachtregiment* Berlin," a guard unit, by volunteers from all over Germany.
As an Infantry regiment GD took part in the Polish and French campaigns. In April 1942 armoured units were added, and on 23 June 1943 GD was made up to a Panzer Grenadier Division. As such it fought at Kharkov, Kursk, and later south of the Dnieper.
In November 1944 GD was renamed "Panzer Korps Grossdeutschland" and fought its final battles in the German retreat west.)

Notes to Diary 17 March to 9 June 1942

Erich reports that the German Army was still taking the threat of gas seriously, as the troops' gas masks were being tested. Most soldiers by now used the metal gas mask containers as a waterproof carrying case for cigarettes and alcohol.

What soldiers would not like the duty of guarding a brewery? The officers let the soldiers drink some but not enough to reduce their efficiency. Erich notes "of course" they obeyed!

Throughout the diary Erich records his love of girls, music, dancing, and the cinema and theatre. Also stressed is the importance of mail from home to the soldiers. The interest of the War Correspondent would improve morale, as the film and pictures would be shown in Germany and possibly be seen by relatives and friends.

The constant entries about the weather show how important this is for soldiers who are exposed to the elements constantly and whose survival may depend on it. April first is celebrated with the traditional humour. Erich takes pride in his Company's achievements as shown by the noting of the awards presented.

On the fourth April Erich records one of the many atrocities against civilians on the Eastern Front. This time it seems like Soviets who have slaughtered some women. This was done to Soviet citizens who had aided the Germans or had relationships with them.

Throughout the diary there is constant Soviet air activity and opposing German anti-aircraft fire (Flak). This had a morale reducing effect on German troops, as they were constantly on alert and found little rest or uninterrupted sleep. As the Germans were always short of armour they used all the captured tanks they could. Erich relates that even Soviet tanks that could not be moved were dug in as strong points.

Erich notes new arrivals and the posting of his fellow soldiers. He also fraternises with allied Hungarian soldiers. Food is a common language to soldiers, and as an Austrian he would be aware they had a lot in common before the First World War.

On 26 April Erich records the *Fuhrer's* speech but not its content. The arrival of new tanks is more important, as is the scarcity of food on 15 May.

On 21 May new tanks have arrived: the Panzer III with the long 5 cm L/60 gun, and the Panzer IV with the long 7.5 cm L/48. These gave the Germans a much better chance when fighting Soviet armour, such as the T-34, which was appearing in large numbers.

German soldiers enjoyed regular home leave passes, far more than in the British and American armies. In this diary they seem to have been allocated by a system of drawing lots, so it would have been up to luck. It was more usual to allocate leave to soldiers with the longest service at the front. Perhaps in elite units, such as Panzer Divisions, they could not have a lot of highly trained personnel on leave at one time.

On 31 May Erich shows his pride in his tank commander getting the German Cross in Gold by underlining the entry in his diary. This was the second highest decoration after the Knight's Cross. Such awards reflected on the whole unit and were celebrated as such.

Chapter 8

Diary 10 June 1942 to 11 August 1942

Written in a light grey Russian school notebook.

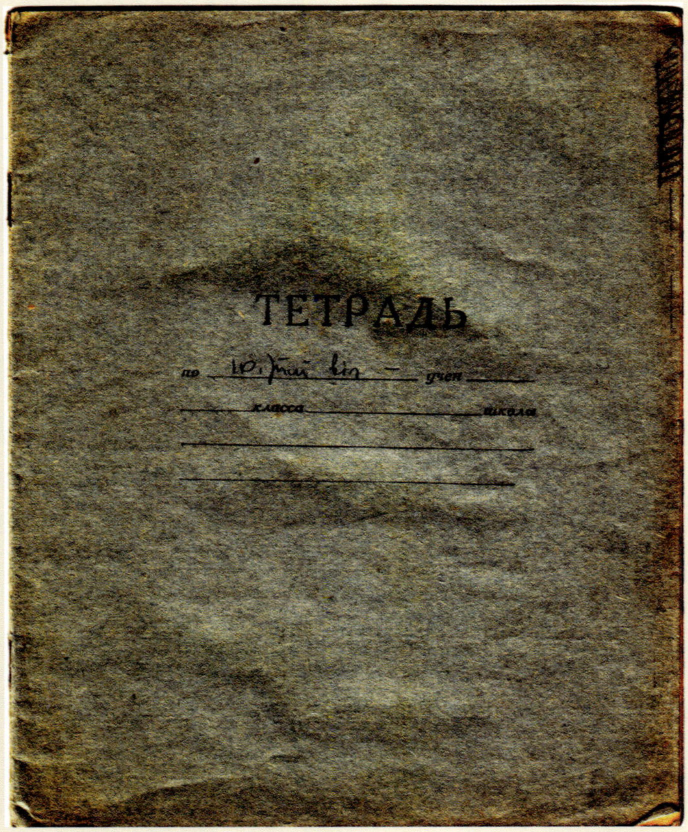

Diary cover.

Wednesday 10 June. Battle practice with 5 Pz IV commanded by Ltn. Berger. On the way home three shells explode in the tank of *Feldwebel* Triese. Both Baumgartner and *Feldwebel* Triese were blown out of the turret by the blast but were unhurt. They were very lucky the head of the shell did not explode. New Fz (*Feldzeug* – Ordinance) drives through.

Thursday 11 June. Early radio practice, I am in charge. GefFz (Ordinance corporal) and I go in the direction of Mzensk.
Not much else happening, practice shooting.

Friday 12 June. Sniping the whole day. Russians bombed the airfield, destroyed six Heinkels and a hangar. One T-34 shot up. Great, the shot goes through.

Saturday 13 June. Vehicle watch with *Kubelwagen*. A lot of nonsense. 0430 parade of tanks and weapons commanded by Ltn. Beyer and Spiess. In the evening aircraft attack as usual.

Sunday 14 June. *Soldatenheim*, then sentry duty. Got a letter. Richana killed in Finland.
1700 Alarm! Have to go with the tanks and am relieved of sentry duty. Tanks are put into groups, my group at the front. Uffz. Schnaider is our gunner, Dietrich our driver. The tanks are loaded with full equipment.
The Russians are attacking BOLCOW.

Monday 15 June. At 0200 advance on BOLDOW. In a small village called FATKENO we move in and put up tents. See a lot of aeroplanes overhead but they don't see our tanks.

Tuesday 16 June. Alarm during the night. It has quieted down.
Got new radio equipment. It's raining so we stay in the tents.
Quiet life.

Wednesday 17 June. Air battle over the Rollbahn.
Surprise, Gef Comes back from leave. Make pudding and hot chocolate in the tents. Rains all day.

Thursday 18 June. Who are we going to get as Company commander? Will it be Gef? Until the right person is found Ltn. Berger stays as my Tank Commander. Gef will probably lead the *Abteilung*.

Friday 19 June. Springer goes on leave. On the 26th Spiess and Uffz. Welker go on leave. When will it be our turn to go on leave?
Raining the whole day, lying in the tent.

Saturday 20 June. *Abteilung* lined up for inspection. The Regimental Commander comes up and the *Abteilung* is handed over to Gef. *Hauptman* Gosler leaves. I am on sentry duty. One bag of post arrives. 10 leave passes available for 1 to 14 July.

Sunday 21 June. Gef says goodbye to Ltn. Lange, who leaves the *Kompanie*. In the evening we have beer There are several promotions: *Feldwebels* Treuter and Grosse to *OberFeldwebel*. Werrel and Schondorfer to Uffz. The rest will be promoted in Orel.

<u>1 Year in Russia</u>

Monday 22 June. Have to get up at 0330 to return to OREL, but there is an Alarm, as the Russians are attacking and we stay here. If only we could get back to that city RIMOTZ, this morning might decide if we can get back. It's been really cold all week, I wish the sun would come out again. At 0700 we prepare to move out but our tank will not start. Konz drives to OREL without us. Broken down, we stand alone. Uffz. Garnsberger comes with the trucks and rations and we travel with the Zug back to FINOWOE for soup and a brush with the Spiess.
Stuck in a swamp at 1200.
(Anniversary of the start of Operation Barbarossa, the German invasion of the Soviet union.)

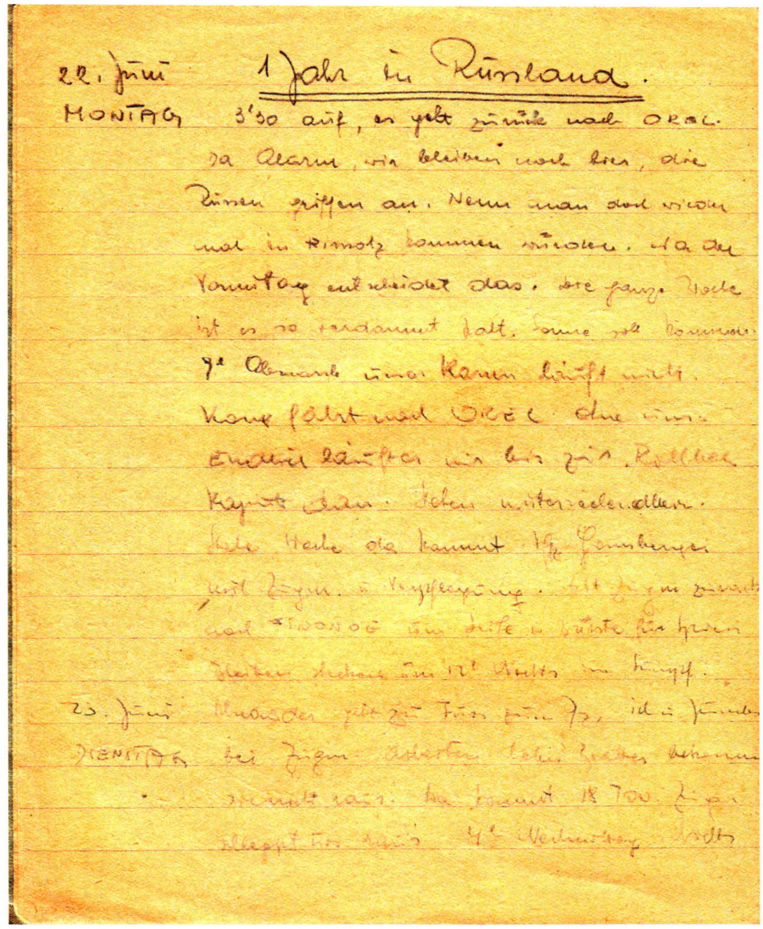
22. Juni
MONTAG
1 Jahr in Russland.
3'30 auf, es geht zurück nach OREL.

Diary page "One year in Russia."

Stuck in a swamp.

Tuesday 23 June. Schneider goes back on foot to our tank. The others and I stay with the trucks, which we try to get out using planks.
The 18 ton Famo Half Track recovers the tank and brings it to us at 1600 hours. There is nothing we can do as the tank is still broken down.
In the evening we get it started and it covers 2 km then breaks down again. We stay with it overnight and, as all the villages are too far away, we put up our tents.
(The Famo, or Sd.Kfz. 9, was the largest half-track used in WWII. It recovered armoured vehicles on a trailer or towed those that could run. Three Famos were needed to tow one 56 ton Tiger tank, however.)

Wednesday 24 June. Early in the morning Garsberger comes and the tank limps forward. In the afternoon we manage to leave and in the evening arrive at the *Kompanie*.
Yesterday leave passes were given out but I missed them, as I was with the tank. Kaiser got to go on leave after winning the last pass in the raffle that they had.

Thursday 25 June. Today the *Kompanie* is moving to the outskirts of OREL. We are billeted in rooms which we decorate.
I am on sentry duty again.

Friday 26 June. Have another raffle for a leave pass. *Funker* (Radio operator) Muller got the winner. Unlucky me! Work routine duty, to make the pathway even.

Saturday 27 June. Living in the tents and sleeping in the rooms.
Work detail until 1700. In the evening go to Toni to visit a comrade who had been buried alive after an explosion and is now in hospital.
Spiess goes on leave.

Sunday 28 June. Had a bath this morning in the *Soldatenheim* and wrote ten letters. Returned to the *Soldatenheim* later and drank a few beers. In the evening went to Wally's and got to know Ania, she is a great dancer.

Monday 29 June. Practice in the morning and work until evening. Otherwise not much happens. *OberFeldwebel* Gross and *Feldwebel* Volk back from leave.

Tuesday 30 June. Practice involving the lead platoon and *BruckenKompanie* (bridging company) from *Abteilung*. *Haumptman* Kaiser also there. 7th *Kompanie* watch as spectators. At the end the radio is broken and all the radiomen get a telling off from Ltn. Berger. We drive to the repair depot. A fuse has gone in the radio. The tank gets a new engine. We don't get home until 1900.
There's a violent thunderstorm.

Wednesday 1 July. Lots of special reports on radio. Sevastopol has been captured. Rommel is just outside Alexandria. The German Army is marching forward in the middle and south of Russia. Everything is quiet in our area. Russians have bombed the airfield but did not hit anything. Four Russian planes were shot down by Flak. *Feldwebel* Fromm is working towards his goal.
We get stuck in the swamp again and don't get home until 2000.

Thursday 2 July. Battle practice again for 6th *Kompanie*. Battle shooting for the zugs of the *Abteilung*. All the Officers are there. Everything goes well. I have responsibility for the radio.
Get Vaccination then Technical Duties.

Friday 3 July. Technical duties.
Every night aircraft attack, won't they let us sleep! All the windows are broken by the blast.

Saturday 4 July. Tank shooting practice in battle formations. The *Abteilung* commander is there. Things don't go well and we are told off.

Sunday 5 July. Alarm at 0600. Have to get ready immediately and leave in the direction of BELEF. Get attacked by aircraft on the way.
Just outside LOCHOV we stop and wait in a defensive position. Then drive and attack immediately. We have only the 6th *Kompanie* under Hptm. Kaiser with 11 Pz IV. Three of our tanks are knocked out.
4th *Kompanie* is kept in reserve to complete the task. The Russians are kicked back from the HKL (front line). They return at 2300. We shot at two T-34s. I go with *StabsFeldwebel* Hachel as my tank goes for repair.
Four Russian planes shot down. In total 47 Russian Tanks attack us, some from the USA (M3 Lees). 35 enemy aircraft seen. Russian artillery shoots at us but does not do any harm.

Monday 6 July. *Abteilung* attack the Russians. My tank is on the flank on the right. Steiner shoots at two T34s. I have the machine gun and cover some of our troops. *Nebelwerfer* fire goes overhead (rocket launchers).

"Heavy Russian Flak gun."

We are in the area of *Grossdeutschland* division, which is getting ready for another attack. Our *Abteilung* is split into *Kampfgruppen*. Zug Stab. (Platoon Headquarters) is at Oberstltn. Somstron. We drive forward to another position. The Russians are in front of the HKL and reach our position. Too late for a counterattack, as it is 2000. Many wounded. The Russian Artillery is shooting but don't hit anything.

"Briefing – Ltn. Volkendorff. Hptfldw. Geissler fell on 8.4.43. Obfldw. Trauter, Fldw. Gofrörer, Uffz. Mayer. and Obgefr. Zehntner. Gefr. Rüber fell July 1942."

Tuesday 7 July. Hard day. Nine hours of attack and it is really hot. Always encountering enemy tanks. Steiner shot at 4 tanks and certainly knocked out two T34s at 200 metres. Casualties: Mekler, Adi, and Toni Bauernfeind. Adi is dead, shot through the lungs. The gunner Ebner lost an eye. How unlucky! Martel got slightly injured. We got a hit on the turret right hand side. With Toni there was a 7.62 cm (anti-tank gun) hit in front of the driver. Steiber was lucky it did not penetrate. He got hit in the face but not badly. One more hit on the turret top left hand corner but no one is hurt. Two others get shot. We run out of ammunition. Take ammunition out of Toni's tank, as it has broken down, and fight on with that. Ours is the lone Pz IV left. Thank God that our companies come up from the left flank and then capture the village.
Thirty enemy tanks were destroyed and one Pak. Lots of the Russian tanks were USA (American M3 Lees).
Attack continues with infantry on the HKL. Whole *Abteilung* shoots, shoots, shoots. Russian Artillery and Tanks shoot straight at us. We cannot do anything about it as they are further away than 3000 m (out of range). Ltn. Schmit in a Pz II (Panzer II tank) is killed. Our radio operator is hurt. All in all 6 of our tanks are hit but they do not burn up so can be recovered. Artillery is still shooting at us so stay in the tank.

Return to refuel and rearm at 2000. What a day!
For the Russians to get BOUMOW, OREL, and KURSK they would have to take the flank of the *Sud Armee* (German South Army). That sounds good! An attack is planned. Our tank is to attack with infantry as before.

"Fallen Soviet soldier."

Wednesday 8 July. Had to get ready at 0400. We left, but were ordered back to the original positions in the afternoon. The infantry had to go out again. The attack went on for 8 hours and was really hard.
The Russian artillery fired at us constantly and we had to change position every 5 minutes to avoid getting hit. We attack in two groups: ours under Ltn. Mayer and the other under OberLtn. Heinike to the left of us.
Uffz. Sticht is hit and we knock out a T-34. Suddenly an HE (explosive) round hits us! Engine damaged, Stitzrolle gone (idler wheel for tracks)! No one injured though. Bastard! They were hiding amongst knocked out tanks. They also killed Ltn. Heinnan of 4 *Kompanie* and wounded Ritter Laite. No penetrations by the HE in our tank. A T34 shoots Albert Schriebe. We shoot until we run out of main gun ammo and I fire the MG until it jams Then we return to our position in the forest.
2300 everyone gets some sleep.
There is a sudden explosion at Ltn. Meyer's tank. Nobody knows what happened. Heini Primer got wounded at the hip, Uffz. Sticht got a splinter in the head, and Meyer got hit by a splinter in the foot. It's a mystery, as there were no incoming shell sounds, everything was quiet. I'm really curious to find out what happened.
Our *Nebelwerfer* (rocket artillery) shoot over our heads. Ltn. Ray brought back a T34 but could not see through its vision ports. Nothing gets through.

Thursday 9 July. 0230 have to get up and get ready. Russian artillery is shooting furiously. Stalin Organs (Russian rocket launchers) are firing without mercy. It's one hit after another. Sticht's tank has to go for repair. Wachter instead of Primer to go to Ltn. Meyer. We all take cover in the tank then return to the ORT position, as there have been reports of Russian tanks.

The battle begins at 1200. We have to stay in the same position and fire until our ammo runs out. Rim brings more ammunition. Russian tanks are driving around in front of us but do not see us luckily.
KW1, T-34, and American tanks are all knocked out by our tanks. We must halt the Russians. 35 tanks attack us and 35 tanks are knocked out and burning. On a small hill we see lots more Russian tanks and Infantry ready to attack. Will we withdraw and when? Very hot and nothing to drink. The sweat runs down the face and body.
1400 still standing here at the same place. 8.8cm Flak guns come up behind our position and fire continuously but miss with every shot. The Russian tanks drive in front of us back and forth. The Flak guns are right next to us, I can see every shot miss. Rubbish shooting! Shite!
At 1700 we finally leave the battle and make our way to refuel and rearm with 4th *Kompanie*. Also make repairs.
Get new orders – *Abteilung* is to go into dead ground. We can't continue fighting because of the continual heavy rain. Return to *Kompanie*. At 1800 there is an attack with infantry in the HKL (front line). Our gun breaks, it has to be reset by hand after each shot. Ltn. Meyer's tank has a problem and he returns to base.
Six Pz IV in 4 *Kompanie*, those of Gef, Kabel, Meyer, Friese, Grosse, and Gfrohner come to the hill. They are taken under fire by Russian Pak and Artillery. *Feldwebel* Gfrohner's tank takes two hits, the cannon is burst. The driver Ortner is dead, as is the gunner Mathius Kucher. *Feldwebel* Gfrohrer, Portsch, and the radioman Frans Kaiser are wounded.
Feldwebel Gfrohrer was brought back by *Feldwebel* Frisse. Portsch was brought back by the infantry with major burns. Frans Kaiser had splinters in his arm and back. Gfrohrer had splinters in his head and shoulders. We get a new radio order, but then receive hits in the transmission, front of the tank, and the turret. Tracks broken in three places, but thank God nobody hurt. Our gun is now completely broken and will not shoot. Gef and our tank are the only two Pz IV left.
Gefrohrer's tank burns up. Kucher and Ortner are still in it.
Get back at 2400. Nothing to drink and eat. Tomorrow the same attack.
Our gun is broken so we must wait for compressed air.

10 July Friday. The same attack again. The whole *Abteilung*. Now the fun starts. Get to the village. The shit hits the fan. The *Sanipanzer* (Armoured Ambulance) took a hit. The track flew off. The guys baled out. The regimental commander took a hit, baled out. Hptm. Karen arrived. Took a hit, baled out. Hptm. Borsch came up, took a hit, baled out. Our Gef goes into a bomb crater, gets stuck. Friese got stuck in front of the bridge. Ritzel kaput. Ltn. Mayer also got stuck there. We're the only Pz IV, drive behind Hptm. Kaiser, take 3 villages. Pak firing. 7.62 shells come into our HKL. We come to a small hill in front of us. Russian artillery in position. 3 regiments are supposed to be here. Impact after impact. We think we've had it. Hit in the steering, move on a bit and then back. Track torn off. Have to bale out. Take the most important things and go back. Got the MG out. We set off, pistols in our hands. Artillery hits all around. In the evening we get to our village ERSCHT. No one here from 6 Kp. The Gef's crew also arrived on foot. No Pz IV came back. We are standing here without any cover. Want to try and get a bit of sleep. Friese and Lt Mayer arrive. All the high-up ones were meeting at the Gef's vehicle when the hits were taken and got back on foot going from one shell crater to the next.

11 July. 2 Pz IV ready for action from 14 total. Theiss comes with one Pz IV. Ltn. Schlumberger also arrived without a Pz (tank). Everyone up early to go on foot to our Pz. *Zugmaschine* (recovery half-track) will tow off the Gef's Pz. We go on foot with M.Pi (submachine gun) and get lost, go right through a minefield, but nothing happens. We didn't know at first. Wounded infantrymen assemble one of ours amongst them, terrible the way he was shouting. Finally we got to the Pz. The fan was still running, otherwise nothing inside. One return roller is gone. We try it out and tighten the track. Hard, filthy work, as it's marshy here. 30m from us are 2 Russian PAK, 7.62cm and 4.7cm. All sorts of things lying around here, but we succeed. The artillery firing here and 7.62 PAK. But now in and away. Were well fired at. Get to ERSCHT happy. They all stared at us when we arrived. The *Zugmaschine* with Gef's crew are also here. Nobel and Schnauder Adi slightly wounded by shrapnel in the arm and face. Staying in the Pz, came under fire when recovering the wounded. Pz not to get towed away because of artillery fire. *Zugmaschine* goes and fetches Fldw. Gfröhrer's Pz. Kucher and Ortner are still in it, dead. We got them out here in ERSCHT. Helped. Radio still whole. Ortner's chest torn open and then the shot went into the chest. Kucher's leg gone and shrapnel in his head and chest. Must have been killed outright. Kucher was Commander, Ortner Richtsch (gunner), Fldw. Gfröhrer was the driver. Came under PAK fire as Fldw.'s vehicle was being towed away and had to go back. Ltn. Schlumberger brought wine, cigarettes, chocolate, and cigars. Battle group which is still here got this overview: 5 Pz knocked out since the beginning, Gfröhrer shot dead, the *Richtschütze* torn to pieces. It's 11.30, I'm dead tired. Nowossat is going back. Steuber Rudi is now the driver. Thank God that the guy is away. Changed the road wheels, return roller. There was mail. Tonight the Pz are being collected by the *Zugmaschine*.

12 July Sunday. During the night the Gef's Pz IV collected by 2 *Zugmaschinen*, *Sanipanzer* also. Other tanks towed into the hollow. There were EK1 and 2 again, given to the wounded. Our Commander Stabfldw. Habel awarded the German Cross in Gold. Today we got 6 Pz IVs ready for action. Yesterday Adi installed a new barrel recuperator (the mechanism for returning the gun barrel after the recoil on firing).

13 July Monday. Day off. Schuster Karli is also buried in the military cemetery in BOLCOW, along with Ortner and Kucher. Altweger seriously wounded. He was Ltn. Schmidt's radio operator. Schnaps to drink. We've got 7 Pz IV. We've got 2 new Ltn. Big surprise. General *Oberst* Schmidt is to come.

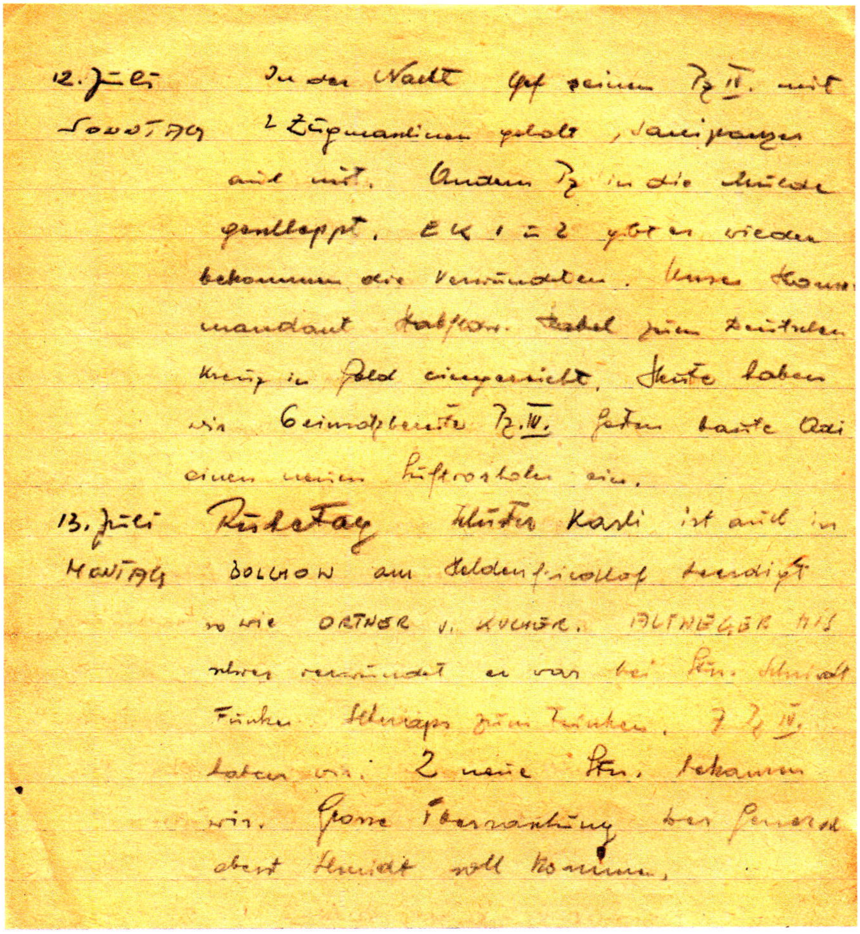

Diary page EK1 and 2.

14 July Tuesday. The General is here. Big surprise. 6 are going on leave. Uffz. Steuer, Martel, Seufert, Hoffran, Flausch, and ME. On 19 July at 01.30 we're leaving from OREL. Day off. The Russians have withdrawn. Quite quiet. Just heard, we're going back to OREL again in the next few days. 7 PM the *Oberstleutnant* presented the E.K. From us Gfröhrer and Uffz. Mekler, both in the field hospital. Uffz. Schnauder E.K.1, also Tremper, Fuchs, Hofmeister, Senkfried, and Pfisterer. Uffz. Hartlein is preparing our leave papers. One bottle of vermouth and blancmange for our crew. Stamminger Hansl is my relief. He's already here, arrived back from leave a few days ago.

15 July Wednesday. Wet day. Not much happening. At midday we 5 are going on leave. To OREL with Schorsch. First to the field hospital to Uffz. Mekler to give him his EK1. Uffz. Hartlein is with us and Fldw. Fromm. Afterwards to the leave centre. Themel is supposed to be going on leave with us, but he crushed 3 toes and is in the field hospital. What bad luck.

16 July Thursday. Awake at 6 AM. We're still on duty here. We go to the barber and to the baths. Fall in at 2 at the leave centre. Uffz. Theiss and Uffz. Sticht are leaving today.

17 July Friday. To the doctor and to delousing. Front assembly point. Then to leave centre.

18 July Saturday. Pack our things. To the station at midnight.

19 July Sunday. Travel via BRYANSK - GOMEL - UNETSCHA - MINSK - BRESTIC.

20 July Monday. BRESTICITOWSK through POLAND - RADOM

21 July Tuesday. DEBLIN - MISOWICE - PRERAU - ODERBERG

22 July VIENNA - LINZ - arrival at 9 PM. 11.30 PM in St Georgen at Uncle Ferdl's.

23 July. ON LEAVE.
(No diary entries between 24 July and 10 August.)

11 August Tuesday. 8.30 departure from St. Georgen. 11.10 departure from Linz.

"21 July – 11 August 1942. Leave from the front."
Erich in black Panzer uniform.

"21 July – 11 August 1942. Leave from the front." Good shot of uniforms.

"21 July – 11 August 1942. Leave from the front." Another view of the three servicemen with someone in civilian clothes.

Notes to 10 June to 11 August 1942

The diary starts with an accident in one of the 17. Pz. Div. tanks and shows it was not always enemy action which posed a threat to soldiers. Erich notes the new versions of the Panzer IV can shoot right through the armour of the Soviet T-34.

There is still a lot of Soviet air activity. Again, post and leave are very important in the minds of the soldiers. Erich feels unlucky not to be picked from the raffle. On 18 June Erich is keen that his friend Gef commands his tank and the *Abteilung*.

17.Panzer Division was reduced to one tank Battalion, or *Abteilung*, when the First Battalion was transferred to 29.Motorised Division as Panzer *Abteilung* 129. This reduced 17.Panzer Division's strength in combat.

Erich celebrates 22 June as the first year in Russia with capital letters and underlining the entry. It was important for soldiers to visit wounded comrades in hospital to check on their well being and raise their morale. The *Soldatenheim*, the equivalent of the NAAFI and PX, is an important place to the troops, as shown by Erich's visits.

Despite all the danger from the enemy, there is still a lot of work for the radio operators. The senior NCOs and officers do not hesitate to reprimand them if things go wrong.

On 1 July Erich notes German successes. This was soon to change! As the radio operator in the Panzer IV Erich had the hull MG 34 machine gun and could use it against enemy infantry, as on 6 July.

In the fierce fighting starting on 6 July, Erich makes notes as and when he can, recording his unit's casualties and the losses inflicted on the Soviets. On 10 July Erich saves the radio codes from his tank. This was one of the Radio Operator's duties. When tank crews were displaced from knocked out tanks they had to fight on with pistols and sub-machine guns as Erich describes.

The fighting continued until 13 July, when the General visits 17.Panzer Division with medals to reward the bravery of some of its personnel. Shortly after Erich is delighted to get some well earned home leave.

"21 July – 11th August 1942. Leave from the front."
Close up of the three men. Erich correctly wears a white shirt and black tie with his Panzer uniform. He has the rank of *Gefreiter*, as shown by the single sleeve chevron, and wears the ribbon of the Iron Cross second class and the Panzer Assault Badge. The *Luftwaffe* man on the right also has the rank of *Gefreiter*. The man on the left appears to be in army field grey, but closer inspection of the buttons shows them to have the *Kreigsmarine* navy anchor. The shoulder straps are pointed and have navy rank on them. The lower tunic pockets are not bloused This means that the uniform is of the *Kreigsmarine* costal artillery. The early issue soutache chevron on the side cap would have been in gold.

Operation Winter Storm December 1942.

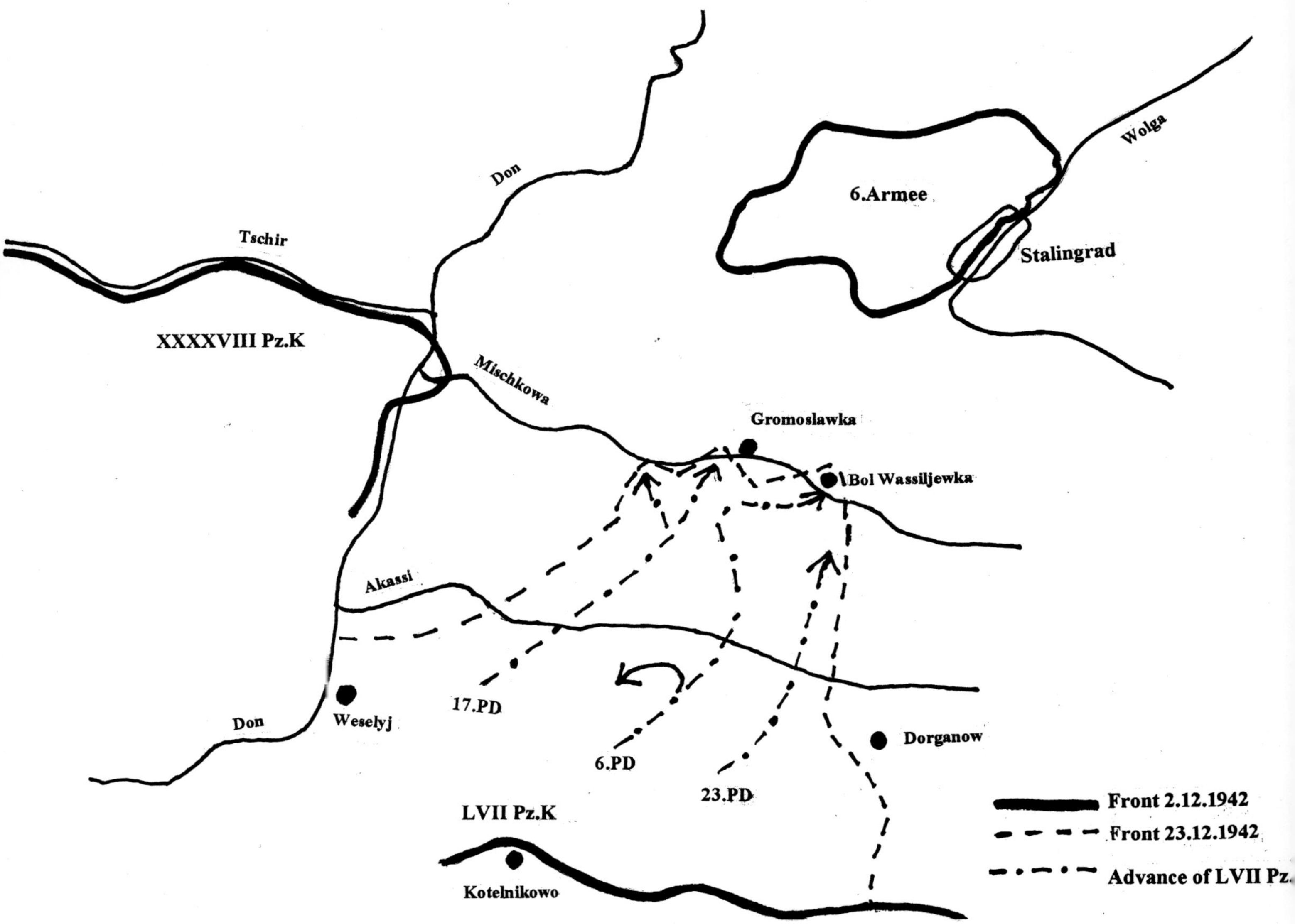

Chapter 9

Diary 11 August 1942 to 26 December 1942

Unfortunately no diary material survives from this time. Erich probably lost his diary during the fierce fighting. Luckily there are some of Erich's photographs that did survive to provide a record of this period. We also have Erich's certificate for his Winter Medal and the original medal. The date on the certificate is 20 August 1942, showing how much later the troops got their medals.

Particularly noteworthy are the photos taken during the attempted relief of the Stalingrad pocket. Very few photographs of this operation were taken, so Erich's are a very valuable record of this fighting.

For more information please refer to the chapter on the 17.Panzer Division's history.

IM NAMEN DES FÜHRERS
UND
OBERSTEN BEFEHLSHABERS
DER WEHRMACHT
IST DEM
Unteroffizier Erich Hager
6./Pz.Rgt.39
AM 20. 8. 1942
DIE MEDAILLE
WINTERSCHLACHT IM OSTEN
1941/42
(OSTMEDAILLE)
VERLIEHEN WORDEN.
FÜR DIE RICHTIGKEIT:
Hauptmann u.- Abt.Führer

Erich's Winter Medal certificate.

Erich's original Winter Medal. Only the ribbon was worn on the tunic.

"Our Gef Hptm. Kaiser. Fell on 27 Aug. 1942 at the SCHISDRA attack north of OREL. Promoted to Major."

"Advance in the SCHISDRA action through sand desert in August 1942."

"KW1 SCHISDRA action in August 1942."

"KW1 knocked out in SCHISDRA action in August 1942."

"Military cemetery north of OREL near SCHISDRA action. Sept. 1942."

"Military cemetery near BOLCOW. September 1943."

"Billet near LYWNI, south of OREL. Into action with 1 Division, where Ltn. Erwin Poetsch was. Sept. – October 1942."

"Destroyed Russian Assault gun. Russian 12.2 cm in the Don bend on the steppe. November 1942. Advance on STALINGRAD."

Advance to STALINGRAD. Kradmelder and Panzer IV Ausf. E.

"Snowstorm on the Kalinsche Steppe. Uffz. Reissinger Hansl and Obgefr. Kellner."

"Knocked out tank. Pz IV of 6 P.D. In the push and attack against the Kessel at STALINGRAD in December 1942. It was 40 km from the cattle collection point." Unfortunately the photograph is damaged, but is included for historical interest.

Advance towards STALINGRAD. Tross.

"Retreat from STALINGRAD. Here with prisoners in December 1942."

Chapter 10

Diary 27 December 1942 to 31 December 1943

This diary is a small German pocket diary "Taschen Kalendar." Erich's entries are in very small writing. In the diary Saturdays have an extra space for notes, which explains why the entries on that day are larger.

Diary cover

"Schirrmeister had fallen in Dec. 1942 at Stalingrad. Place is NISCK-KYMSKI."

Sunday 27 December 1942. Pulled back to HOLSINWOL. Fight after fight, then driving through the night.

Monday 28 December. Everything is going back. Us at the rear with the tank. We counter attack. USTELUSKOZYE

Tuesday 29 December. Tidied up the feeding camp. Lots and lots of Schnaps. Good to get everyday things.

Wednesday 30 December. Attack, attack with lots of our tanks.

Thursday 31 December. Retreat from Stalingrad. We made 4 attacks per day. Got blocked in and boxed our way out. The whole division was involved. Last attack at 2300.

"On the retreat from STALINGRAD. I had just slaughtered 2 pigs and hung them up on the gun. Below are the Gef and Obltn Pictal. In January 1943."

Friday 1 January 1943. Happy time. Saw in the New Year listening to the radio. Travelled the whole day travelling to HoF 3 (Map reference), where there was safety. Here we spent the night.

Saturday 2 January. Retreat again. Whole division brings up the rear. We drive through snowstorm - freezing cold and spent the night outdoors.

Sunday 3 January. *Fuhrerbefehl* (*Fuhrer* order) takes us immediately back to the old position and counterattack. Get new tanks, Panzer 4 with the long 7.5 gun.
(17.Panzer Division repulsed a Soviet assault.)

Monday 4 January. The unit attacked with 40 tanks. Great success and pushed on 40 km. Attacked by 60 soviet panzers - T-34 and KW1. Knocked out 25 of them. All sorts of fighting going on. *Feldwebel* Feber from my unit killed. Commanding officer shot.)
(German assault towards Stalingrad.)

Tuesday 5 January. *Hauptman* Heinz Schonburg returned at Kolonitikaja. Took leave of Feld. Feder. In the evening we had Schnaps, liqueurs, and chocolate. I slept in a school.

Wednesday 6 January. Withdrew 100km in the night. The Spitze was in the lead. Freezing cold overnight. Unit commander Prinz injured in an accident and is going home.
(Soviet units had infiltrated behind 17.Panzer Division positions.)

Thursday 7 January. Moved forward again to our old positions. Attacked against OVERIKI, PRAFRI. Attacks supported by Tigers. (Heavy Tiger Tanks. 17.Panzer Division had been reinforced by a company of ten of these powerful machines.) Fleiss knocked out. Saw a lot of tanks.

Attack supported by Tiger tanks. As normal practice the Tiger leads supported by the lighter Panzer III N.

Diary pages involving T-34, KW1, and Tiger tanks.

Friday 8 January. Attacking again. Formed a bridgehead and took a town. Soviet Pak opposition. Our own gunners came up to support us.
(17.Panzer Division armour was counter attacking Soviet forces. General Rokossovsky, commander in chief of the Don Front, issues surrender ultimatum to 6.*Armee* trapped in Stalingrad.)

Saturday 9 January. Made another attack at the old place. My tank took 4 Pak hits. The tank had had it and was towed away. I was wounded in the finger. Ltn. Mayer and Major Ohkifert shot. Eisenhutte and Kleid dead.
(von Paulus orders surrender ultimatum to be ignored. Battle continues with increased ferocity.)

Sunday 10 January. My platoon deployed with Tigers. They have young crews, shite. (The Germans gave the Tigers to experienced battle proven tank soldiers. If Erich thought that younger crews were being given the new weapons he is possibly irritated that he was not selected. He may also have felt that young crews would not make such good use of the new weapons.)
Tank battle begins again. Many hit by Paks.
(The Red Army opens "Operation Ring," the final onslaught on the battered remnants of 6.*Armee*, with a 55 minute bombardment.)

Monday 11 January. Fighting retreat to SALSK, PROLETARSKAWA, and TSCKAKOTSKI. All out attack on KRASSNY.
Feldw. Membeich shot. Russians attack all day. It's great to be in amongst it!

Tuesday 12 January. Went to KOWRINAR. Here attacked supported by *SS Wiking* division. Great attacks! The tanks were there in the thick of it as ever!

Wednesday 13 January. Division deployed in static position. Four Pz II with us. I go to divisional HQ. It's a great life! Heavy snow storm and freezing cold. We secure the area.

Thursday 14 January. Another day in the same place. *SS Wiking* are with us. We started the march at 0400 (15 January) and drove through the night. Only 4x4 drive lorries got through.
(5th SS Panzer Division "Wiking" was formed in 1940 from the "Germania" regiment extracted from the SS Division "Verfügungstruppe," later to become the "Das Reich" Division.
One feature of this division was the high proportion of non-German volunteers from western Europe and the Nordic countries serving in its ranks, including Danish, Estonian, Finnish, Flemish, Wallonian, Dutch, Norwegian, and Swiss nationals.
"Wiking" fought with *Heeresgruppe Süd* and at Kursk. It was trapped in the Cherkassy pocket, and although it broke out most of the division's heavy weapons and armour were lost. Being one of the few SS Divisions that fought extensively on the eastern front, "Wiking" resisted the increasingly strong Red Army throughout Poland, the Vistula, Hungary, Czechoslovakia, and Austria.
Wiking and the 17th Panzer Division were to become the main formations of XXIV Panzer Korps and the Field Army Reserve. *Heeresgruppe Süd* had to get German Army High Command permission to employ them at all.)

"Security at the SAL on the retreat from STALINGRAD. Securing the retreat of the SS Wiking. January 1943." Note the grey primer on the gun barrel showing it had been replaced in the field without time to paint it in *Dunkelgelb* to match the tank.

Friday 15 January. Everything else was left behind. Drove through PROLETARSAWZA and back to MANITSCH. Here we were in action again. The whole unit gathered and quartered together.

"Retreat from STALINGRAD. Here is the ABT during a counter attack at MANITSCH during the attacks on JEGORLIK in January 1943."

"Retreat from STALINGRAD. Here we are in a counter attack from MANITSCH against KRASSNY during a horrendous snowstorm. Back with prisoners. In January 1943."

"During the retreat from STALINGRAD. As our whole Div. was shot up no one knew where to go from here. January 1943."

Saturday 16 January. Into action, straight away to BARANIKI. The Russians occupied half the village and we had the other half. We had gunners from 16 Mot Division - great division!
(16.Motorised Division was nicknamed the *Windhund* ["Greyhound"] Division. At this time it was involved in defensive operations in the Southern sector. In 1943 it was upgraded to a Panzer Grenadier Division and finally in 1944 to the 116th Panzer Division, fighting in Normandy and Western Germany.)

Sunday 17 January. Attacked KRASSNY during a snowstorm. Overran the Russians, killed 50 enemy, took 300 prisoners, 8 PaKs, and some artillery and mortars. My regiment was in command of the operation. Three of our tanks were damaged in the attack.

Monday 18 January. Further attack on HOWOMANITSCH in a snowstorm. Drove through the Russians. It was great! Spent the night there.

Tuesday 19 January. Attack on NOWOJEGORLIK on the same river. Half the village was full of Russians, but we could not dislodge them. They had dug in on a hill and we went back through the Russians.

Wednesday 20 January. Three more attacks from BARANKOWSKODE. The Russians infiltrated the village and captured a supply depot. We have to retreat but where to?

Thursday 21 January. Passed through SALSK at midnight. Bagged two pigs during the journey to LOPINSKODE. Every unit is retreating, retreating! I wonder if we will get through to ROSTOW. Are we completely hemmed in?

"Retreat from STALINGRAD. January 1943."

"At the retreat from STALINGRAD. We were encircled, the whole 17 P.D. We pushed our way out through the Kalinken Steppe. In January 1943."

Friday 22 January. Went immediately to MANITSCH and attacked the first village. The attack was successful against MALSASABADEWIKA

Saturday 23 January. Attack without mortar fire on SWOBDA. Very lucky, as the Russians were stiff with fright, lots destroyed.
Officers Fleiss and Mullhauser of 16 Mot Div fell.

Sunday 24 January. Attack on MANITSCHKODE on the MANITSCH. Were attacked by Russians at BULUTSCHKYN. Just attack after attack!
(Russians take Starobelskiy, near the river Donets, which is more than 250 miles to the west of Stalingrad. Hitler replies by ordering no surrender in Stalingrad. The Soviet offensive towards the Kuban bridgehead is stopped at Novorossiysk and Krasnodar.)

Monday 25 January. Another attack against MALSA, SABADENKA, and SWOBADA. Couldn't make much progress. Lots of T-34s and KW-1s against us. Our tank received a few hits but nothing serious.
(Soviets succeed in splitting 6.*Armee* into northern and southern pockets. Germans evacuate Armavir and Voronesh.)

"In memory of our unforgettable Irwin. Fell on 25.1.43. Remember Irwin from his parents." Perhaps a relative of Erich. By the date Irwin was possibly killed at Stalingrad

Tuesday 26 January. Attacked TUSKULOFF on the MANITSCH. *Feldwebel* Popel shot. 2 men dead and 3 missing. Spent the whole night at this god forsaken place as we were snowed in again.
(Stalingrad pocket is split in two by the Soviets.)

"Snow storm on the Kalinken Steppes during the retreat from STALINGRAD. January 1943."

"On the retreat from STALINGRAD. Obstacles on the Kalinken Steppe. January 1943."

Wednesday 27 January. Early morning tank fighting against T-34s and KW-1s. Building up a supply line. Ltn. Lefulten fell in PKW (Small troop carrying vehicle).

Thursday 28 January. Journeyed to KRASSNY SAMDA. Fuelled and armed tank for attack against a village. Stalin Organs captured and a load of Russians shot up in the attack.

Friday 29 January. We are leading the attack again, but in the afternoon everything goes back. We go to TUSKICOFF to rebuild the unit. There were tank battles in the evening 150m in front of us. Our tanks are roaring forward and we're providing covering fire for them. 6 Panzers are here and we are surrounded.

Saturday 30 January. We drove through the night. Four tanks were stuck without fuel. Ltn. Meyer travels with us and we are surrounded by a Russian battalion. We shoot at everything and collide with Russians. A Russian flies over the tank in front of us- WOW!
Fuel arrives, and we go into a counterattack on the flank and retake the lost ground. Our own tank is supported by 16 Mot. Div. and our own people find the four tanks without fuel, which are recovered and then we withdraw.

Sunday 31 January Gave the tanks to the 4th company and we went to our own company by car. Took the pigs of course! Spent the night with the company.
(In Stalingrad the exhausted troops in the southern pocket have run out of ammunition, and with the newly promoted Field Marshall von Paulus surrender to the Red Army.)

Eastern Front South. Area of 17.Panzer Division operations.

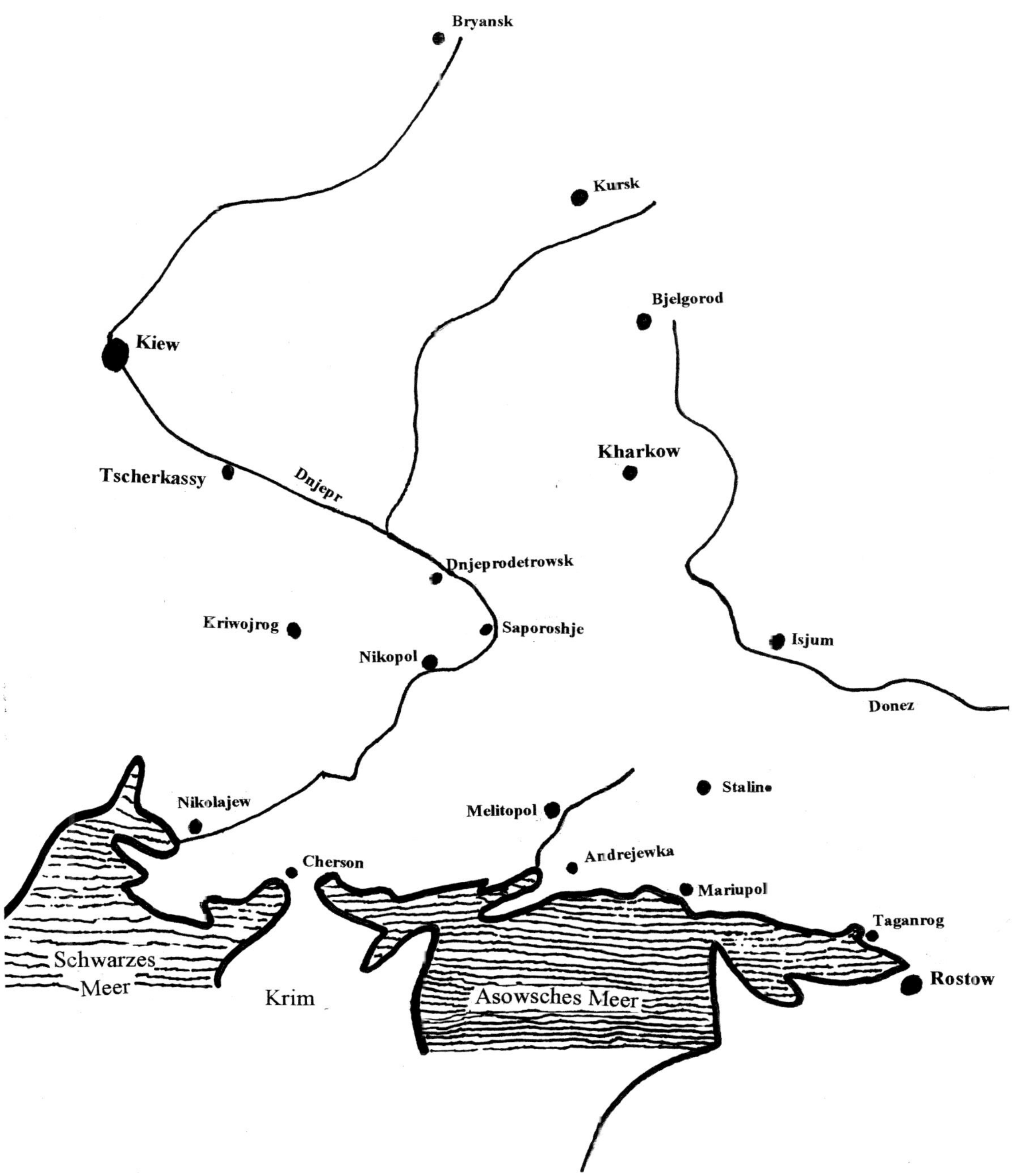

Monday 1 February. Travelled 25 km back on the supply line and quartered. Peace at last!
Made us a roast with the pigs. Gef has to return to 16 Mot Div. to collect more of our own people.

"Our crew: Uffz. Schnauder, Uffz. Schöneberger, and Obgef. Baumgartner, killed 8.4.43. Before Rostow. January 1943."

Tuesday 2 February. Officers Heisinger and Hollinger depart by lorry. It's bitter cold and we are just about frozen. Travel to BATALSK over 5 pioneer bridges to ROSTOW. We get quarters here.
(The last remnants of 6.*Armee* in the north Stalingrad pocket surrender. 96,000 survivors of the 300,000 strong 6.*Armee* are captured. Only 5,000 will ever return to Germany. Soviets celebrate the victory in Moscow with a salute of several hundred guns.)

Wednesday 3 February. Went with the Gef in the *Kubelwagen*, looked round ROSTOW. Lovely town with lovely women! Shame we're not staying there. Elsewhere every unit is retreating, lots and lots of troops.

Thursday 4 February. Divisions are passing through here from the Caucacus. We are waiting for our division. It's bitter cold. Lovely girls in the quarters.

Friday 5 February. Left in a lorry and went to ALEXAMOROWKA in a snow storm.

Saturday 6 February. We are the only ones from our unit here. Stayed the night with *SS Wiking*. Then made our way through GORLOWKA to MAKEJEWKA, where we got quarters and waited for the company. MAKEJEWKA was a lovely town with lovely women. Lots of troops passing through in continual snowstorms.

Sunday 7 February. We have private quarters which are absolutely great. Ltn. Meyer is with us collecting provisions. Gef is back with the company after getting lost.

Monday 8 February. It's freezing cold, but despite that we leave the quarters and take walks, go to the cinema, and get coffee. It's just great for me.

Tuesday 9 February. Company's arrived and we join up with them. We travel the whole night through STALINO to NIKITOWKA, where we get quarters.

Wednesday 10 February. Settled in. Great quarters! I am with Gef in one quarter.

Thursday 11 February. Lots of snow fell and had to be moved. The company is all together. My quarter with Gef is really great.

Friday 12 February. There's lots of Schnaps - everyone's drunk. Great life here but very cold.

Saturday 13 February. Work details and really settled in. Went swimming and to the cinema.
Gef is getting the German Cross in Gold, Ltn. Lucknel and Feldw. Grissler too.

Sunday 14 February. Schnaps again - whole company drunk in anticipation of company's departure tomorrow. But we will still be drunk!

Monday 15 February. Ten crews flying to DNEPRO to collect tanks. Go to airfield at MAKEJEWKA, but there is lots of fog and we can't fly. The fog does not lift all day. Meet men from 3 PD (3.Panzer Division).
(3rd Panzer Division was formed in October 1935, and at this time was fighting in the Southern sector of the eastern front. After this the division fought at Kharkov, the Dnieper, Ukraine, and Poland.)

Tuesday 16 February. The fog is still here. There is no flying. 150 men stuck. Looks like there are personnel from 3 different tank divisions.

Wednesday 17 February. A convoy from the airfield brings us to the station. Here we are loaded on a cattle truck and set off in the direction of DNEPROPETOWSKI.

Thursday 18 February. Continue travelling in the freezing cold with no heater on to SAPAROSHE on the DNEPR.

From here we board buses to DNEPROPETOWSKI.
(In the aftermath of Stalingrad Dr. Goebbels announces "Total War," which starts the employment of women in the war effort.)

Friday 19 February. In a south army tank camp waiting for the new tanks for deployment. The Russians are already 30 km from us. There is a mood of retreat in DNEPRO.

Saturday 20th February. Settling in domestically. At night you can hear the artillery. Planes bomb us every evening and through the night.

Sunday 21 February. It's a great life in the barracks. We eat doughnuts, they're our speciality! The planes are still bombing though.

Monday 22 February. 150 men are accommodated. Fifty men from each division in a large room.

Tuesday 23 February. Played cards all day. Otherwise pottered about working. Went to the canteen. Got *Ausweis* (work papers). Prepared to form *Kampfgruppe* "Sigen."

Wednesday 24 February. Every soldier without *Ausweis* is caught and sent to the front line. Thus they are cashiered.

Thursday 25 February. *Waffen SS* quickly formed *Kampfgruppen* and beat the Russians back again. DNEPRO relieved.

Friday 26 February. We came too late for the first tanks, as they were taken. Lucky really, as everyone was shot. Still no more tanks here.

Saturday 27 February. Did nothing all day but play cards. Horst Hammungen has jaundice. Will he be going home?

Sunday 28 February. Nice weather here already. No more snow yet. I am doing nothing. Planes are bombing us.

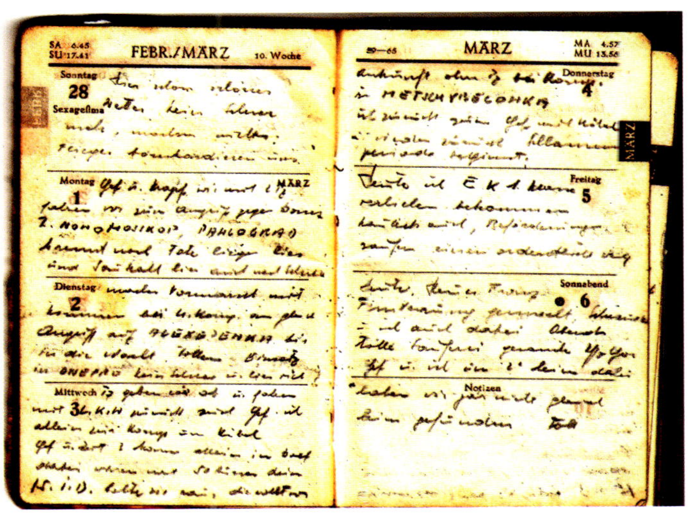

Diary pages. Erich getting the EK1, the Iron Cross first class.

Monday 1 March. My crew, Gefreiter, Krapf, and two tanks go up for the attack against DANEZ, then NOWOMOSSKOP. PAWLOGRAD still burning with dead lying all around. Still snow there and biter cold.

Tuesday 2 March. Advance with the 4th company for an immediate attack on ALEXEDEWKA. This continues into the night. Great deployment at DNEPRO. No snow here.

Wednesday 3 March. We hand over the tanks and travel back by lorry. Gef tells me to make my own way back to the unit in a *Kubelwagen*. Pass a position manned by 50 Russians who are attacked by 15 ID (15. Infantry Division).
(15. Infantry Division at this time was part of LVII Panzer Korps. They had advanced on the Donez at the end of February 1943.)

Thursday 4 March. Arrived at the unit in METSCHUBECOWKA. They were without tanks. I went back to the Gefreiter by *Kubelwagen* and returned again. The mud period (*Rasputitsa*) is beginning.

Friday 5 March. Today I was presented with the EK 1 (Iron Cross First Class). I was also promoted. Had a good booze up!

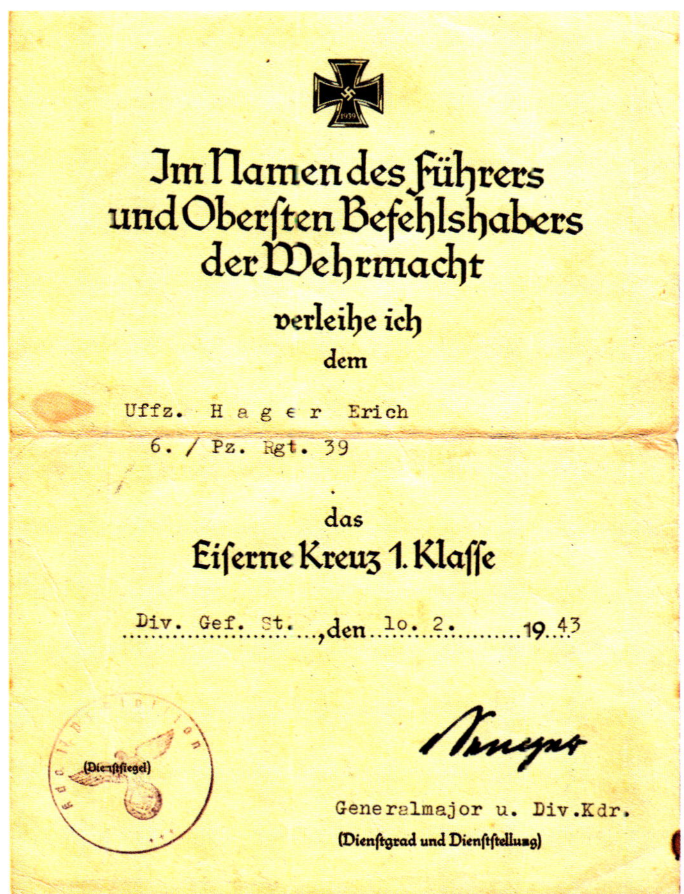

Im Namen des Führers
und Obersten Befehlshabers
der Wehrmacht

verleihe ich
dem

Uffz. Hager Erich
6. / Pz. Rgt. 39

das

Eiserne Kreuz 1. Klasse

Div. Gef. St., den 10. 2. 1943

(Dienstsiegel)

Generalmajor u. Div.Kdr.
(Dienstgrad und Dienststellung)

Erich's Iron Cross first Class certificate. Now his name is Hager. Signed by the Divisional Commander von Senger und Etterlin.

Erich with the Iron Cross first Class, Panzer Assault Badge, and rank of *Unterofficer*.

Saturday 6 March. Today Franz Heiner got married by proxy. Schaulder and I were there too. In the evening we had great celebrations. Gef and I got home at 0200 AM. We almost couldn't find the way home. Great!!!

"Steuer Franz's wedding. Gef Hptm. Pietsch, Ltn. Mayer from Linz, Uffz. Schauder, and me. I got EK1. March 1943. Advance on DONEZ front." Erich is on the left hand side.

Sunday 7 March. Got a hangover from last night! Tomorrow we're going into action again. Going forward by lorry.

Monday 8 March. Departure to the ABCOSE. 4 company to SCHEBELINKA. Immediate action against GAJEWKA with 63 Panzer Gren. Regt. (63.Panzer Grenadier Regiment, part of 17.Panzer Division) at the DONEZ. Russians in fear.

Tuesday 9 March. Day off. Settled in quarters. Re-armed.

Wednesday 10 March. Attack on BINLKIN and GLINITIS. Ltn. Meyer is at the cinema, we are at the DONEZ.

Thursday 11 March. Day off. Technical duty.

Friday 12 March. Attack against KOLOWAJA. Ob.Ltn. Pickle is hit and Gef takes command until the *Hauptman* can take over. Rifleman from 15. Pz. Div. (15.Panzer Division) attack the Russians and they beat it over the DONEZ. After the fighting we catch chickens.

Saturday 13 March. Day off. We roast chickens and celebrate promotions. All of us get drunk.

Sunday 14 March. Day off.
(German armoured forces of II-SS Panzer Korps retake Kharkov.)

Besitzzeugnis

Dem

Erich H a g e r ., Unteroffizier

(Name, Dienstgrad)

6./Panzer-Regiment 39

(Truppenteil, Dienststelle)

ist auf Grund

seiner am 18. März 1943 erlittenen

einmaligen Verwundung — Beschädigung

das

Verwundetenabzeichen

in Schwarz

verliehen worden.

Abt.Gef.Stand, den 14. April 1943

(Unterschrift)

Major u.Abt.-Kommandeur

II./Panzer-Rgt.39.

(Dienstgrad und Dienststelle)

Erich's Wound Badge in Black certificate. Signed by the Commander of the Second Battalion Panzer Regiment 39.

Monday 15 March. Went over to 15. Inf. Div. at GUSSAROWKA. Out in the evening. Tomorrow we will have immediate action.

Tuesday 16 March. Attack against KRASSNY and GUSSAROWKA. During the attack was hit by *Panzerbusche* (anti-tank rifle fire). Staying in the town. Troops forage in the village. Great attack!

Wednesday 17 March. Day off. Our old tank is towed away. Gef. and I get into Feld. Geissler's tank.

Thursday 18 March. Attack! We advance on a hill dominating the HKL (front line, main line of resistance). Ltn. Zech, Meyer, and our tank are hit. Many slightly injured. 6 missing 5 fatally injured.

Friday 19 March. Move from GUSSAROWKA to SCHEWELINKA. Arrive without tanks, as we leave 4 tanks with 15.Inf. Div. all of them shot up.

Saturday 20 March. Day off. Gef away.

Sunday 21 March. Gef, Schmauder and Vanrata going to DNEPRORETOWSK.

"In DNEPRORETOWSK. We are taking over these new supplied S.F.L. but only for a few days. Waiting at this time for tanks which never arrive. In March 1943." The vehicles are SdKfz 138. 7.5cm Pak 40/2 *Fahrgestell Panzerkampfwagen* II (Sf) Marder II. These were tank destroyers. The date would not suggest the light colour to be whitewash, but must be due to a factory fresh *Dunkelgelb* dark yellow finish.

Another view of the Marder II *Panzerjagers*.

Monday 22 March. Spiess (Senior Non Commisioned Officer) inspects quarters. Ober. Ltn. Zech is taking over the *Kompanie* and will be coming to the quarters.

Tuesday 23 March. Day off. Everyone drunk with Schnaps.

Wednesday 24 March. Day off.

Thursday 25 March. Day off. A few *Helferin* (female auxiliaries) come into the quarters with us. Great!!!!!!!

Friday 26 March. Preparing for departure tomorrow. Something is going on again.

Saturday 27 March. Departure for 15. Inf. Div. area. Quartered in SOKOLOWKA. We are the sole unit in the village.

Sunday 28 March. Day off. Great life! All alone here.

Monday 29 March. Day off. Played football.

Tuesday 30 March. Left for KISELLI, where we find great quarters and girls.

Wednesday 31 March. Settled into quarters. Absolutely great.

Thursday 1 April. Heuer and Wertmann have gone to St. Polten. As *Schirrmeister* (NCO responsible for all vehicles, including maintenance and spare parts) and *fahrer* (driver) respectively.

Friday 2 April. Day off. Nothing happening. Played football.

Saturday 3 April. Duty roster and roll call. Nothing happening. We all drink schnaps. Everyone gets drunk.

"Before the attack on the bridgehead on the DONEZ. Uffz Gelage. April 1943."

Sunday 4 April. Day off. We have a football match. Officers take part too.

Drinking session.

Result of heavy drinking or expressing their opinion of Hitler's Generalship?

Monday 5 April. Heard something about an attack against 15. Inf. Div. Wonder if we will be next?

Tuesday 6 April. Went off to attack the bridgehead at MELLOWADA. Found quarters in GLASONOWKA.

Wednesday 7 April. Went into the HKL. We felt our way forward. All the time we get madder. The riflemen are falling in the fire from the Russians in front of us.

Thursday 8 April. The Black Day. Attack on the bridgehead at GRINITSCHYNI on the DONEZ. I am shot for the sixth time. Ober.Ltn. Zech, Olsflohr, Geissler, Kienscher, Etzlinger, Baumgartner, and Ladenbitie fell. We were lucky to still have our life.

"Before the attack on the bridgehead. GRINITSCHYNI. DONEZ. 1943."

"Before the attack on the bridgehead. GRINITSCHYNI. April 1943."

Friday 9 April. Going back with Schleisser to the *Kompanie*. Staying overnight at KISELLI. Will leave tomorrow with Schleisser and Schinokla to DNEPROPETOWSK.

"Etzlinger's grave. Fell on 8.4.43. DONEZ bridgehead."

"Grave of Baumgartner Seppl, our loader. Fell on 8.4.43 in the attack on a bridgehead on the DONEZ at GRINITSCHYNI."

"Graves of Obfeldw. Geissler, Obgefr. Etzlinger, and Gefr. Kiesschen. Our crew. Obgefr. Baumgartner. April 1943."

Saturday 10 April. 0300 AM departure by lorry. We keep getting stuck. Lots of pushing, pushing, pushing! Overnight we stay in the village.

Everyone helps get the truck free. "Pushing, pushing, pushing."

Sunday 11 April. Continued the journey to PAWLOGRAD, where we find quarters. Scheisser and I share. Great women! The road to DNEPROPETOWSK is blocked.

Monday 12 April. Still in PAWLOGRAD. Go to the theatre - great! Got milk. Went to the girls in the evening.

Tuesday 13 April. Going from PAWLOGRAD via NOWOMOSSKOWSK to DNEPROPETOWSK.
We stay here overnight. It's as busy here as home. Such women!!!!

Wednesday 14 April. Do our shopping. Leave the centre and then go via KAMENSKODA to NIKOLADEWKA. Get the things then return to KAMENSKODA, where we visit the cinema. Stay overnight.

Thursday 15 April. This is a sumptuous life - cinema, women. Unfortunately we can't stay here. That would be something for us!!!! In the evening we are away again to DNEPRO.

Friday 16 April. Stayed overnight in PAWLOGRAD. Town totally destroyed. Fighting raged all day. *Waffen SS* mopped up.

Saturday 17 April. Departed the area and rejoined my *Kompanie* in KISELLI.

Sunday 18 April. Day off. Played in a football game.

Football match in May 1943 in KINSELLT on the DONEZ.

Monday 19 April. Back on duty. Got my new tank. Great girls in the quarters.

Tuesday 20 April. Whole *Abteilung* formed up (Adolph Hitler's birthday). Our new commanding officer, Major Matini, spoke. Muller was promoted to *Unteroffizier*.

Wednesday 21 April. I am getting the wound badge. Gross and Dierigen are *Feldwebel*s again.

Thursday 22 April. Left KISELLI for DEROHN BISSCHIN. We are an operational *Kompanie* again. Quartered in houses 2 km from Donez.

Friday 23 April. Exercise in tank and supply line today. *Funkmeister* Hagen came to us from 7th *Kompanie*.

Saturday 24 April. No duty yet. Settled into huts.

Sunday 25 April. Provisions arrive. We get thoroughly drunk. Otherwise nothing happens.

Monday 26 April. Duties begin, also instruction. Otherwise it's a day off.

Tuesday 27 April. Surprise artillery attack on us. The shells miss and nothing happens to our *Kompanie*.

Wednesday 28 April. Duties as usual, otherwise a day off.

Thursday 29 April. Lovely days (weather). Still quiet.
Not far from here is the DONEZ, which is the front line.

Friday 30 April. *Dienstbetrieb* (service duty, in other words the "9 to 5"). In the night Emil (light enemy bomber) flies overhead and deposits his bombs.

Saturday 1 May. Unit drill and exercise with the General. Afterwards there is chocolate distributed to the troops.

Sunday 2 May. Evening with the officers. This was at first great, but Schossl and *Hauptman* Trauter brawled, shame that they were informed on!

Monday 3 May. Schlossl has been punished by his leave being put back for two months and the officer dismissed from the unit.

Tuesday 4 May. Exercise with tanks, riflemen, and artillery. The general was there again. The steppe was set on fire - that's too bad!

Wednesday 5 May. Technical instruction. I am on duty. Had a big row with Uffz. Gor.

Thursday 6 May. *Dienstbetrieb* (Duty). Artillery firing again. Had a football match.

Friday 7 May.
Sprengranate 46 (High Explosive tank gun shell.)

HLB 26 (*Holladung* - High Explosive Anti-Tank, HEAT, hollow charge round.)
Panzergranate 15 (Armour piercing tank gun shell.)
20 *Gurtsacke* 1:1 (MG ammo bags containing 150 rounds in belts, ratio of ball round to tracer 1:1)
Leucht 15w 4r 3g (Flare shell)
(Erich seems to be using his diary as a notebook to record ammunition supply.)

Saturday 8 May. Drill. Because of the row all officers have to undergo officer training. That will hurt. Regimental HQ went home to form up a new tank regiment. Such luck! They are in St. Polten first.

Sunday 9 May. Heinz Schanenberger, Valenst, and Alexander are with us as drivers. Reisenger is a gunner.

Monday 10 May. Artillery is firing at us. The relief has gone on ahead and we're clearing out tomorrow towards ISSUM.

Tuesday 11 May. Departed from MERCHNY BISCHKIN to a new rest camp in the forest. Camping at WOLWENKOWO.

Wednesday 12 May. North of ISSUM and settling in. 15 ID are here and behind us 19 PD.
(19.Panzer Division was formed from 19.Infantry Division in 1940. It fought on the central sector of the eastern Front before being transferred south. Later fought in Poland and Czechoslovakia.)

Thursday 13 May. So long as it's nice we live well here in the forest, in tents and under the tank.

Friday 14 May. Everyday at 0830 Ivan comes - hasn't discovered us then. Thank God.

Saturday 15 May. Present strength 14 Pz IV.
4th *Kompanie* Pz III with 7.5 KwK (7.5 cm tank gun. This would denote the Panzer III N, the last in the Panzer III variants. It was armed with a short 7.5cm KwK L/24 gun.)
5th *Kompanie* Pz III and Pz IV are also here in the forest but a bit further away.

Sunday 16 May. Schneider back from leave. Alexander ill. Day off sunbathing.

Monday 17 May. Gefreiter gone to hospital. Alexander too. We're alone. On duty.

Tuesday 18 May. A long spell of rain beginning. Damn! Lying in the tent.

Wednesday 19 May. Uninterrupted pouring rain. No duty as impossible.

Thursday 20 May. Day of rain. Duty often interrupted by rain.

Friday 21 May. Day of rain. *Dienstbetrieb*.

Saturday 22 May. Day of rain. Divisional command to dig bunkers also for lorries during this time of rain.
"Bunte Buhne" (Coloured Stage) put on by Russian girls. I was fascinated. Played to us in the forest.

Sunday 23 May. Day of rain. Dug bunkers. Always damn well covered in dirt!

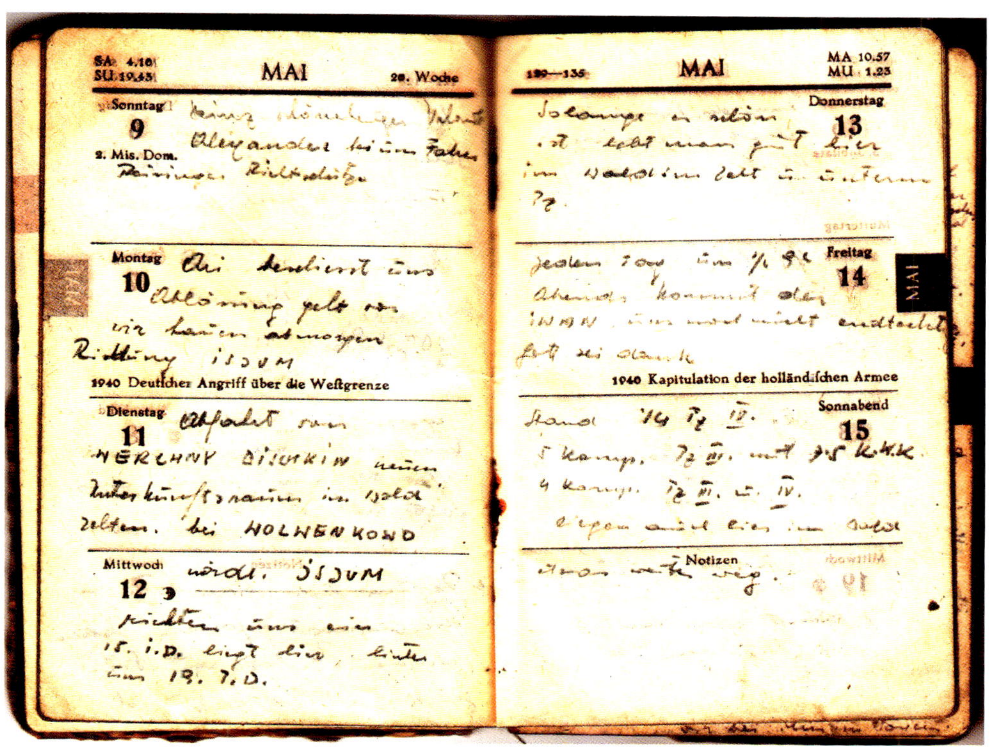

Diary pages. Erich listing ammunition and tank strength.

Monday 24 May. Day of rain. Dug bunkers.

Tuesday 25 May. Day of rain. Dug bunkers.

Wednesday 26 May. Day of rain. Dug bunkers.

Thursday 27 May. Day of rain. Duty. Dug bunkers.

Friday 28 May. Day of rain. Duty. Dug bunkers.

Saturday 29 May. Permanent Alarm. Day of rain. Half hourly sentry duty.

Sunday 30 May. Day of rain. Becoming a learner driver.

Monday 31 May. Beginning of driver school. During the instruction all shit broke loose. 7.5 cm shells hit our positions. Ltn. Mayer wounded, also Schisser, Prochaska, Ortner, and Karbaum.

Tuesday 1 June. Went to LOSOWENKA and back. Technical instruction.

Wednesday 2 June. Instruction – Technical duty.
Gef back from hospital.

Thursday 3 June. Driving school in WOLOWENKOWO, went swimming there. Then travelled to LOSOWENKA and back. Taking over the *Funkgeschafte* (Radiowork). *Feldwebel* Hager going on leave.

Friday 4 June. Exercise of the tanks and supply vehicles. Got told that I'm going on a training course at *Kompanie*.

Saturday 5 June. 0700 departure to 2 *Kompanie* N (*Nachrichten*, Signals) *Abteilung*. Arrived at midday, camping. Officers and men from the whole division gathered here, 70 men. Lovely village, swimming planned for tomorrow. One more day with the *Kompanie*.

Sunday 6 June. Up at 0400, started duty at 0600 'til 1100. Instruction on radio 1400-1600. Today I start, course begins tomorrow.
Now very hot each day!

Monday 7 June. Up at 0400. Duty started at 0600, then 5 hours of lessons. Continuous wave. Medium wave signals (Blitz sign) and UKW 4. (UKW, Ultra Kurz Welle, ultra short wave. In terms of frequency vhf, very high frequency.)
In the afternoon swimming. Then in the evening meeting girls 'til 2100. Great here. Swimming just superb.

"Uffz. Kummer 4Kp. Swimming with the trainee radio operators at the N.A. 27 in June 1943." N.A.27 was the Signals battalion of 17.Panzer Division.

Tuesday 8 June. 0600 duty. Lessons, then practice on 6 radio stations, Ami (American), SFL, 40, 6S, and Ausf KA 17. All great guys here. Practice in changing frequency. Swimming as every day. In the evening at the girls'. Great!

Wednesday 9 June. Exercise to LAGE. I was the overnight leader of the exercise. Great.
Good grades. Lessons then swimming. Great.
Skat for an hour. Girls.

Thursday 10 June. Exercise the whole day. I had a great swim during exercise. Swimming again in the afternoon. *Very* hot. Skat.

Friday 11 June. Exercise again. I played Skat all morning. Afternoon two hours lessons.

Saturday 12 June. Lessons 'til 1100 then free. Swimming – really hot, otherwise great life. In the evening, girls. A medical student from the Reich here on holiday. She's a Russian employed in Berlin.
On the 15th should have gone on leave but can't because of the course. Hard luck! Maybe on the 22nd. Hopefully nothing will get in the way.

Sunday 13 June. Day off. Really hot. Today there are provisions goods, cigarettes, champagne, wine, and beer. In the evening we get drunk together. Absolutely great. Swimming.

Monday 14 June. Today duty. Radio operator instruction. Really hot. Swimming as usual in the afternoon. Emil bombs us at night.

Tuesday 15 June. Radio operation until 1100. Then instructions then swimming. In the evening Skat with Ari, Hans, and Fritz. All sat down together.

Wednesday 16 June. Called back to unit so course immediately stopped. Division moved. Where to? We went back to *Kompanie* by tank. Took leave of the others. Very hot. *Kompanie* packing up to move off.

Thursday 17 June. 0400 departure. Went singly to Schewtschenko. Staying here overnight.
Swimming. Hot.
Tanks with metal panelling. (This could refer to extra armour bolted or welded onto tanks or the metal plates hung at the sides of the Panzer III and Panzer IV to give extra protection.) Hollinger going off to officer training school today.

Friday 18 June. 0400 departure to GOSOWAJA, where we arrived at 0800 and waited until 1600 to load. Very hot. Quite lovely women here. Everyone has women. The railways are very lively.

Saturday 19 June. Travelled all through the night and unloaded in ARTEMOWSK at 0700. Staying here until 1700, when we are to march off. Where to?
Lovely towns here. Everything is going towards the Donez overnight. Emil bombing all night.
Our division is fully deployed. 15 SFL. (*Selbst Fahr Lafette*, self propelled carriage – self propelled artillery. Twelve had been delivered to Panzer grenadier regiments 40 and 63 on 20 May.) Just great. Only GD (*Grossdeutchland* Division) have them.
General Senger und Etterlin leaving to become Commanding General in Sicily. Shame.

Sunday 20 June. The village we are in is SSEARFIMOWKA.
38. Inf. Div. (Infantry Division) and 62. Inf. Div. We are under the command of 62 as *Angriffgroupe* (unit for counterattacks).
Artillery firing in front of us on the hill. Hot day.

Monday 21 June. Day off. Lying in a fruit plantation. Everywhere full of troops, artillery, Pak, SFL (Anti-tank and self propelled guns).
63 *Schutzen* Regt and some of 28 ID are a few kilometres away.
(28 Infantry division later became 28 *Leichte*, or Light Infantry division.)

Tuesday 22 June. Second anniversary of the war with Russia. There's beer. Day off. Hot days.
Gef going into the village.

Wednesday 23 June. Went 5km with Reisinger, Prediger, and Uffz. Speilen. Skat. Injections. Hot day.

Thursday 24 June. Duty as usual. Otherwise nothing happening.
Rainy day. Played cards in the evening.

Friday 25 June. Driving school again. All day to ARTEMOWSK. *Soldatenheim* – great coffee. Home in the evening. Got a row from the Gef.
Driving instructor is Prediger.

Saturday 26 June. Went out with driving school in the morning. In the afternoon picked cherries and raspberries.
Talked to commanders of 32. Inf. Div. They are Berliners.

Sunday 27 June. Driving school in the morning. Afternoon played cards.
Tomorrow the exam; I am going for 1st Class driver.

Monday 28 June. Up at 0300. Left at 0400 for the workshops. Exam by pen at midday in the barracks. I passed both exams. Joy! Five failed: Wendel, Senkfried, Schneider, and Lutz. On the way home Lutz broke his foot. Got home at 2300.

Tuesday 29 June. The march off was delayed again for our *Kampfgruppe*. Parole, Krinsk going away. Uffz's card kitty is dissolved. Everyone gets 61 *Reichmarks*.
Four are going on leave - I'm not sure if I am one of them.

Wednesday 30 June. Gef. away. Pretul has come to the unit.
The Turkestaners are fighting for us.
Doing nothing.
(The Germans raised units of anti-Bolshevik Russian citizens from the satellite states of the Soviet Union. The Caucasian people were traditionally freedom loving and had always fought against invaders. The Czar had settled Terek Cossacks amongst them and the Soviets had persecuted the minorities in the Soviet Union.)

Thursday 1 July. *Dienstbetreib* (Technical duty).
Gefrörer, Mertel, Schramm, and Höller away on leave.
Played cards in the evening. Emil came as on every night.

Friday 2 July. Shooting with the *Kompanie* rifles (k98s).
Hauptman Pietsch back with our *Kompanie*.
The Turkestaners are here again with us.
Played cards in the evening.

Saturday 3 July. Whole *Kompanie* picked raspberries and cherries. Whole avenues are here for tomorrow.
Dindoling instruction
John is the *heute Spiess* (senior sergeant major) from today.
Cleaned sick bay. Played cards. *HauptFeldwebel* Treuter puts his business in the past with John becoming *Spiess* (an argument forgotten).
Hauptman Pietsch here again.

Sunday 4 July. 1200 march off to ARTEMOWSK via VARITE. 30 men. Just great, keen already.
Marched in the direction of SSLAWDANSK. Quiet there. Got quarters after a 12 hour journey arriving at 0300. Stayed overnight.

"On the left Fldw. John, also Uffz. Koubeck."

Monday 5 July. 0900 moved away singly, departure via SSLAWDANSK to LOSSAREWKA, where we arrived at midday.
In the evening go to PRISWOLNY in ISSUM.

Tuesday 6 July. In ISSUM, in the direction of BARWENKOWO. We get quarters here. Great quarters with girls.
Adolf (Hitler) is in his forward command post (to monitor the battle at Kursk.)

Wednesday 7 July. *Technischer Dienst* (Technical duty).
Sorted out quarters. 5 *Kompanie* also here.
Whole division assembled.

Thursday 8 July. Technical duty. *Arbeitdienst* (RAD) put radio in the quarters.
Swimming in the evening. Lovely girls. Lots of fruit here.

Friday 9 July. Technical duty with the *Arbeitdienst* (Labour service).
OberFeldwebel Grosse has come back up to the *Kompanie*.
When will I go on leave?
Swimming in the evening. Provisions come. Lots of wine. Everyone drunk.

Saturday 10 July. I went to the dentist with Heinz at SSLAWDANSK, 36 km away. Lovely women there. Beer again from the provisions.
Big *Kesselschlacht* (encirclement battle) has begun at BALGOROD and South Urals.
Americans have landed on Sicily on the 10th.

(Operation Husky, the allied invasion of Sicily, took place on 9/10 July. The British 8th Army landed on the Southeast of the island and the U.S. 7th Army landed on the south of the island. This was the start of the invasion of Italy, and after the capture of the island caused a change of government and the Italians to pursue an armistice with the Allies.)

Sunday 11 July. Day off. Swimming. Picked cherries.
Had a hectic party with women. Listened to the radio in the quarter. Otherwise just chatting.

Monday 12 July. To the *Abteilung* HQ. Taking down orders.
Bombed during the night. One man dead on the landing strip.
Otherwise did nothing all day. Few leave passes this month.

Tuesday 13 July. General radio exercise. Three Uffzs' tanks involved until 1600, then get withdrawing orders.
Otherwise nothing happening.
Got 70 pictures. Great! Listened to the radio.

Wednesday 14 July. Going to the dentist in SSLAWDANSK.
Don't get taken again. Found great girls. Came home by train.
Listened to the radio.

Thursday 15 July. MP (sub-machine gun, machine pistol) shooting practice by the whole *Kompanie*.
Sport in the afternoon. Otherwise nothing happening.
Listened to the radio in the evening then technical duty.

Friday 16 July. Tank parade. Heinz has to go to Gef for a dressing down. Me to ABT.
Because of the exercise *Feldwebel* Makowitz is NO (Signals Officer). Russians attacking on the whole front. Exercise cancelled. Action!
(The Soviet Voronezh front joins the counter offensive after the German failure to break through at Kursk. It attacks the 4th Panzer Army and Army detachment "Kempf" to the south of the Kursk salient.)

Saturday 17 July. 0200 march off towards ISSUM. Action! Travelled 'til 2000 then spent night in village WERNAPOLDE before ISSUM. *SS Wiking* next to us. 2. Inf. Div. in front of us.
Russians attacked the whole DONEZ front. Lots of plane activity on both sides day and night. Great air battles.
No bloody chance of leave.
Vancatie and Grim going off on leave. Nobody hears me!

"Before the action at ISJUM. KRAMATORSKASA."

"At our battle stations near ISJUM. 1943."

"Before the attack in July 1943 at ISJUM."

"Uffz. Prediger, Uffz. Brandstetter, Uffz. Link, Uffz. Mangold, Obgefr. Schindelar, Obgefr. Goraus, Obgefr. Sommer Karl, and Gefr. Karbaum. Near ISJUM 1943."

"1943," another view of tank crew. The tank is a Panzer IV Ausf.G.

Sunday 18 July. Lots of air activity. An unparalleled army cooperation. 0100 march off – Battle Stations. March until 1200. We're ahead. Whole unit attacking. *SS Wiking* is attacking also. We're supporting. Our artillery is magic. Planes banking magnificently here. 317 have been lost. None today. Great shots.

Monday 19 July. 1200 march off. 30 km journey south. Assembled in a wood. Great air activity on both sides. Russian artillery is having a good shoot at us.

Tuesday 20 July. Sitting in the middle of a great artillery barrage. Russian attack on the hills as far as the DONEZ. Artillery fire all the time. Bomb crater next to our tank. Russians reached the DONEZ.
Advanced with riflemen 'til 0200, slept in wood. Russians came at 0600 and broke through. Immediate counter attack. Retook village. Only one tank in front of us. Five tanks involved in the attack on the hill. Gef and I got 2 hits each. We took the hill and returned to the wood. Russians attacked again, us to the fore, counterattack right away.
In the evening went to GOLADA DOLINA and stood the whole night there. We're bombed with the heaviest bombs.

"At our battle stations before the big Russian summer offensive in July 1943 at the DONEZ front near LISSITSCHAWSK. Uffz. Heinz Schönenberger and I writing."

Wednesday 21 July. Early attack against village. We have to go back to retake it. Lots of Pak fire against us. Opelik shot. Another attack!
Whole *Abteilung* involved. 40 SFL (self propelled) artillery. Place taken after a hard struggle. 5 tanks from our *Kompanie* hit. Host, Zukunft, Krause, Aust, Pfisterer, and Ortner missing. Many wounded.
Returned to fuel up, then immediately into the attack. Took the hill. Our *Jager* (Infantry) are getting them (the Soviets) well.
Tremendous air battles.

Thursday 22 July. At midday we and 7 *Kompanie* are up front at battle stations. Must repulse attacks. Artillery and Pak guns are firing at us. SS units should be advancing towards ARTEMONSK. Pfisterer and Ortner seem to have been taken prisoner.
Everything is going on here in GOLADA DOLINA. We've got the Russians!
Guard duty all night.

Friday 23 July. Guard duty until midday. Artillery and mortars firing at us almost by order. Major transferred. Gef to lead. The ABT (*Abteilung*) making a damn attack. Order from division to contain and mop up the enemy breakthrough. Order from Division. We're running around like dogs. Tank battle in the village, two T-34s knocked out.

Saturday 24 July. We're in command of the village. More tank battles with T-34s in GOLADA DOLINA. Two more T-34s knocked out.
Enemy attacked again, 5th *Kompanie* settled that alone. In total 4 T-34s, 4 other tanks, and 1 armoured reconnaissance car knocked out. Splendid!
Whole night radio messages non-stop. *Hauptman* Krause leads 6 *Kompanie*. I'm going on leave 31 july.
Our General Schilling fell on the 21st (Commander 17.Panzer Division). Our ABT Commandant on the 23rd replaced him. Gef leads the ABT

Sunday 25 July. New *Abteilung* commander is here - Major Dunsel. Artillery really firing at us, I am always ducking under the tank.
8 tanks return from the workshop. Aircraft are bombing us as well as artillery. There is always something going on. Russians attacking but are repulsed. Always manning the radio, as we are the point *Kompanie*.

Monday 26 July. Aircraft bombed us in the night. Artillery attacks all the time, forcing us to crouch under the tanks repeatedly.
The *Abteilung* falls in and the *Abteilung* commander says a few words. EK (Iron crosses) are handed out and leave passes ordered.
More artillery fire lands in the woods. In the evening we listen in and do guard duty. A T-34 is repaired for our use. (The Germans often pressed captured armour into their service, as they never had enough of their own. These were known as "Beutepanzer.")

Tuesday 27 July. Birthday today.
Standing guard in town. Artillery and mortar fire - you can't get out of the tank. New radio instructions received at 0200 orders to attack at 0600 - a lousy command! Everyone feels like that and it was a bad attack. *Hauptmann* Krause and *HauptFeldwebel* Trauter seriously wounded, everything at the level of their balls. That on my birthday!
Relief from duty.

Wednesday 28 July. Finally a quiet night. Now and again Artillery fire.
There's sparkling wine, chocolate, and cigarettes. Will I be relieved tomorrow? Harburger should be radio operator.
Gef yesterday before the attack, we realised he should be sacked (some mistake by the officer?). We feel strongly about this.
Our armoured cars came under attack. One took a direct hit. Three dead.

Thursday 29 July. At midday *Obergefreiter* Harburger relieves me. I go to the supply lines in GRIGAROWKA. Finally finish duties and work.
In the evening Schossel and I go to PRIWOLDE. Then I go to Wera. Slept at her place 'til 0200.
Now it's true I'm going on leave. Great joy!

Friday 30 July. By locomotive to KRAMOTORSTRADA. An SF train takes me to LOSOWADA at 0400. Travelled until 2100. Replacements come for our division. Must be approximately 1000 men. Stayed with them overnight. Everything here is in ruins. Aircraft still here. Field rations are all there is to eat here.

Saturday 31 July. This must be my happiest day because of leave! 0900 departure. First to doctor for check up. Travelled via POLTAWA, which we reached in the afternoon. Played Skat. Great!
Will I go on leave or not? My only thought!

Sunday 1 August. Today travelled through KIEW, KASATIN, GOSTOW, and BANT-SCHOW.
Reloaded weapons, finished applying markings. On guard.
We're travelling through the most dangerous partisan area now.

Monday 2 August. Standing in OLIGA since 0600. Line blown up 6 times. Did not leave until 1600. That's the time we should have left DEOST.
Played Skat. Hungarians unloading. Villages burning.
2000 reached Brest. Am the first at the delousing. Here 'til 0200.

Tuesday 3 August. Stayed overnight. At 0600 my train goes west. Sitting in a café. Then proceed to *Soldatenheim* in town.
0100 assembly, march to station. Get second class carriage – great!
Now we're going on leave and now we hear the sounds of home.

Wednesday 4 August. Journey through DEBLIN, RADOM, and MISSOWITZ via PRESSBURG through Slovakia to Vienna!
Visit Rita – not home.
At night further on to Graz.

Thursday 5 August. Half past 11 arrive in Graz. Visit aunt Bertha, slept.

Friday 6 August. Visit café in St Georg.
Tomorrow depart for Linz.

At the café. Erich is in the centre.

Another view of the group at the café.

Saturday 7 August. 0800 off to Linz. Train crash, 6 hour delay. Tickets stop at Linz, no quarters for us. Only coffee for the overnight stay.

Sunday 8 August. Get home.
Ferde Miessinger and Fritz Friede here. Saw Rudi arrive today.

Monday 9 August. Brunnhofer Rudi, Pfanzagl Rudi, and Thomas Rudi waiting at the local ferry.
Seidl and Poetzel are already gone. Fritz Friede had a farewell celebration.
Great!

Tuesday 10 August (No entry in the diary)

Wednesday 11 August. Rupert Lobmayer came back from Serbia. Toni Schimpferd is a tank Uffz. in the *Waffen SS.*

Thursday 12 August. Fritz Friede left.

Friday 13th and Saturday 14th No entries.

Sunday 15 August. Linz – partied 'til early hours of Monday.

Monday 16 August (No entry in the diary)

Tuesday 17 August. Going to Berchtesgaden. Just great there. Made a friend – lovely girl, Rosi - didn't come along.
Going to the Königsee (deep glacial lake near Berchtesgaden, which is a municipality in the German Bavarian alps near the Austrian border.)

Photo of Bartholme at the Konigsee, near Berchtesgaden, Bavaria.

Wednesday 18 August. Back to the Königsee. Going with Annilee to the Watzmann – great!
(Watzmann is one of the mountains near Bechtesgaden, the third highest in Germany.)

Erich on the Watzmann mountain near Bechtesgaden.

Thursday 19 August. Today at the Predigstuhl (another mountain). Bad Reichenhall. Evening out with girls.

Friday 20 August. Today at the salt mines. Great.
Leave in the evening.

Saturday 21 August. Hans Hindner arrived. I also have to go back. Evening out with Rosi.

Sunday 22 August. Florian also here. The three of us get together. All kinds of music at the Schiesstatte (a pub).
30 wounded here from Linz.

Monday 23 August. Went with Hans and Florian round and about in Linz. Air raid alarm. Visited Villa Ostende.

Tuesday 24 August. Home early.

Wednesday 25 August. Back to Linz with Hans. Returned in the evening.
Take photographs.

Thursday 26 August. Said goodbye at home at 2000. Difficult to leave. Linz – overnight with Aunt Kathe.

Friday 27 August. Brunhofer away today to Passau.
0515 leave Linz for Vienna.
0930 leave Vienna with vehicle commander of 1st and 2nd carriage.

Saturday 28 August. 1200 arrived in Brest. Meet up with 6 of my regiment. All sorts of things going on at the *Kompanie*.
1730 departure from Brest. Few hours delay on the line at night, blown up 14 times. I was in the first carriage. Not pleasant.

Sunday 29 August. Nothing happened in the night. The journey goes on to KIEW.

Monday 30 August. This morning we went over a mine. 1 dead, 3 wounded. The timing meant the 6th carriage went up.
In the evening we got to GOSOWADA, where there were lots of wounded.
(Erich was unlucky to travel at this time, which coincided with "the War of the Rails," which lasted six weeks from August to September 1943. This was a large scale partisan offensive on the rail network, lead and strictly controlled by NKVD teams, the political troops of the USSR. Partisans had been taught the most advanced techniques of sabotage.
In all 167 partisan units were involved, more than 100,000 men using 150 tons of explosive, 150 km of cable, and 500,000 detonators.
The "War of the Rails" covered territory 1000km wide and 500 km deep. On the first night 42,000 explosions took place, and this increased over the following nights. In the offensive 836 trains were blown up, and 184 rail and 556 road bridges were destroyed. Vast quantities of equipment and ammunition were lost. Large numbers of German troops had to be deployed to fight the partisans and defend the rail communications.
After the Soviet victory at Kursk and the counteroffensive to push the Germans back, a second operation on the railway network called "Concert" was carried out. This was on a similar scale and lasted until October 1943.
Erich witnessed first hand how effective the Partisan action was.)

Tuesday 31 August. Rudi Haas gone today to SS Panzer *Abteilung*. Today I went to DASSINOWATADA, travelled all night, we were bombed.

Wednesday 1 September. Today went to STALINO, and from there to MAKEJEWKA. Our division is on the MIUS. We were bombed with phosphorus bombs – terrible! Further on to MOSBINE, supply line here.

Thursday 2 September. Early move to the *Kompanie*. All sorts going on. Furinger, Burger, Walker, Gehlemann, Wachter, Mertel, and Rübig wounded. Murgel, Franke, and Reichlardt fallen (killed). I went up with Gefreiter in the car – here we go again. Gef is the *Kampfgruppenfuhrer* (Battle group leader).

Friday 3 September. Immediately into action, counter attack. Humm shot. Gef leads alone. Then back. New action 'til evening. Then withdraw back to *Kompanie* positions.

Saturday 4 September. We're holding the bridgehead. At 0300 there's a strong attack; we have to go back and give up the bridgehead. Pity, as it's a well constructed position. Forward again in the evening, firing all the time to contain the enemy. Then back to the supply line to rearm and refuel.

"Tank attack on the bridgehead at NIKOPOL. 1943."

"In front of the line with the entrenchment task force at the bridgehead NIKOPOL in September 1943. Uffz. Schramm, Obgefr. Kaufmann, and I." Eric is on the right.

Sunday 5 September. Early morning forward again. At the command post there is firing. Our position is a great one, and today we get a bit of peace.
Lots to drink, 40 bottles per crew. Troops still retreating.

Monday 6 September. Still quiet. Schnaps again. We don't know each other, we're so drunk. How long can we hold the position? We're the furthest east division.
(Soviets separate Army Group Centre from Army Group South)

Tuesday 7 September. Enemy tanks penetrate the position. We're up front and knock out one T-34 and two are knocked out by others. In the evening another attack – must be Russians firing from our own trenches. This goes on 'til 2300.
Overnight up front.

Wednesday 8 September. Midday immediately moved south to 3 *Jager* Division where Russian tanks had broken through. We knocked out 2 T-34s and the others fled.
In the evening we received orders to return to our own positions.
17 PD is still the furthest forward. Travel through the night. Into defence again.

Thursday 9 September. Italy has unconditionally surrendered. I saw it coming. 17PD is holding a hill with 40 vehicles. Standing defence.
In the evening go to 3 *Jager* Division, as the Russians have broken through. Retreat then to ALEXANDREW.
(Italy surrendered on 8 September. A deal was struck between the new Italian government and Lieutenant General Maxwell D. Taylor of the 82nd Airborne Division, who had been parachuted in to represent the Allies. Mussolini had been arrested on the orders of King Victor Emmanuel on 25 July.)

Friday 10 September. 0300 move back again. Russians are behind us already in the next village. Russians attacking. Panic in NOWOTROTZKODE – everything clearing out. We're among the houses, three T-34s knocked out then back to our position.
Our tank is kaput so retreat again. Rendezvous by refuelling.
Russian tanks and cavalry are coming. Panic – we're surrounded!
We are the spear point platoon. Defend desperately. Break out four times with Gef.

Saturday 11 September. 0400 three T-34s knocked out then retreat. Our own forces right and left retreating. Russians are constantly there as we retreat. We counter attack with four tanks and two on tow.
Two men dead and two missing, including *Feldwebel* Wummer amongst them. We re the point platoon. Retreat. No more troops arrive, all tanks now kaput. We struggle back with T-34s behind us again and the river in front. We have to get through and finally link up with 3 *Jager* Division. As the Russians haven't caught us we can think ourselves lucky. Defence against T-34s attacking the village. We have to go back – they want to get us here.
In the evening we retreat, Poles are shooting at us. Reach the supply line at STALINO at 2200.

Sunday 12 September. One tank ready for action from the whole division. We're being relieved by 5 *Kompanie*. At 1200 return to the supply line, where we find quarters by 1800 in POLOGI.
Gef comes in the evening. Have great music.

Monday 13 September. Settling into quarters. Everyone who was present reports to the Spiess' battle report. Marching orders straight away, 135 km, that is 35km west of SAPAROSCHE. 10 men report, replacements from St. Polten. Travel by *Kubelwagen* without convoy. Spent the night in the workshop with Heinz.

Tuesday 14 September. Got up early to go further on. The road is full of retreating troops. This retreat is worse than any before. *Abteilung* has no tanks yet. Move to TOMANOWKA. What will happen here? What will they do with us?
No post arriving or leaving either.

Wednesday 15 September. Day off. Afternoon to the cinema, "Dance with the Kaiser." Heinz and Dietrich back from the workshop.
In the evening – a boozy evening, *OberFeldwebel* Grosse and us.
At midnight to the Gef's. Drank there 'til 0200. Everyone drunk.

Thursday 16 September. Reported for duty in a sleepy state – drunk – kept on drinking. Uffz., Gef, and everyone drunk. Rained all day – filthy weather. Played the gramophone. Otherwise quiet. My division has pulled out completely. Wrote 10 letters. Had a booze up. Civilians are still walking through.

Friday 17 September. Day off. Day of rain. Roast half a pig. Moving in to new quarters of Ltn. Opelik. Eight men here. Two women. Great! Have to manage rooms ourselves. Ltn. Guggenhagen visited us. He's from 33 Tank regiment (9th Panzer Division). Booze up.

Saturday 18 September. Complete roll call. Went to quartermaster to hand in things that are superfluous. Ltn. Guggenhagen still here.
Went to cinema to watch "His Best Friend." Invited to Gef in evening. Gef and three of us - Heinz, Adolf, and I - party. Doctor back from leave, brought pictures with him. Until now drunk every day. At Gef's also drank three bottles of Sekt (Sparkling wine) and Cognac – great music.

Sunday 19 September. Nice day. Aircraft in our area again, otherwise nothing happening. Go to the cinema.
Russians pulling back every day.

Monday 20 September. More troops arrive.
Nice day. Light duty. Otherwise nothing happening.
Drank schnaps.
(Army Group South, *Heeresgruppe Sud*, withdraws to Melitopol-Zaporozhe line.)

Tuesday 21 September. Up at 0400. We have to go to the front trenches. Forty men by lorry. Bombed in SAPPROSCHE.
Division travels 130km to WOADIWIROWKA with 63 Panzer Grenadier regiment. Slept in barn – Damn!

Wednesday 22 September. Construction of defences. Yesterday in the building of these we had one dead. 7.62 cm Pak firing at us in artillery mode. Two wounded in 40 Pz Gren Regt.
About 40 *Luftwaffe* in action at WASSILEWKA.

Thursday 23 September. Everyday making entrenchments from 0100 to 1700, sixteen hours. Freezing cold. Just like a punishment unit.
Machine guns, mortars, and artillery firing at us.
Luftwaffe went over. We're protecting the trenches. We are infantry now.

Friday 24 September. From today we only make entrenchments at night. Russians attack every day. We're on fatigues also. Lots of Russians about. *Aufklarungs Abteilung* (reconnaissance unit) took prisoners. 1700 away in the HKL.

Saturday 25 September. Entrenched position.
Emil is firing at us as before – six at one time. Russians attack at night with Feltol (some kind of Napalm).
0300 to village, slept 'til midday. 0100 away again That's how it is. Every day the Russians attack with Feltol, then ours reply with Feltol. They caught us doing that In the village artillery fire.

Sunday 26 September. Shovelling 'til early on, then moving to SELENY GAI. Slept in tent overnight. Evenings shovelling. Emil visits.
(Erich is probably referring to the Russian Er – 2 long range bomber. "Emil" was the German phonetic alphabet for "E.")

"Construction of defences – command post at the bridgehead at NIKTOPOL. Providing food for themselves after slaughtering in SELENY GAI. Uffz. May, Uffz. Schramm, Obgefr. Kaufmann H., and me. September 1943."

Monday 27 September. From today we have to take over defence in the Franken position. At night making entrenchments. In the day as Infantry. That's what it is for us. Shit!
(Germans withdraw all forces in the Ukraine to the west bank of the river Dnieper, where they set up positions.)

Tuesday 28 September. Shovelling at night. Today at 1st *Kompanie* 53 Pz. Gren. Regt. Russians attacking with Feltol. Machine gun fire whistling over our heads. Mortar fire. Six Emils shooting at us. Great artillery barrages.

Wednesday 29 September. Our side making a counter attack with every man of all units. Russians broke through with tanks. Knocked out ten in close combat. Great air battles every day here.

Thursday 30 September. Ltn. Luckel dead. Hit from shrapnel, also 15 from 3 *Jager* Division. 4 *Kompanie* returning and getting tanks.
6 and 7 *Kompanie* still here. Three men from *Stab* (HQ) still missing.

Friday 1 October At night shovelling as ever. In the day defence
Meeting up with Fritz Wein from 7 battery in VB (supply) great.
Air battles – lots of Stukas here. That's the way it is.

Saturday 2 October. Shovelling. Russians attacking as usual.
Pioniere (engineers) away in front of us making a counter attack. They succeed in a magic of fire, rifles, machine guns, mortars, and artillery.
Emil bombs the whole night. No chance to wash.
Our life is played out at night. Daytime is defence in front position. Washing is impossible. Heavy bombardment coming from the Russians as well as attacks.

Sunday 3 October. Shovelling and building trenches as usual.
Air battles again, just great. Rocket launchers are here now.
Flak firing on Emil.

Monday 4 October. *Feldwebel* Froschl came. The NCOs are being relieved, 20 officers too. Stupid! Air battles with Stukas. More strikes in front of us making dust. Shovelling at night.

Tuesday 5 October. Listening in from the trench. Me, surveillance over the Russians all day. Thomas Hoffman in the field hospital. Fifty men shovelling in threes again. Every night 200-300 men working here.

Wednesday 6 October. Digging in today at the outpost.
For one day Fritz is here. I meet him. We are under machine gun fire.
Day time - air battles. Three Russians crash near us – Great!
Artillery is firing at us, otherwise fairly quiet.

Thursday 7 October. Digging in every night. Defences finally completed. We look like pigs. There's mail and a few cigarettes. I've foot problems and remain behind.

Friday 8 October. Air activity, otherwise quieter. Days very hot, nights very cold. Still no rain. Listening to radio at U3 station.

Saturday 9 October. Overnight change in the weather – rain!
Heavy bombardment begins, Russians attacking on the whole front. Great! We forage. 15 Chickens, delicious food. A tank unit should be on the way for our Division. Beat back attack by evening. Our artillery played the main part. There was lots going on.

Sunday 10 October. Digging in with 5 *Kompanie*.
Luftwaffe attack until 0200. Artillery and mortar fire on the front positions. Russians attacking again. Nothing yet at 3 *Jager* Division.
143 Russian Tanks knocked out. Bitter cold. Lots of air activity.

Monday 11 October. 0400 Russians attack. Today built artillery position for 5 Regiment. Bitter cold. One plane came down 200 metres behind us. The HKL shaking with heavy bombardment. Lots of dust at 3JD (3 *Jager* Division), like a sandstorm. Lots of tanks knocked out.

Tuesday 12 October. Up at 0400, command to push forward. Ltn. Dietrich, our reconnaissance officer, had a bad accident. He was knocked down and suffered internal injuries. The driver drove away. This happened at KALINOWKA.

Wednesday 13 October. Digging in at the advanced position. Incoming artillery and mortar fire. Day time defence as usual.
Lying in the fresh air at night. Beastly for us here.
(Soviet advance reaches Melitopol.)

Thursday 14 October. 4 and 5 *Kompanie* going to MELITOPOL.
Artillery and Pak fire on our position. Radio operator comes with post. I get a parcel from home. Digging in at 40 Pz Gren Regt position.
(Germans evacuate the Zaporozhe bridgehead, their last bastion on the eastern bank of the Dnieper.)

Friday 15 October. Artillery and pak firing at us. Wide area of impact, left and right of us. We, the 17PD (17.Panzer Division), are at the most easterly point. Digging in at night as ever.

Saturday 16 October. Now it's getting serious. Infantry come back into our position. Alarm squads are detailed. One bunker built. Russians speak to us with a loudspeaker but come to a dead end. Wet day.
(Soviets attempt break out from Bukrin bridgehead south of Kiev. They start an offensive to cut off the 1st Panzer Army on the Dnieper.)
Cleared up 30 Russian shells. Our Artillery are firing phosphorus again. UO already in front of us.

Sunday 17 October. I write 10 letters. Pouring with rain. I have to go early with coffee to the position as no lorry driver can take me. I arrive absolutely filthy and soaked.

Monday 18 October. Russians attack again. We reply with artillery, Pak, phosphorus, mortars, and ground attack aircraft, R2s.
Built bunker. Bitter cold, digging at night.
(The Germans used the R2 designation for bomber/ground attack aircraft, e.g. the Bf 109 G-1 R/2, which was the ground attack version of the Me 109 "Gustav.")

Tuesday 19 October. 0500 Alarm! Manned the forward position. Russians have broken through both 40 and 63 Pz Gren Regts. We're in the position and reply with artillery and Pak firing phosphorus all afternoon. Great!
Max and I are relieved and travel straight back overnight by *Zugmashine* (half-track tractor).

Wednesday 20 October. Looked for fuel. Got a lorry standing in front of NIKOPOL but can't get there. 4 *Kompanie* have no tanks, as they were all shot up at MELITOPOL yesterday. Five men dead.

"In the repair shop at NIKTOPOL. Obgefr. May and Krill." Panzer IV Ausf. H under repair.

"Tank repair shop at NIKTOPOL. Obgef. Griesmacher – fell on 29.4.44. Obgef. Krill." The vehicle is a one ton light half-track Sd.Kfz. 10 *Zugmaschine*.

Thursday 21 October. Up at 0430. travelled to workshop. See Ferdinand from 4 *Kompanie* at midday. Finally peace and quiet. Moving in with Heinz and Adolf. Finally able to wash and shave. Such luxury!

Friday 22 October. Collect my things together, Write letters. New Uffz. Afternoon – radio instruction. A cinema is also here. We were heavily bombed in the evening.

Saturday 23 October. Uffz. shooting practice. Great! Me and 4 *Kompanie* 'til midday then stopped. Harburger failed, he's going back to the *Kompanie*. I'm going to radio operator training.
At the front our people were sent in as infantry with 63 Pz Gren Regt. *Feldwebel* Frosche wounded. He's going back. Damn!

Sunday 24 October. Today a morning drink in the *Soldatenheim* in NIKOPOL. Gef is also there. Great, everyone got drunk. Back at 0100. Went to bed as I am exhausted.
(Red army takes Melitopol after 10 days of heavy fighting.)

Monday 25 October. Infantry *Kompanie* is drawn up. That's what's happened to us. No point in thinking about it. Things can't be harder. Duty is great otherwise.

Tuesday 26 October. Leave stopped. Post stopped. Situation shitty. Otherwise nothing happening.
Partisans have shot 12 infantrymen in the next town.

Wednesday 27 October. 0500 departure for NIKOPOL.
I am at the optician's. Didn't get taken until 1100.
Beginning to tidy up. Today Alarm. Set up for new tasks and perhaps the last battle of the unit.

Thursday 28 October. Infantry training in the morning. At midday the march-off orders. 150 km northwest. The division is there in peace. Will it go on like that? Should I go back to the quarters and pack our things?

Friday 29 October. Departure at 0500. Only two armoured tanks with *Feldwebel* Grosse alone. Travel through NIKOPOL, OPOSTOLAWAKA, KAMEWKA, and ALEXANDOWKA to BELINKI. Not a house still standing here. To KAMUSNA, where we get quarters. We're with the Gef in the command post.

"Ferry from NIKTOPOL."

"At the quay at NIKTOPOL. 1943."

Saturday 30 October. Going away at 0800. 5 Uffz and 9 men. Lorries are parked for transport. The supply line is set up and we sort out our quarters. Listened to the radio. Great music.
Schrauder going back to GRIGORDEWKA.

Sunday 31 October. Nothing exciting happening. Still lovely weather. Great music on the radio. Today veal cutlet for lunch.

Still no post here. Heinz, who dropped out, got here today. Adolf is also back.

Monday 1 November. Promotions – Adolf becomes *Feldwebel*; Pilshofer, Tietze, and Gernhardt become Uffzs. Gef moved out. We three alone in quarters. Got one tank for training.

Tuesday 2 November. *Feldwebel* Schnauder going to NIKOPOL. At midday the *Kommandos* (special squads) are going out again as a patrol. Gef, all the *Feldwebel*s, and three Uffzs are there too.
I'm alone in the quarter. All duties are being done by *Feldwebel* Reichhart. Passwords go to all concerned to aid the others back.

Wednesday 3 November. Nothing happening. Lay in bed all day reading. Adolf visited me.
In the evening went to the radio operator, as there was music, and listen to this on the radio. Gloomy days. 3 *Jager* Division going through here. Lorry parked up again.
(Red Army offensive from Dnieper north of Kiev begins.)

Thursday 4 November. Nothing happening. Go to village and get milk and eggs to make custard. Lying down and reading. *Kommandos* come back, then we get orders for moving out planned towards the southwest. Therefore further back.
In the evening invited to a meal at the Gef's, Adolf, Heinz, and I. drank liqueur and beer.

Friday 5 November. Get things ready. Waiting on the last lorries. Load provisions – Sekt, Schnaps, wine, and cigarettes. Had a small drink in the evening. Went to Gef, who was left to organise things.

Saturday 6 November. 0400 away with *OberFeldwebel* Zollmeister. Lorry to take rank and file. Only seasoned troops in the kubels (*Kubelwagen* light cars). Artillery firing all the time. We organised clothing and distributed food.
In the evening joined up with the division. Stayed overnight in KUPANI. Played Skat. Replacements for riflemen already here. NIKOLADEF under attack. The division is not in CHERSON. That would be something for us as CHERSON is a great town. Great women!
(Russians take Kiev and break the 4th Panzer army in three.)

Sunday 7 November. Find our forward command and drive to our new positions above NIKOLADEF, 15km north on the INGUL. Unloaded supplies and returned to NIKOLADEF again. All kinds of clothing for us still to organise.

Monday 8 November. 0500 departure for NIKOLADEF with *OberFeldwebel* Zollmeister. Carried combat suits, letters etc. NIKOLADEF quite a beautiful town and such women! FF (unknown expression)! In the evening back with the company.
Who would have thought we would land up at the bow (supplies).

Tuesday 9 November. Nothing happening. Read the whole day. It has rained. Yesterday the *Führer* spoke. The whole company is together again.

Wednesday 10 November. Duty started. Three hours of instruction and terrain duty. In a storm and heavy rain we have to go to positions at a farm by boat on the Ingul. Everyone swearing, rudder broken, stuck in the mud. We've had enough!

Thursday 11 November. Gef – instruction.
Midday went to the cinema – "The Sanctimonious Florian." Great story from Bavaria. Laughing. Juptner and Sturmer transferred to 4 *Kompanie*, who are on defence here. I have guard duty too.

Friday 12 November. Quite a lot of instruction. The first snow is not lasting here. Went to the cinema to watch "The Mountaineer" immediately followed by the "Journey in Adventure." Two great films – lots to laugh about.

Saturday 13 November. Drill - whole company. Gef gives instructions. Afternoon back to the cinema, "The Mountaineer" for the second time. Lots and lots of laughing. The evening to the Gef's to listen to the radio. Also get a few Schrapel (unknown term) from him.

Sunday 14 November. Slept 'til lunch – veal cutlet.
Otherwise did nothing all day. At Gef's in the evening. Listened to the radio. Great music.

Monday 15 November. Lessons all day. Also at Gef's, who has a pain in the head.
Evening to the cinema "The Two Sunday Children." Great film.
Ban on leave lifted.
3 *Kompanie* received 5 Panthers (new medium tank, given to 1st Battalion in each panzer regiment. Here at platoon strength.)

Tuesday 16 November. Lessons all day. Ltn. Zech took his leave. He's now leader of 7 *Kompanie*. Me to the cinema to watch "Sinful Village." All drivers ordered back to the *Kompanie* and away to NIKOLADEF to collect 10 tanks.

Wednesday 17 November. Adolf away as advance party. Division in action again. At midday the drivers came with 10 tanks. Two new men from Linz are here. Lots of work. Took over tanks.
Evening cinema – Operette. Great! Division northeast of Gessau.

Thursday 18 November. Technical duty. Get vehicles ready. Clean weapons. New radio equipment on board – make ourselves familiar with it. Ltn. Pilshofer, Karl, and Organasch got the EK1 (Iron Cross First Class) today. 10 crews with no officer. Our Gef is there.
When are we off?

Friday 19 November. Get tanks ready and test equipment. 7 *Kompanie* has taken over 8 Panthers from 18.Panzer Division.
Otherwise nothing happening. Got no post.
In the evening – cinema – operette again. Great music.
Sleep, as there is nothing going on here.

Saturday 20 November. Train journey to ABHARSCH. The march command for 6 *Kompanie* arrives too for 6 *Kompanie* for tomorrow 0615. Pack everything. Received fur hats. We're going 125 km via NIKOLADEF, then CHERSON and North along the DNEPR to TRAGINKA on the DNEPR. Our division is going into action there. *Abteilung* is not going into action until Wednesday. Also the other *Kompanie*.
Got one more tank. *Feldwebel* Wimmer is taking it over. Now we have 11 tanks.

"Setting off for action to TRAGINKA via NIKOLADEF – CHERSON to the DNEPR in November 1943. Uffz. May, Uffz. Schramm, Uffz. Koubeck, Uffz. Seemann, and me Uffz. Hoffmann – died April 1944 in the field hospital."

Gef is getting the RITTERKREUZ (Knight's cross – the highest level of the Iron Cross awards. The date agrees with the award to Werner Pietsch, who was awarded the RK on 16 November 1943.)

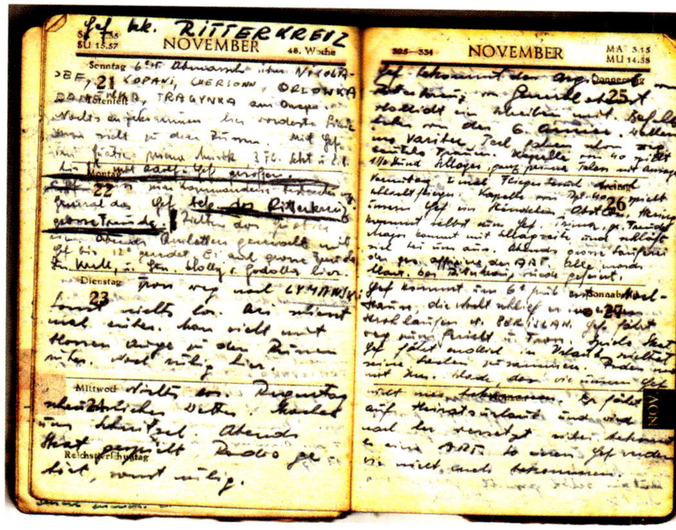

Diary pages, "Gef is getting the *Ritterkreuz*."

Sunday 21 November. 0615 march off via NIKOLADEF, KOPANI, CHERSON, ORLOWKA, DANEWKA, and TRAGINKA on the DNEPR. Here is the front line. You can see over to the Russians.
With the Gef in quarters. Great music. Three bottles of Sekt and Liqueur. Drank with Adolf and Gef until dawn.

Monday 22 November. Gef went to speak with the General at the *Kommandeur* (headquarters). Gef is getting the *Ritterkreuz*. *Great Joy*. Sort out the quarter. In the evening party. Talked to Gef until midnight. Also great joy for him. Ltn. Krull and Ltn. Scholling also here.

Tuesday 23 November. Supply depot away to LYMANSK. Otherwise nothing happening. Artillery firing across our lines. You can see over to the Russians with the naked eye. Still quiet here.

Wednesday 24 November. Nothing up. Rainy day. Terrible weather. Made *Schnitzel* (veal cutlet). Played Skat in the evening. Listened to the radio. Otherwise quiet.

Thursday 25 November. Gef gets a copy of the *Ritterkreuz* from *Generaloberst* Hollicht, a senior commander with the 6 Army.
They want to go to the Music Hall but, hard luck, it's already blown away. German band of 40 Pz. Gren. Regt. play for one and a half hours. All the hits – just great. War songs with love songs.

"On the day of the presentation of the *Ritterkreuz*. Our Gef with Obltn. Schmidt who fell December 1943." The Gef here is Werner Pietsch.

"After the presentation of the *Ritterkreuz* to our Gef. The music from Pz.Gr.Regt. 40. With Obstltn. Hessing in TRAGINKA in front of our billet. November 1943."

"Our Gef received the *Ritterkreuz* and our tank driver received the EK1 today, 23 November 1943 in TRAGINKA on the DNEPR. Our crew and Gef's PKW driver. Hptm. Werner Pietsch, Fldw. Schnauder, Uffz. Schöneberger, Gefr. Knutzler, Obgefr. Vancata PKW driver, and me." Erich is on the right and Pietsch is third from the left wearing the officer's peaked cap.

Friday 26 November. In the morning we get two visits from Russian aircraft. They drop anti-personnel bombs three times.
The band of 40 Regiment plays our Gef a serenade (usually a congratulation song).
OberstLtn. Hessing himself comes to Gef. Great, great joy!
Major comes three sheets to the wind and sleeps it off with us.
In the evening there is a huge booze up of all the officers in the *Abteilung*. Everyone is drunk. With the *Ritterkreuz* it's celebrations again.

Saturday 27 November. Gef did not come home 'til 0600. He slept in a haystack near BERISLAW. Gef is going away to the replacement and supply depot. I play Skat. Gef finally going on leave. Gets his things together. The radio is still with him.
Shame we will no longer have our Gef. He's going on home leave and will be transferred afterwards. Surely he will get an *Abteilung*. We'll never get another Gef like him.

Sunday 28 November. Collect radio instructions from Ltn. Makowitz. Gef takes his leave. Hands over the *Kompanie* to *Hauptmann* Klass. He comes from *Stabs* (HQ) *Kompanie*. We talk to him. He hasn't yet led a *Kompanie* into action. He has been a soldier for 14 years already. Brought a turkey with him.

Monday 29 November. Spiess looked in and brought canteen provisions with him. Another new Ltn. transferred to us, name of Wiese. Something happening today. Women were raped by Uffz. Pilshofer, Schnee, Orgonasch, and Steimmaier. *Feldgendarmarie* (Military policeman) Lottin arrested them.
That's the limit!

Tuesday 30 November. *HauptFeldwebel* looked in. Brought post.
Our own attack over the DNEPR by 63 Pz. Gren. Regt. was executed successfully. Bridgehead at GESSOWER established.
Otherwise quiet. Radio and reading.

Wednesday 1 December. 0800 alarm over whole *Kampfgruppe*. Great numbers of MTW's all on tracks. (*Mannscaftstransportwagen*, troop transport vehicles, here probably the half-track Sd.Kfz. 251 series.) Finished at 0930.
Music hall coming back. Going to variety show, played by the infantry themselves. Great music. Herring and Busch also here.

Thursday 2 December. Rained all day.
Divisional order – tanks have to be dug in. People from supply sent as labour service. Learned that I can have a pistol again.
Kfz 69 broken. Go to *Kompanie* on foot.

(Kfz 69 was a small lorry or tractor built by Krupp as the L2H43. Commonly known as the "Boxer" for its flat four cylindered, air-cooled engine. It had a unique independent suspension and had 6 wheels, the rear four being driven. It could reach speeds of up to 70 km/h. The personnel transport was Kfz 70, but the artillery tractor Erich refers to here was the KFZ 69. This was designed to tow a 3.7 cm Pak 36 and had ammunition storage down both sides. Crew was the driver and five men. Also known as the "Protze," which was the term for a first carriage on the German horse-drawn artillery.)

Friday 3 December. Dug in the tank. Spiess still here. Getting colder already, otherwise nothing happening. Batman and driver going to *Stabs* (HQ) *Kompanie*. Music. Went to the *Abteilung* where there were welfare materials. Played in the evening. Gef also there. On 1 December there had been a radio broadcast about Gef and his *Ritterkreuz*.

Saturday 4 December. In the morning we built a roof. Very good. Gef still away. Duty due on Monday. Had a bath. Baths every 4 weeks. Listened to the radio and played straws as every day. Women here. My pistol is back again. *Stabsgefreiter* (HQ corporal) Ebeet caught it. He's now in the field hospital. Will that be that?

Sunday 5 December. Duty starts.
Training - Uffz. training with Gef. Otherwise nothing happening.
Listened to radio, played straws with Gef.
(Period of intensive NCO training in 17.Panzer Division.)

Monday 6 December. Duty in the morning. Training.
Those on leave are departing. Speiss drove up to us.
Received 12 tanks. In the afternoon all Uffz. were in disgrace.
In the evening played straws with Gef, listened to the radio.
Finally post.

Tuesday 7 December. Technical duty. Trebport got 7 days arrest because of petty thieving. He stole my pistol and gave it to Zier. What a rotten thing to do.
Listened to the radio. Played straws.

Wednesday 8 December. Duty just great.
Birthday celebration with Schnaps. Heinz drunk, I cut his hair. Great.
Today marching off. We're being loaded up.
In the evening, Alarm. 2300 march off.

Thursday 9 December. We'll be loaded up at CHERSON. Gef leading this, but where are we going to? North?
We are the tank *Abteilung* with 35 tanks, *Aufklarungs Abteilung* (reconnaissance), 17 Flak battalion, *pioniere* (engineers) and infantry are with us. Jofer is attached to us. 6 *Kompanie* has 17 vehicles.
Zugwetter. (Weather or metrological unit.) Departure from here.

Friday 10 December. Drove via KR8WO1-R04 (presumably a map reference) and unloaded in KUSZOFKA. Russians have broken through here. Immediately into action; our *Kompanie* to attack BOGNOTNOVSE and return. 4 *Kompanie* is also here. We attack along the road towards NEWESNIKOW after reconnaissance on foot. *Sturmgeschutze* (assault guns based on the Panzer III chassis) are also here. All sorts going on. We're turning like mad back and forth. They're shooting at us. Heinz is wounded. Eight of our tanks are out of action, mostly hit in the drive sprockets and running gear.

Saturday 11 December. Russian aircraft bomb us. Alarm – the other *Kampfgruppe* is put into action. Koubek is here with us as driver.
All sorts going on here. We counter attack from KUSZOFKA along the road against infantry and tanks. Defence all night. Bitter cold.
Russians behind us again. Reimer knows what he is doing. The Russians have assault guns here. In the first attack two tanks are put out of action because of failure in the drive sprockets. This must be sabotage at the workshops. Will such *shite* be in my all Bavarian company?
Five tanks ready for action. The *SS Totenkopf* and the 384 Infantry Divisions are at KEROWOGRAD - KRIWOROG. Ltn. Schee and *Obergefreiter* Schmidt wounded.
(384 Infantry Division had been destroyed at Stalingrad in January 1943. It was reformed in February 1943 and fought on the Eastern Front until being finally destroyed in Romania in August 1944.
SS Totenkopf had been originally formed from concentration camp guards and moulded into a formidable fighting unit by its commander, Theoder Eicke. It fought in the western campaign and in the northern sector of the Eastern Front, where it was encircled and broke out of the Demyansk pocket.
After refitting in France as a Panzer Grenadier Division, *Totenkopf* helped stop the Russian offensive after Stalingrad and took part in the recapture of Kharkov and the battle of Kursk as part of II *SS Panzer Korps*. The division was renamed 3 SS Panzer Division "Totenkopf" and fought at Warsaw, Budapest, and finally Vienna.)

Sunday 12 December. Russians attack BODGANOWKA. We're still standing in defence and attack in the flank. We knocked out three assault guns, an armoured car, and a few Paks.
Retreat. The Russians have outflanked us round KUZROFKA, which is evacuated. Three more T-34s knocked out. Four of our own tanks here.

Monday 13 December. Up at 0330. Attack against a hill near BATISMANN. Our *Kompanie*, 3 Pz (three tanks), 4 *Kompanie* with three tanks All sorts going on. Lots of Russian tanks and Paks against us.
Ltn. Weiss shot, Dietrich wounded. Uffz. Muller from 4 *Kompanie* got hit. Our fighter-bombers were working great.
Attack again as yesterday against BATISMANN 'til midnight. Two tanks, the whole unit. *Sturmgeschutze* also there. Damn Russian counterattack! We're out again on the point.
(Attack by armoured battle group Pz.Kpf.Gr., consisting of II./Pz.Rgt.39 and I./Pz.Gren.Rgt.40 south of Novgorodka.)

Tuesday 14 December. Orders. At 0200 leave for KUSZOFKA. Attack against NONGORODNA with 11 Panzer Division. At 1400 the advances took BODGANOWKA and KATENKOWO again. Ten Russian Paks (anti-tank guns) destroyed. Uffz. Schecker shot. Turm and Schmidt got hit.
The pocket must be closed. Has it or not? The attack continues and the battle lasted until midnight. We have eight tanks supported by SS tanks and *Sturmgeschutze*.

Wednesday 15 December. Attack in front of NOWGORDONA. Our *Kompanie* attacks a Pak front (anti-tank gun defence line).
Five of our tanks knocked out. Ltn. Schmidt dead – Gfrörer and Heller wounded. Four of our tanks kaput.
Action - two platoons have to find a way round. There are Paks as we look up and down. Russians make a counter attack. *Kompanie* attack with 5 Panthers. Two of our tanks are knocked out. Ltn. Kunkel fell. We're going back to KUSZOFKA.

Thursday 16 December. Went further back with the tanks to the supply line via DOLIWSKE. Find the supply line on the march. Franz Heun and Sepp Frosche finally get there. Find quarters in NOWOROMANOWKA.
Uffz. Thomas dead yesterday.

Friday 17 December. Writing a battle report with Gef. Two Iron crosses added with Grosse and Gfrorer. Post arrives and finally able to wash and shave in peace. Adolf, Heinz, and I in the quarter.
The pocket came to nothing.

Saturday 18 December. Russians continue to break through.
At midday Falke and Gef go by *Kubel* (small Volkswagen car) to the *Kommandeur*. Gef is getting the EK1 (Iron cross 1st class, given automatically due to the higher award of the Knight's Cross). That was some journey.
Tiger tanks were unloaded in DOLEWSKADA as well as 13.Panzer Division.
We got home at 0200 drunk. Pocket not yet closed. 11. Panzer Division has now taken NONGORODNA, hard battles here. *Abteilung* allowed to have 8 tanks up front. Our old tank which came to grief in the lake is not to be recovered. The Russians are already there. Five tanks completely lost in the *Kompanie*.

Sunday 19 December. *Vorkommando* away to a new hard fought over area. Otherwise nothing happening. Six tanks have gone forward.
Feldwebels Dierigen and Hager with Ltn. Godolla shot. Dierigen with a head wound. Today we got 300 cigarettes and four bottles of Cognac and two bottles of wine.

(A *Vorkommando* was an advance unit that went ahead to see everything was in place for the Division when it moved to a new location.)

Monday 20 December. We left for NOWOGRIGAREWKA in a *Kubel* travelling on our own. 25km further to the east. Sort out our quarters. Up front *Feldwebel* Frösche shot. Uffz. Muller killed by a hit on the radio operator's station (in front of tank).
Made ourselves punch. Great drink. *Hauptmann* Pichel visited.

Tuesday 21 December. Yesterday Ltn. Preisseger transferred to us. Ltn. Zech gave up front tank over to him.
All kinds of provisions delivered again. Have a good old booze up. One Uffz. and three men arrive as replacements. Listened to music. Played straws. Murmann got three days arrest, then was awarded the EK2 (Iron Cross second class).
(Soviets called off their offensive against 17.Panzer Division, but the Red Army demolished the German bridgehead on Dnieper at Kherson.)

Wednesday 22 December. It's snowing again, otherwise nothing happening all day. Ltn. Godolla died. Ltn. Preisegger wounded.
Two tanks in action. It's as on the first day we arrived.

Thursday 23 December. Gef ill, otherwise not much happening.
5 *Kompanie* are going to have a Christmas celebration in the school.
I am guard commander for 5 *Kompanie*. Eat a good Schnitzel. Write a few letters. Snowing heavily. *Hauptmann* Sudhof killed.

Friday 24 December. Our celebration of Christmas in the school.
Speech by Gef. Promotions: Gfrörer to *Funkmeister*, Velk becomes *OberFeldwebel*, Gamsberger becomes *Feldwebel*, and Mangold becomes Uffz.
Gef was up front with the *Abteilung*. One of our tanks knocked out. Karl Sommer injured already, to lose a foot. *Hauptmann* Rösler, 63 Pz. Gren. Regt., seriously wounded. Celebrations very cold. Am on duty at 2200.

Saturday 25 December. Gef resting, rather hung over from yesterday's booze up. Otherwise not much happening. Playing cards.
Got all sorts of things. We got half a kilo of chocolate as well as many other things. In the evening a short walk before going into action. Four tanks with Ltn. Jofer.
What will be happening with us? Our division might well have had it. The infantry lost two Battalion commanders: Haupt. Södhof of 40 Regt. fell, and *Hauptman* Rösler of 63 Regt. seriously wounded. ObstLtn. Opper of 63 Regt. is also gone. We have four tanks in the whole *Abteilung*. What will they do with us then?

Sunday 26 December Bit of a thaw, otherwise not much happening. Play cards, then in the evening, straws. Make a punch.
It rained all day. Karl Sammer is losing both feet. He is lying here in a *Hpt. Verhandplatz* (main medical aid station).
Develop the film, arranged by Haupt. Pictel.

Monday 27 December. Still a thaw, otherwise not much happening. Ltn. Weise and Spiess going to Karl Sammer, *Kommandeur* Major Gruel driving at 1200. Gef has to give up the *Abteilung* this evening. Heinz and I took pictures 'til 1200. We took 30 photos, just great. Karl Sammer becomes an Uffz. tomorrow.

Tuesday 28 December. Gef to see Major.
We are transferring. Tanks still away today to KIROWOGRAD.
Loaded up. Where to? SHITOMER? Us to follow a few days later?
Play cards, then straws in the evening. Ltn. Preisegger back from the field hospital. There is mail. Wendel, despatch rider, goes to division with difficulty.
(17.Panzer Division was being transferred to the area of Vinnitsa.)

Wednesday 29 December. Ltn. Preisegger made EK2.
Our tank is recovered. Wrote a few letters. Otherwise nothing happening. Played cards then straws in the evening. Gef still ill.

Thursday 30 December. A new ObLtn. and Ltn. came to our regiment, both transferred to us from 39 Panzer Regiment HQ in France.
Have all sorts of things to tell from here. March off for certain on 2 January. Got more parcels and letters. We played cards, and in the evening straws with music.

Friday 31 December. We're celebrating New Year.
In the morning I was in the workshop. In the evening the fun starts.
Gef lying in bed. First we had a drink at our quarters and then went from quarters to quarters drinking, singing, and firing our guns.
2300 went to Oberfldw. Adolf and Sepp. 2400 we went to Ltn. Opelik, Grosse, Gfrörer, and Voek. Eventually went to bed at 0230.
March off order for tomorrow at 0600. Have a bath and pack my things. Soon to bed.
We still belong to our Panzer Regiment 39. The commanding officer is Knight's Cross holder Major Schneider von Mohlefski. The regiment is based in France on a training area south of Cralon.

Notes to 27 December 1942 to 31 December 1943
This diary, the longest of all Erich's individual accounts, was written in a small notebook. The handwriting was much smaller than usual and required great patience and diligence to read.

Erich's record starts with the retreat from the attempt to relieve the Stalingrad pocket and the fierce fighting that ensued in dreadful weather. He mentions the march on 5 February and the difficulties with deep snow, which caused vehicle breakdowns. Erich refers to the fact that only tracked units like his could get to the allotted area on time.

On 7 January, 17.Panzer Division got the help of Tiger Tanks, which must have been very welcome with their thick armour and hard hitting 8.8cm gun. However, on the 10th Erich shows displeasure about the youth of the Tiger crews, recruited fresh from the replacement Battalions. He probably believed veteran soldiers like himself should have had the chance to man such new and powerful machines.

Erich relates the transport to Dnepropetrovsk on 18 February. The Division was to attack the flank of a Soviet advance east of the town but was too weak to make much progress.

The 5. SS Division "Wiking" gets several mentions as a neighbouring unit. This was probably much appreciated, as "Wiking" was one of the premier *Waffen SS* Divisions. 17.Panzer Division repelled enemy attacks on the right of "Wiking's" area. This was during the battle for Kharkov, where 17.Panzer Division was part of Army Group South reserve with "Wiking" and 23.Panzer Division.

Despite the confusion of fighting and the soldiers having to scavenge for food, Erich could still meet pretty girls! On 24 February Erich relates the desperate situation on the front line, as every soldier was needed.

On 5 March Erich got better news when he was awarded the Iron Cross First Class (EK1). As usual he celebrated with a good "booze up." Throughout March, in a quieter period Erich gets the chance to have days off, go to the cinema, and meet more women, "Great women!" Erich was certainly a ladies man.

In May Erich is to be found digging bunkers, which were essential for defence against the fierce Soviet attacks. The Division was occupying defensive positions on the Donets river. Erich mentions the move on 14 May into Izyum for refitting.

Erich was also training as a tank driver. The Germans believed in soldiers having skills in other areas to their speciality to replace crews killed or wounded. This contributed to their efficiency in combat.

On 2 July Erich noticed the Turkestaners as German allies. It must have been strange after Nazi ideology for German soldiers to be allied to such exotic and "non-Aryan" people. Also in July, on the 7th Erich takes as much notice of Adolf Hitler's speech as he does to the fact that he has quarters with girls. The latter was probably much more important.

Erich records the fighting starting on 17 July, when the Soviets attacked round Izyum. This went on until they withdrew on 27 July. Erich comments on the 28th being a "quiet night." No doubt welcome after the fierce assaults on the Division's positions!

Leave is always in Erich's mind, and on 29 July he is overjoyed when he has home leave. This is taken from 4 August. On returning Erich witnesses the effectiveness of Soviet partisan activity with their attacks on the railways.

On his return Erich records the move to relieve the trapped XXIX Korps near Stalino on 28 and 29 August. In early September Erich's notes reflect the German tactics of using their armour to blunt and repel Soviet breakthroughs. Erich takes pride in the fact that 17. Panzer Division is the furthest eastward unit.

On 9 September Erich shows no surprise at the Italian capitulation. The Italians had a low standing in the eyes of the German military. This was unfair, as they often fought bravely, especially those units on the eastern front, but were let down by their chronic leadership and logistic system. Later in September the importance of alcohol to soldiers is well documented.

From 22 September Erich and his comrades are busy building defences. He shows annoyance at a duty he feels is below him as a Panzerman. This was in common with other elite and highly trained troops. Later in the war large numbers of *Kreigsmarine* sailers and *Luftwaffe* specialists were drafted into Infantry and *Volksgrenadier* units and they proved ill trained and motivated.

On 26 Septenber the Soviets started a major offensive against 17.Panzer Division's area. The Division was below strength but fought well, and Erich experiences this fighting.

On 4 October Erich feels that the loss of experienced officers and NCOs is stupid, probably as the loss of such men will weaken the division. The next day Erich is listening in to the Soviet radio, a practice that both sides carried out continually. On the 9th of the month the importance of foraging to supplement the troops' diet is again well illustrated.

On 10 October Erich records 143 Soviet tanks knocked out. The Germans inflicted much higher losses on the Soviets than they took themselves. The Soviets, however, could replace the losses in men and materials, while the Germans could not.

On 16 October Soviet propaganda used loudspeakers to relay messages to the German troops. This was a common practice to encourage desertion and/or attempt to lower morale. About this time the Soviets started to use Germans captured at Stalingrad to send the messages and relate stories of their good treatment as prisoners.

On 26 October Erich reports more German deaths at the hands of Partisans. This was a war in which no quarter was given by both sides, and where no German soldier could feel safe even behind the front line. On 16 November came better news for the Division, with the arrival of the first Panther Panzer V tanks. This much increased the armour protection and firepower of the German armoured units and gave them superiority to much of the Soviet armour.

On 20 November and again on the 22nd, Erich shows his great joy and pride when Gef was awarded the Knight's Cross, the highest decoration. He underlines the entries made in capitals. These awards reflected on the whole unit the officer was in charge of in terms of bravery and effectiveness in combat. Gef got a copy of the Knight's cross on 25 November. This was an Iron Class Second Class made to look like a Knight's Cross and was worn until the real medal came. Some officers and soldiers continued to wear the copy in battle and kept the real medal safe.

The Division had at last obtained half-track carriers for Panzer Grenadiers in October, and Erich observes their movement on 1 December. He takes part in the move to Kherson for rest and refit. Early December was a period of intensive training of NCOs, and Erich records his involvement in this.

Erich records his horror at the German soldiers who committed rape on 29 November. Another incident which causes him concern is the possible sabotage on 11 December. This could have been caused by defective materials, as manufacturing was getting tougher in Germany.

Between 14 and 16 December the Panzer *Abteilung* joined forces with the First Battalion of Panzer Grenadier 40 and counterattacked the Soviets, who were pushed back. Again, Erich records his part and what he saw. Christmas Eve saw a major Soviet offensive which caused Erich and the division to be moved to the Vinnitsa area to help repel it.

December 25th finds Erich uncertain about the future of the Division due to its high losses in battle, but on the last day of the year he records his pride in his tank unit, the 39 Panzer Regiment.

Chapter 11

Diary 12 April 1944 to 9 June 1944

Written in small notebock, no front cover, red back cover.

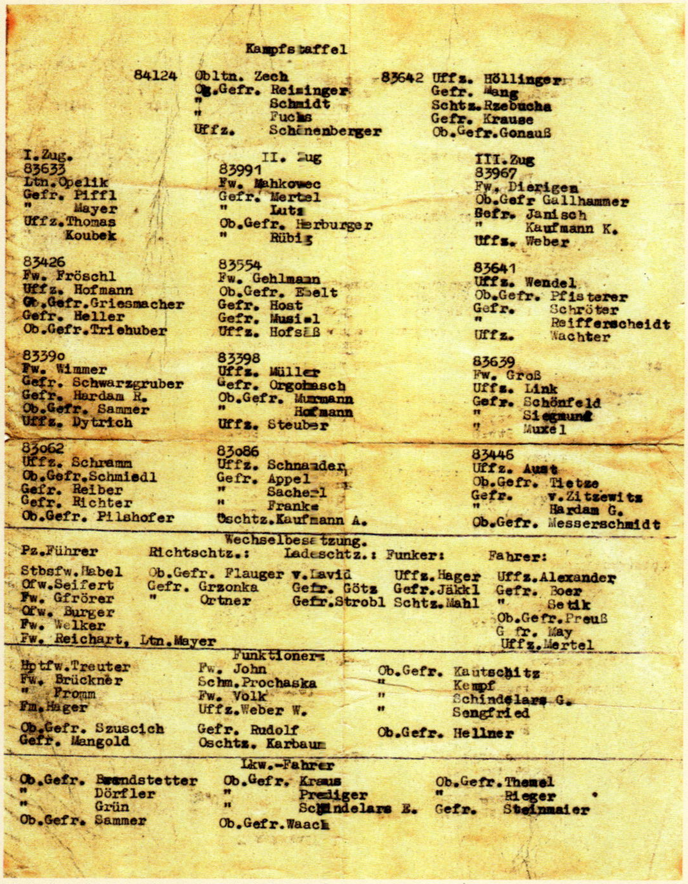

Kampfstaffel

84124 Obltn. Zech — 83642 Uffz. Höllinger
Ob.Gefr. Reisinger — Gefr. Mang
" Schmidt — Schtz.Rzebucha
" Fuchs — Gefr. Krause
Uffz. Schönenberger — Ob.Gefr.Gonauß

I.Zug. / II. Zug / III.Zug

83633 Ltn.Opelik, Gefr. Piffl, " Mayer, Uffz.Thomas, Koubek
83991 Fw. Mahkowec, Gefr. Mertel, " Lutz, Ob.Gefr. Herburger, " Rübig
83967 Fw. Dierigen, Ob.Gefr Gallhammer, Gefr. Janisch, " Kaufmann K., Uffz. Weber

83426 Fw. Fröschl, Uffz. Hofmann, Ob.Gefr.Griesmacher, Gefr. Heller, Ob.Gefr.Triehuber
83554 Fw. Gehlmann, Ob.Gefr. Ebelt, Gefr. Host, Gefr. Musiel, Uffz. Hofsäß
83641 Uffz. Wendel, Ob.Gefr. Pfisterer, Gefr. Schröter, " Reifferscheidt, Uffz. Wachter

83390 Fw. Wimmer, Gefr. Schwarzgruber, Gefr. Hardam R., Ob.Gefr. Sammer, Uffz. Dytrich
83398 Uffz. Müller, Gefr. Orgohasch, Ob.Gefr. Murmann, " Hofmann, Uffz. Steuber
83639 Fw. Groß, Uffz. Link, Gefr. Schönfeld, " Siegmund, " Muxel

83062 Uffz. Schramm, Ob.Gefr.Schmiedl, Gefr. Reiber, Gefr. Richter, Ob.Gefr. Pilshofer
83086 Uffz. Schnaader, Gefr. Appel, " Sachetl, " Franke, Oschtz.Kaufmann A.
83446 Uffz. Aust, Ob.Gefr. Tietze, Gefr. v.Zitzewitz, " Hardam G., Ob.Gefr. Messerschmidt

Wechselbesatzung.

Pz.Führer	Richtschtz.:	Ladeschtz.:	Funker:	Fahrer:
Stbsfw.Habel	Ob.Gefr. Flauger	v.Lavid	Uffz.Hager	Uffz.Alexander
Ofw.Seifert	Gefr. Grzonka	Gefr. Götz	Gefr.Jäkkl	Gefr. Boer
Fw. Gfrörer	" Ortner	Gefr.Strobl	Schtz.Mahl	" Setik
Ofw. Burger				Ob.Gefr.Preuß
Fw. Welker				Gfr. May
Fw. Reichart, Ltn.Mayer				Uffz.Mertel

Funktioner:

Hptfw.Treuter — Fw. John — Ob.Gefr. Kautschitz
Fw. Brückner — Schm.Prochaska — " Kempf
" Fromm — Fw. Volk — " Schindelars G.
Fm.Hager — Uffz.Weber W. — " Sengfried
Ob.Gefr. Szuscich — Gefr. Rudolf — Ob.Gefr. Hellner
Gefr. Mangold — Oschtz. Karbaum

Lkw.-Fahrer

Ob.Gefr. Brandstetter — Ob.Gefr. Kraus — Ob.Gefr.Themel
" Dörfler — " Prediger — " Rieger
" Grün — " Schindelars E. — Gefr. Steinmaier
Ob.Gefr. Sammer — Ob.Gefr.Waach

Tank crew list for second battalion Panzer Regiment 39. Erich is listed under the *Funkers* (signalmen) of the crews without tanks. The date is not recorded. The numbers refer to the factory number of the tanks. Numbers starting with 83 generally signify the Panzer IV.

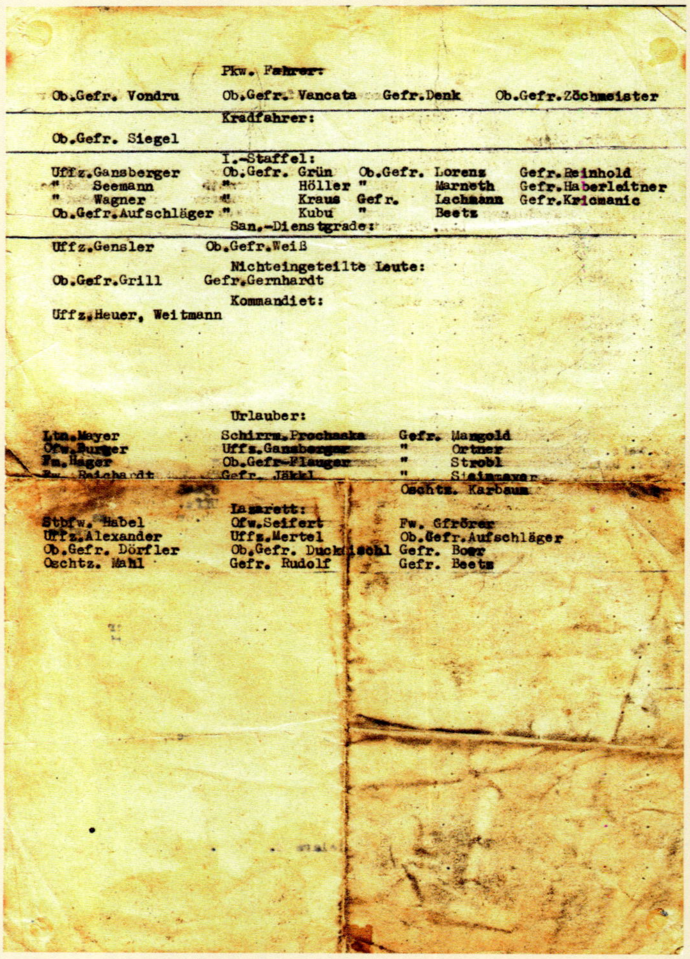

Pkw. Fahrer:

Ob.Gefr. Vondru — Ob.Gefr. Vancata — Gefr.Denk — Ob.Gefr.Zöchmeister

Kradfahrer:

Ob.Gefr. Siegel

I.-Staffel:

Uffz.Gansberger — Ob.Gefr. Grün — Ob.Gefr. Lorenz — Gefr.Reinhold
" Seemann — " Höller — " Marneth — Gefr.Haberleitner
" Wagner — " Kraus — Gefr. Lachmann — Gefr.Kricmanic
Ob.Gefr.Aufschläger — " Kubu — " Beetz

San.-Dienstgrade:

Uffz.Gensler — Ob.Gefr.Weiß

Nichteingeteilte Leute:

Ob.Gefr.Grill — Gefr.Gernhardt

Kommandiet:

Uffz.Heuer, Weitmann

Urlauber:

Ltn.Mayer — Schirrm.Prochaska — Gefr. Mangold
Ofw.Burger — Uffz.Gansberger — " Ortner
Fm.Hager — Ob.Gefr-Flauger — " Strobl
Fw. Reichardt — Gefr. Jäkkl — " Steinmayer
Oschtz. Karbaum

Lazarett:

Stbfw. Habel — Ofw.Seifert — Fw. Gfrörer
Uffz.Alexander — Uffz.Mertel — Ob.Gefr.Aufschläger
Ob.Gefr. Dörfler — Ob.Gefr. Duckwischl — Gefr. Boer
Oschtz. Mahl — Gefr. Rudolf — Gefr. Beetz

Reverse of the same document.

"In memory of the Gef radio operator Uffz. Hager. Russia 10.1.44. Pietsch Hptm."

"Our driver Uffz. Alexander. Fell on 8.4.1944 in the big Kessel at ZALESZYKI." Uffz. Alexander wears the early Panzer jacket as shown by the pink *Waffenfabre* piping round the collar. He has a lanyard for an NCO's whistle looped round his top right hand button.

"Grave of Walter Musiol. Run over in march by his own tank. 1944."

"Grave of our Hptfldw. Geissler. Fell on 8.4.44 in the attack on the bridgehead GRINITUINI on the DONEZ."

12 April. Stationed here 10 SS PD (*Waffen SS* "Frundsberg" Division), H J. PD, (*Waffen SS Hitlejugend* "Hitler Youth" Division), 106 G.D., 387 Infantry Div, in addition 365 Infantry Div. The battle group stays in readiness until DOBROMYSL. The battle HQ orders radio silence. 3 Pz (Panzers, tanks) up ahead for security. 3 tanks here. It's rained all day. Everywhere is full. We're quartered with 365 Infantry Div (Recruits' Division), all 17 years old.
Artillery firing like mad. The terrain is like at home. You'd think you were travelling through the Vienna Woods. Lovely houses. Has already been the World War Front. Here the battle has long been taking place down river. A.A.A. (*Aufklarungs-Ausbildungs-Abteilung*, Reconnaissance Battalion) already on the other side of the DNESTR.
(17.Pz.Div. was part of the German defensive line on the Dnestr with the other units.)

13 April. Sunny day. Everything is lousy. As lousy as everything is, as never before. *Stalinorgel* (truck mounted rockets), anti-tank firing at us. Our artillery is firing like mad. In these battles it's a dreadful noise. Our tank is kaput. Gears, 3 road wheels ripped off, track broken. Everything depends on spare parts. Work 'til the evening with 2 detachment on the fourth (tank). Finally got the track back on without 2 road wheels. Can't do anything about it!! Tanks all around us. We're always under cover.
Artillery fire all day. Supply 1 sitting in PZREMYSL. *Oberst* Grün snatched up all the people from 17 PD. They would have gone to the *Reich* otherwise.

14 April. New battle tank arrived for us. Came from Div. I didn't get in. Travelling with Ltn. Kohlberger in the *Schwimmwagen*. *Stalinorgel*, anti-tank guns, and artillery. Went up into the gun emplacements with Gef to see how things are. No Russians to be seen.
Artillery fire very strong up front. 21 Stukas bombing heavily 500m in front of us. Assault guns - 7 from 249 section digging in. Are to cross the DNESTR with us. Engineers are building a ferry. There's leave again. That's the best bit. Otherwise nothing happening. Tidying up the command post.

15 April. Went on foot with Willi to the tanks to check the radio. Snipers firing on us. Got through safely, though artillery, anti-tank (firing) at us just like every day. Order to cross (the river) for 5 PM. Piffl and Krim as well as 3 *Richtschütze* (gunners) Haupt. Puhle, and Tietze relieve people from 16PD (16.Panzer Division). At the ferry point there are infantrymen upon infantrymen about the 1000 who all want to get across. 1 *Schwimmwagen*. It takes ½ hour to ferry one tank across. When will we be finished? General also here.
Gef and us go across with the Volkswagen. Just the heaviest 15.2 cm (artillery gun) firing. Firing with a vengeance and water flying all over the place - it was OK though. Our company and people from HQ company and 4 company are relieving the people who have been thrown together today, and they are going back to their unit. Fröbl Sepp unlucky again, had an accident - the small ferry sank. 3 comrades drown as it is already quite dark. Ferry done for. Sepp and his tank are still on it.

16 April. Mail again. Ltn. Gern stuck in the mud with 4 tanks. Got them all out. With 5 Panzer IV and 2 assault guns we go to NIZNROW to Schönfeld. Ltn. Grosse leading the company. Grosse and Fröbl, *Zipführer* Westfehl attacked. Ltn. Kohlberger, Anbauer, and I staying here. Fröbl Sepp now coming early too. Grosse and Brylrum later. Jüptner still missing. Firing going on all over. You can hear T-34 tanks turning, anti-tank guns, heavy artillery, machine guns, Pz. Busch (anti-tank rifles). General here too. Ltn. Fron and Hammisch have come back wounded. Ltn. Fron by artillery, Hammisch by machine gun.
Wachbrenner took our *Schwimmwagen* back to the ferry. I tied both up. Fröbl Sepp leading the company 'til Grosse gets here. OberLtn. Wöfl has to lead the company. Link came and took me in the tank to the Gef. *Befehlswagen* (Command tank) kaput. Gef got in at the start, not me.
Attack continuing against a village which was taken - BRATYSZOW. 3 T-34s knocked out. (Troops) massing. Command vehicle back here. Gef gets into it. Ltn. Preisegger here leading the company. Everyone took part in this attack. Schramm welding the (tank) track. Piffl helps. Command to fall in. *Stalinorgel*, Pak (anti-tank guns) firing at us. Have to push on 8km - we're at the front - unpleasant feeling. Mayer a casualty. Juptner a casualty, both because of burning vehicle. Piffl and Schramm still working. Push on. Horror - very tortuous, woods, houses. T-34s always ahead of us. You can hardly believe it. At night stop before a wood. Dig in. Assault guns also there. Hptm. Zorn and Schramm also made it through. Piffl knocked the track off, working on it. At night I'm also in the turret. T-34s thundering in front of us all night.

17 April. 4 AM relieved by Burk, go to command post. Big mistake, should have got into the command vehicle with Gef; he didn't say anything but drove off right in front of me. I ran behind with Muli. Still got there. Ltn. Kohlberger told me to go in the command vehicle. Slaughtered a calf. Go back to NIZNROW, can't find our *Schwimmwagen*, and Willi has provisions. Go over the DNESTR to the supply line. Get something to eat in the kitchen. Leave passes have arrived. Mission with Fldw. Syviklam. Set up base in NIZNROW. Go with Muli for fuel and munitions, then to the ferry, which doesn't take us. Stand there for hours. One aircraft attack after another. Nothing happens. Flak brings one down. Go to NIZNROW on foot. No peace from the aircraft. Almost nothing left standing of this little town. Corpses lying around, it looks dreadful here.
Ltn. Preisegger - fall in again at 5.30 with Obfldw Grosse, Fldw Brylaum Fech, Fröschl, Verim, and Schramm.
Wait for Ltn. Kohlberger to drive ahead of us. Fldw. Fröschl was unconscious yesterday, relieved today. *Richtschütze* (gunner) made commander. Heitkamp made *Richtschütze*. Aircraft are continually here. Stukas up to 60, then down to 11. The Russians - always rubbing their nose in it. Want to write a few letters. Don't manage it again.
(On this day 17.Panzer Division was part of a German offensive.)

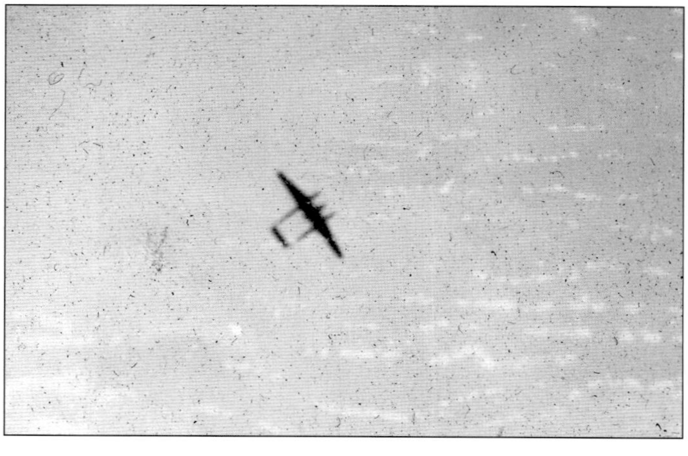

"1 Fokker Wolf reconnaissance plane."

18 April. Runway bombs were here all night. 5 at a time. The bombs roared all night beside, left, and in front of us. Lots of duds. Early in the morning we saw that they had been dropping stones. Hard to believe. We just stared at them. Marching off at first light, me as forward detail with Ltn. in the *Schwimmwagen*. Went to BRATYSZOW to Jüptner, Toru, and Mayer. Toru - his car broken up. Mayer has had enough. On to Piffl, who has lost his way and was waiting for Mayer, who lost the track. Onwards to seek quarters at OKNIANT. I'm staying back alone and waiting for the unit. Stukas coming, then the Russians again. A few now and again round the house. Artillery and *Stalinorgel* deafen me.
In the evening the *Abteilung* arrives. I'm billeted beside the kitchen. Steuber came today from up front. Ltn. Preisegger - his car a casualty. Ltn. Preisegger and his crew got out in time. Fldw. Brylaum here - he's slightly wounded by pieces of shrapnel. Advance going calmly on. Russians retreating. The town of TLUMALZ in our hands. 5 Pz IV in action. Slaughtered 11 chickens. *Schirmeister* (Vehicle or Supply Sergeant) goes up for fuel and munitions.

19 April. Stukas here again. Hptm. Pietsch arrived here with ObLtn. Kühne. Major Bauer has been transferred. In the afternoon march off to quarters. I travel in Ltn. Mayer's *Kubelwagen*. Through the town of TLUMALZ. The left hand runway strip in the direction of HORADENKA to GRASSKA - no quarters here. Schramm out. Fifteen 7.62 cm Pak here. Loads of lorries kaput. Artillery, *Stalinorgel* firing on us. In the evening back to the town of TLUMALZ and billets. Play cards. Ltn. Preisegger shot again (wound badge in silver). Obfldw Grene outside turret, drove over a mine - seriously wounded - already at the main dressing station. 4 Pz (Tanks) in action.
(17.Panzer Division had been reinforced by a Tiger tank unit and had had a delivery of new Panzer IV tanks. It was involved in attacks to 5 May.)

20 April. New quarters here in the town. Anbauer and I together. Write 11 letters. Lovely weather. Great women. Getik shot in the back. Ltn. Preisegger was in command and is wounded. Tietze seriously wounded, burnt, lots of casualties. Leave passes here. *Tross* 2 also (Supply train 2). Am already over the DNESTR. Ahead 1 Panther (Panther Tank) unit in action with us. It's raining.
(Erich records no entry to celebrate Hitler's birthday.)

21 April. Anbauer travelled on early. Spiess stays here. All sorts of things to tell. Uffz. Mertel missing in the fighting. Obfldw. Gefrörer is platoon commander with the infantry. Obfldw. Volk is messing officer with the infantry. Koubek is working with Ltn. Markowitz. Supplied with 17 Pz IV. There are also reinforcements (Ltn. von Zitzewitz). Fldw. Piffl drove over a mine. Wounded (main dressing station). 4 Pz IV still in action. Up front 15 tanks were knocked out by Russian tanks. *Buchse* 2.8. (Tapered bore anti-tank weapon that fired Tungsten cored shells). Lots going on there. An anti-tank brigade in action there.
1 PD and 16 PD withdrawn again - on their way home. They were only here for 4 months. Every PD with 3 tank units. What have we done wrong that they are not taking us out of here? Have we to be forced under? There's something uncanny!
Heinz is in the field hospital in Metz? What can be wrong with him? Third time, he's so unlucky. Günter Hoffmann, our *Richtschütze*, died in the field hospital. Our Uncle Bummi died. Got to know great girls.

22 April. With the Spiess, *Schubarbeiten* (nozzle work, refueling), done from the time when *Tross* 2 was down. Otherwise nothing happening. Fldw. Webel, Uffz. Aust, Uffz. Koubek, Siegfried, Organahl, and Steinmayer. They've got the combat section. It's raining.
At night I go to the town. Danced a lot and was in great mood. There are women that we think are from home. Slaughter a pig. In the evening, send-off for Major Düwel who's been transferred to Juderian.

"Briefing during action at TSJOM. Major Düwel Abt. Kdr. and Hptm. Pietsch Gef."

23 April. Collect the *Gefechtsbezeichnung* (combat description) from Ltn. Kohlberger. Then Obflw. Grosse, Link, Reiniger, and I are going back with Muli. Stops every 100m - such crap.
In the evening to the Company. *Hauptmann* Pietsch did not go today with Obflw. He flew to the *Reich* to the Headquarters of *Generaloberst* Hüte. All sorts going on. Mangold Heinz and Hardam have to go off. Uffz. Muli to DARSCAROW. Grün transferred to HQ. Haberleitner with a vehicle and Ligl with motorbike and sidecar. 6 Company still the company to go into action. Obflw. Volk has come back. The Spiess is all in because the people have to go away. He's alone on the *Abteilung* command.
17 Pz (tanks) are here. 7 officers - Ltn. Zitzewitz and Ltn. Jupotka have come to us. Ltn. Eckart a right young one.

24 April. They do what they want with 6 Comp? Perhaps there's mission? Leave would be the only good thing. Loader training. Am trainer. We've got 23 recruits.
Lovely weather all day. Washed all our things.

25 April. Did a bit of sunbathing. Vancata arrived with the *Kubelwagen*. They had an adventurous trip. There's mail. Mangold away. Uffz. Schulz gone to Warsaw. 2 Pz IV gone ahead.
In the evening phone call from Gef. Got to go up right away. Go with Sepp in the *Kubelwagen* to the Gef in TLUMALZ. Again radio operator for the Gef.
In the evening with a girl. Also got a letter from her. Great!
10 o'clock go on up with the *Kubelwagen*.

"Our crew and the Gef. Kubel driver Vancata from Vienna." Erich is in the centre.

26 April. 6 Pz IV the Company. Fldw. Jüptner *Richtschütze* (Gunner). Waiting for the attack to begin. In the afternoon it got going. At 7 o'clock 267 Infantry Division fell in. *Nebelwerfer* (multiple rocket launcher), everything here. A real battle. Major Zahn. 17 Tigers, 17 Panthers, 15 Pz IV, 10 *Hornissen* (Self propelled anti-tank guns, 8.8cm on a hybrid Panzer III/IV chassis). The infantry going forward well.
It started to rain, quite lightly all afternoon. Ask Gef about radio operator training. He's not against it. Adj. Ltn. Kohlberger has just come I said to him. He spoke immediately to the Gef and I will be put forward. That would be my life-long dream. Ltn. Kohlberger wants to take me with him immediately. Gef says I have to go into this attack first. I hope it works out - that would be just fine. The Spiess is also here and also knows about it. *Stalinorgel* firing on us. Anti-tank fire also. Otherwise not much happening.
In the evening to the supply line with Muli. That was some journey.

27 April. The worst day of my military life. Ltn. Kohlberger went to Division and settled the thing about the training. He arrived and told me that the application was already too late and a late application was not acceptable because the General has already been informed and names already given. I have had it, totally slapped in the face.
Went and made Schnitzel in the kitchen with Willi. Suggestion that Hartkamp be given the EK2 (Iron cross second class). In the evening went up in the tank. Kaufmann can drive back.
Aerial combat over TLUMALZ. One Russian shot down. No rain today. There are canteen goods again but nothing interests me. I should have been able to go back to the *Reich* tomorrow. Hard luck! - hard luck - that cost me an effort.

28 April. *Nebelwerfer* firing like mad. *Stalinorgel* also and artillery. Aircraft all day. All sorts going on.
For our *Kampfgrüppe* no orders yet. Canteen supplies are here. Sekt, schnaps, cigarettes.
I'm really feeling down. I have real bad luck. Leave passes have also arrived. Otherwise nothing happening. Aircraft also here all the time.

29 April. Here to say good morning are the Russian planes - a whole load of them. Orders arrive - form up at 9 AM for *Kampfgrüppe* 10 - that's now 30 Tigers, 24 Panthers, 16 Pz IV, 18 *Hornisse*. Attack on CHOCHNIERZ. Go there at 12 o'clock. Piffl and Wendel shot in the attack. Wendel's vehicle came for him. Preuss, driver, is dead in the vehicle. Griesmacher, *Richtschütze*, seriously wounded. Reissinger brought him back. He had died by that time. 2 old ones gone again. Piffl's lot got off without a scratch. Further attack - quite difficult terrain conditions. 3 Tigers went over mines. 1 Panther set alight and put out of action. Everything gets stuck in the mud. We wanted to go through a wood but everything gets stuck. Not everything has got out yet. Today's goal for 334 (Map point reference) will soon be reached. The whole *Kampfgrüppe* (battlegroup) will reach the target. The radio operator for Karl Wendel is also dead, stayed in his vehicle and burned. He was Zimmer, a new man who had only been here for 6 days.

"Obgef. Griesmacher killed on 29.4 44. Obgef. Krill, Obgef. May." Elderly SdKfz. 251/10 A. This vehicle was armed with a 3.7 cm. PaK 36 and was used by platoon leaders and engineers. It is surprising that one of the first of the series should survive to the introduction of the three colour camouflage in 1943. Unusually the vehicle is named on the front and sides "Leopard."

30 April. 4 AM supplies arrived for everyone. At 5 AM preparations for a further attack. 6.30 AM finally ready against 359 (Map reference point). 1st attack because of the huge damage done from the flank. Panthers stormed through the wood. Of course we got stuck again. What terrain. Perhaps something going on here. All calibres of artillery and anti-tank firing at us. Tigers and Panthers being lost like never before. Uffz. Link arrived. *Hornisse* have knocked out 4 T-34s.
Attack on 45 finally gains the hill, after our Division secured the hill. Still being attacked as never before by *Stalinorgel* and artillery. It's bitter cold. Aircraft attacking us. 100 were here - maybe double that. 1 T-34 destroyed. 2 Pz IV casualties (Fröbl and another). Link drove into a gully, couldn't get out.
Getting a new commanding officer – OberstLtn. from GHQ. Pictal leaving. Hard luck. Jüptner got splinters in his head from the *Stalinorgel*, because he is continually running around. One other is shot. There were air attack in waves. Perhaps we were small fry. Ready for action: 6 Pz IV, 1 from SS, 1 in repair. We are sleeping in a haystack.

1 May. Formed up at 6 AM against 2 hills (45 - 52). Things going on there again. Fldw. Karf a casualty, unlucky. We went on ourselves as last in the track. There was a bang and I was covered in powder-smoke, and I was thrown out of the vehicle. Went over a mine - no one hurt. Left suspension units away. Tracks torn open. Our comrades don't follow. The artillery firing at us. We have to get out quickly. Securing position at 10 AM. Jump into an old field position and wait. All alone on a wide meadow, no infantrymen. Only the Panthers and Pz IV are further forward.
The Baron has to go to the Panzer. (Note - the word "he" is in capital letters, even in the middle of a sentence, when referring to this person!) HE took 2 prisoners - both Ukranians. Now HE wants to attack. The holes are still full. Thank God engineers are coming at midday, who have to clear mines. We took 27 more prisoners. Before, when we were alone we were constantly being shot at. We couldn't lift our heads. That was hellish. Our own *Nebelwerfer* and artillery were firing at us. Everything came together. Above us stood 2 T-34s and anti-tank guns. They fired constantly and just about deafened us. Mortar and artillery came dubiously close. The engineers have cleared 65 mines. We were clearly infantrymen. We've got one machine gun and we are firing with it. 1 Panther also went over a mine.
In the evening Pz (a tank) cleaned out of a ditch and went back to ZERBUKOW to the Company all round defence position. Supplies here also. Order has come that Jüptner, Toni, and Griess have to go back immediately as they have to go to weapons' training school. New orders!! Had a few hours' sleep. Reisinger and Wölfl brought in casualties.

2 May. We have no tank. Wölfl with 4 tanks to attack on Hill 359 - for the second time. 7 Panthers, 15 Tigers. We, Gef and I, are sitting with the artillery observer and watching. Bad position. Continuous anti-tank fire at us. *Stalinorgel*, mortar, and artillery all mixed together. You can hardly lift your head up. Major Zahn also here now. Observer VSH Pz (*Vorgeschobene* Panzer, Observation and signals tank) with 2 turrets coming up on to the hill. Fire 3 shots and away again. You can hardly believe it. They look as if they are standing still.
From 6 AM we've been lying in the hole - now 12 o'clock. In the afternoon it gets worse. You can't raise your head. Constant anti-tank fire. Heavy artillery hammering us. They are getting closer to the hole. We are making ourselves look small. The PZ (tanks) are attacking. On the left the Tigers. On the right hand side on hill 359 the Panthers and Wölfl with 4 Pz IV.
1 Tiger is knocked out. 1 Pz IV, Frönll, of ours. A direct artillery hit - 3 wounded, including Frönll, 1 Pz IV damaged by artillery, others casualties. In the evening night activity against Hill 359 with 3 Panthers, 1 Pz IV last. If it is successful then the armoured *Kampfgrüppe* will be pulled out. In this undertaking one tank is kaput - a mine - our last Pz IV, Wölfl's. Gef and I on foot to LERBOKUW. There they are firing like mad. We're dismantling again and going to Gef at *Kampfgrüppe* Zahn. Sleep here.

3 May. Task force Zahn pulled out, falling back to the area round DEZIERZAWI. Gef and I walking and meeting ObLtn. Wölfl in the truck. Go with him. Had something to eat at the Field canteen. Then with the *Schwimmwagen* to TLUMALZ. Got washed here. New commanding officer, now have *Tross* 2. He's called ObstLtn. Weiss-Tavanke. Move into my quarters. A girl coming soon. Sleeping here beside 2 girls in TLUMALZ. But having to travel on straight away. No vehicle here.

4 May. Our tailor also here. Have to do all sorts of things for ObstLtn. Still waiting for a vehicle to get back. At 3 AM the Gef and I go with the *Schwimmwagen* to supply line I. Staying here. 6 Kp pulled out. Kitchen and V lorry (supply vehicle) coming back this evening. Another quarter with a radio - we've been missing that for a long time. Finally some peace. Hope it lasts for a while. We've deserved it. Gef experienced all sorts of things with the *Abteilung*. Now training is starting again. Sort out the quarters. Polished the Gef's decorations Early this morning Jüptner, Kriess, and Rühle went off to officer training.

"Our tailor Obgef."

5 May. Up at 7.15. I'm doing the layout of past battles for the crews. I am standing at the front of 67 men. Gef doing the training plan. Training for 4 crews - Obfldw. Volk, Fldw. Bröder, Uffz. Gernhardt, and Uffz. Klannecker are doing tank driver training, etc. Training starts tomorrow. Nice day. Today quite busy. Otherwise nothing special going on. Kitchen and supply wagon came back today. Slowly everyone is coming back.

6 May. Training starting under the leadership of the Gef. Abt. Kdr. Koubek (*Abteilung* Commander) coming this afternoon to see what's going on. I'm our unit commander - for the first time. In the afternoon with Obflw. training, on the course. Otherwise nothing happening. Our people slowly all coming back. Post again. Evening great - listened to the radio.

7 May. Sunday. Duty as yesterday. Course. No instruction today. Burial of Griesmacher, Preuss, and Zimmer. Otherwise nothing happening. We're leaving here soon. Advance HQ going off tomorrow morning. When will it be my turn for leave? 32 men have done leave over 8 months.

8 May. Course. Write a few letters. Otherwise nothing going on. 2 wireless messages. 1st message: Send 4 drivers and 1 Uffz and 3 men to Pz transport at TLUMALZ. Uffz. Müller, Uffz. Klannecker, Obgef. Lachmann, Lorenz, and Jäger, Neudel. 2nd message: 1 Uffz. as trainer to the B.A.O.K. (*Befehlshaber Armeeoberkommando*, Army Command), 1 elsewhere. Uffz. Schramm going to TLUMALZ this evening, tomorrow to Division and then away. Otherwise nothing happening. This afternoon I have to teach on the course.

9 May. Nothing in particular happening. Our Company has dwindled somewhat. Almost no Uffz. In the Div there are only 7 Uffz. That's all. Hopefully there will be promotions. We're about 50 down in the Company. Did nothing all day. Listen to the radio. In the evening all the seven Feldws. came with a bottle of Schnaps. It did the rounds. Paula was really drunk. Made a racket for 10 (of us). The other companies have to transfer to TLUMALZ. We are staying here. Got a nice letter for Trudi. Invited me to Innsbrück!!

10 May. Uffz. Mop has to go to the Field Hospital. Broken his fibula. Has been lying here for more than 14 days. Otherwise nothing happening. Course, as every other day. I'm doing nothing. Played football in the evening. Uffz against enlisted men - we won 4:3. Today from St Polten came Uffz. Brandstätter Lois, Uffz. Rutting, Uffz. Müller. 3 tank drivers. Goetz and Sonugel and 1 Obgef. - a new one. Listened to music in the evening. Soon going to bed. Zier made 30 amulets. Am NCO of the watch.

11 May. Course as every day. Had to instruct again. Nothing much happening. Schirmeister and Kaufmann A. going on leave. Gave Kaufmann a packet with 1000 cigarettes to take away. Played football again in the evening. Revenge. We won 7:1. Everyone exhausted, us included. Haven't played for such a long time. 1 new Fldw. came to the Company. Soon be new promotions. Rudi to be Fldw., Deichuter and Kaufmann to be Uffz. Got a new uniform.

12 May. Steuber Rudi going to TLUMALZ to relieve Obfw. Hager from the forward command post. Course as usual. Otherwise nothing happening.

13 May. Course as usual. Sunbathed a bit. In the evening inoculations. Radio instruction then Gef instruction from 7 - 8 in the evening. There are canteen goods - cigarettes and Schnaps. Otherwise nothing happening. There are only 20 men because of leave. When will it be my turn? End of June, if all goes well. To Division for radio operator training - Giller, Peteck, Prenzig.

14 May. Made up a parcel. Gave it to Obgefr. Setik because he's going on leave with Fldw. Fromm and Uffz. Seemann on the 16 May. Today there is KiK increase, chocolate, coffee. Otherwise nothing happening. Today's Sunday. Did battle symbols.

15 May. Monday. Panzer training ended. Instead of that, new U (*Unterofficier*, NCO) training in which various Uffz. are taking part, but once again for everyone and 15 more crews. Instruction from the Gef. That's not bad, though. 1 hour in the morning, 2 in the afternoon. Steuber Rudi, Deichuter, and Kaufmann have to report to ABT (*Abteilung*, Battalion) for inspection because of promotions. Schramm not with them. Only Rudi becoming Fldw.

16 May. Duty. Otherwise nothing happening. In the evening Ltn. Opelik came. He's back from leave. A Fldw. also back from leave. Alert company drawn up. Ltn. Freischütz leading it. Each Company assigned 2:15 (Officer to enlisted man ratio). Quite far away. To set up 2 positions. Taken further forward by train from STANISLAW. In the afternoon *Geländedienst*. (Training under field conditions at company level without logistical support.) The last time.

17 May. Alert company left. Of our Company 8 men are staying behind on duty. I've never seen that before. No one doing the training any more as there's no one here. We've got 40 spaces in the Company. The Spiess wanted to play the big man again because we played cards in the afternoon. Got the Fldw. annoyed with us again. In the afternoon sport. Otherwise nothing happening. Have extra duties, NCO of the Watch. I'm 10th in line for leave. I can maybe take it in the middle of June. It would be nice. In the whole Company I have first place in the number of battles fought with 74 attacks. At level 4 for *Pz Kampfabzeichnung* (Tank Battle Badge), 1 more attack needed. Rudi Steuber is in second place with 63 attacks.

18 May. Nothing happening. Instruction training continuing. Hard luck. Wrote a few letters. Hot day. Our kitchen maid was handed over to the Labour Exchange. It was my Saint's Day today. Forgot about it completely. On 25 May I remembered it was my Saint's Day.

"1944." Wrote a few letters.

"1944." Stuff being collected today. Erich is second from the left.

19 May. No duty. Nothing happening. Wrote a few letters. Weather close. When will I get leave? End of June? This evening we went hunting – Gef, Fldw. Brückner, and I with 2 rifles. Walked from 7 - 9 PM through the woods but didn't see any deer. The walk was wonderful, just like at home. Absolutely quiet. Was worth it.

20 May. Saturday. With the Spiess. Instruction about garrison duty. Otherwise nothing happening. Music Hall arrived. Called The Happy People from Innsbrück. Was 3 ladies, elderly sort. 5 gentlemen, old boys. Since early this morning big divisional exercise with Stukas, Tigers, and Pz IV. 96 mSPW (armoured half-tracks Sd.Kfz. 251 series) - all kinds of things. Live firing. In the afternoon the music hall performance in the open air. Was just great, so I was told. I wasn't there. Have guard duty again. A thunderstorm. It's pouring down. Ltn. Gross came back from leave. Obgfr. Gonauss came back with a lorry from the repair workshop. Entered up another attack; 'til now 75 attacks, Level 4. (This counted for the Tank Battle Badge that Erich was entitled to.)

21 May. Sunday. No duty. Hot day again. Canteen goods again. Stuff being collected today. Food good today. Beef, olives, soup, and custard. In the afternoon wrote a few letters. Got a lovely big photo from Evelyn. Otherwise nothing happening. In the afternoon a storm 'til evening. In the evening lovely and cool. Sat in front of the house 'til 10 PM – Gef and I. He played the mouth organ.

22 May. Instruction with the Gef - then promotions.
Uffz. Rudi Steuber becomes *Feldwebel*
Geschisher becomes Uffz.
Kaufmann K Uffz.
Griesmacher, deceased, and Preiss, deceased, become Uffz.
In the afternoon cinema from 1 - 7 PM. 3 things – "Harald erscheint um 9 Uhr" (Harald appears at 9 o'clock), "Gefährtin meines Sommers" (Companion of my summer), and "Traummusik" (Music of my dreams). Great. Canteen goods. Each 1 bottle of Schnaps. For Uffz. Pilshofer we are collecting cigarettes to be sent to him. There is chocolate for the crossing over the Dnestr on 15.4.44. There is mail.

23 May. Uffz. Kaufmann K and Gef Strobl went on leave today. It's very cold. At 2 this morning the Gef went hunting. Otherwise nothing happened all day. Division band will play for us today. Important: according to H D V (*HeeresDiensVorschrift*, German Army regulations) there is no need for radio operators for a Pz Unit. Hard luck for me. Can never become a radio operator. Company is only entitled to 1 G Uffz. Unit. 1 radio operator. In the afternoon I have lesson again at the Pz school. Division band arrives. In the afternoon they played for 130 minutes with a mixed programme. Was lovely. In the evening the Fldws. were celebrating Rudi Steuber's promotion.

24 May. Company stripes given out. Otherwise nothing happening. Bitter cold. Rains, then sunshine again. Then rains again. Like in April. Weapons inspection. Aircraft machine guns had to be remounted. (A MG 34 machine gun was mounted on the tank commander's cupola to fire at attacking aircraft. This was moved from the position in the tank front hull.) Ltn. Opelik, Fldw. Kröger, and Uffz. Wagner went to a training yesterday in TARNOW. Am NCO of the Watch again today. For *Pilshofer* Karl we have collected cigarettes. Fldw. Wimmer is sending them to him. Today I'm anxious again. The *Jankers* (Americans) were over Kärnten and Steiermark, north and east (areas of Austria) at midday today. Hopefully not near our house. Am NCO of the Watch again. From 6 - 7 AM had Company instruction.

25 May. 2 visits from aircraft Machine guns did not fire. Big to-do. In the morning we had to do tactical maneuvering instruction with the Gef. In the afternoon attacks at the front. I was not there. Dörfler Ernst made me an egg-flip. Was good. Zier going on leave tomorrow. Otherwise nothing happening.

26 May. Zier away at 7 AM In the morning more training. Drawing sketches. Schurf and Reiber came back from *Schanzkommando* (a group of soldiers who were assigned to digging trenches and dugouts). 1 new Uffz. from 1.27 (first company, *Abteilung* 27) came to us. Uffz. Wolfram Günter. Already 3 years as Uffz. and 7 altogether as a soldier. In 1941 I was in the 3 *Abteilung*, *LehrAbteilung* 2 *Staffel* (3rd education unit 2nd detachment). Otherwise nothing happening. New orders. Guard over the civilians at entrenchments works at the Dnestr. No one at all from the Company here. 9 Fldw., 7 Uffz., 18 men. Otherwise always cold, still raining.

27 May. Early Company instruction from the Gef. Otherwise nothing happening. There's chocolate again for the DNESTR crossing. All sorts of things going on in Italy. Mail again. Windner Hans is sitting in quiet Denmark. Lidel and Wissinger are in Paris. Otherwise an evening like all the rest.

28 May. Whit Sunday. A lovely day. No duties. Had a bath. Otherwise nothing happening. In the afternoon drank a bottle of *Advocaat* with Steuber Rudi and Wolfram. Gef away at *Abteilung*. Coming back, then were are going shooting with pistols and rifles. Today for the first time our huntsmen found 3 deer and resting places of wild boar. That will be a good hunt. NCO of the Watch today. We were invited by Ltn. Goss. Steuber and I drank with him 'til midnight - 2 bottles of *Advocaat*. 4 Kp and 7 Kp have gone off in the tanks. Up front there is a lot of trouble again.

29 May. Whit Monday. The only happy one for me. The Spiess let it be known that 8 leave passes are here. On the list I am 9th due to get leave. Hopefully I'll be lucky. In the morning there are battles at RI (Infantry area). We are firing with machine guns. Today there is a big Officers' meeting, Commanding officer, even divisional commanding officer, Major-General von der Meden (Divisional commander) is here. Firing here. No duty otherwise. Fldw. Wimmer becomes Oberfldw. The Fldws. are boozing in the morning. Tomorrow Fldw. Gensberger and the HQ Gef are going on leave. Hot day today. Lovely weather. Gef with Trouble. Too much drunk again. Gef Beetz came after 6, brought the lorry back.

30 May. Up at 2 AM. Went hunting with the Gef and Fldw. Bruckner and Dörfler. Saw 1 stag and spotted 1 wild boar but did not get to shoot. Shame. In the morning instruction then duty. In the afternoon played football - 14 men in total. Quite exhausted. Then swimming - great. In the evening went hunting again but didn't spot anything. Pz (Tanks) have arrived for 7 Kp. (7th Company). Drivers had to go away in the evening but came straight back. Fldw. Junkuas stayed outside all night at the hunting stand.

31 May. The following arrived from St Polten today: Fldw. Gern, Obgefr. Bitrus, Sengfried, Orgohasch, and Gefr. Boer. All former members, as well as more boys as replacements. Instruction all morning.

HERAUSGEBER: PANZER-PROPAGANDAKOMPANIE

GRABENZEITUNG

DES „Panzer voran"

FOLGE 35

MITTWOCH, DEN 31. MAI 1944

Zwischen Küste und Albaner Bergen

Neuer Schwerpunkt des feindlichen Grossangriffs in Italien — Wirksame Gegenangriffe unserer Truppen — 94 amerikanische Flugzeuge vernichtet

Führerhauptquartier, 30. Mai 1944.

Das Oberkommando der Wehrmacht gibt bekannt:

Der Schwerpunkt des feindlichen Gegenangriffs lag gestern am äußersten Westflügel der italienischen Front von der Küste bis in den Raum der Albauer Berge. Dem hier mit massierten Infanterie- und Pauzerkräften angreifenden Gegner gelangen an einigen Stellen örtliche Einbrüche, die durch Gegenangriffe sofort bereinigt oder abgeriegelt wurden. 25 feindliche Panzer wurden dabei abgeschossen. Östlich Velletri scheiterten zahlreiche in Bataillonsstärke geführte feindliche Angriffe. Südlich und südwestlich Valmontone zerschlugen unsere Truppen alle Angriffe, die der Gegner mit zusammengefaßten Kräften führte und gewannen bei Fortsetzung des eigenen Gegenangriffs weiteres Gelände zurück. Im Raum beiderseits Ceccano griff der Feind mit überlegenen Kräften unsere Stellungen an und konnte in den von Nachhuten zäh verteidigten Ort eindringen. Östlich des Saccoflusses wurden bei der Abwehr feindlicher Angriffe bei Pofi 22 feindliche Panzer abgeschossen.

Kampffähren der Kriegsmarine schossen im Golf von Genua ein britisches Schnellboot in Brand.

Im Osten kam es auch gestern zu keinen Kampfhandlungen von Bedeutung.

Über dem Finnischen Meerbusen schossen Wachfahrzeuge der Kriegsmarine sechs Sowjetbomber ab. Sieben weitere wurden im Luftkampf vernichtet.

In der letzten Nacht führten deutsche Kampfflugzeuge wirksame Angriffe gegen die Bahnknotenpunkte Kasatin und Shmerinka, die Brände und Explosionen in Betriebsstoff- und Munitionslagern hervorriefen.

Nordamerikanische Bomberverbände drangen bei Tage von Süden und Westen in das nord-, mittel- und südostdeutsche Reichsgebiet ein. Besonders in Leipzig, Posen und Cottbus entstanden Schäden. Die Bevölkerung hatte Verluste. In heftigen Luftkämpfen und durch Flakartillerie wurden 94 feindliche Flugzeuge vernichtet.

In der vergangenen Nacht warfen einzelne britische Flugzeuge Bomben im Raum von Wien und Hannover.

Deutsche Kampfflugzeuge führten wirksame Angriffe gegen die englischen Hafenstädte Plymouth und Portsmouth.

Zusammenhängende Front von Nettuno bis zur Adria

Das hervorstechendste Merkmal der Schlachtentwicklung in Italien während der letzten Woche ist, daß Generalfeldmarschall Kesselring im Zuge der beweglichen Kampfführung seiner Verbände die deutschen Truppen an der italienischen Südfront wie auch am Landekopf Nettuno zurückgenommen hat, was sich so auswirkt, daß jetzt in Italien von Nettuno über die Gebirgsketten bis zur Adria eine zusammenhängende Front entstanden ist. Der Feind hat damit sein Ziel, seinen Landekopf Nettuno in seinen Frontverlauf einzubauen, ein halbes Jahr später als beabsichtigt, erreicht. Ihm ist aber an keiner Stelle ein Durchbruch gelungen. Er muß sich immer wieder durch unsere Bergstellungen durchfressen mit einem Materialaufwand und mit Blutverlusten, die ins Unvorstellbare gehen.

Der OKW-Bericht der beiden letzten Tage meldet, daß der Feind seinen Großangriff unter Einsatz neuer Verbände mit Schwerpunkt südwestlich Velletri fortsetzte. Alle Angriffe scheiterten aber nach harten, wechselvollen Kämpfen, die vornehmlich gegen weit überlegene Panzerkräfte geführt werden mußten. Südwestlich Ceprano warfen unsere Truppen im Gegenstoß über den Saccofluß vorgedrungenen Feind zurück. Bei Ceprano selbst griff der Feind mit vielen hundert Panzern an. Panzergrenadiere und Fallschirmjäger zerschlugen aber die ersten Angriffswellen des Feindes, ein weiterer Vorstoß wurde durch zusammengefaßtes Artilleriefeuer verhindert.

Der Pfingstsonntag stand dann im Zeichen erfolgreicher Abwehrkämpfe unserer Truppen. Im Abschnitt Aprilia—Valmontone schlugen unsere Divisionen die von starken Panzerkräften unterstützten Durchbruchsversuche des Gegners in erbitterten Kämpfen zurück. Das bisher von unseren Nachtruppen zäh verteidigte Trümmerfeld von Aprilia wurde dem Feind überlassen. Südlich Valmontone wurde der Einbruchsraum der letzten Tage durch Angriffe von Ost und Nordwest weiter eingeengt.

Das Ritterkreuz für Vitèz Lakatos

Führerhauptquartier. Der Führer verlieh das Ritterkreuz des Eisernen Kreuzes an den Befehlshaber der ungarischen Ostfronttruppen, Generaloberst Vitèz Lakatos, in Anerkennung seiner Verdienste im Angriff, sowie in der erfolgreichen Abwehr der feindlichen Angriffe im Raum von Kolomea.

Deutschland und Japan

Führerhauptquartier. Der Führer empfing den kaiserlich-japanischen Botschafter Oshima zu einer längeren Aussprache. Die Besprechung des Führers mit Botschafter Oshima behandelte aktuelle Fragen der deutsch-japanischen Zusammenarbeit in der gemeinsamen Kriegführung der beiden Völker. An der Aussprache beim Führer nahm Reichsaußenminister v. Ribbentrop teil, der mit Botschafter Oshima noch eine längere Aussprache hatte.

Front line newspaper for armoured troops.

Tomorrow Fldw. Brückner and Obgefr. Reiber going on leave. A hot day. Company do, lots of people. In the afternoon I went swimming with Brandstätter Lois and Rübig Otto - naked, of course. Listened to the radio. Got mail. Thunderstorm in the evening. 2 leave passes are following on, so I'm going on leave.
1. 1 pass for tomorrow (these words scored out)
5. 2 passes
7. 1 pass
8. 1 pass
10. 2 passes
14. 2 passes - I'll go

June '44
1. Today solemn handing over of 17 Pz IV to 4 Comp and 7 Comp with music. Whole Abt fell in. Abt commanding officer held a trial run then march past of the tanks. Was great. In the afternoon Officers firing with rifles and machine guns - various shooting targets.

Rifle shooters	1st prize	Obfldw. Wimmel
"	2nd "	Fldw. Gern
"	3rd "	Ltn. Gern
M.Pi. (Submachine Gun)	1st prize	Uffz. Link
"	2nd "	Gef.
"	3rd "	Obfldw. Wimmer

In the evening a booze up 'til everyone was drunk of course. Drank at least 10 different hard Schnaps.

2 June. Hangover from it. Duty all morning. In the afternoon entrenchment task force - we are area defence. Got quite soaked again. In the evening I'm on guard duty again. Otherwise nothing happening. Wrote a few letters.

3 June. Awake at 4 AM, duty at 5 AM. No duty in the afternoon. Today our company railway guard with 2 : 12 men (NCO to soldier ratio). Surveillance at the entrenchments. We are 1 : 5 men. No one else left over. Fldw. Gern and Uffz. Brichisten are bringing 1 assault gun that we acquired (from a division that was going home). Otherwise nothing happening. Uffz. Vogelsanger and Uffz. Rübig going to SANCK in Poland in a tank. 2 other drivers are leaving. They're lucky. Vogelsanger going on leave. Nothing happening at all in the afternoon. In the evening went hare hunting with the Gef. Then chatted with Ltn. Gern.

4 June Sunday Fall in at 9 AM. Am NCO of the Watch again for railway surveillance and at the same time for the company. Otherwise nothing happening. Valk now the Spiess as John and Rudolf go on leave tomorrow. Today is Whit Sunday for the Poles and Ukranians. On 14 June I'll probably go on leave. Hopefully nothing will get in the way of that. Yesterday evening I got a letter from home. My parents are getting divorced. I am dumbfounded.

5 June. Spiess and Rudolf away on leave. Bustle. Not much happening as we are still surveillance task force. 4 Company is doing Pz (tank) firing. Junker for the aircraft guard. Hot day. In the afternoon instruction with the radio operator with Ltn. Bart as N-Offz (Signals Officer). Aircaft activity:
Surprise
1. : I'm going on leave on the 10th
2. : Americans and Tommy in Rome
I got a letter from Heinz. Am curious about when Uffz. Vancata is coming with the *Kubelwagen*. It's about time.

6 June. Bustle and entrenchments for all round defence. Lovely day. Aircraft were here again. Not on duty. Hot day. Nothing happening.
1st surprise I N V A S I O N began in the night. Mouth of the SEINE – Cherburg (D-Day landings)
2nd surprise: Going on LEAVE on 8 June.
In the evening we are going hunting and having sapper training. Gef, Dörfler and I. At 9 AM a ram came out near me and I shot 100 metres to the side of it. That was rotten! Dörfler shot 5 times at it. In total I shot 4 times. Didn't get anything. Gef annoyed. Going to Company. Gef shot twice at a hare but did not get him either. Bad luck all round. Nothing hit at 100m. Heard more news about the invasion. There's never a dull moment. For us it's strange that the Russians haven't attacked!! But that will come soon. (Erich was predicting that the Soviets would react to the D-Day landings with an offensive of their own on the eastern front.)

7 June. No duty. Had a bath. Neumann has gone on leave. Lovely day. Otherwise nothing happening. Packed my things together. Tomorrow? !!!! Went to the doctor. Rained in the afternoon. Leave papers are ready. Great. Got uniform. I have my things ready. Toni Jüptner wrote to me and sent me a picture of Luischen. In the evening hunting with Gef and Schnauder - saw a few deer but didn't get to fire. Back at 12. Got leave papers ready. I have to be away at 3 AM. Vancata coming with the *Kubelwagen*.

8 June. Up at 2 AM. Go to the repair shop and go by lorry to STANISLAV, away from there at 11.30 to PZREMSYL, not much of a journey, quite good, find a few comrades. It's raining as we get into LEMBERG. Drive 'til 2 AM.

9 June. De-lousing etc. Our train going at 16.30 sharp. It's going to the homeland. That's another feeling. Via KRAKAV - ODERBERG - LUNDENBURG, then to Vienna North. Tried to find Father, had to run around 3 barracks, but couldn't find him. Learn in a pub that he has been shunted off to NORTH RUSSIA, apparently to a *Schlachter Kompanie* (Butcher Company). 1 AM left Vienna and got out at St Polten and went to Schnauder's sister for half an hour, then went on to Linz. Met Franz Hager from Lingitz with his wife from LODZ (Poland). He's an Uffz. with a Tiger unit in ITALY.

Taken when Erich was on leave. Note the use of his best tunics: M42 for the *Feldwebel* on the right of each picture and M43 for the other soldier. The *Feldwebel* wears the Iron Cross second class, General Assault Badge, and the Black Wounds Badge. He also has the white tress on his shoulder straps which shows he is an officer aspirant.

Notes on 12 April to 9 June

This diary starts with a lot of action and Erich in the thick of battle. 17.Panzer Division was part of the defensive line along the Dnestr river with the other Divisions. April 15th shows the confusion and desperation of retreat when troops would not wish to fall into the hands of the Soviets. The large rivers on the eastern front hampered advance and withdrawal alike.

On 16 April Erich records the horrors of war, and on the 18th is amazed at the Soviet aircraft dropping large stones. They had obviously run out of bombs! Later on the 21st Erich is surprised that 17.Panzer Division has not been relieved as the other divisions have been. As an old soldier now he can be sceptical of the youth of a new officer.

Despite all the action Erich still meets girls and seeks out food. At the end of April Erich is clearly disappointed by not being able to get on the radio operator's course in Germany. However, in May he becomes a trainer in the Division and is so busy he forgets his Saint's day. The Anglo-American bombing raids caused much damage and casualties, so Erich is worried about his house when he hears that Austria has been targeted. He and his comrades seem to have a new hobby - hunting - which they hope will provide extra food.

On 27 May Erich reflects on his comrades in sunnier and quieter places of duty. The month finishes with him working out his chances of leave. It must have been a stunning surprise for Erich to have to learn that his parents were divorcing when he was far away serving at the front. The next day he notes sarcastically about the continual Soviet air activity.

The historic day of 6 June 1944 is recorded by Erich in capitals and underlining. A better surprise for him is his leave, which he again writes in capitals. The diary ends with his leave.

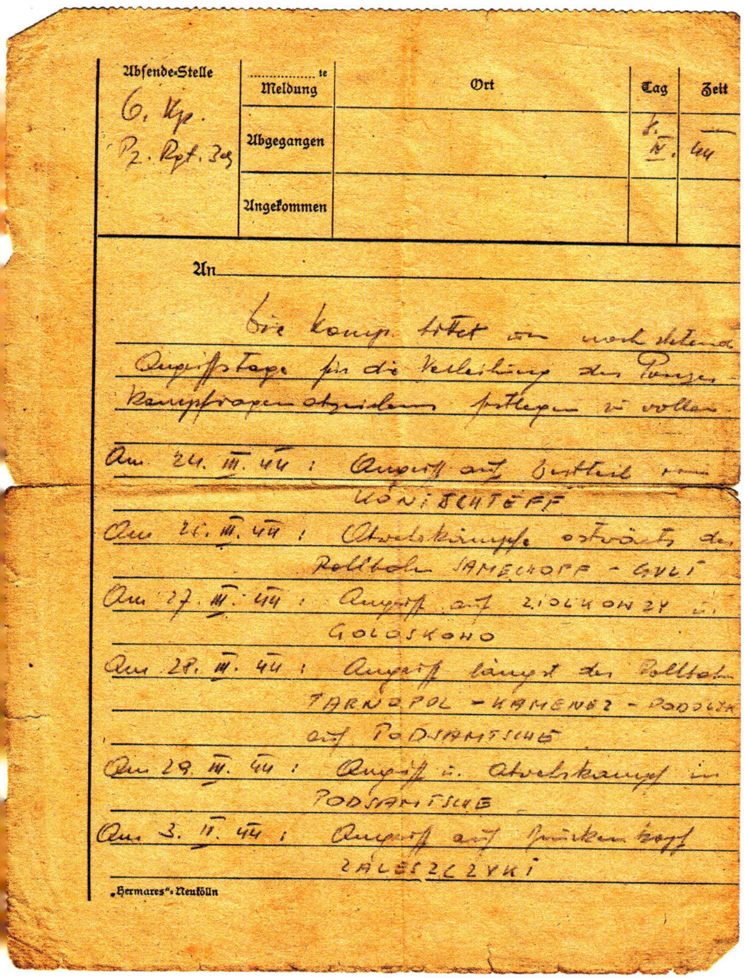

Absende-Stelle	....te Meldung	Ort	Tag	Zeit
6. Kp. Pz. Rgt. 39	Abgegangen		6. IV.	44
	Angekommen			

An

Am 24. III. 44 : Angriff auf Ortsteil von KONISCHTEFF

Am 26. III. 44 : Abwehrkämpfe ostwärts der Rollbahn JAMECHOFF - GULI

Am 27. III. 44 : Angriff auf ZIOLKOWZY u. GOLOSKOHO

Am 28. III. 44 : Angriff längs der Rollbahn TARNOPOL - KAMENEZ - PODOLSK auf PODSAMTSCHE

Am 29. III. 44 : Angriff u. Abwehrkampf in PODSAMTSCHE

Am 3. IV. 44 : Angriff auf Brückenkopf ZALESZCZYKI

„Hermares"-Neukölln

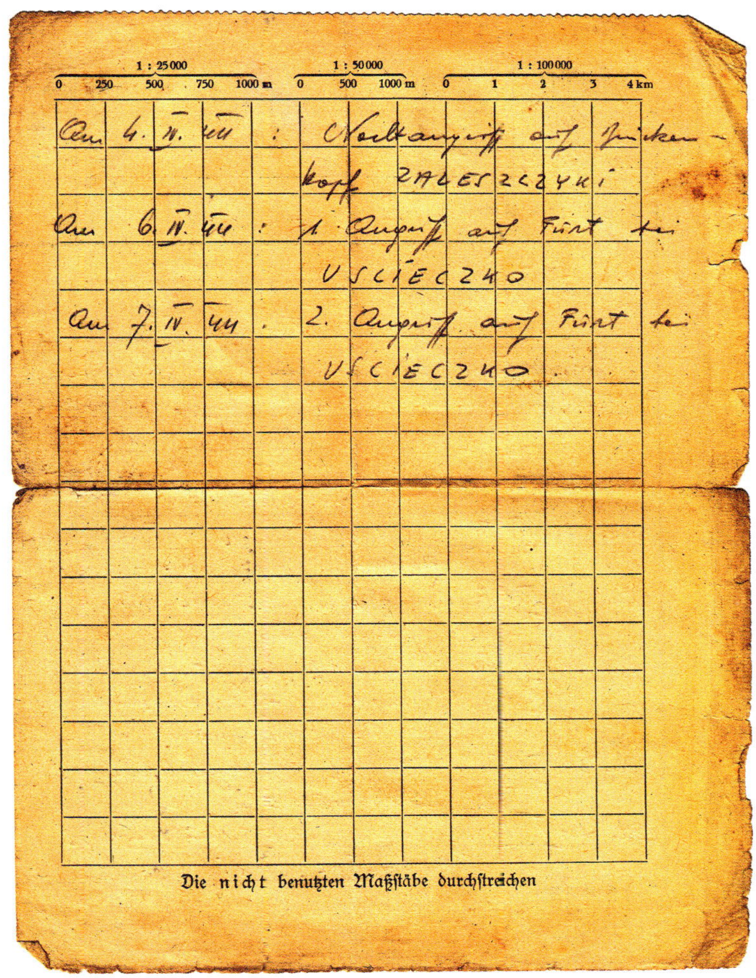

1 : 25000 — 0 250 500 750 1000 m; 1 : 50000 — 0 500 1000 m; 1 : 100000 — 0 1 2 3 4 km

Am 4. IV. 44 : Nachtangriff auf Brückenkopf ZALESZCZYKI

Am 6. IV. 44 : 1. Angriff auf Furt bei USCIECZKO

Am 7. IV. 44 . 2. Angriff auf Furt bei USCIECZKO

Die nicht benutzten Maßstäbe durchstreichen

List of attacks made by 6.*Kompanie* Panzer Regiment 39 in the early part of 1944.

Chapter 12

Diary 2 July 1944 to 13 September 1944

Written in a notebook without cover.

Erich mans an MG 34 set up in an anti-aircraft role. By the barrel sleeve it is one that has been mounted in a tank. Erich wears the M43 Panzer Cap.

Started again after the loss of all my things on 17 July 1944 in DOBRACEF on the Bug near SOKAL-KRYST.... Written up from the 2 - 21 July from my memory.

2 July. Left home, go by horses to Linz. Kammberger Hans picked me up. Arrived in the evening in Vienna; we catch up with all soldiers on leave. Leave passes collected. We're taken in to the arsenal. Stayed overnight.

3 July. To the Rennweg barracks, back to the arsenal; many were kept, going to France or Italy and my unit drawn up. Get my leave pass, but was taken away again, finally, I'm lucky, can go back to my old unit. Go to the Prater, there I meet several of our Kp (Company), Raiber, Sachmann, Vondru, and Beetz, find out here that the Div. is in Romania and that the Spiess is in the field hospital. Many of our company are here. Fldw. Brückner went to Romania today. However, I've got to go back to PRZEMYSL. Div is to be transferred again, where to? Departure from Vienna at 11.30 PM. Was at the cinema: Blutzeugen "weil ich dich liebe" (Martyrs … because I love you). Saw it twice.

4 July: Travelled through Oderberg, Lindenburg, stopped outside of Krakow, Heldenklau, caught again, Tanks …. But can go on. In Tarnow I see our Josef, he waves and I wave, but that's all. Arrive in PRZEMYSL, report in, but nobody knows anything about our Div, stay here and report in again tomorrow. Went out to the cinema in the evening: Johann. Went for a bit of a walk. Went to bed. Uffz. Hansk from repair shop and I in a parked train, 1st class.

5 July. Wakened up and the train is moving; we got out quickly because it was travelling slowly, go to the camp, make the acquaintance of a Red Cross nurse, arrange to meet her and meet in the afternoon. Go to the cinema "die Kochstaplerin." Great woman, married, husband missing for a long time. In the evening at 6 directed on to STRV, said good-bye to both at the train with a kiss, of course.

An endless journey with a slow train begins. All got out in SAMBOR during the night. Wait.

6 July. Went on again to DOB (illegible), got out again, wait all day. Didn't go on again 'til evening, were in the leave station. Endless day. Bed in a private home.

7 July. Travelled to DROWOBIETSCH, got off again. In the evening on to STRV. Arrived at night, reported in, have to go to STANISLAV back to the old area. Stay overnight here, Hansl and I in a private house again. In the morning the train is overfull, can't go onwards 'til afternoon. There Uffz. Gernhardt, Rudolf, Gruss, and Neumann arrive. Hansk and I go into the town, get to know a W.H. (*Whermacht Heer* - Army) helper, also quite nice. Several of the ABT (*Abteilung*) now here. Arrived in STANISLAV in the evening. Advanced detachment of the Div just here. Report in, but have to come back again tomorrow. Look for private accommodation. Great, then go to the cinema "Johann" again. Later to the leave centre.

8 July. Report in, sent on to TLUMAC to the old battle area. Departure not until midday. Go to the leave centre, meet a few of the ABT (Obfldw. Raab, Abschirrer, Deissinger, etc). At midday travelled on by slow train. That was some journey, in a cattle wagon, jammed together. Dreadful! Got off near TLUMAC. How do we go on from here? Then horses arrive. Nothing else but to get on with it. Go a bit, then we meet a vehicle from the ABT that takes on. Then we learn the most surprising thing: new formation of the ABT in ROMANIA, 6 Company has been disbanded, became a supply company. Weapons came to the reconnaissance platoon in the HQ company, the other people home to St. Polten. The ABT had to send home more than 200 men, according to a new order. Each Company no more than 9 tanks. Reconnaissance detachment should have 9 but does not have as many. Those on leave mostly sent home! And what will happen to us?? Arrive. Ltn. Kohlberger directs us to 7 Company as Hptm. Kloss with V (Supply) Company is not yet here from Romania. Look for billet with Uffz. Neuworth, Gef, Feber from ObLtn. Wolfl (7 Kp.), Hptm. von Kunendorf (5 Kp.), Hptm. von Lebezow (Reconnaissance), Obtln. Krall (4 Kp.), Hptm. Kloss (V-Kp.), ObLtn. Kuhne (HQ), Obfldw. Grosse to St Polten.

9 July. 1 AM alarm. Get ready again immediately, vehicles being loaded up. We got up at 6 AM as march off was not until then. We're going with Obfldw. Strauß in his tank. In the town! We stand for a long time, in the afternoon in boiling hot temperature again, on to STANISLAV. We got out here for a bit. Ltn. Mang greets me (4 Kp) now. Go to the newly-opened brothel. Unbelievably busy, and you meet half the ABT there. Great women here. ObLtn. Krall is just sorting out the people who are going home to St Polten, sending old people away (Fldw. Hartmann, Hederich, Uffz. Meindl, Fenzl, etc). Away at night. We're in the cattle truck, meet Uffz. Vogelsang.

10 July. In LEMBERG we stand for a long time. We sunbathe. With the crew are also ObLtn. Wölfl, Uffz. Lornez from Linz, Faber, all great guys. Then onwards to the north, where to? No one knows!! Königsberg? All sorts going on!!

11 July. Go to SOKAL on the Bug, unload here in the early morning, now going by Muli and Elefant, which belong to our Kp. V Kp (Supply Company) not here yet. We stay in the pub all afternoon, meet Burgstoller and Knitzler. Then go with them. We look for the ABT and come to 4 Kp, go with them up front. Now over the border in Russia again. 4 Kp moving in battle formation. What do we want there? It's very very loud here. Must go back again in the evening, to the place where we've already been twice. Stayed overnight with Steuber Rudi.

12 July. Supplies. Our Gef Hptm. Kloss and Ltn. Opelik and Ltn. Kleie, who all belong to 4 Kp. Gef takes me back to the Komp in the *Kubelwagen*. Go through SOKAL along the Bug to DOBRACEF near KRISTVNAPOL. Schauder and several others are here. Move in with Obflw. and Stauber. Immediately get a mission to signpost the road. Back in the evening. Seek out the old ones in the evening.

13 July. Read my mail. So I am with V Kp. (supply Company) as chief radio operator. Gublinge from HQ Kp sent to me, great guy. I tidy up my things. Uffz. Grün is the ABT quartermaster. Move into a new billet, a nice one. Get settled in. In the billet, Obfldw. Geillinger, Zitek, Neumann, Orgowasch, and I. Radio and everything there. Reisinger Hansi and others visit me.

14 July. ABT in action. All sorts going on up front. So much aircraft activity, never seen it like that. Uffz. Hager Rudi dead, Uffz. Neuwirte, Burgstoller, and Ltn. Kleie all wounded by aircraft. As medium wave radio operators are Gefr. Karbaum, Hassler, Petik, and Bayer. Search out a few remaining old ones. Write a few letters.

15 July. Up front all sorts of things going on. Hptm. von Lebezow dead, ObLtn. Wölfl and his whole crew dead. Direct artillery hit. Several Pz (tanks) knocked out. Gef fallen. There's plenty going on there.
We've started with medium wave ϟ (Signals) training. In the village there is also a wedding. Every day people come on leave. Uffz. Willi Webel, tomorrow there will be a drive back to St Polten.

16 July. Heavy fighting up ahead. Russians pushing us back a bit. We give up a bit of ground. Gef of 5 Kp Hptm. von Kunersdorf dead, all of 4 Kp knocked out, ObLtn. Krell wounded. They had to blow up 5 tanks (to prevent capture by the enemy). 4 Kp have no more Pz (tanks) at the front. These are really hard operations. Everything going to pot. 5 Kp had 2 Pz blown up. Ltn. Eckhard also knocked out. Fldw. Krüger changed over, now here in the repair shop. (Rübig, driver) arrived from St Polten. Obfldw. Breithard, Uffz. Schwarz. To 4 Kp, Fldw Hering, Uffz. Bissinger 5 Kp who were out in the winter. We are doing ϟ training. Got our own vehicle and loaded up. Obgefr. Süssenstock - driver.

(The Brody pocket had trapped 40,000 German troops. 17.Panzer Division was part of the force trying to relieve it.)

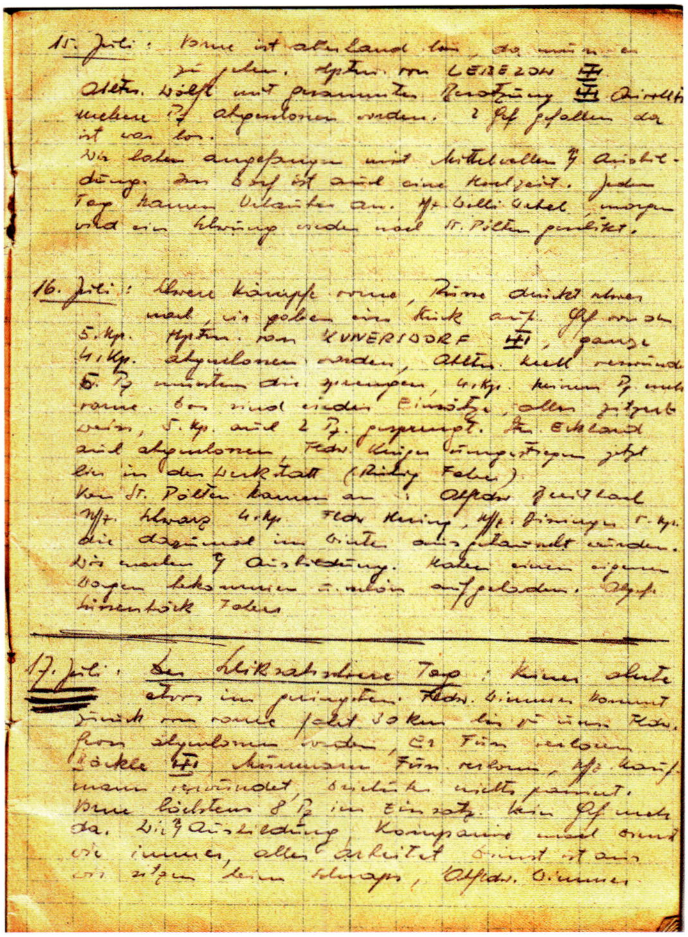

Diary page for "The most awful day."

17 July. *The most awful day.* Nobody had the slightest idea. Fldw. came back from the front, drove 30km to us. Fldw. Gross knocked out. He's lost his foot. Böckle dead. Hussmann lost his foot, Uffz. Kaufmann wounded, nothing happened to Deichüter. At the front at most 8 tanks in action. No Gef there any more. We have ϟ training. Kp doing duty as usual, everyone working. Duty is finished. We're sitting with Schnaps, Obfldw. Wimmer, Obfw., Fldw. Harteich, Uffz. Rübig, Uffz. Brandstätter, Uffz. Deichüter, Fldw. Brückner has just said that he has just been shot at on his way back from foraging. Someone was firing close by, once, twice. Everyone said that repair shop is doing some adjustment firing, then there was a loud bang close by. The Fldw. came running, the bomb crater was beside the shooting range and tore the Gef Lang to pieces - dead - direct hit! Now we're all astonished. The order get ready immediately. Russians have broken through. We're 30km behind the front line. Russians with tanks over the Bug and in the forest. Vehicles ready and loaded up, then begins continuous firing - all tanks firing, we can't believe our eyes, 2 T-34s going through the middle of the village and block the road back. No vehicle can get out. Infantry following on behind. T-34s come slowly backwards firing like mad. What can we do, nothing other than run into the cornfields. Everyone runs just as they are. Over the fences, Bissinger and I together to the cemetery. There 2 T-34s in front of us and getting ready. We go back. Houses are now burning down. We're just about the last. Over a hill to the next village, being shot at the whole time. Gef Budra of 5 Kp dead. A tank of ours is knocked out on the right of me. Nothing happened to crew of Obfldw. Canz. 1 tank further ahead got a direct hit in the turret, learn later it was Rübig's vehicle. Commander. Fldw. Harteich hopped it. Vehicle goes on, all repair shop vehicles, so not ready for action. Gerik has the *Kubelwagen* from the repair shop. Ahead, behind, right and left the craters. Schlächter comes - our own and fires. Left of me a T-34 on fire. We run for our lives through water that came over our knees and on through the fields 'til we got over the hill. Here 6 infantry from a replacement battalion who have also just about-turned. Are we glad and also exhausted that we're out of the range of the T-34 and MG (machine gun fire). All anyone has is what they are standing in. We march on. Soon it will be dark. 2 assault guns are here but also retreating. Geiblinger, Petek, and I climb on. It's raining. We're perished with cold, all our boots full of water. Who cares. We're completely exhausted. At 12 midnight the convoy is standing still, everything in a mess, we go into a house, take off all our clothes, leave them to dry and go to sleep. Obgefr. Janisch also missing. We assume he's dead. (The attempted relief attempt on the Brody pocket by 17.Panzer Division and 16.Panzer Division had failed, and Soviet reserves were counterattacking. XIII Korps, which had been trapped, was totally destroyed on 22 July. 17,000 Germans were taken prisoner. Some of the trapped troops did breakout to the German lines.)

18 July. At 6 AM I'm up and about, look out of the window, not a soul to be seen. We get dressed, and go, the whole village empty. We make sure that we get away as quickly as possible, on foot to BELEC; here finally everyone here, repair shop and everyone from our Company, but ¾ of us missing. Gef not here. Take an LKW (Lorry) and drive up again with Uffz. Dattler and several LKW drivers. We try to get there. En route we meet Obfw. Ganz, Fldw. Kotz, then Ltn. Vrede, Obschirrer, Griesinger. We drive on, then Ltn. Vrede, Fldw. Kotz. 1 Fldw. from the HQ, Uffz. Dattler and I go on foot to the previous god-forsaken place, but don't go in, walk round to the left. Our village is alight, there is firing on the right of us in the market place, T-34 again. We turn back and run for our lives through the cornfield; running here exhausts you, boy oh boy, in the field you see rifles suddenly looming up. We thought they were Russian, but who is it? Fldw. Brückner with 20 men who were in the infantry. We go back together. Russians come chasing after us. Gef is still down with the Pz (Tank) where the repair shop was. Then we go back with the tracked vehicle, the others with a MTW (troop carrying vehicle). In BELEC everyone is getting out. Us too, to WAREZ, a bit further north, en

route had got lost and we were left on our own there. The two half-broken Pz go out of action and stop. Fldw. Kotz leads the rest - 7 LKW. We keep going to HRUBIECOW, 60km north, absolutely no vehicle from our Div is to be seen here. Everyone is getting out of here too. We head off westwards to ZAMOSK; we're not left alone here, a strong partisan area. We're a bigger convoy, after 7 o'clock no more vehicles. *Inspektor* Müller now running the show. We find quarters. Uffz. Nassar (7 Kp) and I have already picked up two girls. We went to the billet, great they're ethnic Germans, but we already have marching orders. There are a lot of Germans here, also shops, businesses, register office, everything here. Food's good here and I have a great bed. Nassar sleeps next door. Yesterday and today I have run for my life and in the evening I'm sitting with a pretty 21 year old girl and buttering her up. Life is funny indeed.

19 July. We have to be there at 5 AM. Want to go to TOMASKOW. *Inspektor* Müller now travelling alone. We have to wait 'til he comes back. Nassar and I are going into the town. Great. Everything here. You can have everything and we've got lots of money. All Germans are leaving today. When we were in the middle of the town a German man came running up and asked what we are doing! He asks us to become witnesses to his marriage. Nothing like that has ever happened to me before. We do him this favour, of course, although we are wearing battledress and are quite dirty. But it has to be quick for him. Have never been to one before but it will be alright. She is a shopkeeper, he is a pub landlord. Everything goes well and we joined in with them. Look for the brothel but it doesn't open 'til 2 o'clock, we go to the civilian brothel. Here it looks like in the underworld but the women just great, sweet Poles, spent the whole morning here. Made the best use of it. Departure should be at midday, again nothing, went to bed, am quite exhausted. Feet like lead. Sleep 'til 4 o'clock, then to the hairdresser, then to the old billet, girl from the shop also here again. She's in charge of the entire baker's shop, earns good money. Sleep there again. Don't go into the town again.

20 July. Up at 7. 8 o'clock departure, have to go to KORMANOW, everything is gathering there. Get fuel in the town first. There also see the woman that we were with from the civilian brothel, really nicely dressed, even elegant. You can see women here, just the thing. I also meet the girl form the billet again. Finally departure. Driving, it's quite easy-going in large convoys of ethnic Germans who are making their way back. Then we meet our forward supply line with Fldw. Brückner etc, wait here, then comes along our Gef. The Kp is also following on, the few vehicles we have, they are sitting on the drivers' cabs and on the running boards. Find out even more. Fldw. Hartlich was taken prisoner, fled and was shot, dead. Civilians told us. Gef Neumann dead, 5 others dead and missing. Where's Schnauder? Our LKW also to pot, W u G (weapons and equipment) also, kitchen retrieved but the Russians have plundered everything. Uffz. Lang (clerk) was also taken prisoner. He got away during a Stuka attack and came back to us. Civilians said that the Russians have taken several of us prisoner. They took all their boots away and their trousers. Am curious to know how many still are missing. We've just stopped and we've just got to march off again. There's never been such a situation before. Ari is coming into the village with us. Now we're staying here. Such a mess!!

21 July. 2.30 awake, immediate march off. Left of where we are, very loud roaring. Good, then we'll go away. Orderly room and pay sergeant with money, all lost, Ivan's got it. What we've got on is all we have. Travel via ZAMOSK, westwards to SWERSHINESS, lovely little town, a really great billet!! Finally can get a really good wash. But we've still got to count on marching off soon. Everything retreating. Komp fall in, and established who all is missing. Are quite a lot of us: Schnauder, Voghauger, Reisinger, Rüdel, etc. Where can they be? At midday advance detachment away, we're away at 2 o'clock. Going northwest. Towards LUBLIN, near TURVBIN billets. Still had to go through a partisan forest with weapons ready for firing, nothing happened, have Pz with us. (Partisans would have no weapons to take on tanks). The convoy before us was shot at. 7 LKW kaput. Immediate halt, everyone fall in, Pz crews 17 needed, not so many here as 4 Kp is sitting in JAROSLAV. Pz to be had in ZAMOSK. ABT still has 1 Pz IV in action, 14 km east of ZAMOSK. That's as far as we've got. Billets. Me, immediately on guard duty and therefore get a sleep. Here a big partisan area.

22 July. Nice place but everyone here partisans. Otherwise nothing happening! Hot day, other units just arriving, bringing our assault guns, then another anti-aircraft workshop. Here we are again, to be ready for march off, how can this go on then? Obfldw. Hager has been up at the front since yesterday at 6 AM with the Gef. Supposed to go there apparently. We're currently 45km southeast of LUBLIN. Was at the Gef meeting. Nothing like this has happened before, front broken up, no one really knows what's going on. The Russians appear here with tanks and then somewhere else. Where we were yesterday, 40 T-34s have now come there. Then they've put down airborne troops in the forests, you're not safe anywhere. Russians are appearing everywhere. We must see that we reach the Vistula on time, otherwise we're KiK north and south of us, he's on the same hill already. Everything is in such a muddle. Div is pushing northwards to head off a spearhead. Tanks are already in action. Tomorrow I've got to go to the front and fall in as acting master radio operator. Obfldw. Hager also back in the evening. In ZAMOSK all sorts of things were being pinched. There's beer. This place here is ROSKI near ZIOLKIENKA.

23 July. Awake at 4 AM. Ready for march off. My orders - to go up to the battle detachment with Obgefr. Schindelar. V-Wagen with canteen goods, but have to search for the battle group, got given a map and then we were off. Went via ZIOLKIENKA to GOROSK, then a lane to IZBILA, then 5km further on, here in a wood the whole ABT. Report to Kdr ObstLtn. Gave out goods. I don't need to stay here,

go back. Obfldw. Wimmer and Uffz. Brandstätter go with me. Ltn. Mang with a tank Gonders with alternative crew also with us. We travel further on alone. Road completely blocked with *Bespannten* units (horse-drawn, as was about 80% of the German Army. This slow moving traffic could prove a problem for the faster motorized units), 291 I.D., Ski Div. (291. Infantry Division and a Ski Division). Our *Bespannten* units an endless convoy. It was moving along slowly and each one stubborn 'til the cows come home. Finally in the afternoon back in our old billet. No other soul still here. Now have to look for our Kp. On the road it looks like the whole Front is in the middle of being disbanded, simply terrible. Everyone's making sure they get over the Vistula. Try to drive further to WYSOKIE via TURABIN, everything is turning back there. T-34 firing at TURABIN. We turn round back through our town, through the partisan area in the forest to WYSOKIE, a small town in the middle of the forest. Already 9 at night, we have to stay overnight. *Bespannte* also here, pouring with rain, it's lousy. We've just got settled when firing begins Kauz and Geier, alarm, partisans are coming. Finally it was only half as crazy. Stayed overnight. Load up 9 wounded. ObLtn. Figil seriously wounded by partisans.

24 July. Moved on early. Road just a quagmire that you get through. There is a lot of stuff lying around from infantrymen who've been attacked here, pieces of uniform, vehicles, etc. We get stuck here for 4 hours, everyone says to set it on fire, but we worked and got out. On we went to WYSOKIE, reporting centre, don't know anything, go on to KRASSNIKI, only through lanes and fields. Everything full of *Bespannte* convoys. Are lucky and get through. KRASSNIKI report in to Major Hermann, get sent on to ANAPOL on the Vistula. The repair shop has been sent on there. Stragglers are all being cashiered. Over the Vistula to OZAROW. Dropped out on the way, no fuel. No LKW gives us fuel. Our General v. d. Meden (17.Panzer Division Commander) comes by and asks what's wrong. I tell him and *he* gives me 20 litres of fuel. First rate, I can say. It's already pitch dark. In OZAROW handed over the wounded and looked for a billet. Town really lovely.

"Advance in the Steppe." Quagmire roads.

25 July. Drive on and finally get to our Komp. Hand over the note from ObstLtn. Weiss to the Gef and organise the ϟ station (Signals station). Fldw. Schnauder here. Voglsauger, Reisinger in St Polten with the whole of 4 Kp. Here's something - Geiblinger and I set up the ϟstation. ABT in action, first attack 4 Pz IV lost. Fldw. Fahnenzucker, Piffl Wilfried (Linz) dead, Gef Breier, *Richtschütze* dead. Obfldw. Wimmer handed over the car to him yesterday. Situation not yet clarified. Wonder if all the troops will get out of this mess? Try all day to get through. No luck. New command for order to salute (the troops were to give the Nazi salute after the bomb attempt on Hitler's life to prove loyalty) still "*Deutscher Gross*." Got washed again. We still haven't got any clothes. No one can change their underwear. What a life. How will it go on? Set up a B-set (type of radio) in order to be able to hear the news. We're in JANOWICE near OPATOW.

26 July. Still no connection, otherwise nothing happening here. Each of us got 2 pairs of socks today. Gave the radio LKW a good tidy. Continue training. ABT Kmdr. ObstLtn. Weiss also here. 8 tanks were still in action. Explore whether there are possibilities for loading here at the train station. We're to be loaded up again. Where to? We suppose to REICHSHOF. In the evening Dr Göbbels gives a really good speech and the information about the *Führer* assassination attempt. Interesting. Hopefully things will now be different. Have guard duty.
(On 20 July 1944 a bomb was exploded during a staff meeting at the *Wolfsschanze* near Rastenburg, East Prussia, by Colonel Claus von Stauffenberg. He was a leading member of a group of officers who plotted to kill Hitler and take power to stop the war.
Four officers were killed, but Hitler was saved by the stout oak table. Afterwards the *Gestapo* arrested over 7,000 people; about 4,980 were executed, and others who knew of the plot, like Rommel, were forced to commit suicide. This destroyed the resistance movement, but Hitler and the Nazis stayed paranoid about the army.)

27 July. My birthday; a day just like any other. Otherwise nothing much happening. Whole Abt is to come here and load up. Wimmer and Steuber visiting, beer. Drink some wine and Schnaps. At home there have been the first bombings. 500 USA bombers. Curious to know what is going on. Göring Works. Otherwise it's quiet here. Training - go to the workshop with the radio set. All sorts of things going on up at the bridgehead. A few of our tanks knocked out again. Obgefr. Dank seriously wounded. Lost an eye. Today busy with the Abt up front. Sent a few messages. ObGefr. Lehrer and StabsGefr. Kendert arrived this evening.

28 July. Training in the morning. Early on Company lecture. March off should be today at 17.00. Just heard that our tanks had to turn round again, as Russians have broken through again near KRASSNIK. We are holding a bridgehead here. How long will we be able to hold it? I got 2 letters from Jüptner Toni. He's already on his way to the Infantry. Lots of us have joined - Raiber and Kellner and Uffz. Klaniecker too. Now the time has come to move off, it's raining again. Advance V-detachment also arrived here, lots of work. Radio came. 2nd radio set will be set up with Ltn. Opelik. Hahn and Düber from HQ Company have to take it over. At 2.15 march off via SABOTKA - SANDOMIERS - MIELICZ to DEBICA.

29 July. 2.15 march off, pitch dark and rain, awful journey. But then lovely asphalt road, drive to DEBICA, lovely town, then turned back and moved down into a small village. Set up our radio. Took it down again in the evening. Advance detachment – ObLtn. Hager went off again. Where to? This place here bombarded. The Russians are already behind us again in the north and the south. We're stuck again. How is it going to end this time? When are new troops going to get here? The 23 PD, 24 PD, 3 PD, and GD (*Grossdeutschland*) have arrived with us. The way things are here you can't work it out. I've never experienced anything like this in all the 3 years I've been in Russia. Everything's going wrong everywhere under the sun. I hope the situation changes soon. Will we be able to halt the Russians at the Vistula? Otherwise we'll find ourselves at the Oder!! (Erich has realised that the Soviets can push into Germany itself. On the previous day the Soviets had arrived at the Polish border, and on the 29th had reached the Baltic sea, cutting off Army Group North in Estonia and Latvia.)

"Company comrades. Left Heuer Franzl Uffz., then Weiss, then Usach, who fell on the 29.7.44."

30 July. Last night some of our LKW went to Reichshof foraging, brought back 72,000 cigarettes, 300 litres of sour milk, lots of boxes of red wine and apple juice, etc. Gef says I have to take our LKW immediately to the new accommodation area. Drove via DEBICA - ROPLYCE - SEDZISCOW to SIELEC. Set up the radio. Here lovely quarters, could easily spend some time here. Company not leaving here 'til 12.30. It's Sunday. Great music on the radio. At 2 o'clock the Abt arrives. If I hear correctly what the situation is, the Russians are firing into REICHSHOF. The railway from SANDOMIERS - DEBICA has already been disrupted. Our tanks cannot get to us at all. 23km from here to REICHSHOF, we'll probably get away from here tomorrow, as we can't lose any more LKW, otherwise we'll be walking. Who on earth will be able to stop the Russians? In the evening, 2 radio messages came from I.G. (*im Generalsstab* – General HQ): 10.30 immediate departure. Travel via SEDZICZOW - KOPCZYZE - DEBICA.

31 July. After DEBICA stopped on the road, then pulled into a few houses on the left of the road. Obfldw. Hager drove up ahead. We set up the radio. Something must happen soon or we'll be sitting back in the Reich. Surplus people being sent to the base. Otherwise not much happening. Whole day radio operations. Learned new cipher procedure. Rainy day. Curious to know when things will change. The mood is quite bad here with us. We're supposed to get some mail. Today got one letter, the first since 1 June from home. We've still been given nothing to wear, still running around in the same clothing. It's the same for all of us, nothing to change into. Today pinched 2 geese. In the evening ate really well, drank nice wine afterwards. Gef has just come and joined us, also had something to eat and drink. Played Skat 'til 12 o'clock. On radio stand-by during the night.

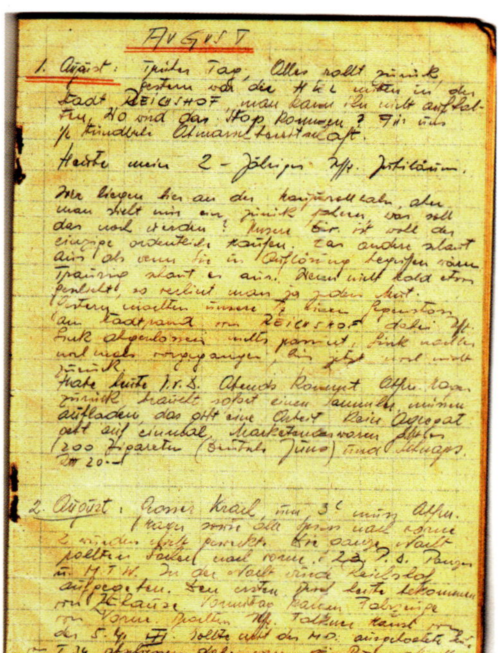

1 August 1944 diary page.

AUGUST

1 August. Dismal day. Everything is moving back. Yesterday the HKL (main line of resistance) was in the middle of the town of REICHSHOF, you can't stop it. Where will the stop come? We have to be ready for march off at half an hour's notice. Today my second anniversary of being Uffz. We're sitting here on the main runway. We realise we're retreating. What is going to come of it next? Our Div is the only bunch in good order. The other looks as if it might be disbanded. Things look dismal. If something doesn't happen soon then we'll lose heart. Yesterday our tanks made a counter attack at the edge of REICHSHOF, Uffz. Link knocked out, nothing happened. Afterwards Link went back up front, not yet back. Am officer of the watch. In the evening Obflw. Hager back, needs an assembler immediately, have to charge it up, that's a lot of work. Suddenly everything goes quiet. There are canteen goods, 200 cigarettes - deutsche Juno and Schnaps, 20 bottles.

2 August. Huge noise, at 3 o'clock Obflw. Hager as well as all the Spiess to go up front. 2 of us were not wakened. All night long things were moving to the front. 23 P.D. tanks and MTW. During the night REICHSHOF was surrendered. Got my first letter from home today. In the morning vehicles were coming back from the front. They brought Uffz. Falkner Hansi from 5 Kp - dead. Was trying to shoot down targeted people from a T-34 with the MP (sub machine gun), but the Russians were faster. Uffz. Link here again. Obflw. Hager again here, needs a new transmitter, another one broken. In the morning charged up the assembler. Load of work. A few radio messages came again. Otherwise not much happening. Have a bath in the evening. Obflw. back again. Fröbl Sepp also back, going on to the base.

3 August. All night long things were moving up to the front. Tiger, Panther from 23 PD. Write a few letters in the morning. Gef comes, says we'll probably be moving back a bit again at midday. Still dismal weather, no trace of summer. At 3 o'clock move off, have just had a good lunchtime nap. Travelled via DEBICA - TARNOW - SGORWIZA near TARNOW. It's raining. Billet not good. Everything stowed away. Immediately set up our radio position. In the evening our ABT commander came. Today a celebratory meal for us. Lehner cooked a hare and a chicken with potato salad and soup, then a bottle of wine. Gef comes and has a bite to eat with us, also treats us to a great bottle of white wine. Afterwards filter coffee. Fröbl Sepp also here with us. 12 o'clock to bed.

4 August. Saturday. Dismal day. Otherwise nothing special happening. 3 PZ (three tanks) in action at the front. Do radio training. A mess. There are canteen goods - wine, R6 cigarettes, biscuits, etc. In the evening made myself a great meal - salted roast potatoes with eggs, gherkin, and potato salad, soup, and filter coffee with biscuits, then 2 bottles of wine. Gef also here again. He always arrives in good time.

5 August. A nice day again. Write a few letters. Otherwise nothing happening. In action - 10 Pz IV. Now it looks a

lot better for us. The situation has changed. Things are stabilising for us more at the front. Played skat in the evening.

6 August. Sunday. Got post again. Lovely weather. I think summer is now arriving. Until now only had rain. Otherwise nothing special happening. Today we're supposed to be finally getting clothing. There are quite splendid girls here but not down here with us. I can't get away. Endless duty. Write a few letters. That's the whole of Sunday!! Today arrived from St Polten those who had been taken back: Ltn. Kleishaut, Hptfldw. Kaupke from 4 Kp. Of ours: Uffz. Voglsanger, Zier, and a few boys. Gef gives them a terrible telling-off.

7 August. Black Monday. Lovely hot day. During the night a great fire fight, Flak and bombs. Do training. Take 30 messages error free, at a speed of 40 there's still something wrong. Otherwise nothing happening. Drive to TARNOW to the baths, then stroll around for an hour, lovely women here, go to the cinema "Leichtes Blut," very good, afterwards to the soldier's leave centre, also lovely girls. Radio very busy. Back at 9 o'clock.

8 August. Received clothing. Lots of radio activity. In the afternoon whole Abt assembles in black (Panzer uniform). ObstLtn. Weiss-Karanke gives out some decorations. Also speaks about the situation. According to statements from Poland, they want to make some kind of rebellion here where we are. That means we should have hope. Hot day. Now we have summer.
The whole situation: Russians have turned left from Warsaw, southwards, and are approaching KRAKOW, so far behind us. We're probably going to get into a pocket. But 1 P.D., 16 P.D., 17 P.D., 23 P.D., 24 P.D., and 3 Inf Div are being deployed to thwart and cut off this wedge. We're not going back from here.

9 August. Hot day, lots of radio activity. In the afternoon the radio message came through - it is to be reckoned that today at 16.30 there will be a rebellion of the Poles of the whole general government. We have to secure ourselves for that. But the time passes here and nothing happens. But we can't know. No one can go around unarmed any more. Everyone has to take their rifle to parade. Wonder whether something will come of it. In the evenings we play Skat. Otherwise nothing happening. Obfldw. Volk becomes Hptfldw. from today. In the evening a celebration. 12 men stand guard the whole day. Police are in the next village.

10 August. Muggy day. Visit Weber Willi, who was transferred with a kitchen to 7 KP. Got great sausage. Redid my battle record. Otherwise nothing happening. At the front in action all sorts of things going on. Ltn. Schwarzgruber, ObLtn. Talakerer, and Fldw. Ulrich knocked out. With 3 tanks they had to attack a village in which 10 T-34 were standing. Fldw. Ulrich dead and several more from the Company. Spending the evening with a girl but soon going home. In the kitchen all sorts going on each day.

11 August. Do radio training. Otherwise nothing happening. Got a terrible row from the Gef. Apparently I was supposed to have received a message from I.G. (HQ) at 2 AM. Setting up our own guard 'til 2 AM. Orgomasch comes to us again. At the front we have 2 tanks in action. Of them Obfldw. Canz of 4 Kp knocked out. He's wounded. Post arrived in the evening. Got a letter from Trudi with a photo. Got delicious sausage again from Weber Willi. Got my battle record with signature. I've got 75 (Panzer attacks), the only one who has.

"Remember me fondly. Trudi. Innsbruck 29.7.1944."

12 August. 17 Pz (tanks) will arrive again and almost no one here. A few of ours as well. Orgomasch, Karbaum have to go back. Today is going to be a lovely day again. It will be difficult to get back into a tank again. Lots of radio activity. Otherwise nothing special happening. In the evening we have a lovely roast pork with roast potatoes and we made gherkin salad.

13 August: Sunday. Lovely day. Nothing special happening. Write a few letters. In the afternoon was with the Gef's girl

for a while. In the evening the cooks made a big meal. Just great. Have they got things to eat! We had everything and drank a load of wine. Lots of girls here. A harmonica player from HQ Company and a gramophone and we had a great dance. Often dance with G (unreadable name), good dancer. During the night it rained.

14 August. Lots of radio activity. Lovely day. Bad midday meal. Gef gave Fldw. Bruckner a terrible telling-off. Go swimming and to the cinema in TARNOW, met great girls there again. Girls from the front theatre of 23. Pz. Div. Was top-rate. That was something!!! Afterwards to the leave centre. Beer, Schnaps, and a meal. In the evening more radio activity. 17 Pz (tanks) have arrived, with ObLtn. Krell and Kellner Otto, Raiber also there. Hardam from Uffz. training school also with them. Mangold on leave still. Lots of radio messages because of that. From HQ Company Schadanix has gone off. Hit and run. Was supposed to go to the Straf Kp. (*StrafKompenie* – a unit of soldiers who had broken rules.)
(The Soviets had started an offensive from their Vistula bridgeheads. 17.Panzer Division was one of the German units assembled to try to repulse the attacks.)

15 August. The tanks are still here. Abt commander comes and promotes Lurich to Uffz., Schnauder Adolf as *Richtschütze* (Gunner), and Schleier to *Ladeschütze* (loader). There's a whisper about transferring to East Prussia!!! Ltn. Lois Hollinger also here, spent 3 hours with me and we chatted about everything. He's got married, his old sweetheart, Käthe. He's a great guy. However wants to get away from us again. Commander lets him go as he is going to SS Div Hitler Youth. Uffz. Heinrich Seufert also here, come to the reconnaissance group.
In the evening Gef promotes Geiblinger Hans to Uffz. Overjoyed, of course. Now there are two of us as Uffz. The tanks are moving off tonight. We had two hours radio duty because of this. Tanks already loaded. Maybe to East Prussia? Or even to the South of France? For the moment everything is uncertain. Obgefr. Sacherl and Schtz Brenzek came back from Pz radio operator training course.

16 August. All night activity, endlessly to the Gef. Half hour warning for march off. It's again come to having to move back. No password this time. Lovely day again. Radio activity. In the evening went for a walk with Höllinger Lois (Ltn.) and Brückner Martin, then went to Steuber Rudi and Seifert and drank beer and Schnaps. Chatted 'til 11 o'clock. We're definitely off tomorrow.

17 August. 7 AM march off via KRAKOV, a beautiful city. You can see very elegant women here, lots going on there. Journey continues to KIELCE and we are staying here overnight. Whole Abt in 2 houses. High risk of guerrillas here, all sorts going on here. In the evening at 9.00 still on alert. Discovered the neighbouring house, 20 year old girl, great woman.

18 August. Staying here all day, and there is maybe something going on. Round about us, wherever you go in private there are women. There are about 10 in the area. There was fun all afternoon. You can meet the whole Abt there. Great women. I've never experienced anything like that. We really let off steam. In the afternoon parade and confined to quarters for the whole Abt. A few talked nonsense there. Sitting in the evening in front of our house. A few tarts come by. Crazy things happen there. In the night I went out again but it was already too late. No one has any more money. Hopefully we'll get paid again soon. We only get money once a month on the 21st day of the month.

19 August. Are still here in KIELCE. When will we move on? Have heard that 5 Pz IV have been knocked out by Polish partisans. That really is the limit. In the hinterland there will soon be more shooting than at the front. This bandit activity. We're not allowed to go out, just lying around. 12.30 departure on a road to RAOMVIA- STARACOWICE - KAMIENNA -WITZIK - RUDNIK. This is where we were aiming for. Journey great again. Area very pretty. From the beginning the journey has only been on asphalt roads. This is like at home. Big factories, a business and life. *Kradmelder* (motorcycle messenger) and commanding officer come back from the front. Our Abt cut to pieces during an attack on a Pak-Riegel (anti-tank gun screen with several guns), 12 Pz IV immediately completely lost. All knocked out. 4 Kp there, 15 dead and over 20 seriously and slightly wounded. Amongst them Karbaum dead, Götz missing, Setik and Argomasch seriously wounded, Brandstätter has burns. Fell in with 23 Pz IV, now after 2 days 4 are left. You can say what you like, but you can't launch any more attacks with Pz IV. Otherwise there will be more losses than in an infantry company. We also had bad luck with our car, got stuck in the sand in front of the billet, had to unload everything and pull it out, also had to report to Kdr. Obfldw. cleared off beforehand. Had signal trouble with HQ. Radio connection re-established. A few messages. In the evening Lehner and Bager came back. Now 10 men in a room. Guard duty 'til 4 again.
(17.Panzer Division had broken through to German troops trapped by the Soviet offensives from the Vistula bridgeheads. With other units it tried to push the Soviets back to the Vistula, but this had limited success and was called off on 23 August.)

20 August. Quarrel again early in the morning with the Obfldw. 5 minutes, can't go past without him having something to moan about. Lots of seriously wounded in 4Kp. Obfldw. Breitbach, Uffz. Kietz (lost a leg), Uffz. Fenzl. Fldw. John and *Feldwebel* Schmidt dead. The Russians are firing new tank munitions. The old ones are dying in these brutal attacks. What else will happen to us?
Schramm has come back from the training school, he's also fed up. They had to do infantry training. Schramm visited me in the evening. Told him about Schauder Adi and Brandstätter Lois and chatted. All day combat unit upon unit have been coming in. Here are 1 P.D., 3 P.D., 4 P.D., 16 P.D., 17 P.D., 22 P.D., and 24 P.D. That's just great seeing so many things going to the front. You get a completely different feeling. I wonder if it will be successful. Will

they be able to close the Kessel at ANAPOL-KRASSNIK completely? It is still open for 4km; 17 Div (17.Panzer Division) has got the Russians sitting in there, subdued like mad. The 4km are a bit much.
Our 5 Kp is going back to the Reich in serried ranks, to collect new tanks. Sunday has gone by again. It's been extremely hot as every day. Radio guard duty at night again.

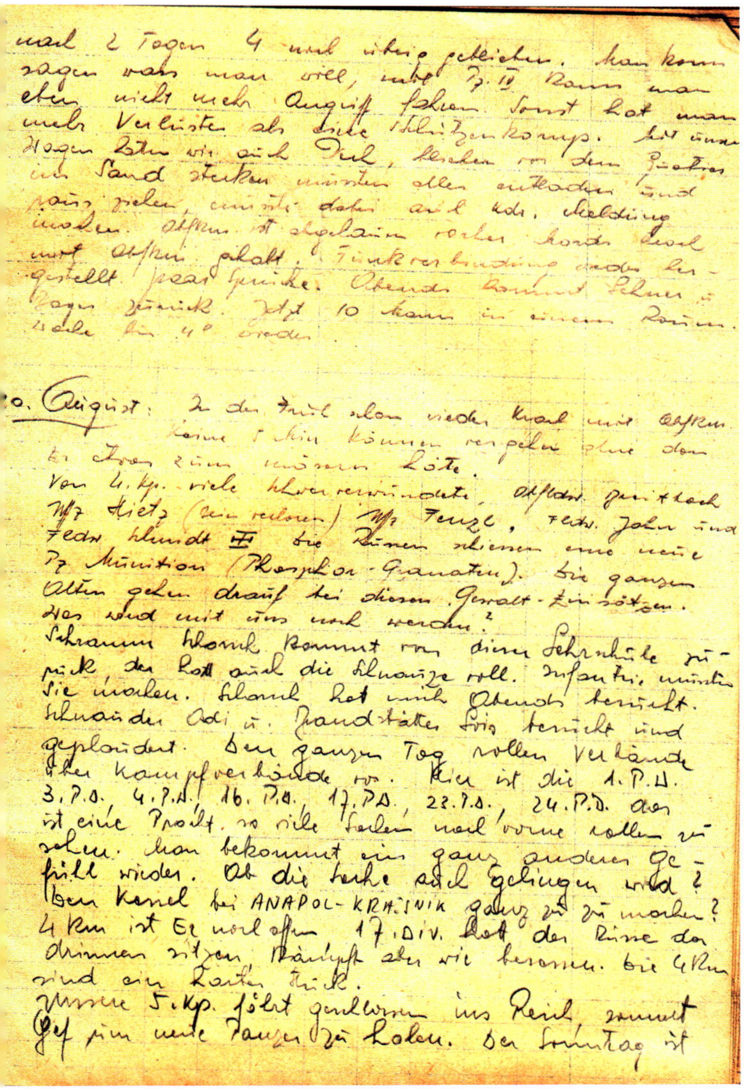

Diary page listing the Divisions involved.

21 August. This is the day of the month when we are paid. Do training, intensified, hot day. There is a lot going on at the front. Today they are bringing in the first <u>Königstiger</u> (King Tiger). That's the tank that you can really do something with. 40 have gone to the front. The attack is beginning today. It's really noisy. In the evening I'm going swimming. Great, pleasant.

22 August. Uffz. Quischen is dead. We still have 4 or 5 Pz IV. Paid today.
Otherwise intensified training. Every day troops are going by. We have all sorts of things. It just can't go wrong. Hot day, going swimming in the evening. Otherwise nothing special going on here. Going back to St Polten tomorrow are Uffz. Heuritsch, Obgefr. Beetz, and 4 of our men. Our infantry captured 40 USA Studebaker LKWs. (American trucks given as war aid to the Soviets.) Approximately 200 of our Pz (tanks) were in the attack. All kinds of things.

23 August. We've got the first post again. Training all day, soon get to speed 70. Hot day. Swimming in the evening, great. Otherwise nothing special happening.

24 August. Training as every day. Hot day. No summer 'til now. Radio activity as usual. Apparently 5 Company has to go to St Polten. Otherwise nothing special happening. Going swimming again. In the evening I went to see Weber Willi. Has a lovely girl in his kitchen. In the evening Ivan is coming bombing as he does every day.

25 August. 2 Pz in action. Uffz. Janichek knocked out and dead with the *Richtschütze* dead. Still one tank at the front, Uffz. Högner. Our ABT commander Weiss-Karanke, ObstLtn., took over leadership of all the tanks of 3 P.D., 2 Tiger ABT, 501, 509, as their Commander was a casualty. In the evening I went again to Willi, helped him slaughter and prepare a pig. Chatted the girl up a bit. Going to the cinema at 6 o'clock. 30 men from the Company, "die lustigen Vagabünden" (The Happy Tramps), a really good film, we killed ourselves laughing, that was just the thing for us infantrymen. Cinema was in a factory which was attacked 3 weeks ago by partisans and is quite badly damaged. On the way home we were bombed by Ivan, the bombs whistled by quite close.

26 August. Our I troop (maintenance) here again. At the front Uffz. Högner also knocked out in the afternoon. *Richtschütze* dead. None of our tanks left at the front. In the afternoon there are canteen goods, wine and cigarettes at MERLORKOVA. At Willi's kitchen, 7 Kp, I drank almost 2 bottles of beer, in a good mood. Today Geiblinger signals tested us. I took 70, Boyer 40, Petek 30. Go swimming with Gotek. There are now 11 of us in the billet. In the evening ate chicken and drank wine. Important messages. The Div is gathering for an attack south of Kamiernov. V detachment (supply) to us tomorrow.

27 August. V detachment arrived. 12 men have come to us as radio attendants. It's Sunday and we have to work all day. Hot day like all the days before. Geiblinger Hans drinking like mad with Lorenz and now sleeping it off in the open air. Take a message from I G (Infantry HQ) alone. Soon we will have march off from here. Tomorrow for sure. Gef at 17.00 to I G (HQ). Hans has slept it off. Going swimming. All radio operators drunk, Lorenz, etc. In the evening quite an important message came for us again. Afterwards visit Bischof and Lorenz, but they've had it. Listen to some great music. Vehicles have to be loaded

up. Fromm N.G. gone ahead as advance detachment. Petek and Mayer from us.

28 August. Loaded up the vehicles. March off is after lunch. Waiting for the radio message from V detachment to find out where we are going. Took down the transmitter at 12.00. 13.15 march off via KAMIENNA - STARACOWICE - KIELCE and 2km further on to DOMASCOWICE. The journey was great. Area is lovely, just like home, lovely roads, pine forests, arrive at 16.30. The greatest joy. We radio operators have a billet for ourselves with 3 beds in it - very nice. Obfldw. in a terrible temper. We couldn't care less. Immediate radio activity again.

29 August. Today, after a long time, dismal weather. Finally a bit of peace and quiet from the Obfldw. Radio activity as ever. Otherwise not much happening. Prehofer Uffz. going home on marriage leave, give him letters to take. Perhaps he'll bring me a parcel back. He comes from St Valentin.

30 August. 8 anti-personnel bombers come and drop bombs and incendiaries on KIELCE, 2km from us. Quite a fire. They leave us in peace. The general situation is now not rosy. You have the feeling that the war will not last too much longer. However, it has to go in our favour. If it went the other way we would be poor wretches.
Radio activity as usual. Otherwise not much happening. Lorenz was here. From 1 September new code procedure in force. Got a buzzer device. It even lulls you to sleep.

31 August. Utmost economy with fuel. The situation in Romania!! (The Soviets had captured the Romanian oil fields at Ploesti on the 29th that the Germans depended on for fuel.) What will the next period of time bring? Fighting already at PLOESTI. What if we lose that? Tonight 4 Pz drove up, 2 knocked out, 2 into the attack, 1 immediately knocked out. Uffz. Seufert Heinrich dead, his first attack as commander. On 14 August he came back from St Polten. Lots of radio activity. In the evening made a great meal.
(17.Panzer Division made a final attack on the Vistula bridgeheads, but the Soviets were too strong and this operation was called off on 5 September.)

1 September. New code, good start, didn't receive any messages. I.G. sign established, thank God. 5 new medium-wave radio operators arrived. Curious to know what they can do. One has come to us, quite a nice boy, 18 years old. Otherwise nothing happening! Lovely weather as usual!

2 September. Lots of radio activity. Gef here a few times, otherwise not much happening all day.
The battle in Finland broken off. Connection to Germany severed. The same in Bulgaria. I'm flabbergasted. I'd never have thought it. What's going to happen next? (Germany's allies, the Finnish and Bulgarians, had changed alliance and sided with the Allies.)

3 September. Sunday. Radio duty as usual. In the afternoon 2 films: "Alles um Gloria" and "in Flagranti," both very nice. I'm now the only one in the billet. The wider picture not rosy, France quite lousy. Curious to know what's going to happen!! In the evening I went to the radio post of Regt 40 (Panzer Grenadier Regiment 40).

4 September. Radio operations. Now cold weather, write 5 letters. Otherwise nothing special happening. One day like all the rest. Got a letter from Father, he writes: Hummer, Fendl, Predl, Weiss from Luftenberg, Lobinger dead. More good friends gone!! Things going on here again. Russians have pushed in a bit again. Our commander is leading a battle group again, Pz IV from 16 P.D., assault guns and our 3 Pz IV.

5 September: Lovely day. Otherwise nothing happening. Gas masks have to be carried. Marching off again tomorrow. Battle detachment already transferred back into the old zone they were in before, near OSTROWICE. Throwing us around again? Advance detachment already gone. Otherwise quiet.

6 September. Not moving off 'til tomorrow at 8 o'clock. Nothing happening all day. Lots of radio communication! The big surprise, in the evening the Obfldw. comes and tells me I have to take over the radio post in the repair shop tomorrow and set it up. My dream becomes reality. I have Gefr. Adam of 4 Kp with me.
Get my own radio post.

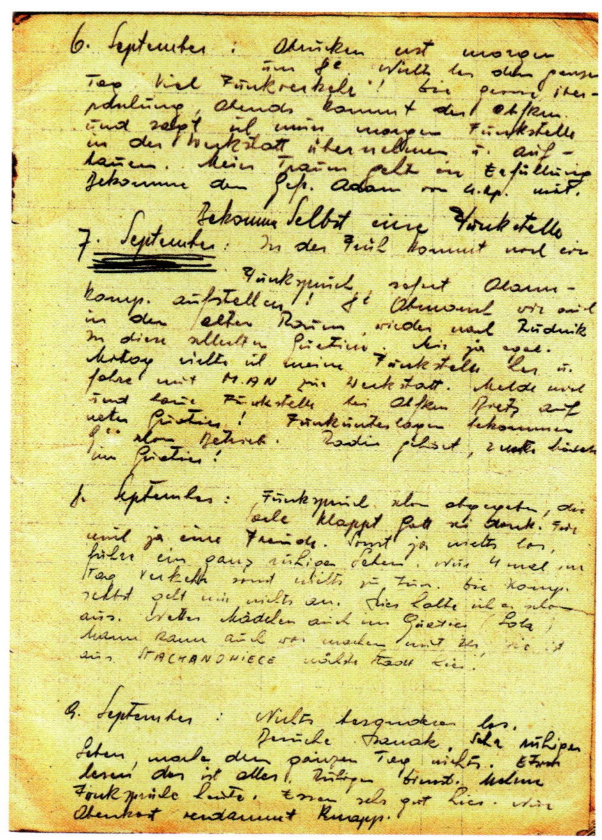

Diary page, "Get my own radio post."

7 September. In the early morning comes another message, set up air raid company immediately! 8 AM march off, we've also got to go into the old zone, back to RUDNIK again. Into the awful billet. Doesn't matter to me. At midday, set up my radio post and go with Man to the repair shop. Report in and set up radio post in a nice billet with Obfldw. Pretz Got radio instructions. Busy working at 9 o'clock. Listened to the radio, 2 nice girls in the billet!

8 September. Already delivered a radio message, the thing works, thank goodness. A pleasure for me. Otherwise nothing happening, leading quite a quiet life. Only activity 4 times a day. Otherwise nothing to do. The Company itself has got nothing to do with me. I'll be able to stand it here. Nice girl also in the billet, Lola. You can have fun with her. She comes from STACHANOWIECE, next town from here.

9 September. Nothing much happening. Very peaceful life, do nothing all day. A bit of reading, that's all. Quiet duty. Take messages today. Food very good here. Only the evening meal is damned meagre.

10 September. Sunday. Quiet here, as with every day. 3 P.D. and some divisions pulled out of here. It's also quieter at this bridgehead of Ivan. Counter attacks were successful. Swim in the river, water still warm. Lots of radio activity today, in the afternoon was vaccinated! Music loudspeaker already for a few days. Danced with Lola. She's a great dancer.

11 September. In the afternoon I sent Adam to the Komp to get post etc. and also a few letters. Otherwise nothing happening all day. It's gradually becoming cold. Football match - team of Uffz, 12:2 for the team. In the evening listened to music and read. There's wine, a bottle for 4 men.

12 September. Already very cold at night. Lovely and warm in the day. We're getting 34 tanks, all of them Panzer IV again. Collection squad already gone to the station. Write a few letters. Otherwise nothing in particular happening. One day goes by like the next. In the evening 17 tanks arrived, from Linz, no people. Celebrate the birthday of Obfldw. Pietz with 2 bottles of wine and fast music. I broke the Company gramophone with it. Obfldw. Klotz was also at the celebration.
(17.Panzer Division had received the Panzer IVs on the 9th.)

13 September. Got a rude awakening. Infantrymen, 3 P.D. come and have lots of men. There was screaming from the women, terrible, went on all afternoon. Gef lets me call, I have to give Gefr. Adam over to 4 Kp as Gef radio operator. The reconnaissance platoon have taken over the tanks, 4 Kp, 7 Kp. today already surrounded. Schnauder Adi at the commanding officer's as *Richtschütze*. He visited me in the afternoon. Warm day again. Very cold at night!

Notes for 2 July to 13 September

Erich starts the diary by noting his loss of possessions, and that he wrote the first part of the diary from memory. He does not seem to have made a bad job of it! This could explain the gap in Erich's records for June 1944. He must have lost the diary or diaries at this point.

The reason for Erich losing his belongings was that the Soviets had encircled XIII Korps near Brody, and 17 Panzer Division was one of the units desperately fighting to free them. Fierce fighting went on through the month of July, but the Soviets were too strong and the relief units were pushed back with heavy casualties.

Leave is an issue again, and Erich is much more uncertain about the Division's mission. The cinema again provides a welcome distraction. Erich continues his interest in girls, but now frequents brothels. Presumably there was not the time to get to know women as he had done in the past. By his account the brothels were popular. I suppose we cannot be surprised, as these were young men at war who could not know if they would live much longer to see their loved ones.

Throughout the diary Erich notes with sadness the loss of the "old ones," i.e. the veterans of the division like Erich. Casualties are heavy in this period, and Erich himself barely escapes with his life from a rampaging T-34 on 17 July.

A happier event occurs on 19 July when Erich is asked to witness the marriage of ethnic Germans. There were many ethnic Germans living in the territories occupied by the Germans and many were forced to join the German army, while others were forcibly repatriated to the Reich.

We can only imagine why Erich calls a civilian brothel "like the underworld," but he describes the women as "sweet." Erich does show a mark of respect for these ladies of the night as he describes how elegantly dressed they were when he met them later. For Erich it seems they replaced girlfriends when they were not available.

Partisans become a very real military threat. Erich relates on 27 July the Soviet practice of reinforcing Partisans with elite paratroops. These were specially trained in raiding and sabotage. Erich states what the Germans commonly found on the Eastern front, that nowhere was safe. Even the well armed Panzer troops were not immune from Partisan/Soviet special forces attack.

On 22 July Erich gets more responsibility as a master radio operator. This is a post that Erich has been after for a while. The next day Erich bemoans the slow progress of the horse-drawn units. As about 80% of the German army was so equipped this was not unusual. It gave them a distinct disadvantage against the fully motorized Allies. The Soviets still had cavalry combat units, however. Other German motorized units often found the same problem when trying to quickly deploy into a new position. It is interesting that it was 17.Panzer Division's commander himself who gave Erich fuel.

On 25 July Erich comments on the bomb attempt on Hitler's life. The next day he listens to Göbbel's account of the incident, no doubt heavily tainted by Nazi propaganda.

Erich cannot have been the only German soldier to notice the worsening military situation on 29 July, and he then realizes that the Soviets could invade Germany. This is why the troops appropriate all they can as shown on 30 July, after which the Soviet threat gets bigger.

On 1 August Erich celebrates his one year anniversary as an *Unteroffizer*. The beginning of August is cheered up with food, drink, and cigarettes, but Erich still records "Black Monday" as the day that the Division took heavy casualties in a previous year.

Erich realizes that the division has a real possibility of being trapped in a pocket with no hope of escape on 8 August. This would have been a worrying thought to any German soldier given the previous pocket battles. An interesting note is the transfer of a soldier to the 12. SS Panzer Division "Hitlerjugend" on 15 August. This *Waffen SS* Division was made up of volunteers and had taken heavy losses in the Normandy battles. Experienced NCOs and Officers from both the *Waffen SS* and army trained and led the young grenadiers from the Hitler Youth, who were commonly aged 17 or 18.

The Panzer IV tank has been described as the "workhorse of the German Army" in WWII. Erich realises that it was not a match for the latest Soviet weapons and ammunition on 19 August He regrets the casualties of his comrades. German industry could not make enough of the Panther or Tiger series of tanks, so the Panzer IV had to be kept in production right up to the end of the war. Erich is impressed with the sight of the heavily armoured and armed King Tiger on the 21st. Although much heavier, this tank only had the same engine as the medium Panther, and this restricted its mobility.

The lack of armour is shown on 20 August when Erich reports tank crew training as infantry. He sarcastically refers to him and his comrades as "infantrymen" on the 25th. This was common in the German armed forces, as specialists, such as *Luftwaffe* air and ground crew without planes and sailors from the *Kriegsmarine* without ships were hurriedly trained as badly needed infantrymen. The lack of time, training, and inclination often had disastrous results.

The fact that 17.Panzer Division captured a large amount of U.S. supplied trucks on 22 August shows the extent of aid America gave to the Soviets. All the wheeled transport of many Soviet units had been supplied by the United States. This gave the Soviets the chance to concentrate on tank and armour production. The Germans were pleased to capture U.S. trucks due to their high quality of manufacture, toughness, and reliability.

On 26 August Erich is tested on his radio skills, and possibly as a result gets, to his joy, his own radio post.

At the end of August the collapse of the German military machine continues, as Erich records the Rumanian oil fields being over-run and the resultant shortages of fuel for the German forces. This is followed by Germany's allies Finland and Bulgaria changing sides and fighting against the Germans. The Diary ends with two of 17.Panzer Division's companies being surrounded and more Soviet attacks.

Chapter 13

Diary 14 September 1944 to 30 November 1944

Written in a light red covered note book with a map of Poland on the back.

Diary cover.

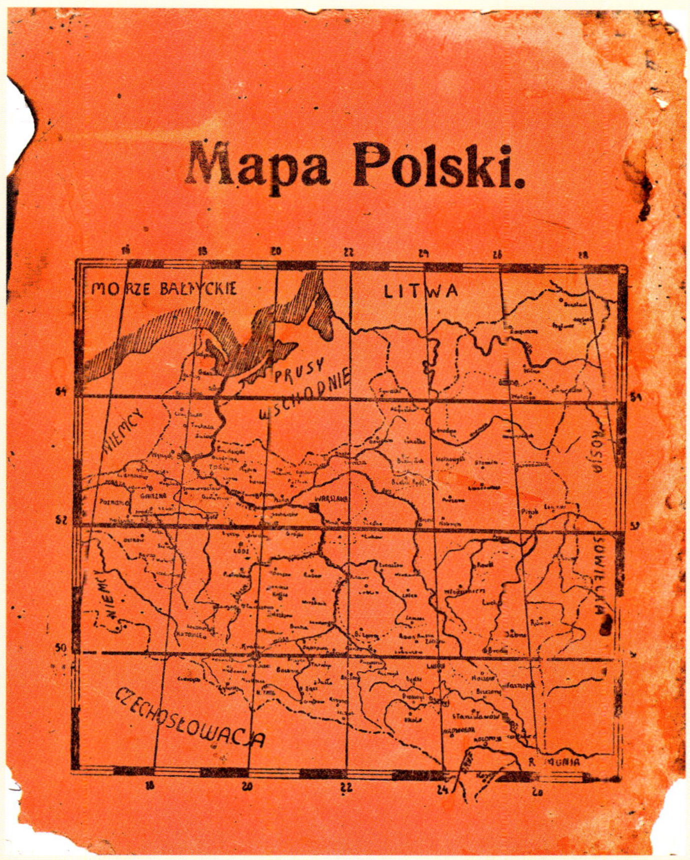

Diary back cover.

14 September 1944. Now I'm quite alone here, don't know what to do all day. Schnauder Adi visited me. Otherwise nothing happening. Few radio messages.

15 September. One day here like all the others. The 17 Pz came again for testing. Petek visited me. He's with 4Kp, now the radio operator. Otherwise nothing happening. Lovely music on the radio. Wrote a few letters.

16 September. Not much happening. The whole time we sit by the radio listening to all the news. What will the next days and weeks bring? 2 of our engineers were with the *Führer*, they got *die goldene Nahkampfspange* (the close combat bar in gold). He spoke quite optimistically to them, keep holding out 'til late autumn.
Without fail its coming to an end. Here in our area the Russians have pulled out their whole attack division. Setting up a defence. We will soon be going then too.

17 September. Sunday. Nothing happening, quite quiet here now. Sleeping, reading, listening to music. Got bread from our bakery. 1 man dismissed.

18 September. One day just like the next. That's doing me good. Tanks have already gone up ahead. They're near OPATOW. Great music again!

19 September. Nothing happening. Great music in the morning already. Otherwise calm, calm. 30 men had to go away as the entrenchment task force. Read a few nice books.

20 September. We're having lovely autumn days, very warm, not much going on. Great music on the radio. Reading and writing, that's all. Danced in the evening, all alone with girls. Music from the radio. Nice.

21 September. There are canteen goods, thank goodness, also 180 cigarettes, Schnaps. Otherwise nothing happening all day. Wrote a letter to father. Great music!! Reading a great book.

22 September. Still lovely mild autumn weather. Tanks not in action. Otherwise nothing happening. Great music!! Cards and games every day from 11-12!
In the evening mostly danced and pleased myself! Just at lunch just now. There's roaring and whistling. We get outside. There's a shell and 2 *Schlächter* (ground attack aircraft) are firing at and bombing the train at the stop. We're under cover again and again. They come near. The *Lufttorpedo* (rockets fired from planes or sometimes from the ground filled with liquid TNT) are whistling by, where the orderly room is and the large part of the repair shop. They hit everything. A fuel vehicle as well. Several dead, but all civilians. The women are screaming "God take pity." The infantrymen are running around to save what can be saved. Confusion. The wooden houses have dried out and burn quite quickly, and the wind is helping. I can't leave my radio post. Curious to see how much has been damaged.
Everything has calmed down a bit already. Only the women making a dreadful noise. All the houses there have burned down. Nothing's happened here with us. Radio messages still coming.
Total radio silence from immediately. Now I have got a bit of peace.

23 September. Peace, peace, spending all day lying down. At midday hear on the radio, battle blunder over the eastern Danube. Immediately write a letter home. I'm a bit perturbed. In the afternoon 2 *Schlächter* here bombing the runway next to us.
Otherwise I am reading. Still lovely weather. I think we'll march off soon. It's much too quiet here. In the evening it came through on the radio: Hptm. Burmeister, commander of s.Pz.Abt 506, Tiger tanks, to get the *Ritterkreuz*. Know him very well. We were in the *Kessel* (Cauldron Battle – where the forces were surrounded by the Soviets) at KAMENEZ-PODALSK-VNON together. At that time he was leading a battle group (southern battle group). Were in the tank for a lot of time. He led the Tiger Abt. 506. A fine man and officer. I'm pleased for him.

"Paul Matschlich. Obfldw. Grave is beside the school. KAMENEZ - PODALSK."

"The Kessel at TSCHERKANNET at KAMENEZ – PODALSK."

24 September. Sunday. At midday Gerblinger came and brought me a parcel from Prehofer from home. Delighted to have bacon, sausage, pastry, cigarettes, razor blades, and writing paper. Having a good feed! Then an unwelcome piece of news, am back on duty tomorrow as there is no radio traffic.
Today we are going to a football match: repair shop against bakers – Score-2 : 2 - great. Girls are here from the butcher's and the bakery. Russian girls from Duzansk and Arel. In the evening listened to music. Otherwise nothing happening. Handed in my things at the orderly room. In the evening the radio operators came with Schnaps and we drank here and played Skat. Obflw. Klotz extremely drunk.

25 September. Working in the radio workshop. Can learn something from it. Obflw. Pretz moving out to Obflw. Klotz. I'm alone. Write a few letters. Rained all day.

26 September. Lovely day. Working in the radio workshop. Tanks here. Schnauder Adi also. New ObLtn. von Hagen as *Einschieber* (Pusher, presumably the officer who got things done) here. Write a few letters. Listened to the radio. Otherwise nothing happening.

27 September. Working in the radio workshop, making the command tanks. Otherwise nothing happening. Uffz. Ötzl coming to us - a great fellow. In the evening Schnauder Adi came to visit and drank my Schnaps. Peaceful up at the Front.

28 September. Working in the radio workshop. Otherwise nothing happening. There are canteen goods. Wine and apple juice.
In the evening Ötzl and I drinking. Obflw. Klotz, and Schnauder Adi came and drank with us. Had a great conversation. Went to bed late.

29 September. Big change-round in our Division. General, v.d. Vredin, I.a. (operations officer), ObstLtn. Neckelmann, Commander of the Grenadiers, Oberst Drux, our commander. ObstLtn. Weiss-Kaffanke, as well as Hptm. Grebenzoll, Gef of 7 Company, left today from our Division. As General and Div commander came *Generalmajor* Demme. Hptm. Kloss is the *Abteilung* temporary commander, Hptm. Sühne the Company commander.
Up front peaceful - too peaceful. Otherwise nothing happening. Write a few letters. Listen to music.

30 September. ObstLtn. Weiss-Kaffanke, our commander, has taken over the grenadiers. 40 Regiment. Today building security with 4 men as all-round defence. In the afternoon 1 on duty. Geitlinger brought me radio documents. Otherwise nothing happening. Aircraft bombing the runway.

<u>October 44</u>
1 October. Early played (at being) infantry. Had to secure KRINKI. Back at 10. Then duty 'til 1 o'clock. In the afternoon football against Jäcker and Fleinher. Broke off the game at 2 : 2. This time we should have got a win. We shouted like mad. Otherwise nothing happening. Quiet here. Wrote a few letters. Lovely music.

2 October. Nothing happened all day. A few tanks here are being prepared. Work all day in the radio workshop. Quite quiet up ahead as well. Dismal autumn day already.

3 October. Am still alone. Ötzl not yet back from Krakau. Nothing happened all day. Made myself a lighting circuit. In the afternoon field duty - that was 2 lovely hours. Fldw. Klötz is platoon leader. We've never laughed as much. He handed over the platoon to me. I should be able to, he said. Now we're doing great things - snooping around a village. In the evening went back in an organised fashion. Eggs, 1 goose, 5 hens What a meal! In the evening did a bit of dancing.

4 October. A dismal day like the other one. Otherwise nothing happening. Quiet here! Ötzl still not here! Still on my own! Ate a chicken in the evening. Great. Listened to music and wrote letters.

5 October. Working at the radio repair shop. New orders for the tanks arrived. In the afternoon no duty. Slept and read a good book. Wrote a few letters. Listened to music and every day soon sleeping.

6 October. Building trenches with 2 men. Otherwise nothing happening. Schnauder Adolf is coming. He's going in hospital - jaundice! ObstLtn. Weiss-Kaffanke back with us. Ate the second chicken. Otherwise nothing happening. In the afternoon I worked in the command vehicle. Listened to music in the evening.

7 October. Saturday. In the morning making trenches with Ltn. Koum. Great stuff as lovely warm weather. After duties given out, I'm free. Low alert stage becomes big alert stage. Kik : kak (handball game). Otherwise nothing happening.

8 October. 8.30 high alert stage. Everything rushing. Company goes into position. (Soviets started an offensive on 6 October near Arad, in Hungary, and planned to destroy the German Army group South. This involved 64 Divisions, 750 tanks and 1,100 aircraft.) I stayed at home. Thus the morning passed. Wrote a few letters. Otherwise nothing happening. In the afternoon we played football, during that an alert, 2000 partisans are trying to attack us. In the evening we fell in. Tomorrow the day of the potato.

9 October. Monday. 2.30 awake. 3 lorries. Via KUNOV, OSTROWIECE, OPATOW, into the evacuated area. Met ObLtn. Krell, talked to him. He's *Landwirtschaftsoffizier* (farming officer) for the Division. The whole Division has to dig potatoes, 400 tons have to be dug and loaded up for Augsburg. We worked 'til 16.30, about 700 tons were dug up. Binhof says Kloss wants me in the tank.

10 October. In the morning I was in the entrenchment task force. Lovely weather. In the afternoon off duty. Ötzl Gustl back from Krakau. At 8.00 Obfldw. Pietz came and said I have to go to the ObLtn. tomorrow at 04.00.
Dismantle the radio station here, there take over as commander of the command vehicle that came from Headquarters.

11 October. 5 o'clock departure with the *Bergezug* (recovery half-track). Going to V Company (Supply). They didn't know anything about it. Go to Adj, Ltn. Gross, come to HQ Company and am staying there. Stabsgef. Rieger from my old Company is my driver. Rained all day today. Company strong. 3 Uffz., 15 men. Wrote a letter.
Visit Lorenz (Fldw.), Flänk and Berg, he's Spiess. Quarter in school. Village 2-3 km from the Front.

12 October. As radio operator I also have got Schutkz and Tomaschek, two young ones. Sorted out the tank. Gef of the HQ Company is Ltn. Barth, N.O. (Signals Officer). ObLtn. Kohlberger, Adj on leave. Peaceful life. There's firing all day long but not as far as us.
Am NCO of the Watch, yes. Uffz. Winzig here at HQ Company as W. and G. (weapons and ammunition) - used to be with our old 6 Company *Richtschütze* (Gunner). In Orel, Russia, he was in charge of the soldiers' leave centre.
In the evening I was with Ltn. Barth and we spoke about the tank and its action.

13 October. 1 hour's instruction in cleaning the munitions. In the afternoon filling up with fuel at V-Staffel. Visited Uffz. Vancata, Gernhardt. Our Prochaska Franz, *Schirmeister* (Vehicle NCO), Gansberger, Wagner, Seemann.
In the evening entrenchment task force. My crew was not there. Today quite unsettled at the Front.

14 October. Not much happening. Still quiet here. Listen to the radio! The only job! Went to Ostrowice by lorry to load up. Bought some white bread - 1 piece was 35 zloti. What else have we got to do with our money! Wanted to visit a few women but the time was too short.

15 October Sunday. With my tank to *V-Staffel* (Supply). Went with Olomer to V Company, VROD. Want to get my canteen goods. Learn about it this afternoon.
In the evening stay here. Borrow some black togs (Panzer uniform of black wrap around jacket and trousers). At 5 PM it starts. ObstLtn. Weiss-Kaffanke, Hptm. Kloss wearing the new *Pz Kampfabzeichen II Stufe 25* (panzer battle badge for 25 attacks). Arrived today Ltn. Gross, Ltn. Barthel. Are splendidly decorated. 2 meals with pork Schnitzel (cutlet). Flan with ground coffee. Sandwiches, 130 bottles of wine, Schnaps, beer, *Glühwein*, and tea. Also speeches, songs, and music, Hesse, Kaplunger, and Dissing.
In the evening Bunte Bühne from OPATOW (theatrical company) came, 5 girls with them. They danced. I must say everything was there. I'm sitting opposite ObstLtn. Weiss, Kaffanke, Kloss, and Kühne. All sorts offered. Of course I had a good drink. ObstLtn. also spoke to me about my 75 attacks being the most of anyone in the Abt. Until late on we sat there with the girls between us. I also danced a few times. It was great! Until 4.30 AM, then home to ZOCHZIN in the *Kubelwagen* with Hptm. Kloss. Everyone was drunk. I pinched 3 bottles of wine. Got home at 5.15 AM.

16 October. Met 2 radio operators who were roasting chicken, great soup and meat. I'd just got into bed at 6.15 when the alert went up - get ready right away. Sort out the tank, collect the radio documents. Bischof Rudi is also coming with his vehicle. Pioneers going around here. General here, also O.B. (*Obersterbefehlshaber*, supreme commander) of the Army.
At midday there was stand down. Back to quarters. Bischof Rudi is staying here with his tank and its crew. Lovely music on the radio. In the evening digging entrenchments. I'm NCO of the Watch, therefore no sleep.

17 October. Radio instruction, otherwise all day not much happening. Lovely music on the radio. Write a few letters. Aircraft visit us each day but no bombs falling yet.

18 October. Go to HKL (Front Defense Line) and dig potatoes. Artillery fire a few times near us. Morning passes. Almost stepped on mines. Lying all over the place here. In the evening lovely music, got a parcel from Father with 2 tins of fish (sardines). My 2 radio operators made a great meal, Knödel (dumplings) with butter sauce. Sausage with vinegar sauce.
Führer command - People's Army set up. Everything's at stake.(*Volkssturm* - males of ages 16 to 60 not serving in the armed forces - were called up and given small arms, usually of obsolete and/or foreign types. Ammunition was in short supply. Only a short basic training was given. This, the shortage of heavy weapons, and the age and physical condition of the men led to poor performance on the battlefield. Certainly a last ditch effort of the Nazi Party.)

19 October. Raining. Doing radio instruction. The Gef Schladanix was to have been shot yesterday, everything already arranged, then came the announcement that in the night he and a Pioneer broke out handcuffed together and fled. With a penknife the door hinge came out and the sentry was going up and down. They have not yet been caught. Another big map reading exercise. O.B. (*Obersterbefehlshaber*) Gen. Obst, Div Gen, and many officers here. Major Heinz also here as ABT *Schreiber* (to take notes), as well as Schönfeld with 4 Kp and Schuer Lois as radio operator for Kloss.

20 October. Another map reading exercise is going on near us. Quite quiet. At 10 o'clock the order - at 11.00 I have to go to the commanding officer in black. Fldw. Steuber, Hoffbauer and Schuer too. Report in uniform and he will present to us the *Panzerkampfabzeichen* III Level (Panzer Assault Badge) for 50 attacks (Silver). Mine for 75 attacks, Pz.Kpf.Abz IV Stufe in gold, is not yet here. Am very pleased. Great. A distinction. Otherwise nothing happening all day. In the evening liqueur was made and a great meal, dumplings with cream, etc. Silly week!

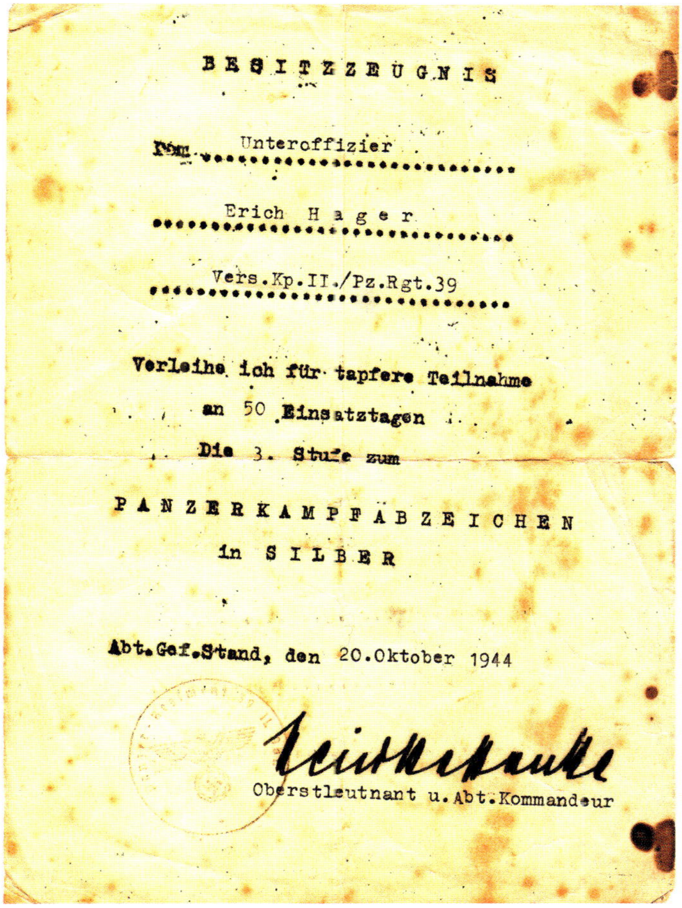

BESITZZEUGNIS

Dem Unteroffizier

Erich Hager

Vers.Kp.II./Pz.Rgt.39

Verleihe ich für tapfere Teilnahme
an 50 Einsatztagen
Die 3. Stufe zum

PANZERKAMPFABZEICHEN
in SILBER

Abt.Gef.Stand, den 20.Oktober 1944

Oberstleutnant u.Abt.Kommandeur

Erich's certificate for the rare Panzer Assault Badge, class 3 for 50 attacks. Signed by the *Abteilung* Commander.

Erich on the right with another well decorated soldier, a *Hauptfeldwebel* who is wearing the filed grey assault gun version of the Panzer uniform.

Erich on the left wearing the Panzer Assault Badge, class 3 for 50 attacks.

Another view of Erich with his comrade, who is an *Unterofficier* or *Feldwebel* and an officer aspirant, as shown by the cord looped round his shoulder straps.

21 October. Weapon cleaning. Tomorrow weapons inspection by Obfldw. Klotz (repair shop). In the afternoon got the tank in tip-top clean condition. At 06.00 radio contact with Div. because in the evening came the order to prepare immediately for loading up in the night. At 20.00 Bischof Rudi and I have to go in our 2 command tanks to 4 Kp and we'll be loaded up with theirs. 2 hours' sleep and march off.

22 October. Sunday. Army travel day. 01.00 departure for OSTROWIEC in the pitch dark and it's raining. I drove along in the ditch. In OSTROWIEC loaded up. Travelled via KVNOW - RVONIK past the workshop - STARACIOWIEC - KAMIENNA - KIELCE. Where on earth are we going? To HUNGARY? That would be nice!! Kept on going in the direction of KRAKAU to JEDRZE (lovely town, peaceful). Unloaded here at 17.00. Now we are on the other side of the bridge to BARANOW. ObLtn. Kohlberger back from a duty journey, leave. I report to him. Journey continues to BVSKO -ZGRAJ - NIKULOWJCE - NOWO-NIES. Stop here overnight. Small village.

23 October. Departure at 06.00. Back on almost the same route, then another road to HOLLENDRY. V Company, Abt (Tank Battalion), and HQ Company are here. Set up here. Area here is completely flat and lots of bogs. Lots of water. In one short distance we went over 20 bridges. Everything flat, few villages. Bischof Rudi and I move into a house with our crew.
Quarter is lousy.

24 October. Überraulung Bös, Hptfldw. is here again. He is first word again. Castrated rams here. Am with HQ Company. V company right next to us. Road construction going on here in peace. 16 PD ¥ (This ¥ is the insignia of 16. Pz. Div.) also here as reserves. 20 I.D. (Infantry Division) left of us. 2 new command vehicles are also here. What kind of job are we going to get? Workshop is in JEDRZEJOW, that's a small town, great women there and even *Gasthäuser* (pubs).

25 October. Technical duty Already quite cold. Otherwise nothing happening. 17 tanks have arrived again. Now the ABT has over 55 Pz IV.
Write a few letters. It's bitter cold. Make the tank clean as a new pin.

26 October. *Sturmpanzer* have arrived. (Heavily armoured assault vehicles based on the Panzer IV chassis. Armed with a 15 cm gun, these were designed to assault fortified positions based on the German experiences on the Eastern Front, including Stalingrad.) Am curious to see what they look like. Have heard a whisper that a 6 company has to be formed again. 55 tanks ready for action. Got to hand over my tank. A crew from intelligence Abt here. Sollner, Kitzinger. Technical duty, otherwise nothing happening. Vehicles already topped up. Bitter cold.

27 October. Handed over my tank to Briedhof Rudi and took over with Rieger. A new Pz III (Panzer III tank) half broken, instead repair shop has to work on it. All kinds of things to do. There was a goose today. Very cold already. I don't have a crew yet. 17 more tanks are to come, so we'll have 72 vehicles. Quite something.

28 October. The new *Sturmpanzer* are becoming 6 Company. Ltn. Jafer is leading them meantime. Getting as crew Gefr. Pulai and Wurtka. Working on it. Gef instruction. Also reconnaissance platoon here. Steuber, Schramm, etc.
Very cold. It's raining. Repair shop here. Starting mine tomorrow. In the afternoon no duty. Otherwise nothing happening. Rations half less. Very hungry. Write a few letters. In the evening 2 geese slaughtered.

29 October. Sunday! No duty! Roasting meat all day and great dumplings made as well. An A1 meal. Afterwards great jazz music. We've got a radio operator from 17 Abt - from Cologne. He's got his jazz harmonica with him. A likable lad. Plays like mad. Plays in the Div jazz band.

30 October. Repair shop working on our tank. Got an overall. 17 Pz (Panzers – tanks) have arrived. In total 76 tanks, a real heap. The *Stupa* (short for *Sturmpanzer*) now number 6 Company and are staying with us. My new tank will also be staying. In the evening great music again and popular songs. Black Panther, etc. All sorts of things to be heard.

31 October. Drill with the Company. Repair shop working hard on the vehicle. Soon be finished. Today we have Company firing. Write a few letters. Got a parcel from Father. Field firing exercise going very well. My platoon the best - led by me. Weapon cleaning. In the evening we made *Kartoffelpuffer* (potato pancakes). At 23.00 I was wakened and told that tomorrow I've to go to BUSKO-ZGROS to a convalescence camp from Choz with N.S. (National Socialist) recreational course.

1 November. Awake at 05.00. Gerlinger Hans and a Gefreiter Koh from 7 Company also there. We went on foot to CHMELNIK, hitch-hiked to BUSKO-ZGROS (30km), arrived, got ourselves deloused. A lovely little town, a Polish mountain resort (*Luftkurort*). Lovely villas and parks. The rich Jews lived here. Approximately 100 men here together. Communal lunch in the games room, everything so luxurious. Here you can really get a rest for 6 days. Women also here. 4 men in a room - us and a Fldw. from 7 Battery - our Div - a great guy. He's from the Jutti, which I know so well. Hptfldw. Fauss. Supper is served spread on rolls. Just great. Service is good and prompt. In the evening we play Skat! To bed at 23.00.

2 November. Awake at 07.00. 08.00 breakfast together, then meeting with N.S.F.O. from Chon - ObLtn. Bärsch, then political lecture from Party member Winter,

Professor from Hedleberg. Great things offered. Lunch together with music and simply great food. Bed rest 'til 15.00. Wrote a letter home. 16.00 coffee and cakes. In the evening cinema. At coffee time excellent jazz music. Cinema "Ein schöner Tag" (A lovely day), very good. Sound was poor. (N.S F.O. was a National Socialist Leadership Officer. A serving soldier thought loyal to the Nazi party. These were appointed due to the Nazis' suspicion of the Army. They were to keep the unit true to Nazi policies and report on individuals who infringed these.)

3 November. Awake at 07.00. 08.00 breakfast together. 09.00 singing, then lecture from an ObLtn., 16 PD (16. Panzer Division) N.S.F.O., former H.J. (*Hitlerjugend*) leader - great. Unforeseen event - our course leader talked about some ill feeling. I'll stay with the first outlook. There will be war again. Political lecture. Meal all together. Went for a ½ hour walk in the town. Lovely women. 16.00 afternoon coffee (cake with music - hit music). Evening meal at 20.15. Club night. Got as much beer as you wanted, ½ bottle of Schnaps and 20 cigarettes. Great programme from 304 I D (304 Infantry Division), great music, great atmosphere. It was great fun! We get on great together and everything stayed within limits. Many activities here - great things presented. The last ones finished at 01.00.

4 November!! Wakened at 07.30, waking is hard work. 08.30 breakfast together, hangovers. Lectures as usual! Great things we hear. Things you never read in the newspapers. The background to the retreat. Meal all together. Walk. 16.00 relaxed afternoon coffee break with cake and great music (played Skat). In the evening film - "Ouase der Buschpilot" (Ouase the bush pilot). Very good.

5 November. Awake at 07.00. 08.00 breakfast *quite private discussion*, "top secret." Lecture, espionage, sabotage. Lunch all together, bed rest. 15.00 singing. 16.00 the General is expected. Doesn't arrive. Great cake again and an extra parcel with chocolate and baking, and great music along with that! Played Skat. In the evening we ate together and at 20.15 leisure time with poetry and we sang 3 songs – "Oh, Deutschland hoch in Ehren," "Wohlauf Kameraden," and "Ein junges Volk steht auf zur Stimme bereit." Was very nice and solemn. Afterwards a cosy gathering. Have found a nice group, all of them Fldw. and Obfldw. We tell stories and sing 'til 12.30. Thus the lovely course with rest and recuperation is coming to an end!

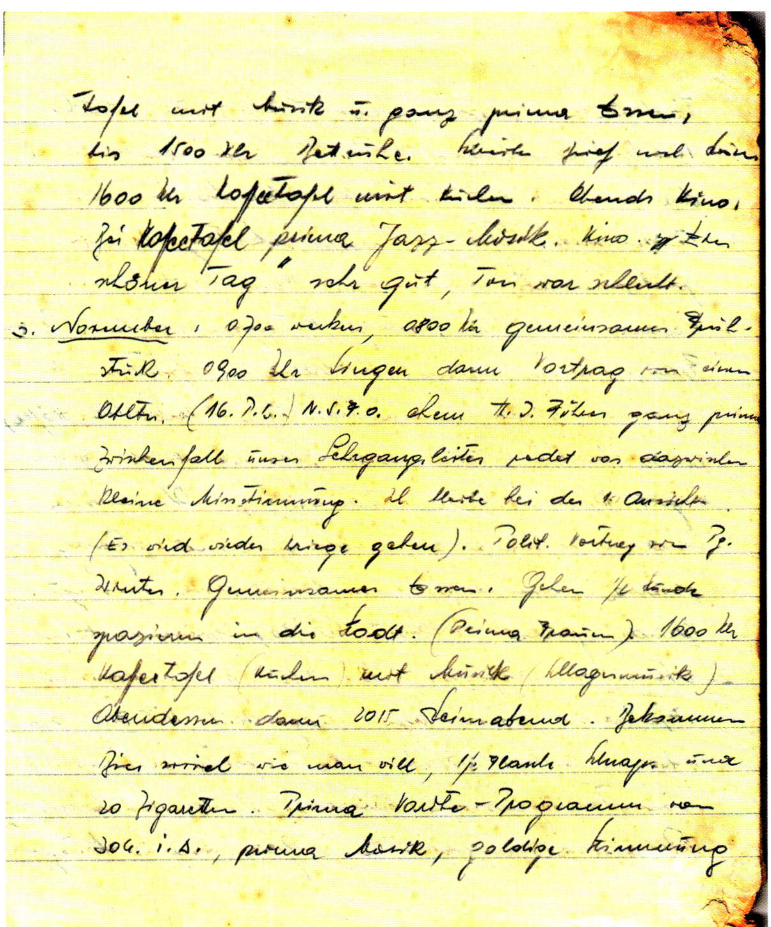

Diary page for the National Socialist course. "Quite private discussion."

6 November. 16 P.D., 17 P.D., 20 Gr Div. - we're leaving earlier. 08.00 breakfast and leave the residence, hitch-hike to CHMELNIK and from there to Hollendrie to our village. Arrived at 10.00, everyone still asleep. Today is a section day of rest because there were night exercises. Obfldw. Hager tells me that I have been transferred to HQ. Satisfied with that. In the afternoon Uffz. Gallhammer and Kroll are here. Uffz. Koubek and Obgefr. Heisinger and Gef Zechmeister here again - they've been transferred to us! Also meet Uffz. Daicner, who is with 6 Kp. Still here are Ltn. Sattler, know him from Linz, Uffz. Reisinger Hans and Gallner of 7 Kp. Aufkl. (*Aufklärer*, reconnaissance) *Zug* (Zug, platoon), Schramm and Brands. Rieger was my leader in the medical centre.

7 November. Section entrenchment day. Not going. A bit of technical duty. Adi Schnauder is back from the field hospital and is going straightaway to an armourer's course in Berlin. Left at 11.50 - took my leave of him. Fldw. Gansberger is taking meat on leave with him. Fldw. Gallhammer of 6 Kp. - had a chat with him. 16 P.D. is getting out of here. Have gone. We've grabbed the quarter. Making ourselves at home. With a radio and electric light. Otherwise nothing happening. Am NCO of the Watch, guardroom.

8 November. Rest of the Company marching off to the reconnaissance platoon. I'm staying here, doing nothing! Write a few letters. Awful weather - "the first snow" - gone away again though. We've instruction with Lorenz. Otherwise nothing happening. Lovely music on the radio. Today met Koubek, Hesich, Kroll, and Zechmeister! V2 flying to London!! (Rocket propelled "Vengence weapons." Part of Hitler's promised new weapons that would win the war. The V2 was the first ballistic rocket to achieve space flight. Over 3,000 were launched, causing 7,250 military and civilian deaths. However, the V2 had no effect on the outcome of the war except to boost Nazi propaganda. It is estimated that for the cost of the V2 program Germany could have built a further 48,000 tanks. These might have been of more use to Erich and hard pressed units like 17.Panzer Division.)

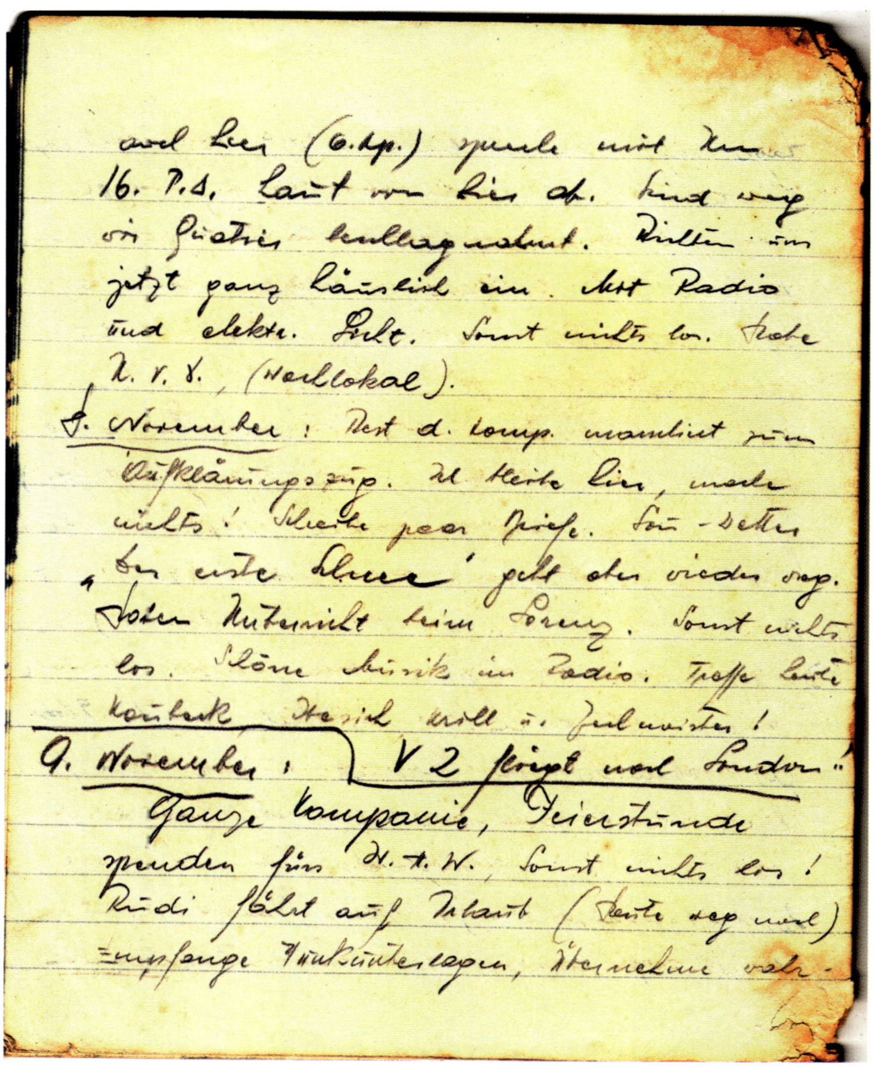

Diary page "V2 firing on London."

9 November. Whole Company leisure hour giving money for H.T.W. (Winter Help Fund for the poor). Otherwise nothing happening. Rudi's gone on leave today. Received radio documents. I'll probably take over his job. Otherwise nothing happening.

10 November. Friday. Vehicle again broken down. Now I have as my crew Driver Obgefr. Günther, Pulai, and Schlutka. Otherwise nothing happening. It snowed for the first time but didn't lie.

11 November. Saturday. Gef instruction. Singing lesson. Hour of commemoration. In the afternoon parade, black (black Panzer uniform). Otherwise nothing happening. Great music on the radio. All quiet. Snowing.

12 November. Sunday. Instruction about cartridges 2, 3, and 60 (refers to power and ranges). Afterwards with V company. In the afternoon nothing happening. Lovely and warm in the quarter. Listened to the radio. Thoughts wander home. *Very peaceful.*

13 November. Monday. Radio instruction. Am picked up, taken in a car with the Company driver to the exercise as *Radioüberwachungsleiter* (radio control leader), in the morning to 7 Kp with Hptm. Liebenrath. ObstLtn. Weiss also there. Didn't go right. In the afternoon with the reconnaissance platoon of our Company. Div leader Demme also here. Didn't work at all, didn't work again 'til 5.30 PM. There was a real telling-off for Eckert, etc. Am frozen through in this *Kubelwagen*. Lovely music on the radio.

14 November. Tuesday. Radio instruction. Went with the *Kubelwagen* to the Gef. Today we are not going to the exercise. Div leader complained because there were so many vehicles there. 1 S.P.W. (armoured half-track), 1 *Schwimmwagen*, and 1 *Kubelwagen* with us. Therefore wrote a few letters. Got a parcel from Father, fish. Otherwise nothing happening. Commemoration. In the evening lovely music. Bitter cold!

15 November. Wednesday. Radio instruction. In the afternoon parade, black (Panzer uniforms). Otherwise nothing happening. Repair shop arrived. Lorenz did my vehicle. StabsGefr. Thaler, V Kp, the first victim of typhoid. 6 of us in the field hospital. Thaler getting worse. In the evening it rained and snowed.

16 November. Thursday. A snowstorm today like in the Kalmücken Steppe. Almost knocks you over. Mayrhofer Lois finally going on leave. New gunner went to Vienna. Ltn. Eckhard transferred to 4 Kp. Therefore Ltn. Jegodka has taken over the reconnaissance platoon. Since the exercise was poor, therefore radio instruction, gas instruction. Snow storm. Guard duty. Write a few letters.

17 November. Friday. Overall situation, all still staying in the same place south of the bridge head still in reserve for the Korps. Injections morning. In the afternoon gas mask inspection. Otherwise nothing happening. Brandstätter Lois now Commanding officer's Panzer driver. Fldw. Hoffmann is in a conundrum. Weiss-Kaffanke is leaving on Monday with Mutzler. New tank, change round of tank crew: Günther, Schutka, Schlesinger, and I. Tomaschek - repair shop.

18 November. Saturday. Singing, march off of pilots, investiture of Gef Commander. ObstLtn. Weiss-Kaffanke takes his leave. We all appeared for this. Otherwise nothing happening all day. Lovely music on the radio.

19 November. It's snowing again. Company goes route marking. Stay at home alone. Write a few letters. Got nice and warm in the afternoon and played cards, great music as well. Otherwise nothing especially new.

20 November. Monday. Instruction. During that new commanding officer arrived - Major Kratschwill. Saw him for the first time. He went to school with Lorenz, Fldw., for 10 years. Geitlinger Hans knew him from the Dragoons in Ems. He is from 10 district (Military district). In the afternoon road building. Schlesinger coming into our quarters. Recovery platoon has left here.

21 November. Order from Commanding Officer - all vehicles and tanks have to be dug in because of heavy aircraft attack. It's coming from the west. He had that experience there. Heavy digging starts. Have NCO of the Watch guard duty. 2 hours. Duty Uffz.

22 November. Wednesday. All day digging and shovelling. Tank buried. Just the turret showing. Completed the digging. Otherwise nothing happening. In the evening we played cards. Tomorrow is shooting.

23 November. Snow is away again. Firing cancelled. Constructing a cover over the tank. Otherwise nothing happening. Played cards in the evening. Great music.

24 November. Friday. Finished the tank cover. Otherwise nothing happening. Wrote a few letters. Otherwise quiet at the Front. Great music on the radio.

25 November. Saturday. Instruction 'til midday. Follow up work on defences. Have guard duty.

26 November. At 09.00 our new Commanding Officer is coming. ABT Kdr. Kratschwill is going to have a look at the command vehicle. Mine's the first, I'm the sentry. He asks how many attacks (Erich had taken part in), what a compatriot. Afterwards the Gef comes with Ltn. Larte and says to dig in the tanks, as they are not 100m apart. Digging 'til 17.00, already dark. No radio. Damn.

27 November. Monday. Gas mask inspection by ABT. Gas Uffz., then technical duty. In the afternoon signals training and loader training. Got parcels and a letter from home. Rammersdorfer killed in Holland, bombs. Gammer Noz and Roman and Windner Ernst missing in France. Radio again today. Great.

28 November. Tuesday. Firing with live ammunition. Instruction in school. Examination by doctor with instruction. Gef instruction. Great music in the evening.

29 November. 3-day close combat training begins. *Panzerfaust* Kl 30, 30, 60, and 100. (Single shot anti-tank weapon. The numbers refer to the ranges that increasingly powerful variants could knock out a tank.) In the afternoon Uffz. Kutz not happy being a flop. All sorts going on. In the evening radio, great music. Variety "20 nackte Beinchen" (20 naked legs) - great. Women FF (Possibly a comment about the women!). Music CHMEZNIK.

30 November. Practice firing on the open terrain with *Panzerfaust*. Ltn. Eckland, Gef went through the quarters checking the walls. Am NCO of the Watch. They noticed in my quarters. Write a few letters.

Notes to 14 September to 30 November 1944 Diary

On 16 September, Erich's comrades tell him of the conversation with Adolf Hitler. Many have stated that Hitler had an amazing ability to convince even hardened front line soldiers that the war could be won. Erich seems to doubt this by the nature of his entry.

After a quiet time in September Erich is horrified by the effect of an air attack on civilians. More welcome on the 24th is a parcel from home containing food. Football playing is popular in this diary, as is food and listening to music as before.

Partisans are always around, as shown on 8 October. Few people would have believed that Panzer men would be farming and collecting potatoes as on the "day of the potato," 9 October and later on the 18th.

Throughout October Erich listens to the action at the front, perhaps wondering when the next major Soviet breakthrough would come. The close relationship between officers and men in the German army is shown by the great social evening on 15 October. On the 20th Erich takes soldierly pride in his high award of the Tank Battle Badge for 75 attacks. Few tank men survived to achieve this decoration.

17. Panzer Division took charge of *Sturmpanzer* IV in late October. It was one of the few tank divisions to do so. They were thickly armoured machines armed with a 15cm howitzer and based on the Panzer IV chassis. *Sturmpanzers* were designed to take out strong points in the attack, but probably were not much use in the defensive fighting the Germans were required to carry out this late in the war.

An interesting reference is made on 29 October to the playing and listening to of jazz music by the troops. Jazz music was despised by the Nazis, as it originated from African American sources. Either the frontline troops ignored Nazi doctrine or it was tolerated to keep the troops' morale up.

Erich attends a National Socialist recreational Course starting on 31 October. These were organised to give Nazi propaganda to the Army, which was seen as a reactionary organisation. Hitler's mistrust was increased after the bomb attempt on his life.

Erich does not record the subjects of the political lectures but relates the ill feelings by some. We can only guess if this was over racial hatred of the Jews or by the Nazi lecturers trying to make out that the front line situation was not as grave as it was. Not everyone believed in the Nazis' promises of "wonder weapons" or their overly optimistic view of how the war was going.

Erich underlines the private - read secret - nature of the lectures. He does relate that the Nazis were blaming spies and saboteurs, a common Nazi tactic, and he believes that there would be another war. The troops were well looked after, with plenty of good food, drink, and cigarettes. This would be to show the Nazi Party in a good light. Erich takes it all as good rest and recreation and a chance to socialize with his comrades.

After the course, on 7 November Erich is pleased to take over comfortable quarters from 16.Panzer Division, since for the troops comfortable living is always welcome. Strangely, even in late 1944 gas defence is still taken seriously by the inspection of gas masks.

On 21 November Erich records the first air attack from the west. This was presumably made by the western Allies. The tanks have to be dug in to hide them, as they would be a priority target. The troops have to pretty well bury them, so movement is not planned for Erich's unit. Allied air attacks in the west greatly hampered German armoured movement.

The diary ends with *Panzerfaust* training on 19 November. This was a one shot throw away anti-tank weapon. Although a very effective weapon in determined hands, being able to knock out any Allied tank, it was an infantry weapon. The training of tank crews in its use shows that the Germans knew they did not have enough tanks to fight the Soviet masses. The situation was becoming increasingly desperate.

Chapter 14

Diary 1 December 1944 to 28 January 1945

Written in light green coloured school notebook.

Diary cover.

1 December Friday. Up at 05.00, as construction squad away to live firing with machine guns and *Panzerfaust* at the forester's house WOLA ZYLINSKI. Am barricade sentry at the forester's house. 200 lovely girls here. One of them shot. In the afternoon instruction. In the evening music.

2 December Saturday. Going swimming in CHMELNIK with Ltn. Eckhardt 'til 12 o'clock. On foot. In the afternoon cleaned the quarters. Made an *Adventskranz* (Advent wreath). Playing cards. Great music on the radio.

3 December Sunday. All day no duty. Room lovely and warm and we play cards. Bitter cold outside. Am NCO of the Watch. Who came at 16.00? Bischof Rudi, back from leave. Got some lovely cakes from him. Brought news of home.

4 December Monday. Radio instruction. Weapon cleaning. Weapons' inspection Spiess Winzig. Went past me. Listened to the radio and Rudi tells me about home. All sorts of news, good and bad. Rudi now Z. b. V. Panzer (*Zur besonderer Verwendung* - Armoured unit for special purposes). No longer S.P.W. (Armoured half-track, SdKfz 251 series.)

5 December. *Richt- und Ladeschützenausbildung* (Aimer and loader training). Rudi away to A.A.17 (*Aufklarungs Abteilung* 17, the Divisional reconnaissance unit) to fetch a S.P.W. (armoured half-track personnel carrier) for us. Not made yet! At 11.30 we're going to K. (*Kanone*) Company. Here are assembling all the *Commandants* and *Richtschützen* (Gunners), as well as all the officers of the Unit. The awards shooting is taking place. Led by Ltn. Sattler Erich, 6 Komp. I went to school with him for 4 years in Linz. He still remembers me and greets me. We chat about long-gone times! Meet lots of old (comrades). From Gehlmann I learn that he's Fldp No. of 6 Komp. 05889D (Field Post

Number, postcode or "Zip" used to send letters and parcels to the troops), and you could have knocked me down with a feather. Luischen wrote to me that her brother is with this Feldp No. and is Uffz. I ask and find out he is here - Uffz Sorn Theo. We make one another's acquaintance and arrange to meet up on Sunday. He's a great guy! Tells me about Luischen!!
Firing finished at 18.00 and we go home. Here there's a parcel from Luischen. Great joy!! Night exercise 'til 23.00. Change the road wheel, etc.

6 December. Do technical duty with my crew. Yesterday Rudi fetched an S.P.W. from A.A.17. Otherwise not much happening. Write Luischen a letter straightaway about my meeting up with her brother Theo.
Instruction in the afternoon, political, then Uffz. instruction, cancelled because there was no desk. No snow but bitter cold. At 15.00 already dark.
Tomorrow *Korps* entrenchment day. In the evening canteen goods.

7 December. Awake at 04.30. March off to CHMELNIK, whole Abt here. Ltn. von Zitzeortz in charge. Met Uffz. Sommer Hansl from 6 Komp. Were together in the infantry in Kaplitz. Now he's head radio operator for ObLtn. Jofer. No commanding officer at the entrenchments, so I skipped off and went home! Tidied up the digs. Radio on. Lovely and warm. Light snow. Am alone! Our Div leader is now Oberst Brux, leader of Grd Rgt 40 (Panzer Grenadier Regiment 40) - *Eichenlaubträger* (Knight's Cross with Oak Leaves award winner).
In all, recent nights all sorts of things have been trundling back going west? Tanks. Flak again. How long will we stay here? Still quiet! 6 Panzer Div sitting here in peace 3, 6, 17, 18, 19, and 24 Panzer Divisions, and then also Grd Div. (Grenadier Division). Spiess just said I should get ready to fetch 1 S.P.W. large (Sc.Kfz. 251 series vehicle) from 63 *Schützen*. Lovely job. Hear that Grd Rgt 63 have to be disbanded?? Why is that? They don't need to go! Deeg goes. Do nothing all day. It's a fact: big regrouping in the Corps and Div. Our Div more or less disbanded. Rgt 63 away, 1 Btl to 40, 1 Btl to the Corps. All the replacements away from us. 1 Sani-Company away from us (Medical company). We are becoming a Pz Regiment again. Heavy Abt. already underway with Reg. H.Q.!!! There is a *Korps* reinforcement. We're the assault group.

8 December Friday. Training, otherwise nothing happening. Increased aircraft activity from Ivan than ever before! Is this an early indication of future attacks? Chief instruction. Technical duty!! In the evening night exercise. Route march in march time from 18.00 - 23.00. Bischof Rudi and I together. We walked and walked in march time 54 km and found no one. Came to SOCHOWOLA to our Div HQ. We went too far. Home via CHMELNIK along the railway line. Arrived dog tired.

9 December Saturday. Radio instruction. Listen in to the Corps radio channel. Technical duty. Big map reading exercise with General, etc. 1 tank from 6 *Komp* and a turret must stand as a symbol. Korn Theo there with his tank. He visited me and we had a chat about everything 'til 17.00, then he can go home. I think Luischen will be the right woman for me. Learn all sorts of things!!! Had a lovely bath. In the evening lovely music on the radio. Our Company to get a Pioneer platoon and Flak-platoon again. All sorts of troops!!

10 December Sunday. Visit Kern Theo!! 6 Company is 1km away from here - LIPNIK!! Otherwise there is church service in the morning. Take the bus at 11.50 to LIPNIK to Theo. Have a great conversation. Had to go home on foot. Was lucky. Murik was here for the service and was being driven to CHMELNIK. Go with him and then go by lorry to CHMELNIK, wanted to go and visit girls but go straight back to KOLENORY. Home at 18.00. Gefr. Mann, jazz harmonica player, has been transferred to us, coming into my vehicle. Listened to music! Rained all night! Winter??

11 December. Radio instruction. New distribution. At midday weapons inspection. My machine gun not noticed, all others checked by Obfldw. Kloss. In the afternoon gas training. Wore gas masks for 2 hours. At 16.00 MAYRHOFER HANS came back from leave and brought me presents, approximately 8kg packet. Great, great things! My delight!! Great!! Am NCO of the Watch. General situation: the fun will soon start. You hear all sorts of things!! Will we attack this time? We'll see!! Tomorrow *Korps* entrenchment day again!
Write a few letters.

12 December Tuesday. Radio instruction. Fldw. Fläsch and I and 8 men away to 4 Company to the firing range on foot, a good walk. Lousy weather! Was outpost for the tank firing of our Company. Only the *Richtschützen* (Gunners) were firing! Lasted 'til 4.30 then home by lorry, thank God. Then we learned the unbelievable. Ltn. Jegotka, *Deutsches Kreuz* in Gold, etc., our reconnaissance platoon commander, Ltn. von Zitzewitz of 5 Company, and Ltn. Ernst Sattler, my school friend at Linz, now 6 Company, were with the driver Obgefr. Heiter, HQ. They were attacked without warning on the road from KRAKAU-KIELCE. All 4 dead. Shot by machine gun. Was their own fault. Did not wait for the convoy, went on alone at night. A terrible blow for the *Abteilung*.
Am dead tired and soon going to bed. Bischof Rudi and driver Uffz. Klosterknecht used to be *Leinmeister* (unidentified appointment) of 6 Company, now demoted, are going by S.P.W. to the workshop. Great music on the radio!

13 December Wednesday. Firing again with reconnaissance platoon. Have a sore foot. Don't go. In the afternoon political lecture from a party member about the "build up in the East!" Very good lecture. At 19.00 night exercise again. Bitter cold! Under my leadership - Combat engagements and bogs 'til 22.00.
Now we're getting frost!! No snow yet. Receive Christmas cards!

14 December. Radio instruction. Today already bitter cold but no snow. Stayed in my room. Great music. Listened to the radio. Uffz. Kühn going on home leave. In the afternoon political instruction, then Uffz. instruction! Otherwise nothing happening. Made a wreath for Ltn. Jegotka. He's being buried in Krakau!
(Date of 15th rubbed out here and this added) Radio instruction. All day nothing particular happening. Great music on the radio. In the afternoon instruction. In the evening there is Schnaps. We're having a big party, having a small Schnaps. Played jazz harmonica music like mad. We're in a really good mood.

15 December Friday. *Nachrückenzug* (advance signals platoon). Tank firing. Big washout. My tank not ready for action. Frick's vehicle frozen up. Bitter cold today. At 10.00 firing began with 2 Pz Bef. (Command tanks) 5 cm guns. Fired 16 shells. In the afternoon technical duty. I-troop (*Instandsetzungstrupp*, repair and maintainance troop assigned to a mechanised unit) comes.
Great music on the radio.

16 December Saturday. Bischof Rudi came back from the repair shop during the night. Today political instruction from a Party member. Learned great things!! Company instructions!! Technical duty.
Great music on the radio! They play great things.

17 December Sunday!! There's supposed to be a joint reception. Didn't come on the radio, though. What can be wrong?? Have a good wash. Wait for Theo. Have a bit of a party as no duty. Lovely and warm and we play, play, and play to forget.
In the evening cinema, "The singing nightingale." We've had to wait for a long time for a film! Major and all the Officers came. Ltn. Bartl, our Gef, said unexpectedly that I'm to go on a master radio operator course? Words failed me! And do I want to!! We'll talk about it tomorrow, he says. I can't sleep all night. My pipedream is coming true!!!

18 December Monday. Day of gas mask and gas room test. I'm desperate to be able to speak to the Boss about the training! He is Commander at the exercise. Finally at midday I go over and he agrees, he's putting my name down for the training! I'm overjoyed. At 14.00 news, the big news. Our troops since yesterday morning at 05.30 lined up for attack from Upper Venn to Luxemburg and the Americans completely surprised. (German surprise attack in the Ardennes. Operation "Wacht am Rhein." Known as the "Battle of the Bulge" to the U.S. and British. Last ditch attempt by Hitler to defeat the Western allies using powerful Army and *Waffen SS* Divisions and what remained of the *Luftwaffe*.) Immediately Company fell in. Statement from Boss about it! Everyone delighted. Will we manage to beat the Americans convincingly?? Hopefully!! We are looking towards the West, but are not forgetting our Front either. That was a lot in one day.
Was NCO of the Watch and wrote a few letters.

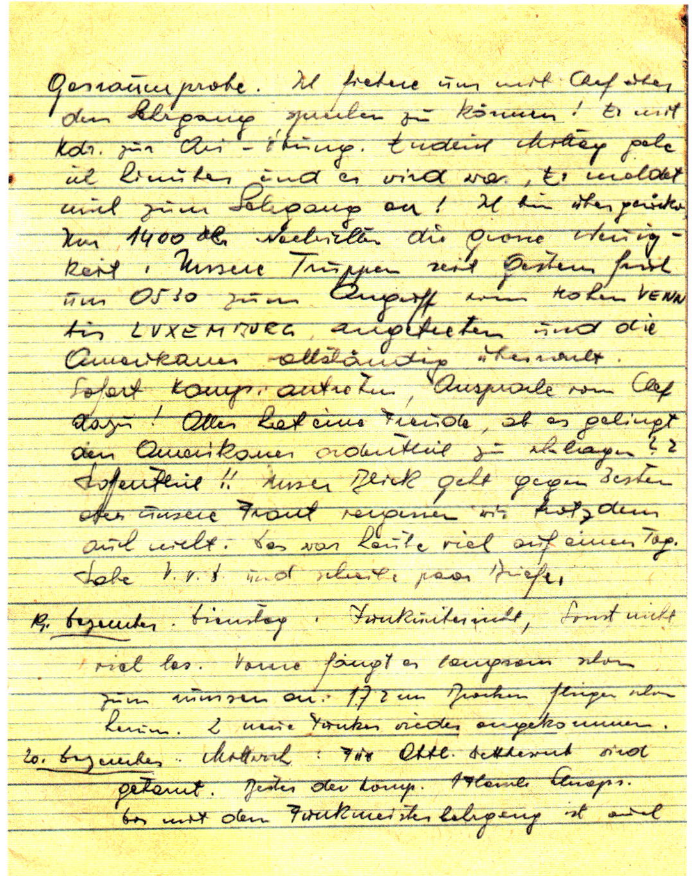
Gasmaskenprobe. Ich freue mich, mit Chef über den Lehrgang sprechen zu können! Er ist Kdr. zur Ausbildung. Endlich mittags gehe ich rüber und er sagt ja, er meldet mich zum Lehrgang an! Ich bin überglücklich. Um 1400 Uhr Nachrichten die grosse Neuigkeit. Unsere Truppen seit gestern früh um 0530 zum Angriff vom Hohen VENN bis LUXEMBURG angetreten und die Amerikaner vollständig überrascht. Sofort Komp. antreten, Ansprache vom Chef dazu! Alles hat eine Freude, ob es gelingt den Amerikaner ordentlich zu schlagen?? Hoffentlich!! Unser Blick geht gegen Westen aber unsere Front vergessen wir trotzdem auch nicht. Das war heute viel auf einen Tag. Habe U.v.D. und schreibe paar Briefe.
19. Dezember. Dienstag. Funkunterricht, sonst nicht viel los. Vorne fängt es langsam schon zum [illegible] an. 15,2 cm [illegible] schon [illegible]. 2 meiner Funker wieder angekommen.
20. Dezember. Mittwoch: [illegible] gefeiert. Bester der Komp. 1 Flasche Schnaps. [illegible] mit dem Funkmeisterlehrgang ist auch

Diary page relating to the opening of the Battle of the Bulge.

19 December Tuesday. Radio instruction. Otherwise nothing much happening. Ahead it is already beginning to start. 15.2 cm guns firing. 2 of my radio operators arrived back.

20 December Wednesday. Celebration. Best in the Company. 1 bottle of Schnaps. It's not clear about the master radio operator training. Phoned and asked V. N. 5 *Nachrichten* Abt. (5 Signals Battalion), any news? They don't know anything about it. A blow for me. I don't believe anything about it any more. Was really too pleased about it! Building shelters for tanks.

21 December Thursday. Building shelters again. Bitter cold but no snow. Up front artillery are firing like mad. Every day we are waiting for Ivan. Still aircraft here. Aircraft look-outs, etc. An artillery Captain here called Leitz got into the vehicle by the radio. I explain the tank to him. A great human being and officer. In the evening I've got the cinema "Die romantische Brautfahrt," very nice piece from Vienna.

22 December Friday. The firing is becoming stronger and stronger. We could march off for attack any time. New radio documents and orders. Will we be able to celebrate

Christmas in peace???? Busy evening after night exercise, such a fuss. I work like mad. Bitter cold and route march. Came home at 2.30, go immediately to Lorenz to receive my radio instructions. Tomorrow morning the fun should start apparently!! There's heavy firing. Heavy fragments are flying here. Our Boss has become ObLtn.

23 December Saturday. It's quiet. Well, you never know!! Today Christmas celebrations should take place. The situation has calmed down again somewhat! I think we'll celebrate in peace! In the morning and afternoon we set up the room in a school. The celebration started at 18.00! Commandant's office and Adj also here. First of all the solemn part, then the jolly, merry part. Good meal first, then bottles of white wine and good Franken beer. Biscuits, chocolate - 2 pieces, cigarettes, and a Christmas Stollen as a present. "Jonny" Mann played tune on the harmonica. Promotions. Uffz. Müller becomes *Feldwebel*. Saudam and Eidenberger become Uffz A few HQ Gefr. and Obgefr. Schutka and Tomasck become Gefr. At this late time we made a party. Jonny played "auf die Schrage Masche" for me. Kdr and Adj quite impressed. Ltn. Eckhard also back here. Comic programme first class. Music quite splendid, Barcelona, schöner Panther. Went home at 02.00.

24 December Sunday. We got up at 08.30. Had cake for breakfast. Ia (first staff officer, operations officer who could strand in for the Divisional Commander) here with his command group Div leader Obst. Brux here, looks at my tank. Won first prize yesterday at the turret competition, prize a bottle of Schnaps. Otherwise off duty. Had to go to the Adj to an interrogation because of the stubborn, sickening crew that didn't come to our Christmas celebration. Had enough of that. In addition to that the whole Company had guard duty. Also for V Company (Supply or ration company). I was NCO of the watch of our own Company. Today forward command from Rgt HQ arrived. Parts of the pioneer platoon, all old fighters. Motorcycle platoon gradually pulling out to another poition. V Company moving into forest. There's another big change-over. Rgt HQ will surely come here to HOLENDRI! Sit now in the evenings in the village pub, a little Christmas tree next to me and with my thoughts back home with my loved ones. What will they all be doing? Christmas!!! To celebrate this lovely festival in the bosom of my loved ones would be my nicest dream! When will that be? If the war were only over for me! In the night everyone drunk and I have no sentries. Boss here as well.

25 December. Today in the garrison we want to celebrate Christmas. One man and Günther pinched the Christmas tree from the school, it's already become known, found nothing at our place. The first joke. There were 2 geese going down the street; we were already outside, and for a joke one of us gave sort of signals to the geese and straight away they came into our quarters and we chopped their heads off right away. There will be a roast. Start right away, two rather plump creatures. Jonny will play for us this evening and that will be spot on! In the middle of cooking Theo arrived to visit. Really pleased. Invite him to eat and he stays. Jonny played "da kommt der Jeulerol von Kde." Jonny had to go away immediately with Krad (motorbike) to Pz *Begleitkomp* (tank escort company). Div leader, Brux also there. Shame, we wanted to have such a nice celebration. The goose tasted delicious, then there was cake. We lit the Christmas tree (there would have been small candles attached to the tree and they would have been lit - the traditional German custom!) and think of home. Great Schnaps liqueur with it and we smoked. Theo spoke a lot about home, we spoke about Luischen and dreams. The two of us were alone 'til 02.00. Great music on the radio. Theo slept here!! Left at 05.30!

26 December Tuesday. Back on duty today. I do nothing! When we were falling in, the boss came and handed me a bottle of Schnaps from the ObLtn. as 1st prize in the camouflage competition. In the afternoon the artillery sergeant-major gave instruction about artillery radio. Night exercise cancelled. Wrote a few letters. Ivan has calmed down again! Thank God! Still no snow. The night owl flies round here every night. Otherwise nothing happening.

27 December Wednesday. Practical exercise with M.E. (Fu 8 radioset) as radio telephone, we give the *Korp* fire command, etc., all afternoon. In the afternoon order, make all the shelters for tanks. Heat proof. Lovely work!!! In the evening we chat a bit. Otherwise nothing happening! Soon going to bed! Ivan busy coming at us from another angle and launching flares.

28 December Thursday. Radio training. A Hptm. Benesch of radio company, coming from Div and inspects us. Was with the *Abfunkmeister* (senior radio operator.) He tested me according to H.D.V. 488/5 (Headquarters regulation) for the course. The course takes place in January. Am very curious about when I will get away. Hopefully it will work out. In the afternoon built targets for shooting. Otherwise nothing happening. Pioneer platoon almost building bridges. Got 18 little packets of pastry from Mum. Bitter cold but still no snow!! The situation here with us is still quiet! For how long? Every day we are waiting for Ivan! Ivan is bombing us. 3 bombs next to the house (the last sentence seems to have been added later).

29 December Friday! Technical duty, otherwise not much happening all day. Tomorrow vehicle inspection. In the afternoon sort out the quarters for pioneer platoon and reconnaissance platoon. Installed in the evening. V-detachment (Supply or ration) moved into the bunker in the forest.

30 December. In the morning vehicle inspection. Cover over our shelters better. Otherwise nothing happening all day. It has snowed at last. Not much snow though. Quiet up ahead. It roars now and again (the noise of the battle on the front line). Jonny organising all sorts of things. Building great beds for ourselves in the room - 8 all together. Riot amongst the civilians because of the organisation of bread. All the civilians know us. But now it is quite good-natured. Company a great crowd.

31 December Sunday. New Year 1944/45. In the morning painted the tanks with whitewash. Jonny baked cakes and biscuits. Covered over the shelters with straw and then shovelled sand - such stupid orders. We worked 'til 18.00. Günther roasted chickens meantime. Saw the stores completely full. The food and the good liqueur make us forget everything again. From the company there is only 1 litre of beer, some very thin. We organise 3 litres of Schnaps and make liqueur out of it. I've invited Fldw. Lorenz. We've also set up a radio. Then it starts - roast potatoes with chicken, beer with that. The liqueur, some cakes and biscuits with that. Listened to Göbbel's speech. Get into the swing of things. Jonny wants to go and get his harmonica from V-troop and stayed down there. Rudi and I went down as well and hung around 'til the New Year.

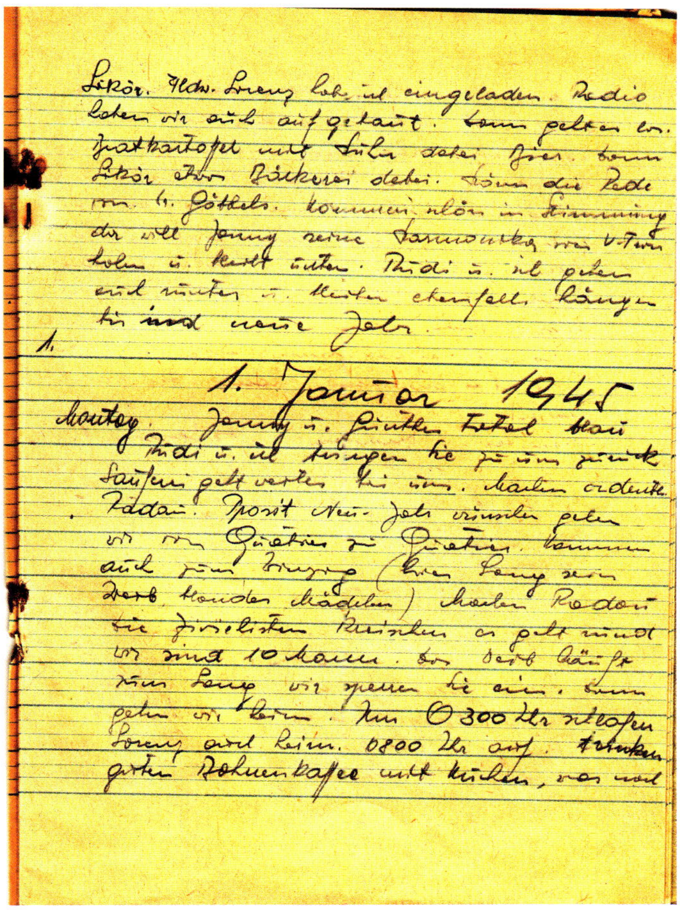

1. Januar 1945

Diary page for the first of January 1945.

1 January 1945
Monday. Jonny and Günther totally drunk. Rudi and I sing their praises all the way back. Drinking goes on at home. Make a great din. We go from quarter to quarter wishing Happy New Year. Came to the houses. Here Leng brought his woman, blond girl. Make a din. The civilians scream, it goes round that there are 10 of us. The woman runs to Leng. We shut them in. Then we go home. At 03.00 went to bed. Lorenz also went home. Up at 08.00. Drink good pure coffee with cake, what was left over from the New Year party. Leng came and wanted to make a fuss because of the woman. Whole company fell in. Commander said a few words to us and read out some articles. Afterwards to the Spiess because of the din. He tries to threaten us, etc., everything falls on us. Lay down because I have a bad stomach. In the afternoon we have to build a T-34 out of wood. Building takes place on the second evening. We are just making the preparations. At 19.00 we start. Fldw. Hesse and Fldw. Lorenz invited. First of all the food and then pure coffee and then good-naturedly mixed the liqueurs, while Jonny plays heavy but quite stupid music!! A great evening, very entertaining and merry - goes on 'til 02.00, but now bed.

2 January. Today duty, not much happening all day. Good mood! Want to go to bed soon as there is a night exercise. Build shelters 'til 23.00. Had enough!! On the radio the announcement of 579 Fl. (Aircraft) shot down and destroyed. A big blow.

3 January Wednesday. Radio instruction in our place. Don't do much. The Regimental commander, Major Reindel, set up quarters here. Jonny is his batman. Our old Rgt HQ here with HQ Fldw. Hebel, Obflw. Host, Uffz. Finler, etc. Have guard duty now 20 sentries.

4 January Thursday. Radio instruction, build shelters, strengthening. Swelling came. Firing. I didn't go. Weapon cleaning. Otherwise nothing happening. It's snowing a bit. However, almost no snow here. Kdr, Div.Nach.Tr. (HQ of the Divisional Signals troop) is being disbanded. Also an intelligence platoon also transferred away. Am curious about what happens. Meyer Hermann, Ltn., is ordnance officer at Rgt HQ. Wants to have us old people.

5 January Friday. Chief radio operators all here for a training. Also take part. ObLtn. Barth talks about communication. Tune in with V.K.H. Uffz. Sommer also here. Tells us all sorts of things. Going to bed soon. At 22.00 Fldw. Lorenz came and wakened me, and told me there was a call from Div. Uffz. Hager to go straight away to radio operator course in Heimat (Germany). I am one of the lucky, so happy I can't sleep. A thousand thoughts are going through my head, all kinds of wishes could come to fruition in the near future. The course starts on 13 January.

6 January Saturday. All morning instruction from the commander. During it I am quite unsettled. When will they send me away? Jonny could go on leave. He doesn't want to!! Would you believe it! His awards on his chest, *Sturmabzeichen* and EK2 (Assault badge and Iron Cross Second class). We need more of such people. In the afternoon I have a really good wash and go to the chief radio operator. We talk a bit about the course. Come back because there's a big change round. Gave up my vehicle immediately to Rgt HQ. HQ Gef. Rieger takes it over and drives it there. Günther in his vehicle. Jonny to Abt

Commander's Pz IV as medium wave radio operator. Set will be installed. Whole intelligence platoon torn apart. Also reconnaissance platoon. This evening a farewell evening, and this time there are even women!! I have 2 letters from Guetier-Denka and Nina. Meal great – *Reibekuchen* (potato fritters), coffee, pure coffee and liqueur. Jonny played music and we danced and then cuddled up. Very nice and intimate 'til 24.00 and then to bed. I had a lovely, pretty girl - Danka.

7 January Sunday!! Off duty. Sent a wireless message to Theo. Took a while. He's coming. Go to the Oberfldw. and say what I've done. He says I should take care of it myself. Theo arrived, but can only stay here an hour. Take him to the bus. Fldw. Rudi Steuber going off to TSCHENSTOCHAV. Then I go to the *Geschäftszimmer* (orderly room), from there to the *Schreibstube* (clerks). They are so stubborn, Leng, the arsehole, afterwards I go to the chief and tell him about it. He kicks up a rumpus, tears a strip off the orderly room and all of a sudden the ball started rolling. Got the dates and go to the orderly room of the Abt. Fldw. Spinkhorn sorts everything out immediately and I take the *Dienstausreiseschein* (duty journey certificate) straight to the Adj ObLtn. Kohlberger, Commander. He signs. Thank God, that's it done. If I hadn't done anything about it myself I would still have been sitting here on the 13th. I've managed to get 3½ days leave. Now I can begin to think about going home. Great joy. Sitting cosily together and telling one another what's been happening. Klosterknecht Rudi and I. Visited "Danka" and said good-bye. Very nice. Commander's batman came and said that something's going to be happening in the next few days. Action? Probably!! Russians attacked in the night and took 1 village, thrown out again.

8 January. *I'm going*. 11.50 leave by bus to JEDREZOW and stop there. Then go on to KARAKAU.

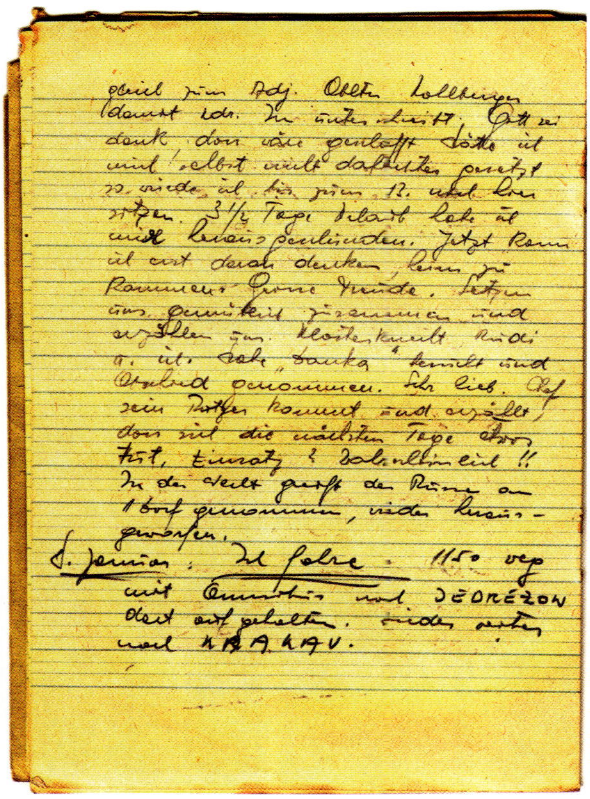

Diary page, "I'm going."

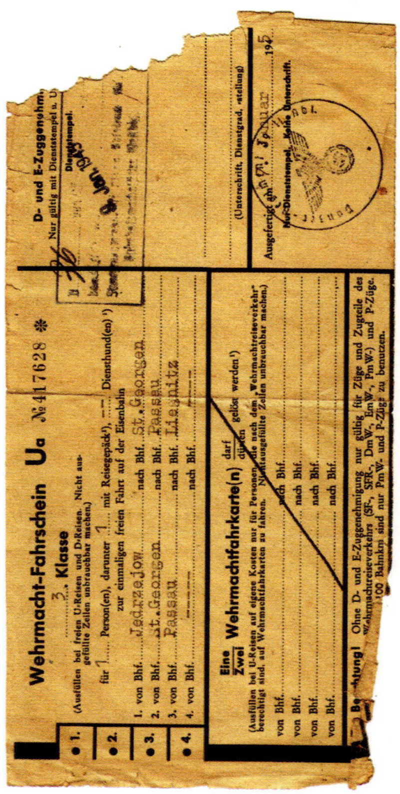

Rail warrant for leave travel home.

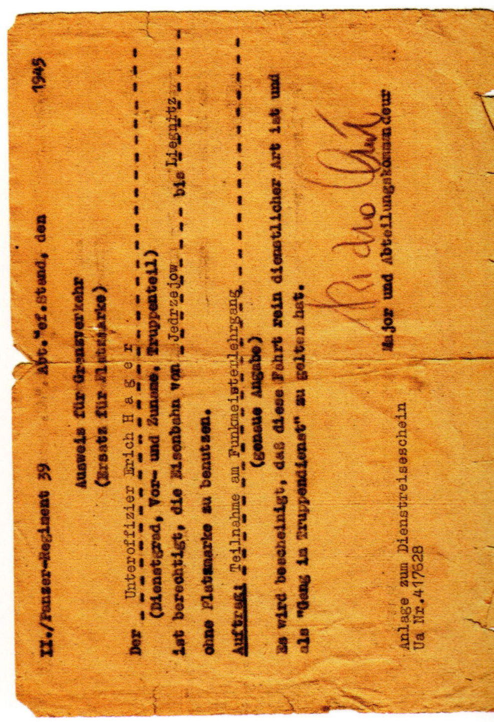

Leave pass signed by the *Abteilung* commander.

9 January. Want to take my short leave via Vienna. Travel under my own steam. At 10.00 in Vienna. Continue by express train to AMSTETTEN. Get off and go to Viehdorf. Big surpirse. Learn Luise and Juli are coming back from holiday at 02.00.

10 January. Travel on. Meet Flak guards *Flakhelferinnen*. Luise Kneroling. (Female auxiliaries in the service of the *Luftwaffe*. Later in the war they manned anti-aircraft guns.) Get to Linz, no train 'til evening. Go to Erma cinema "Opferung" - "Sacrifice." In the evening at 22.00 home.

11 January. Home. Big hello. Seidel Sieglard and Windner family here. Celebrate 'til early morning. Great girls here. Things going on.

12 January. Leave again in the evening via Passau. There I have the books of Franz Hager and go first to Regensburg, from there via Hof - Leipzig - Chemnitz - Görlitz to Liegnitz.

13 January. Arrived at 08.00. More than 60 men (Uffz) registering. Could go on leave but don't want to. Meet 1 Fldw from 60 *Schützen* Regiment. Two of us away. Very busy here. Do recovery service duty straight away. Great coffee - Regina, Zieger, Leichhände, Hoffmann, etc.

14 January. Sleep 'til 10.00, then get shaved and into the town. Great women here. You experience the greatest things. Big site, very busy, I think the Russians are coming to Schlesien (Silesia). The time goes like this 'til 18 January. Every day to bed at 02.00. On 18.1 (18 January) at 08.00 while we're sleeping comes the order to report in and the unbelievable happened, we have to go on leave 'til 30 January. Set off in the evening. And immediately air raid alarm in Breslau, Ivan attacking - only the suburbs. Go by express train to Breslau.
(No entries for 15 to 18 January.)

19 January. You experience the greatest things. The station is closed as it is overflowing with people. I climb into the station, catch an express train for Prague. Could only get in through the window and get into a female *Wehrmacht* compartment. Pretty girls, have a good conversation. One girl wants to go to Linz and joins company with me. It's O.K.

20 January. In Prague went out with Trude. Girl a decent sort. Journey to Linz by express train. Girl deeply in love!! Arrive early at 08.00 home. They can't believe their eyes. In the evening farewell celebration for Siegland in the "schiefe Laterne," noisy business. Hans here too.

21 January Sunday. Big sledging party to Kotsdorf with 2 sledges, 18 of us. Today Linz heavily bombed. Siegi and I watched. 80 killed.

Sledging party. Erich is on the left in M43 Panzer cap.

Erich is just in shot on the left. Note natty goatskin (?) jacket worn by one soldier.

22 January. One day goes by like the last. Hans and I always stand at the square. Nothing happening with girls. Went once to Linz straight away again. On the 27th in the evening a small men's night, Windner, Hans, Hager Franz, Michel, and I. Ate and drank well, 'til 0100. Worked for 2 days at Ferdi's in the butcher's. He's in the *Volkssturm*. And tomorrow on the 28th I'm off.
(No entries for 23 to 27 January.)

28 January. Sunday. Do another sledge trip to Langenschein. In the afternoon to Süngitz. There I went into Franz's, wanted to visit Elfriede. However, she's away to Georgen. The 4 of us sat at Peterzeit, no pretty girls here, went home again.
Sort my things out!!
Pfanzagl Rudi also home on 10 days' operational leave.

Notes to 1 December 1944 to 28 January 1945

On 1 January Erich notes a girl having been shot, but not wether this was an accident or otherwise. A more cheerful entry on the 5th related to his joy at finding old friends are in his Division.

A rare incident of Erich skipping duty happens on 7 January as he notices the withdrawal to the west of many German units. His Division is being streamlined due to the shortage of men. A new commander was appointed on the 2nd of the month from one of the Panzer Grenadier Regiments of 17. Panzer Division.

On the 8th Erich sees ever increasing Soviet air activity. The next day his unit is reducing to a battlegroup while he considers marriage to Luischen. It does not stop him seeing other women at every opportunity!

The threat of gas attack is still taken seriously, as on the 11th Erich has to suffer two hours in a gas mask during an exercise. He recovers when he recieves a large 8 kilogram parcel from home, but suspects the Soviets are planning a new attack. Erich hears with sorrow about the deaths of his four comrades, but concludes they risked their lives by not staying with the convoy.

Erich leads the exercise on 13 December, but finds the ground boggy. During mid-December the troops are subjected to political lectures from Nazi Party members. This was to keep the soldiers loyal to the party and Hitler. Music on the radio seems to have been more important, and probably was much better for morale.

December 17th is a good day for Erich, as there is a big party which helps to forget about the war, and he finally gets to go on the master radio operator's course. The next day comes news of the German offensive in the Ardennes, which many like Erich hoped would knock the western Allies out of the war.

Soldier's graveyard in UMAN.

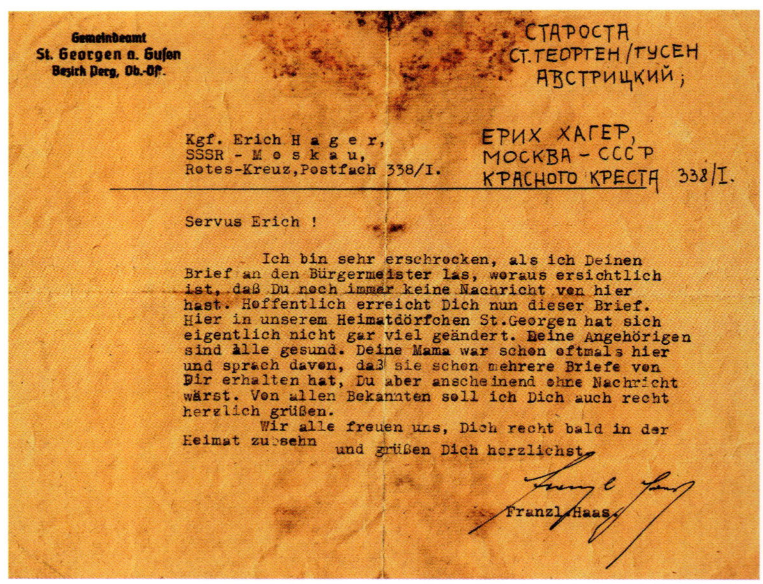

Gemeindeamt
St. Georgen a. Gusen
Bezirk Perg, Ob.-Öst.

СТАРОСТА
СТ.ГЕОРГЕН/ГУСЕН
АВСТРИЦКИЙ;

Kgf. Erich H a g e r,
SSSR - M o s k a u,
Rotes-Kreuz, Postfach 338/I.

ЕРИХ ХАГЕР,
МОСКВА - СССР
КРАСНОГО КРЕСТА 338/I.

Servus Erich !

Ich bin sehr erschrocken, als ich Deinen Brief an den Bürgermeister las, woraus ersichtlich ist, daß Du noch immer keine Nachricht von hier hast. Hoffentlich erreicht Dich nun dieser Brief. Hier in unserem Heimatdörfchen St.Georgen hat sich eigentlich nicht gar viel geändert. Deine Angehörigen sind alle gesund. Deine Mama war schon oftmals hier und sprach davon, daß sie schon mehrere Briefe von Dir erhalten hat, Du aber anscheinend ohne Nachricht wärst. Von allen Bekannten soll ich Dich auch recht herzlich grüßen.

Wir alle freuen uns, Dich recht bald in der Heimat zu sehn und grüßen Dich herzlichst,

Franzl Haas.

A letter written to Erich when he was a prisoner of war. Note address copied in Russian.

Erich hears the increase in firing at the front on the 22nd and hopes to celebrate Christmas in peace. The next day he and his comrades start their Christmas celebrations early, probably since they expected to be thrown into the front line. On Christmas Eve Erich is proud to win a prize, but is annoyed at the crew, who misbehave. Christmas is a hard time for troops away from home and family, and Erich longs to be with his family despite the parties with his comrades.

After the snow falls Erich and his comrades have to apply the winter whitewash camouflage to their tanks. Göebbel's speech does not seem to dampen the New Year celebrations, but the next day Erich and his friends get into trouble due to their noisy celebrations. They must have wondered what the new year would bring for them and if they would survive much of it.

The T-34 made of wood would be utilised as a training aid, probably in the use of the *Panzerfaust* anti-tank weapon. On 3 January the posting of 20 sentries shows the high state of alert. The next day there is further contraction of Erich's unit.

Erich's longing for his course is recorded again on 5 January, and after a party with girls the next day he finally gets his wish on the 7th. As a bonus he is granted some home leave, but takes every chance to meet girls, even on trains. He claims he could only get into a female compartment on the train, which incidentally happens to be full of attractive *Whermacht* female auxillaries!

There are no diary entries for the days of 15 to 17 January and 23 to 26 January. Perhaps Erich partied too well!

This was the last of Erich's diaries. If he wrote another after 28 January 1945 then it must have been lost when he was captured by the Soviets. Erich's writings provide a fasinating record of one man's war on the Eastern Front.

Erich said the Russians that captured him treated him very well. As was usual they took his medals and awards. During his captivity he had to experience temperatures of minus 50 degrees centegrade, however!

Food was scarce, and many of Erich's comrades died from eating frozen, raw potatoes. Erich always boiled his food; his training and time in the Army probably saved his life. Many times in his diaries he talks of preparing food, and no doubt he was an accomplised chef

Clothing in captivity was also scarce, and Erich related that they had to saw the boots and clothes off the frozen bodies of dead comrades.

After being released as a Prisoner of War Erich had to walk the 10,000 kilometres from Siberia to his home in Austria. Some of the Russian villages were so remote they did not know the war was over and insisted on holding Erich captive again until outsiders could confirm the end of hostilities. Erich arrived back in Austria in 1949.

A small metal box crafted by Erich while in soviet captivity. He brought it with him when he returned home.

Chapter 15

Erich's Ladies and Postwar

A selection of surviving photographs.

RAD girl.

Another RAD girl.

"First lambs 1941."

"Easter 1941."

"27.1.42"

"26.6.43, Regina."

"To remember Hilde in September 1942."

"To remember my 'unknown one,' Heddi."

"Remember me fondly. Gudi."

Ema Sack. Film star and/or singer?

Ukranian girl?

Autographed picture.

Post War

Some photos of Erich's life with his family. He was no doubt glad to be home and at peace.

Erich Hager, 17.Panzer Division veteran.

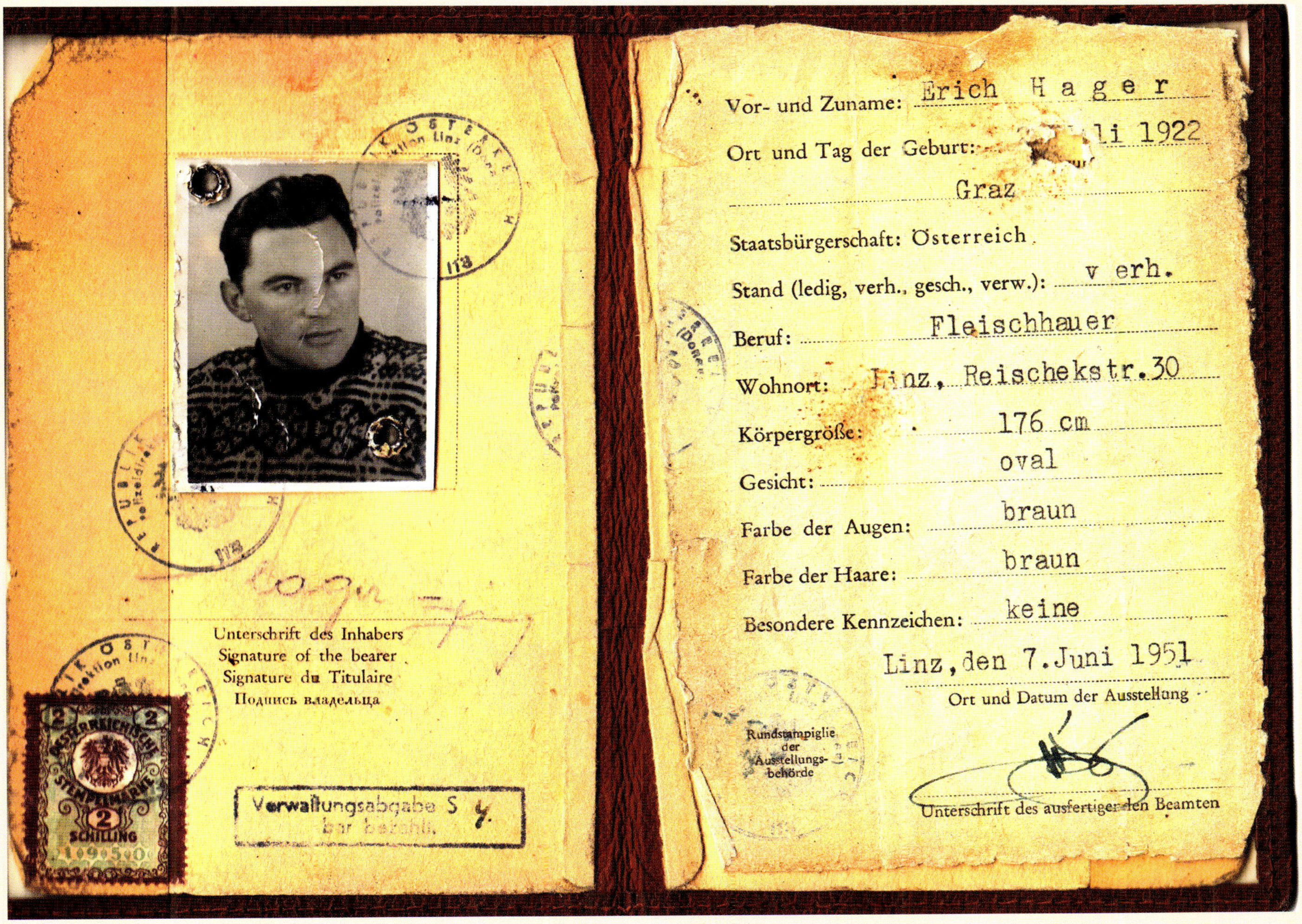

Unterschrift des Inhabers
Signature of the bearer
Signature du Titulaire
Подпись владельца

Verwaltungsabgabe S 4.
bar bezahlt.

Vor- und Zuname: Erich Hager

Ort und Tag der Geburt: li 1922 Graz

Staatsbürgerschaft: Österreich

Stand (ledig, verh., gesch., verw.): verh.

Beruf: Fleischhauer

Wohnort: Linz, Reischekstr.30

Körpergröße: 176 cm

Gesicht: oval

Farbe der Augen: braun

Farbe der Haare: braun

Besondere Kennzeichen: keine

Linz, den 7.Juni 1951

Ort und Datum der Ausstellung

Rundstampiglie der Ausstellungsbehörde

Unterschrift des ausfertigenden Beamten

Erich's ID card 1951. Number 185821.

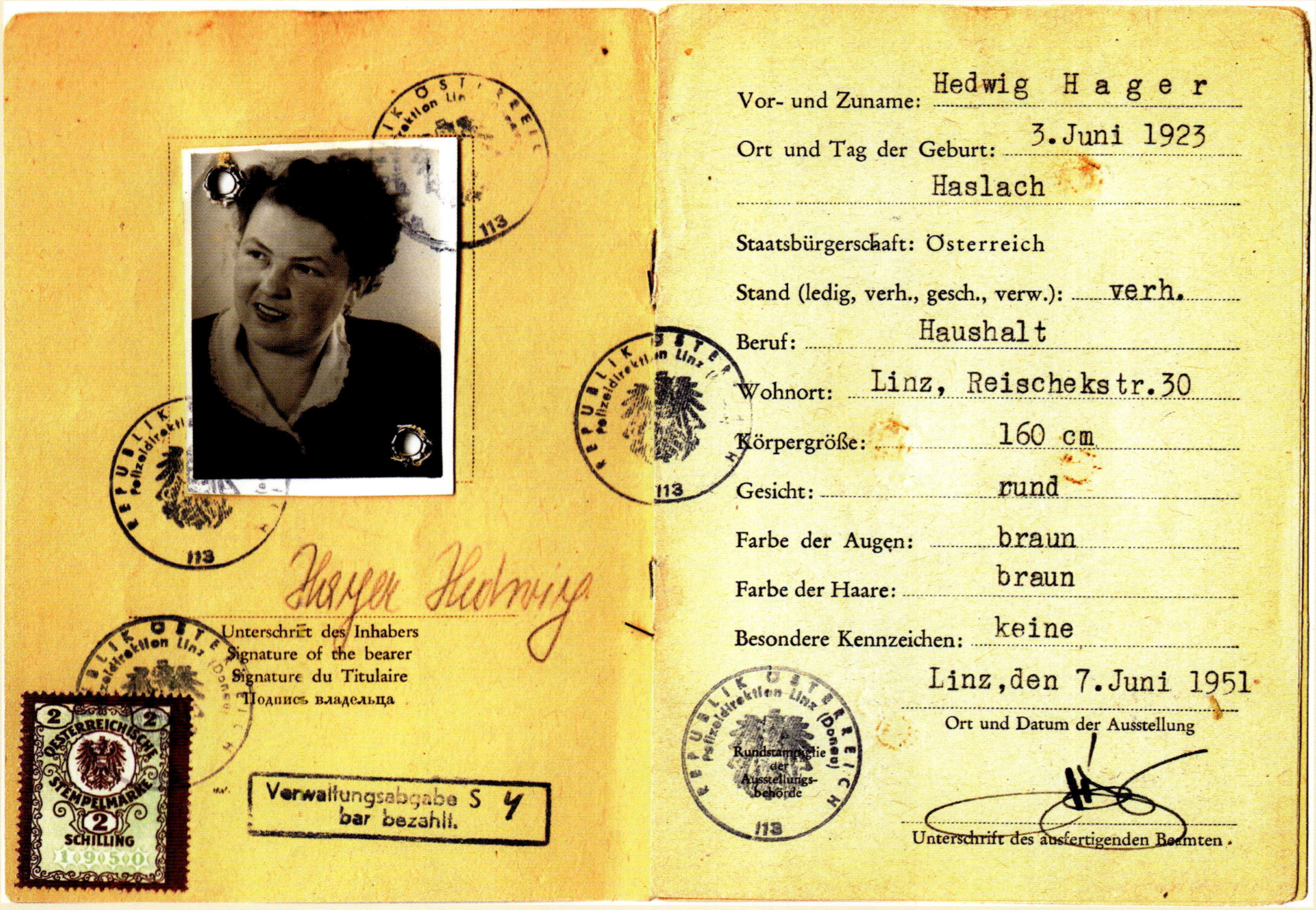

Vor- und Zuname: Hedwig Hager

Ort und Tag der Geburt: 3. Juni 1923 Haslach

Staatsbürgerschaft: Österreich

Stand (ledig, verh., gesch., verw.): verh.

Beruf: Haushalt

Wohnort: Linz, Reischekstr. 30

Körpergröße: 160 cm

Gesicht: rund

Farbe der Augen: braun

Farbe der Haare: braun

Besondere Kennzeichen: keine

Linz, den 7. Juni 1951

Ort und Datum der Ausstellung

Rundstampiglie der Ausstellungsbehörde

Unterschrift des ausfertigenden Beamten

Hager Hedwig

Unterschrift des Inhabers
Signature of the bearer
Signature du Titulaire
Подпись владельца

Österreichische Stempelmarke 2 Schilling 1950

Verwaltungsabgabe S 4 bar bezahlt.

Hedwig Hager's ID card, 1951.

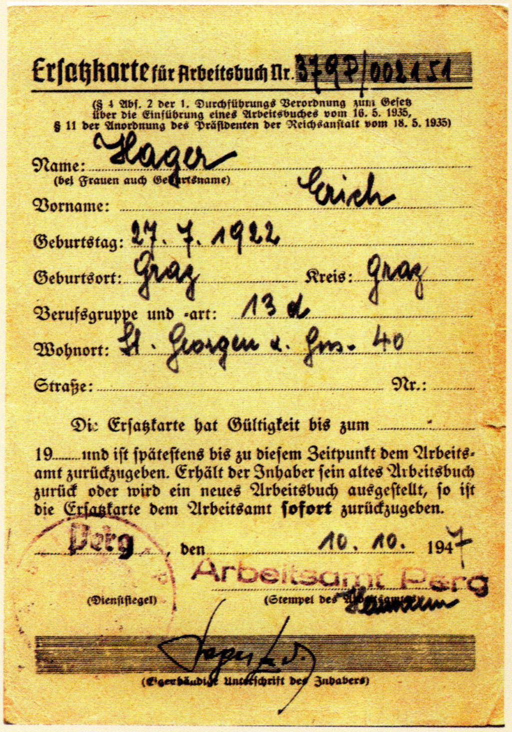

Ersatzkarte für Arbeitsbuch Nr. 379P/002151

(§ 4 Abs. 2 der 1. Durchführungs-Verordnung zum Gesetz über die Einführung eines Arbeitsbuches vom 16. 5. 1935, § 11 der Anordnung des Präsidenten der Reichsanstalt vom 18. 5. 1935)

Name: Hager
(bei Frauen auch Geburtsname)

Vorname: Erich

Geburtstag: 27. 7. 1922

Geburtsort: Graz Kreis: Graz

Berufsgruppe und -art: 13 d

Wohnort: St. Georgen a. Gus. 40

Straße: Nr.:

Die Ersatzkarte hat Gültigkeit bis zum

19 und ist spätestens bis zu diesem Zeitpunkt dem Arbeitsamt zurückzugeben. Erhält der Inhaber sein altes Arbeitsbuch zurück oder wird ein neues Arbeitsbuch ausgestellt, so ist die Ersatzkarte dem Arbeitsamt **sofort** zurückzugeben.

Perg, den 10. 10. 1947

Arbeitsamt Perg

(Dienstsiegel) (Stempel des Arbeitsamts)

(Eigenhändige Unterschrift des Inhabers)

Erich's work book, 1947.

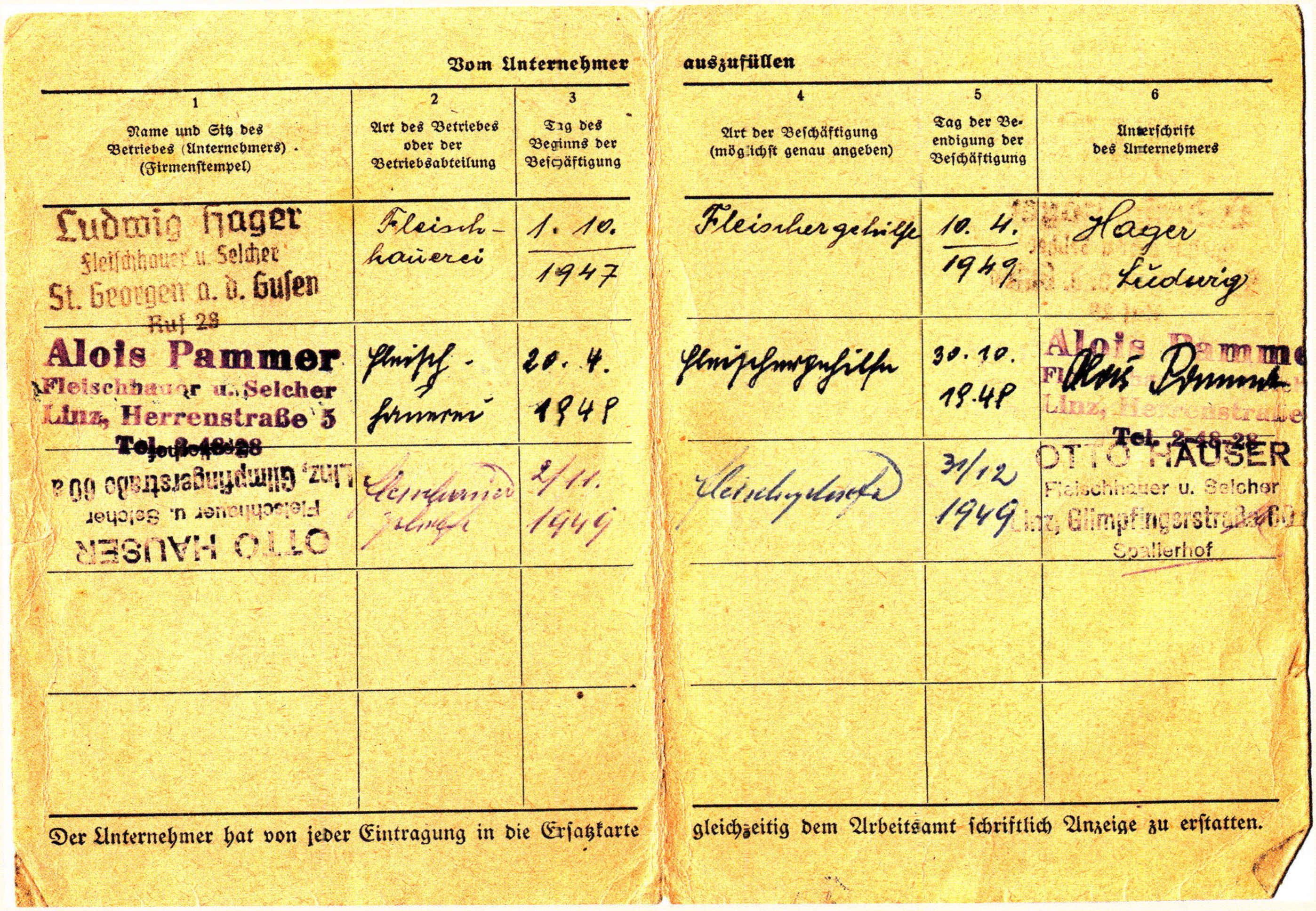

Vom Unternehmer auszufüllen

1 Name und Sitz des Betriebes (Unternehmers) (Firmenstempel)	2 Art des Betriebes oder der Betriebsabteilung	3 Tag des Beginns der Beschäftigung	4 Art der Beschäftigung (möglichst genau angeben)	5 Tag der Beendigung der Beschäftigung	6 Unterschrift des Unternehmers
Ludwig Hager Fleischhauer u. Selcher St. Georgen a. d. Gusen Ruf 28	Fleisch-hauerei	1. 10. 1947	Fleischergehilfe	10. 4. 1949	Hager Ludwig
Alois Pammer Fleischhauer u. Selcher Linz, Herrenstraße 5 Tel. 2-48-28	Fleisch-hauerei	20. 4. 1948	Fleischhauergehilfe	30. 10. 1948	Alois Pammer
Otto Hauser Fleischhauer u. Selcher Linz, Glimpfingerstraße 60	Fleischhauer Gehilfe	2/11. 1949	Fleischergehilfe	31/12 1949	Otto Hauser Fleischhauer u. Selcher Linz, Glimpfingerstraße 60 Spallerhof

Der Unternehmer hat von jeder Eintragung in die Ersatzkarte gleichzeitig dem Arbeitsamt schriftlich Anzeige zu erstatten.

Inside of Erich's work book showing employment as a butcher.

"Hager family 1955."

Visit to the Soviet Union in 1961 with old comrades.
Erich is in the centre.

"March 1963."

Another picture of that 1961 visit.

"In front of the shop. May 1963." This is a first communion photo.

"Klopeunersee 1967. Papa, Mama, Birli, and I in the Ober Hahe Hotel. Also had a few dances." A photo belonging to Erich's daughter Heidi.

"Saalbach. Short holiday. Feb. 1971" Possibly with old comrades. Erich still has the grin that he had in the wartime pictures.

Chapter 16

War Record of 17.Panzer Division

In this section we have used the standard German military abreviations for military units. The arabic numerals in front of a unit's title denote the Company and Roman numerals a battalion. "Div." notes a Division, "Regt." a Regiment, "Batl." a Battalion, and "Komp" a Company. In the same way "Pz." Denotes Panzer, "Gren." are Grenadiers, "I" are Infantry, "Pi." are engineers, and "Jg." are *Jagers*, or light Infantry.

For example, "II./Pz.Regt." 39 denotes "second Battalion of Panzer Regiment 39." In the same way "3./Pz.Pi.Btl.27" denotes "third Company of Panzer Pioneer Battalion 27."

17.Panzer Division was formed at Augsberg from 27 Infantry Division on 1 November 1940 (Bavaria, Military District 7). The Panzer element, Panzer Regiment 39, came from the replacement battalions of the 4th and 33rd Panzer Regiments. The third battalion, III./Pz.Rgt. 39, was created from the first battalion of the Panzer Lehr Regiment, I./Pz.Lehr.Regt. The division was assigned to the 2nd Army while it was in the process of achieving operational status. In May 1941 it was part of Guderian's 2nd *Panzergruppe*.

17.Panzer Division fought exclusively on the Eastern Front, starting in the central sector from June 1941 to November 1942. On 22 June 1941 17.Panzer Division was still under the command of General Guderian in 2.Panzer *Armee*. Guderian, the father of the *Panzerwaffe*, was idolised by his men.

On 22 June 1941 at 0415 hours the advanced units of 17.Panzer Division began crossing the river Bug with 18.Panzer Division by Lazowika, northwest of Brest-Litovsk towards Widomla. *Schützen* Regiment 40 made a bridgehead which the rest of the Division enlarged and used. The tanks forded the river using waterproofing equipment tested for Operation "Sealion," the proposed invasion of Britain. Panzer III and Panzer IV tanks were waterproofed and equipped with snorkels. This allowed tanks to move in water 13 feet deep.

After crossing the River Bug the panzer *Abteilung* advanced towards the Szesrczewo region using the route of march from the bridgehead Lazowika-Lysoczya-Rudawik-Panzerrollebahn II near Widolma-Litewski-Szeszerzewo. The order of march of 17.Panzer Division was Rgt. *Stab*, II./Pz.Rgt. 39, 3./Pz.Pi.Btl.27, I./Pz.Rgt.39, and III./Pz.Rgt. 39.

This march was successfully carried out with only light enemy ground or air activity which did not hamper the advance. Any attacking enemy aircraft were shot down by the Flak units assisted by the other arms.

After a brief halt in Widolma ordered by the Regimental Commander of the Panzer *Abteilung*, the Divisional Commander ordered a technical halt before Szeszerzewo due to the number of breakdowns.

The Panzer *Abteilung* march from Widolma to Szeszerzewo took place successfully. After Litewski, however, the motor transport found difficulty with the sandy roads, and the motor cyclists had to scout out the best way forward. The final 10 km westwards of Szeszerzewo was particularly difficult, and it took some time for all the *Gefechstrosse* (fighting units) to reach the town. The forward *Abteilung* reported the presence of four Soviet tanks east of Szeszerzewo. These drove past the supply train LKW (lorries), but all the German vehicles reached the Panzer *Abtelung* safely.

After a meeting of the Divisional Commander and the Divisional Ia (operations officer) the Panzer *Abteilung* set out on Panzer Rollbahn II towards Pruzana as the spearhead of the Division. The forward units got into a firefight with Soviet forces south of Szeszerzewo, but drove these off to allow the Division to safely move on towards Pruzana. The Division successfully attacked and took Pruzana.

After this the Panzer *Abteilung* was ordered to advance (*Vormarsch*) in the order 4.Komp., Combat HQ Stab., 6.Komp., and 5.Komp. Before Zabin the Panzer *Abteilung* met the spearhead of Panzer Regiment 18 and part of forward *Abteilung* "Weber," but did not encounter any enemy activity until about 10 km southwsest of Pruzana, where the forward German tanks shot up a Soviet tank that was stationary on the road.

Shortly after the *Abteilung* Commnader's tank was passing a dense forest which concealed a Soviet tank with a 4.5 cm cannon. This fired, and the shot hit the *Abteilung* Commnader's tank on the turret. Splinters wounded the entire crew, who evacuated the tank. The *Abteilung* Commander was badly wounded and had to be helped from the sticken vehicle. The German tank men took cover in a roadside ditch under fire from the Soviets.

The Divisional Adjutant was in the tank immediately behind the Commander's. This tank was hit by tank gun fire too, but the shot did not penetrate the armour. When the Commander's tank was hit the column had stopped immediately. The Adjutant's tank had now sighted the Soviet tank, and the 6.Komp. vehicles opened heavy fire on the enemy in the clearing. After these had been destroyed the advance continued. The Commander's tank was recovered by its driver, who had remounted the vehicle under enemy fire. In spite of the Commander's serious wounds he called on his force to continue the advance and succeed in their mission. After a short rest halt Pruzana was taken without enemy resistance.

A German aircraft dropped an aerial message which was confirmed by radio order from Panzer *Gruppe* 2 shortly afterwards that the Panzer *Abteilung* was to advance and take Pruzana airfield and capture any aircraft and military equipment there. This was carried out without difficulty.

After taking the airfield the combat troops of the Panzer *Abteilung* had a technical halt of an hour and then set off towards Slonim. This proved difficult due to the chaotic traffic situation caused by the clogged roads. The Panzer *Abteilung* halted for the night, and the next day the advance could only be resumed after the Commanding general personally sorted out the road traffic problems. Order of March was I./Pz.Rgt 39, III./Pz.Rgt.39, then II./ Pz.Rgt. 39.

The Panzer *Abteilung* was now ordered to attack and take Slonim. Despite trying their best to advance quickly the forward units became tangled up with parts of 18.Panzer Division, as the traffic situation was still difficult. Only when 18.Panzer Division moved off in the correct direction of their advance could 17.Panzer Division make rapid progress without hindrance on the roads from other units.

Divisional orders were to secure bridgeheads near Slonim. II./Panzer Regiment 39 was to move southeast to outflank the town. In the process of this II./Panzer Regiment 39 became involved in heavy tank vs tank fighting with Soviet armour. Likewise, Soviet infantry resisted heavily. A retreating Soviet unit cut off the divisional supply train LKWs for a time. Enemy artillery and small arms fire went on throughout the following night.

The next morning 17.Panzer Division required a break for the technical duty of replenishing fuel and ammunition. By the evening of 26 June 17.Panzer Division had destroyed 15 Tanks, 7 Pak anti-tank guns, 45 Trucks (LKW) with infantry, one goods train, and one passenger train fully occupied with enemy troops.

Next the division received orders to advance towards Minsk. Route of March was to be Slonim-Albertyn-Wygoda-Poleniczyze-Wolna-Mir-Stolpce-Kojdanow-Minsk. Order of march was to be 1.Kp./III.Pz.Rgt. 39, Regts.Stab., 2.Komp./III.Pz.Rgt. 39, II./ Pz.Rgt. 39, and I./Pz.Rgt. 39. Other fighting units came behind.

After the town of Slonim had been taken by 17.Panzer Division some Russian infantry were still resisting against divisional dismounted motorcyclists and a battery of 17.Panzer Division Artillery. They were surprised to be joined by Guderian himself, who manned a machine gun in his armoured command half-track to help overcome the enemy.

Guderian moved on to the headquarters of 17.Panzer Division, finding the Divisional commander, *Generalleutnant* von Arnim, and the Corps Commander, General Lemelsen. While the German officers discussed the advance some Russian tanks appeared pursued by German Panzer IV tanks. Seeing the German officers the Russians opened fire. The Generals were old soldiers and took cover quickly, but two younger officers were wounded, one fatally. The Russian tanks were knocked out after forcing their way into the town.

On the 26th the Divisional Commander, *Generalleutnant* von Arnim, was wounded at Stolpce and replaced by *Generalmajor* Karl Ritter von Weber. 17.Panzer Division arrived in Minsk from the south on 27 June with *Panzergruppe* 3 to find much of the city destroyed. The next day the division occupied Koidonov.

On 28 June divisional command was once again changed when Johannes Streich took over. The wounded von Arnim must have been somewhat cheered up by the announcement that he had been nominated (*eingang*) for the Knight's Cross (RK) on 1 July 1941. While under Guderian's command, 17.Panzer Division unwittingly was the subject of a falling out between the senior commander von Kluge and Guderian.

Von Kluge wanted to keep 17.Panzer Division in reserve in case of a Russian breakout, but Guderian wanted to keep the division with him. According to Guderian he passed von Kluge's order to 17.Panzer Division, who did not receive it and continued to advance. As a similar misunderstanding had already happened in Hoth's Panzer Group, von Kluge suspected insubordination and a conspiracy. He threatened both Guderian and Hoth with court-martial. Another example, after his command in France, of Guderian's bold and stubborn style of leadership. This must have reinforced his place as the 'bad boy" of the German High Command.

After the fall of the Bialystok pocket the 17 and 18.Panzer Divisions were held up by heavy fighting with large numbers of Russian tanks. The Germans had to cross the river Dnieper quickly before strong, fresh Russian defences could be prepared. Von Bock and von Kluge did not want to take responsibility for the command of the unruly Panzer groups 2 and 3. Guderian took charge of the crossing of the river.

As Guderian could see that strong Russian defences would stop the German motorised advance he ordered a crossing of the river immediately. 17 and 18.Panzer

Division were ordered to break off their advance. 17.Panzer Division had recently, on 7 July, knocked out 100 Russian tanks near Senno. Von Kluge wanted Guderian to wait for infantry support, but Guderian pointed out that the Panzers in their attack position would be attacked by Russian aircraft. The attack went ahead as planned.

17.Panzer Division met fierce opposition at Orsha, so it withdrew and attacked again at Kopys with the support of the 29th (Mot) Infantry Division. This time the division with the attached motorised infantry encircled and captured Orsha from the east on 15 July.

The Germans reached Smolensk on 15 July and captured it on the 16th. The Russians counter attacked from the northeast, and Hoth began to encircle them while Guderian sent his XLVI Panzer corps south to prevent the Russians escaping. Meeting heavy resistance, Guderian sent XLVII Panzer Korps in support, but as von Kluge ordered 18.Panzer Division to stay in reserve, 17.Panzer Division was the sole Panzer division. The presence of 17.Panzer Division prevented the Russians from making a breakout by attacking the left flank of Soviet forces from the southeast.

Showing how the German Command lead from the front, 17.Panzer Division had its second commander casualty on 18 July when *Generalmajor* Karl Ritter von Weber was wounded in action. He subsequently died of wounds two days later and was replaced by General Wilhelm von Thoma on 19 July.

On 19 July 17.Panzer Division attacked southeast of Roslavl to cover 24.Panzer Division's east flank. The next day heavy opposition was encountered near Pochep before it was captured on 21 July. Later, on the 25th, 17.Panzer Division attacked from Pochep across the Sudost river towards Trubchevsk to take pressure off 4.Panzer Division so the latter could advance south with 24.Panzer Division. The next day the Division moved to Semzy, where von Arnim received his Knights Cross on 4 September.

Hitler wanted to capture Kiev for its economic importance and the rest of the Ukraine. As Panzer Corps XLVI had been put in reserve, Guderian had only two Panzer Corps, XLVII and XLIV (the latter was exhausted), to attack Kiev.

When Guderian visited the headquarters of 17. Panzer Division he found them under strength, but they still had to participate in the attack on Kiev. After taking Pochinok 17.Panzer Division pushed eastwards and north, trying to link up with 3.Panzer Division and close the Smolensk pocket. This was achieved on 3 August when the Division contacted 20.Motorised Division and 3.Panzer Division

Later on 10 August 17.Panzer Division turned south from Yelnya. On 16 August the third tank battalion, III/Pz.Rgt.39, was renamed I/Pz.Lehr.Rgt. and returned to Germany. This was in line with the current practice of reducing Panzer regiments from three to two battalions. Another Division officer was decorated on 17 August. *Oberst* Rudolf-Eduard Licht was nominated for the German Cross in Gold. (DKiG).

September 10th saw 17.Panzer Division in Gluchov and then Putivl on the 17th. *Generaloberst* von Arnim returned from convalescent leave on the same day and replaced von Thoma as Divisional commander on 19 September. The latter went to 20.Panzer Division. 17.Panzer Division, with its new highly decorated commander, took Bielopolie on 20 September in conjunction with the *Grossdeutschland* Division. However, the next day Divisional units were attacked and partially surrounded near Gluchov. The Division managed to defeat the enemy by the 22nd.

The Division came under the 2.Panzer *Gruppe* (2.Pz. Gr.) on 23 July with 18.Panzer Division and 29.Motorised Division. 17.Panzer Division formed the left flank of 2.Panzer Grenadier Division in an attack from Yampol towards Sevsk. The Division was further honoured when von Arnim was promoted to full *General der Panzertruppen* on 1 October while in Druzhba.

From Sevsk 17.Panzer Division turned north towards Bryansk, capturing bridges over the Nerussa river, west of Dmitrovsk, by 3 October. On the way to Bryansk Karachev was captured on 5 October, and Bryansk itself and the bridge over the Desna river captured from the east on the next day. In doing so 17.Panzer Division captured the Soviet Bryansk HQ south of the town. However, the Soviet commander Eremenko and most of the officers escaped.

The Division now, on 7 October, came under heavy attack from the west while in Bryansk by Soviet units desperately trying to escape eastwards. Despite strong assaults 17.Panzer Division held its ground and formed the northeast side of a pocket forming round Trubchevsk. By 14 October the Soviet attacks had petered out and the Division attacked southwards to clear the Trubchevsk pocket. By the 20th all remaining Soviet troops in the pocket had surrendered. 17.Panzer Division had been an important part in another of the pocket battle successes that characterised the early years of the war in Russia.

Success was not to last. The weather turned bad, starting with heavy rains. In Mtsensk, on 1 November 17.Panzer Division was at a stand-still due to the clogging mud (*rasputitsa*) and lack of supplies that could not get through to the division because of the dire state of the roads.

On 8 November the Division's infantry were attached to XXIV.Pz.Kp. Later in the month on the 17th, the division had a new Commander in *Generalleutnant* Rudolf-Eduard Licht, who took over in Plavsk. General von Arnim went to XXXIX.Pz.Kp.

The new Commander had barely time to settle in as the next day 17.Panzer Division was the lead division in a major assault to outflank Tula, then proceed east and north towards Kashira. Other divisions involved were 3.Panzer Division on the left flank, 4.Panzer Division took the right flank, and the *Grossdeutschland* Division was tasked to capture and hold Tula. By the 20th 17.Panzer Division had captured an important bridge east of Bolochovo on the Shat river and was advancing north towards Venev. This town was captured on 24 November.

Due to strong soviet opposition the offensive bogged down on 30 November three kilometres south of the objective Kashira. On 6 December 17.Panzer Division had to call off the attack and withdraw to a secure line of the Don, Shat, and Upa rivers near Venev. The Soviets counterattacked and made deep penetrations of the German lines, forcing the Division to move further west to Tula on 13 December.

17.Panzer Division was transferred from XXIV Pz.Kp. and tasked with defense along the Plava river south of Plavsk.

The New Year saw the Division in a temporary holding area near Mtsensk after withdrawing from the front line and moving further west to "Winter Line " positions. Like all units of the German armed forces 17.Panzer Division had to endure the terrible winter of 1941/42 ill equipped to do so.

Some joy was brought to the Division when the commander of Panzer Regiment 39, *Oberst* Kurt Cuno, received the German Cross in Gold on 14 January, and on 18 January the same officer received the Knight's Cross. The Division was not to have such a highly decorated officer for long, as on 23 January *Oberst* Cuno was transferred to the *Führer* Reserve. On 1 February the Divisional Commander had been promoted to *Generalmajor*, and *Oberst* Otto Buesing became the Commander of Panzer Regiment 39.

From January up to November 1942 17.Panzer Division was stationed near Orel. The Division remained with Army Group Centre in the Orel sector, being part of German forces preventing any soviet breakthrough during the conquest of southern USSR (*Fall Blau*). The Germans tried to take Stalingrad and the Caucasus simultaneously. The Soviets fell back until they were ready to counterattack around Stalingrad.

On 19 June 1942 Panzer Regiment 39 lost its first battalion, I./Pz.Rgt.39, which was transferred to 29.Mot. Div. and renamed Pz.Abt.129. This sort of practice gave a trained and experienced Panzer *Abteilung* or Battalion to a motorised Division, but weakened the donor Panzer Division, as it had only one Battalion of tanks. 17.Panzer Division was to remain like this for a while which reduced its fighting strength.

In further evidence of the Division's officer quality, on 4 September Heinz von Randow left to become the new Commander of 15.Panzer Division in North Africa, and the next day *Oberst* Karl-Albert Rubsam became the Commander of Panzer Brigade 17. On 11 October the Division got a new Commander in the experienced and able *General der Panzertruppen* Fridolin von Senger und Etterlin. He had served as a motorised brigade commander in the French *Blitzkrieg* campaign and had closely worked with Panzers. As a former cavalryman he espoused the dash and élan of a war of movement.

When von Senger und Etterlin took over 17.Panzer Division southeast of Orel he thought it was of good quality and recognised it as the pre-war Augsburg Division. This warmed him to his new task, and he spent several weeks visiting and familiarising himself with the Divisional units.

However, 17.Panzer Division had only 30 operational tanks and a third of its trucks were unserviceable. 17.Panzer Division remained with Army Group Centre in the Orel sector, being part of German forces preventing any soviet breakthrough during the conquest of southern USSR (*Fall Blau*).

On 14 December 1942 17.Panzer Division was sent to the southern sector as part of 4. Panzer *Armee* to take part in the operation to relieve Stalingrad (codename Winter Storm), crossing the Don at Tsimlyansk. The German 6th *Armee* under von Paulus was encircled around Stalingrad after Hitler had refused to let them withdraw. The Soviets had swept aside the Rumanian forces on the flanks, and the Germans in "Fortress Stalingrad" were 35 miles from the most westerly friendly units. 17.Panzer Division covered the flanks and stopped heavy soviet attacks when the Rumanian resistance collapsed.

General Erich von Manstein, as commander of Army Group Don, quickly planned to relieve Stalingrad. He moved the LVII Panzer Korps under Ltn. Gen. Friedrich Kirchner to the 4. Panzer *Armee* commanded by Col. Gen. Hermann Hoth. These forces took up positions 65 miles to the southwest of Stalingrad in an area, although further from the encircled Germans, that was not well defended and had fewer natural obstacles.

At this time 17.Panzer Division was held in reserve on Hitler's direct orders. The main units in LVII Panzer Korps were 6.Panzer Division commanded by *Generalmajor* Erhard Raus, 17.Panzer Division under *Generalmajor* Fridolin von Senger und Etterlin, and 23.Panzer Division led by *Generalmajor* Hans von Boineburg-Lengsfeld.

Generalmajor von Senger und Etterlin considered 17.Panzer Division very weak in material for its task in the attempt to relieve Stalingrad. He noted it had only 30 tanks, no armoured cars, and only two reconnaissance vehicles. Furthermore, thirty to forty percent of the trucks (LKW) were undergoing major repair. In each battalion one company could only move on foot. These were formed into a battalion which marched behind the Division. This reduced still further 17.Panzer Division's abilities.

After a twelve hour drive crossing the Don at Tsymlianskaya, Frido von Senger und Etterlin and 17.Panzer Division's tracked units arrived on the evening of 15 December at Ovchinnikov and set up Headquarters. The division's wheeled units arrived over the next two days. A thaw had turned the roads into mud baths. Von Senger und Etterlin was unable to go to 4.Panzer *Armee* headquarters, but was told that the enemy was on his left flank. On the telephone von Senger und Etterlin spoke to *Generaloberst* Hoth, whom he knew personally. He reported the "lamentable state of equipment of my division." Hoth replied "At the front some divisions are in an even worse state. Yours has an excellent reputation. I rely on you."

The fighting qualities of 17.Panzer Division were well known *Generalmajor* von Senger und Etterlin, however, had grave doubts about the ability of one complete and two half divisions to advance offensively 100 kilometres to Stalingrad against strong and increasing Soviet opposition. It also seemed ridiculous to von Senger und Etterlin that the 100,000 men in the Sixth Army should not break out to link up to 4.Panzer *Armee*.

6.Panzer Division had been refitted in the west, but the 17 Panzer Division and 23.Panzer Division were well under strength. However, opposing LVII Korps was only a light screen of soviet troops composed of six rifle divisions and two tank brigades, as the soviets did not expect an attack from this direction. The terrain was rolling farmland, with little prominent landmarks for orientation purposes. Rivers consisted of minor tributaries that posed little obstacle to the Germans.

The operation had been named "Winter Storm," and at first made good progress. 6.Panzer Division advanced to Samchin, about a third of the way to Stalingrad. Then the Soviets moved 13th Tank Korps and 4th Mechanised Korps to counter the German force, and 2nd Guards Army was diverted from the encirclement of Stalingrad to stop the German Panzer Divisions.

Despite this increased opposition, the attack continued to take ground on the second day when 11.Panzer Regiment of 6.Panzer Division crossed the Aksay river. A Soviet counter attack by 4th Mechanised Korps pushed 11. Panzer Regiment back to the river, where fighting continued until December 17th.

On 15 December von Senger und Etterlin had information about what faced his Division. The Soviet 65th Tank and 81st Cavalry Divisions had been identified. He ordered Panzer Group Büssing (named after the regimental commander) of 17.Panzer Division to advance to Verkch Kurmoyarskaya via Topolev, where they learned from the locals that the Soviets had withdrawn to the northwest. The motorised elements of the Panzer Grenadier Regiments did not reach Shilovskaya until the 16th because of delays at the bridge at Zymlianskaya.

With better communications established with LVII *Armee* Korps headquarters 17.Panzer Division was ordered to Generalovskii for a surprise attack on the Soviet forces, and to establish a bridgehead over the Askai Yessaulovskii river. This attack showed no enemy - he had moved northwards from Nagavskaya. The tanks moved through Verch Yablotschnii, Nish Yablotschnii, and Verkch Kurmoyarskaya, reporting them free from enemy but mined. There was now an acute shortage of fuel. The roads were turned to mud by the thaw. The road along the Don was reported as impassible, as was the road through Pochlebin, which Korps had instructed the Division to move on.

On the night of the 16th a longed for hard frost set in which allowed fast travel for wheeled vehicles to resume. This started after reconnaissance at 0500 the next day. *Generalmajor* von Senger und Etterlin personally led the Seitz group – Pz.Gren.Rgt. 63, Pz.Jg.27, Regimental Staff, III./Art.Rgt. 27, and a company of Pz.Pi.Btl.27 – along the track through Maiorski, Kotelnikov, and Verch Yablotschnii.

Generalovskii was occupied and the bridgehead established at 1415 on 17 December. The soviet resistance came solely from multiple rocket launchers (Stalinorgan) and low-level attack aircraft. Communications had been cut between the Soviet 65th Tank Brigade and the 81st Cavalry Division, a planned Soviet attack on the supply roads of 6.Panzer Division had been thwarted, and a springboard created for launching an attack on the right wing of the soviet Front north of the Yessaulovskii Aksai, against which the 4.Panzer *Armee* had been unable to gain any ground.

The next day von Senger und Etterlin decided to take advantage of surprise and continue with the advance. He sent Pz.Gren.Regt.63 with two batteries of artillery as the vanguard with II./Pz.Rgt.39 to guard the bridgehead. The frost had enabled fuel to be brought up to replenish the vehicles.

When the tank battalion was relieved it joined the rest of the Division for an attack against the *Kolkhoz* (collective farm) Imeni Vosmogo Marta, which was a strong point in the Soviet defense. The Panzer Commander chose a route which had an icy slope that caused the Panzer IV tracks to slip. *Generalmajor* von Senger und Etterlin rerouted the tanks, and there followed a fierce hour long tank battle at the *Kolkhoz*. Fifteen enemy tanks were knocked out, most having been dug in. The German panzers then withdrew to the west before attacking more enemy tanks that were approaching from the north. The reinforced Pz.Gren.Rgt. 40 protected the left flank during this operation. After this the *Kolkhoz* fell to 17.Panzer Division.

The Division had fought well in a flexible manner that had outmanoeuvred the enemy. The action at the Kolkhoz had warded off a threat of attack on 6.Panzer Division and made a German threat to the Soviet right flank. 17.Panzer Division had taken 50 casualties. Twenty-one Soviet tanks had been destroyed and 150 prisoners had been taken. It was not possible to ascertain the Soviet loss in killed and wounded.

On 19 December 17.Panzer Division attacked Verkhne Kumskii at 0500. The Division had been tasked to take the heights to the north of the town to deny them to the Soviets. These were reached at 0620 by elements of Pz.Gren.Rgt. 63 from the south and Panzers from the north. This force opened fire on Soviet tanks running along the road from Verkne Kumskii to Nizhne Kumskii. German planes bombed 17.Panzer Division positions, as they did not realise the Division had advanced so far.

At 0900 6.Panzer Division had entered Verkne Kumskii from the south, while *Generalmajor* von Senger und Etterlin sent his Division to block the northern exit from the town. He used his precious Panzer IV tanks to guard the left flank. These shot up several enemy tanks and drove off the rest. The German tanks were again mistakenly attacked by Stukas.

By 1100 Verkne Kumskii had been occupied and cleared of soviet troops, with stragglers fleeing in a southwest direction.

As the town of Verkhne Kumskii had been secured by 6.Panzer Division, *Generalmajor* Frido von Senger und Etterlin diverted his Panzer Battalion towards Nizhne Kumskii, on the Myshkova river. He planned to establish a bridgehead at this point. The town had been occupied by fresh Soviet troops as well as those from Verkne Kumanskii. On route the II./Pz.Rgt.39 Panzers routed a Soviet tank attack from the northwest, destroying many enemy tanks and putting the rest to flight. A Soviet counterattack was fought off by a battalion from Pz.Gren.Rgt.40 supported by artillery. Pz.Gren.Rgt.63 was left to link up with 6.Panzer Division. 17.Panzer Division, despite being under strength, had aided 6.Panzer Division and allowed it to advance. The other under strength Division, 23.Panzer Division, had not got beyond the bridgehead at Krugliakov due to heavy Soviet opposition.

Frido von Senger und Etterlin realised that to safeguard any bridgehead on the Myschkova river he would have to protect his left flank. He had only three battalions to cover a broad front of twenty-five kilometres. The enemy had received reinforcements and 17.Panzer Division was short of fuel.

On 19 December II./Pz.Rgt.39 entered Nizhne Kumskii, but couldn't overcome the enemy in the town. There was ferocious house to house fighting and the Germans took heavy casualties from artillery, tank, and rocket launcher fire. The Soviets had destroyed the Myshkova bridges, and there was heavy ice on the fording places. By the night of 19 December 17.Panzer Division had been involved in intense fighting for three days and nights in temperatures of minus fifteen centigrade. On the night of the 19th the division took 275 casualties, the strength of one battalion.

The following day the rest of 17.Panzer Division arrived and captured the town, setting up a small bridgehead on the north bank of the Myschkova. The Germans repelled counterattacks and took 50 prisoners. The total prisoners taken in the 24 hour period amounted to several hundred.

The Division was only about 40 kilometres from the trapped 6th *Armee. Generalmajor* von Senger und Etterlin planned to send his tanks along the south bank eastwards towards Gromoslavka, but this had to be cancelled when the reinforced Soviet forces attacked Nizhne Kumskii in strength. This caused Pz.Gren.Regt.63 heavy casualties in house to house fighting. Oberst Beitz, a battalion commander, was amoung those killed.

17.Panzer Division tanks were sent to push the Soviets out of Nizhne Kumskii, which was secured on 20 December. The tanks set out once again for Gromoslavka but found the soviets had been reinforced (13th Tank Brigade) and had occupied the heights, preventing any German advance.

On 16 December the Soviets had started operation "Saturn" using 1st and 3rd Guards Army with 5th tank army to destroy the Italian 8th Army and Army Detachment Hollidt. This caused von Manstein to withdraw 6.Panzer Division from "Winterstorm" and use it to stabilise the line 100 miles to the west. The German forces now had only the under strength 17.Panzer Division and 23.Panzer Division. The two divisions could only muster 37 operational tanks.

The Soviets brought up more strong forces, as they had no intention of letting the weak German Corps rob them of victory at Stalingrad. 17.Panzer Division was only 30 kilometres from Stalingrad, but had suffered heavily. Casualties could be described as light - 300 men killed out of a division of 10,000 - but the men were exhausted by the fighting and sleepless nights in minus twenty degrees of frost. The panzer regiment had 23 serviceable tanks.

Frido von Senger und Etterlin set up defensive lines in such a way as to give the troops places to warm up close to the front. The tanks were kept in a circular formation well up in front of the other units The Divisional headquarters was kept near to the front line. This put it in danger from the enemy but gave the troops confidence.

17.Panzer Division reported heavy enemy anti-tank fire (Pak) on the night of 22/23 December. The next day Pz.Rgt 39 was ordered to detach and go by Werch to capture Kumskij. This was to be held by elements of the Division while the rest of the fighting units were to advance by point 147.0 and march on Tschikoff. However, on the right the Soviets attacked and cut off the supply units (Verst.Komp.) of I./Pz.Gren.Regt. 40.

At 1300 hrs 17.Panzer Division attacked strongly using its armoured cars (*Panzerspähwagen*), followed at 1500 by the *Panzergrenadiers*. These came into contact with the Soviets at about 1600 near point 121.3. *Panzergrenadiers* from I./Pz.Gren.Regt. 40 attacked this feature on both sides but could not make any headway until reinforced by 12 *Sturmgeschütze* (Stugs, self propelled guns) and part of K.6 of 6.Panzer Division.

At 1700 hours I./Pz.Gren.Regt. 40 reported that the Soviets were advancing westerly. Part of Pz.Gren. Regt. 63 was ordered to support their comrades after point 121.3 to prevent the enemy breaking through and cutting off the roads. Extreme efforts had to be made to defend Point 121.3, and in any case point 146.9 had to be held under any circumstances.

These operations started at 17.45, but Pz.Gren.Regt. 40 reported that the strongly reinforced Soviets had penetrated 2 km and had retaken point 146.9. K17 was on the retreat from Eivsomoj, so the Division found the enemy already 5 km south of point 146.9. Orders by radio instructed I./Pz.Regt. 40 and II./ Pz.Art. Regt. 27 to retake and defend point 121.3 until further notice.

At 2100 Kdr. K.17 announced a *Kampfgruppe* to attack point 146.9 and support point 121.3. The regimental commander of Pz.Gren.Regt. 40 requested support from I./Pz.Gren.Regt. 63, which had been able to advance without contacting the enemy. K.17 ordered that due to its heavy losses Pz.Gren.Regt.40 was to withdraw to the main Division area. December 24th saw the Soviets creeping in between the German units. This made coordinated defence impossible. An isolated battalion was overrun by enemy tanks. On the 25th the divisional staff crossed to the south bank of the Myschkova and a pontoon bridge was erected to evacuate troops on the Soviet side.

It was decided to use 17.Panzer Division as a mobile assault force and they were placed behind 23.Panzer Division. This was achieved under enemy pressure and thirty degrees of frost. Each regiment of the Division was down to about 200 men fit to fight. The Division's only consolation was the Korps' recognition of its ability in smooth battlefield coordination between tanks, infantry, artillery, and supporting units. With von Senger und Etterlin's experience as a cavalry commander, the Divisional command made the best and most flexible use of the relatively small number of tanks left in the division.

The Soviets broke through 23.Panzer Division on 26 December, after which Higher Command ordered a withdrawal to a bridgehead near Kotelnikovo. 17.Panzer Division was ordered to hold this bridgehead, as it was "vital for further operations." The Division possessed one anti-tank gun and eight tanks. As Soviet tanks were deploying in battle formation an assault gun battery (*Stugs*) joined the eight tanks, and together attacked and repulsed the Soviet armour. However, other Soviet armour probed the division's left flank.

A bridge that had been wired for demolition blew up prematurely, killing twelve pioneers. Staffs of 17 and 23.Panzer Divisions amalgamated to organise a joint withdrawal. By 28 December the relentless Soviet pressure forced the Division to retreat to new positions on the Sal River. These were once again out on the open Steppe, and the exhausted troops suffered temperatures of minus twenty degrees. The Soviets had no intention of letting the 6th *Armee* in Stalingrad be relieved. Heavy attacks, one after the other, forced the Germans back. 17.Panzer Division was forced back to Kuberle with 23.Panzer Division.

On 31 December 17.Panzer Division reported it was holding a cohesive front on the Kuberle river. Reported tank strength was 15 Panzer III lg. (long L/60 5cm gun) and 15 Panzer IV lg (long 7.5cm L/43 gun). In addition there were 16 Pak Sfl.40 (7.5cm self-propelled anti-tank guns).

Pz.Gren.Rgt.63 was surrounded and had to be relieved by an armoured attack. Throughout the night its withdrawal involved close quarter fighting in which it lost eighty men, ten per cent of its strength. The infantry particularly suffered from the extreme cold and lack of sleep, which reduced their fighting effectiveness. Lack of suitable winter clothing was a problem. Due to casualties in the *Panzergrenadier* regiments supply train personnel had to be armed and take their place as Grenadiers. This reduced the effectiveness of the supply system, as there were not enough trucks to bring sufficient replenishment to the fighting men. All operational vehicles were pressed into service in the areas west of Proletarskaja and south of Manytsch.

All around the German positions lay the wounded, unburied dead, and wounded prisoners. It was particularly noted that the hospitality and stoic demeanour of the local women seemed to know no limit.

Von Paulus and the 6th *Armee* in the Stalingrad pocket were left to eventual capture after they could fight on no longer. They surrendered on January 31st with 90,000 men going into a captivity few would return from.

At 1450 on the 31st two *Kampfgruppen* (Battlegroups) were formed from 17.Panzer Division with specifically assigned areas of operation.

The first was *Kampfgruppe* “Henrich,” composed of Regt.Gef.Stand, I./Art.Regt. 27 in Swch.Dubowskij and Remontnaja, northwest of the road after Shikowskaja. I./Pz.Gren.Regt. 40 was reinforced with a *Sturmgeschütze* battery. In reserve was the K.17 and II./Art.Regt. 40 in Nassaroff for the defence of the main road between Shikowskaja to Remontnaja. However, folds in the ground allowed soviet troops to infiltrate and the Panzer Company in Hf.3, in the centre of the area, were the first *Kampfgruppe* troops in action.

The second battle group, *Kampfgruppe* Büsing, was composed of Gef.Stand Pz.Regt. 39 in Krjukoff, Pz.Gren.Regt.63 and a *Sturmgeschütze* battery in Werchne Shiroff, and Pz.Pi.Btl. 27 with II./Art.Regt. 27 in reserve east of Werchne Shiroff guarding the bridges over the Ssal river.

156.Inf.Rgt. from 16.Mot.Div. was attached to 17.Panzer Division. Later 5 SS- Pz. Gren. Div. “Wiking” and 503 s.Pz.Abt. (Tiger tank battalion) joined the division on 7 January 1943. 17.Panzer Division gained new strength in the first few days of the year with reinforcements sent by Korps - fifty new tanks on January 3rd, and through its own resources and esprit de corps.

A Soviet attack was repulsed on January 3rd at 0500 at Vessely Gaj. This large village was defended on three sides by the reduced battalions of Pz.Gren.Regt.40. In reserve were the divisional tanks and assault guns. At 0900 the Soviets started a second powerful attack. This succeeded in breaking into the perimeter with tanks and infantry despite stubborn resistance by the exhausted and weakened companies of Grenadiers. The Soviets were repulsed by a counterattack using 17.Panzer Division armour reserve. A further Soviet tank attack in the afternoon was similarly repulsed.

The fighting between 2 and 7 January on the Mal Kuberle and from 7 to 10 January around Kutenikovskaya, along the Sal, was a series of isolated engagements. Divisional Battle Groups could be up to thirty kilometres apart. Success was only achieved by constant regrouping of forces around the concentrated use of armour. Since the infantry lacked anti-tank guns the light artillery batteries (le.FH Bttr.), flak batteries, motorised gun companies, and assault gun batteries were assigned to the Battle Groups.

The Germans were afforded a brief respite, as the Soviet forces had taken ground so quickly that they were suffering from supply difficulties. In addition, their infantry had to spend nights in the open, sapping their strength. Fuel and spare parts were in particular short supply. The German troops were able to rest at least for part of the time. They could shelter in houses and had a reasonable supply of food.

The German high command planned 17.Panzer Division to counter attack across the Sal and move northwest to the Don. Gren.Regt.156 held the bridgehead at Verch Serebriakovka and formed a flanking screen to the north and northwest for the armour.

The offensive started at 0500 on 4 January. A thaw had softened the ground, which made movement difficult. In addition, both tanks and artillery were short of ammunition. The Battle Group crossed to the north bank of the Sal under the cover of the divisional artillery. They were immediately attacked by the Soviets from the direction of Petuchov. This was repulsed with help from the assault guns, and the Division pushed on into the Soviet positions, taking the high ground and destroying enemy tanks and motorised infantry. The Soviets seemed surprised to find such offensive action from a division it had assumed to have been forced onto the defensive. They were pushed back to Prostorny, and the Division reached and cut the road between Semenkinskaya and Romanovskaya.

However, the Soviets were not slow to send reinforcements from the north to help these that had been pushed back. At 1030 a large force was assembling in the Sukhosoleny forest and began to move southwest. Other Soviet units massed to the west of the battle group. Tank fire on these enemy forces knocked out two batteries of field guns and two anti-tank guns in addition to personnel losses. However, the non-stop firing of the battle group was exhausting its ammunition supply. Due to the danger of being overrun because of lack of ammunition the precious armour was ordered back to the bridgehead.

Before this could be carried out the Soviets launched an attack with tanks and infantry from Petuchov against the bridgehead. The battle group counterattacked and drove off the enemy with heavy losses. By 1700 hours the battle group was back under 17.Panzer Division control to the south of Sal-Kuberle. In the armoured battle north of then Sal the soviets had lost 31 tanks (15 burnt out) and 25 anti-tank guns. 17.Panzer Division and the battle group had lost three tanks and 129 casualties. This armoured action had relieved the pressure on the 4.Panzer *Armee*. For a time the initiative had been taken from the Soviets, if only in a limited area.

January 6th and 7th saw the Soviets infiltrating across the Sal river into the northern flank of 17.Panzer Division This caused Pz.Gren.Regt.40 to pull in its northern wing, as it did not have enough troops to hold the south bank of the Sal. The enemy was trying to force 4.Panzer *Armee* to withdraw by using relatively weak forces to exert continuous pressure.

In an attempt to clear the south bank the division's armour attacked Budyenny and Bratzkaya, while Gren. Regt.156 attacked eastwards. The German armour surprised Soviet tanks advancing from Nowaja Serebriakovka by attacking them in the flank. The enemy lost 11 tanks, several hundred dead, and 153 prisoners. At the same time this action removed the threat from Pz.Gren.Regt.40. South of the division assault gun battery 203 drove off attacks on Pz.Pi.Btl.27.

Despite these successes there had been a deteriorating situation behind 17.Panzer Division, and it was planned to withdraw the division behind the Bol Kuberle sector. Pz.Gren.Rgt.63 had already been sent there via Dennisovkii-Ryiska, Nemetzkov-Potavskoye, and Moskovskii. Their main job was to seal the area of the Sal against further enemy infiltration.

On January 8th strong Soviet infantry forces attempted to drive 17.Panzer Division back. At 1200, after a barrage by rocket launchers, three Soviet infantry regiments attacked on a wide front from the area of Nowaja-Serebriakovska to Atamanskii against the eastern side of the German defences. II./Pz.Rgt.39 moved across a bridge east of Versely towards Nowaja-Serebriakovka and attacked the flank of the Soviet infantry Division.

II./Pz.Rgt.39 had been reinforced by a company of ten Tiger tanks. The German High Command had ordered that no Tiger was to fall into enemy hands, so these powerful machines were screened on all sides by II./Pz.Rgt.39 tanks. The Tigers opened fire on the Soviet anti-tank guns from long range, destroying them and leaving the smaller II./Pz.Rgt.39 tanks to annihilate the Soviet infantry.

The German tanks roved through the enemy infantry for hours, causing estimated loses of upwards of 1000 men. Belatedly, at nightfall the Soviets sent 27 T-34 tanks to attack Kutenikovskaya to aid their stricken infantry. These were driven off by the German armour. The divisional artillery's (Pz.Art.Rgt.27) observation officers had ridden with the tanks to allow their guns to participate in the fast flowing action. This action allowed other elements of the Division to withdraw to the new defence line in good order.

On the 40 kilometre front the division was short of anti-tank weapons. It had eight Marder 2 (self-propelled 7.5cm guns), four Marder 3 (self-propelled 7.62cm guns), and only one towed 7.5cm Pak 40. Some of these had to guard the important supply routes. Heavier weapons had been made useless to the Division by the supply of dud ammunition, which would not fire.

The ten Tiger tanks had raised morale and offensive spirit. Their thick armour and powerful 8.8cm guns enhanced the offensive power of the Division, but their small numbers, heavy weight, and slow speed adversely affected the mobile tactics of the Division. The strict orders that they must not fall into enemy hands restricted their deployment. Companies of II./Pz.Rgt.39 were used to act as mobile fire brigades and moved to block enemy penetrations. This was common for all German units in all areas of the Eastern Front.

The Germans were pushed westwards by the relentless Soviet pressure on the exhausted and weakened German units. 17.Panzer Division was too depleted to hardly cover its own operational area. The Soviets, however, refrained from attacking the Division and avoided the heavy losses they had taken in the last few days. Instead they used creeping infiltration tactics on the flanks.

17.Panzer Division tank strength was low, so the Infantry battalions would have to fight without armour and with little artillery support. However, 23.Panzer Division was even weaker and not capable of heavy fighting. This meant the burden had to fall on 17.Panzer Division, which spread its units from the north to the southwest of the LVII Korps' area to prevent encirclement.

The divisional light artillery batteries were allocated to the Panzer Grenadier regiments, while the heavy batteries were under divisional command. Anti-aircraft guns were used in the ground role to give added firepower to the battle groups. The self propelled anti-tank guns were divided amongst the battle groups. The tanks were kept together under divisional command to be used against specific Soviet threats. This often left the infantry without defence against enemy armour.

January 9th saw 17.Panzer Division back to Orlovskaya, then on the Manytch river holding Salsk on the 15th. Tanks carried exhausted infantrymen, wounded, and dead for burial, as well as supplies. Fierce fighting meant that all personnel of the division had to take up a rifle, including Count Castell, commander of Pz.Gren.Rgt.63, and the divisional commander von Senger und Etterlin.

Later, on 22 January 17.Panzer Division withdrew northwest to Sporny and held a bridge head across the Don river at Bataisk and Aksaiskaya near Roshcha. Stragglers from the Rumanian forces joined 17.Panzer Division grenadiers as riflemen. A squadron of Cossacks attached themselves to the divisional staff.

Despite the weariness of 17.Panzer Division its fighting abilities inspired confidence in the other German units. The division held onto the most eastward outposts of German held territory. Even the command of 4.Panzer *Armee* spoke highly of the actions of 17.Panzer Division

Lieutnant Lindenburg of Pz.Gren.Regt.63 was awarded the Knights Cross on 2 Febraury 1943. During the attempted relief operation this young officer had had to take on the roles of regimental adjutant, battalion commander, and regimental commander due to casualties in the regiment's officers. The decoration was personally given by the division commander.

17.Panzer Division crossed the Don river near Rostov on the evening of 2 February, and for the first time since the Stalingrad operation began on December 17, 1942, all members of the Division were out of combat.

The next day von Senger und Etterlin sent a glowing personal message to all members of the division for their efforts in trying to save the trapped 6th Army. He also paid tribute to several officers who had distinguished themselves, including *Oberst* Büssing of Pz.Rgt.39. On 3 February the Division took part in fighting between the Don and Volga and collected in Politotdelskoje. At 1100 an order was received that transferred 17.Panzer Division from 4.Panzer *Armee* to 1.Panzer *Armee*.

On 5 February the Division marched by day in 5 large groups on the route Tschernuchino-Grjewko-Timofejewskij. Vehicles were to be carefully checked, and any unnecessary equipment and baggage was not to be taken. The next day Pz.Rgt.39 reached Dostrojenko, where it received seven Panzer III lang (L/60, 5cm. gun) from the workshops with a promise of three Panzer IV lang. (L/48, 7.5cm gun) later. On 5 February deep snow and the 120 km. march had caused many vehicle breakdowns and several units had fallen behind. This lead to a new order from Pz.A.O.K. 4 (4 Panzer Army Command) for the division to march to Makejewka and then Makejewka-Ilowaisk-Charzyssk. Messages had to be sent by *Kradmelder* (motorbike messenger), as radio silence was observed. This was supervised by an officer from Pz.Nach.Abtl.27. This made it difficult for Divisional units to get messages. The route was policed by *Feldgendarmerie* (Military Police), who could help but not solve all the transport and navigation problems.

The Division had to regroup at Charzyssk, where they found a shortage of billets due to the amount of troops belonging to A.O.K. 6.

Next day, as part of the 1 Panzer *Armee*, 17.Panzer Division moved towards Stalino by route of march Saizewo-Imeni-Kirowa-Dsershinsk starting at 0730. On the 6th it became apparent that some units had not reached the divisional lines, including both battalions of Pz.Gren.Rgt.63, and many tanks and vehicles had suffered breakdowns. Units that were ready with the Division by 1730 included Pz.Gren.Rgt.40, one heavy field howitzer (s.F.H.) battery, the Signals *Abteilung*, and the divisional Headquarters.

Three heavy tractors and seven lorries of II./Pz.A.R.27 had broken down, and this greatly reduced their capacity. Units that were reported as up to strength were three Panzer Grenadier Battalions, the Panzer Pioneer Battalion, and the Motorcycle Battalion. One Panzer Grenadier battalion was reported as under strength. The Division reported 2000 infantrymen, eight light field howitzers (le.F.H.), and four heavy field howitzers (s F.H.) in three Batteries and six serviceable Panzer III lang (L/60, 5cm). All self propelled anti-tank guns (S.fl.) had broken down, and there was only motor transport for 60% of the Division.

On 7 February the Division, as part of XL Pz.Korps, was ordered to attack and hold the line Sslawjansk-Barwenkowo, stopping further enemy movement. This would link up with *Armee-Abteilung* Lanz, which was counterattacking the main enemy attacks south of the Donez. To carry this out the Ia went to liaise with HQ of the XL.Pz.Korps, and the Divisional Commander did the same with *Armee* HQ.

Meanwhile, Pz.Jg.Abt.27 had lost all its heavy self propelled anti-tank guns to breakdowns on the march. Similarly, only two tanks made it to the divisional position; all the rest had broken down. This left the Division in a seriously weakened state. On the return of the Ia (Operations Officer) all *Panzergrenadiers* and motorcycle infantry were combined into one regiment. All the available artillery was made into one *Abteilung*. All other non-assigned troops were made into an alarm company of infantry.

This meant that the division consisted of Pz.Gren. Rgt.63, consisting of one battalion made up of HQ, two infantry companies, one heavy company under ObLtn. Lindenberg, and one battalion of motorcyclists and armoured cars. Officers commanding the units were:

Btl.40 Hptm. Vocke
Btl.63 ObLtn. Lindenberg
Btl. K 17 Hptm. Prugger.

The Division was put under III Panzer Korps to secure the area north of Artemowsk. 17.Panzer Division got motor vehicles from what remained of 24.Panzer Division, which had been destroyed in the Stalingrad pocket. 24.Panzer Division and the other remants of the 6th Army were being sent to France for reforming. This meant that 17.Panzer Division regained some mobility.

On the 8th 17.Panzer Division was tasked with helping 19.Panzer Division, which was defending Nyrkowo to Krassnopolowka. 17.Panzer Division had to defend along the railway line westwards from Berestowaja and secure towards Krassnopolwka. *Panzergrenadiers* had the support of II./Pz.A.R. 27. Elements of Pz.Gren.40 moved towards Belogorowka via Artemowsk and Karpowka. 19.Panzer Division commander liaised with 17.Panzer Division staff.

The Divisional units K17, Pz.Pi.Btl.27, one light field howitzer battery, and all available tanks were to take up position in Karpowka and secure a line Jakowlewka-Krassnopolowka, preparing the area for other attack troops.

19.Panzer Division had to move northwest to block the enemy advance along the railway east of Nyrkowo. Pz.Gren.Rgt. 40 moved to positions at Belogorowka to replace 19.Panzer Division with *Kampfgruppe* K17 in Karpowka. The Ia planned to use K17 to prevent an enemy breakthrough by counterattacking west of a line between Tripolje-Nyrkowo and proceeding eastwards to Kamyschewacha.

Instructions were issued by radio, and the attack started at 1400. Tripolje was taken without a fight, so the Division elements were ordered to go on and seize Wiktorowka. Movement proved to be slow due to deep snow and heavy enemy artillery fire. At 17.20 an order was received to stop the attack but prevent enemy movement to the South.

Pz.Gren.Rgt.40 was sent to Lipowaja and then along the railway line to Kaganowitscha. No enemy reinforcements were found in Wiktorowka, which was to be attacked on the 9 February. Meanwhile, Pz.Gren.Regt. 40 provided security for 19.Panzer Division's north flank. For the attack on Wiktorowka, Pz.Gren.Rgt. 40 was supported by a light field howitzer battery. *Kampfgruppe* K17 was to attack from the southwest supported by a Flak Company and four tanks.

The Division had two tanks available and eleven to be delivered from the repair workshop. A further 33 would not be returned from repair in time. Seven tanks were still on the march from Rostow, and the tanks that were returning from workshops by train after the attacks on Orel had been appropriated by other units. Unit losses on 8 February were two killed, nine wounded, and 3 missing.

The two *Kampfgruppes* prepared through the night; Pz.Gren.Rgt. 40 advanced to the northwest and K17 to the southwest to begin the attack on Wiktorowka at 0800 the next morning. The Divisional commander took position beside *Gruppe* Henrich.

Deep snow drifts hindered the attack troops. The open country around Wiktorowka allowed observers on hill 186.7 to bring down fire from heavy weapons on any attacking troops. Due to 19.Panzer Division's weakness in armour the right flank was exposed without even any artillery cover. Hill 186.7 was steep and heavily defended, but heavy fire and a fierce assault from 17.Panzer Division units took the position. This allowed the armour to cut off the anti-tank and artillery positions, which could no longer rely on observers. However, after turning southwest the division's tanks did run into heavy anti-tank and artillery fire.

The motorcycle infantry were the first to assault Wiktorowka proper after hill 186.7 had been taken. The German units were involved for two hours in fierce house to house fighting, but despite heavy losses could not capture more than half of the town. The attack was stopped until the arrival of all the main Divisional units (Pz.Gren. Rgts.40 and 63 and K17). The Panzer Grenadiers were reinforced by another 830 men, but losses had been 22 dead, 80 wounded, and one missing. However, 17.Panzer Division had captured a lot of enemy materiel, including four field guns and two anti-tank guns.

On 10 February the assaults were repeated with further heavy fighting. The Panzer Grenadiers and motorcycle infantry had taken Wiktorowka by 1330 after fierce house to house fighting. The Division immediately moved on to attack Plotwa, where enemy forces had been spotted in a valley to the west. 19.Panzer Division artillery fired on Plotwa to give support, but had to defend itself against heavy Soviet attacks. Plotwa was taken by 1500 with high losses to the Soviets of men and materials. Pz.Gren. Rgt.40 and Pz.Pi.Btl.27 were used to secure the town and consolidate the defense.

The Division had suffered nine dead and twenty-eight wounded. The Soviets had lost over a hundred killed and eighty-seven prisoners, in addition to thirteen anti-tank guns, four mortars, four machine guns, and five anti-tank rifles.

On 11 February the Division formed two battle groups. The first *Kampfgruppe* was Regiment Henrich from the *Panzergrenadiers* of one Battalion of each of the Pz.Gren.Rgt. 40 and 63 with *Artillerie Abteilung* Hoffman consisting of two light field howitzer batteries. The second battle group was *Kampfgruppe* Trotha, which had part of the division armour and Pioneer Battalion. The Germans watched the movement of the Soviets, particularly their armour.

Regiment Henrich repelled weak enemy attacks with the help of *Sturmgeschütze* (self propelled assault guns). *Kampfgruppe* Trotha destroyed three enemy tanks and several armoured cars west of Wesseloje. The Division suffered three dead and two wounded. The Soviets lost forty dead and 35 taken prisoner, as well as four field guns, six anti-tank guns, two anti-aircraft guns, one mortar, three machine guns, one anti-tank rifle, and sixty vehicles.

The Division, as part of 1.Panzer *Armee*, was given the task of counterattacking the Soviet forces at Niktorovka that had broken through 19.Panzer Division. Three infantry battalions attacked the town through deep snow. Enemy resistance was fierce, and they were held up on the southern exit of Niktorovka. Several batteries of Artillery from 19.Panzer Division shelled the town, assisting the infantry, as well as three tanks from II./Pz.Rgt.39 which lead the subsequent attacks. After bitter house to house fighting the German Grenadiers captured the town. Many Soviet bodies lay in the streets. Prisoners and wounded from both sides were collected at 17.Panzer Division Headquarters. Local women came out and gave assistance to the injured from both sides.

After this success 17.Panzer Division was despatched to the industrial town of Artemovsk. Here the Soviet VIII Cavalry Corps had broken through the German lines. This unit proved to be an elusive enemy aided by the difficult terrain and deep snow, which favoured horses and not motor vehicles. When beaten the Soviets fell back in a southeasterly direction. 17.Panzer Division found the main body of the Soviet Forces to be in the villages of Gorodishtche and Tchernuchino. The road north of these to Voroshilovsk was in Soviet hands, preventing neighbouring German forces from aiding 17.Panzer Division.

Under the personal supervision of the divisional commander Pz.Gren.Regt.63 set out through deep snow and high winds to outflank the Soviets. 6.Panzer Division was advancing from the east on Gorodishtche so Pz.Gren. Regt.63 attacked from the west of Tchernuchino. Due to the deep snow there were problems with truck movement and supply.

On the 17th the motorcycle rifle battalion was sent in to aid the Grenadiers. Divisional artillery guided by radio bombarded the next set of houses in front of the riflemen. Tanks and anti-tank guns protected the flanks. Despite this Tchernuchino held out, so the focus of the German attack switched to Gorodishtche to compel the Soviets to move forces in that direction.

Pz.Gren.Regt.40 had encountered heavy enemy forces in deep snow between the two villages and was held up. Now the tanks of 6.Panzer Division had entered Gorodishtche from the north, finding the enemy had fled. The Soviet VIII Korps had fallen back to the southeast, and 17.Panzer Division was able to enter Tchernuchino on the 19th practically without opposition. The division's losses were small, but it had not been able to capture much in the way of enemy weapons or take prisoners. However, 17.Panzer Division was able to recapture German trucks bearing the symbol of 24.Panzer Division and add them to divisional stocks. Once again 17.Panzer Division received praise for its actions from High Command.

Generalmajor Frido von Senger und Etterlin received the Knight's Cross on 8 February and the Division was out of the line on 16 February.

On 18 February 17.Panzer Division was preparing to attack the flank of a Soviet advance east of Dnepropetrovsk. However, the next day the weak strength of the Division forced it to slowly withdraw west. Contact with neighbouring friendly units had been lost. There was only radio contact with 48.Panzer Korps. The Division was down to that of a weak regiment. It had eight tanks and eleven self propelled anti-tank guns (Pz.Jg.) operational, and the Panzer Grenadiers were down to 1150 men in two battalions. Even weak Divisions were needed, and on 23 February 17.Panzer Division attacked northwest from Vasilkovka area against cut off Soviet units between the Dneiper and Donets rivers

The Division advanced in two parts. Motor Cycle Battalion 17, the tank *Abteilung*, one company of the anti-tank battalion, and a light artillery battery made up the vanguard. The rest of the division followed in reserve and to exploit success.

This action recaptured Petropavlovka and the the bridge over the Samara river on 23 February. The town was occupied after the Soviet troops had fled and the Division took up positions on either side of the Samara river facing north. Among the prisoners were officers of the Soviet III Armoured Corps and from an armoured brigade. The Soviet pursuit was running out of momentum.

Further local success was gained on the 24th and 25th when the Division recaptured Verkhnaya Samara and Burbulatovo respectively. The latter allowed the railway line from Lozovaya to Barvenkovo to be cut, preventing Soviet supplies and reinforcements being brought in by this route. The Division destroyed three tanks, three armoured cars, twenty-five vehicles, and numerous infantry weapons, as well as taking 160 prisoners.

Also on 25 February elements of the Division captured Dobropolye at 0915 in an early morning surprise attack. This proved to be a very successful day, as other Divisional units had captured Aleksandrovka by 1100 and cleared Starye Bliznetsy by 1500. German dive bombers attacked the fleeing soviet columns. 17.Panzer Division captured large quantities of enemy materiel, particularly weapons and supplies. Soviet stragglers were taken prisoner or cut down.

17.Panzer Division was on a roll under the leadership of Frido von Senger und Etterlin. It had advanced so fast into the flank of the enemy that had been advancing southwest that the Soviets could not put up a co-ordinated response. The weak German division had inflicted large losses on the Soviet forces while suffering only minor numbers of casualties itself. The enemy 51st Tank Brigade and its 10th Rifle Brigade suffered severely in dead and prisoners. 17.Panzer Division had captured three tanks, seven field guns (including four heavy guns), two anti-tank guns, eight anti-aircraft guns, ten mortars, twenty-five anti-tank rifles, twelve armoured cars, and sixty lorries. One hundred and fifty-seven prisoners were taken.

On the evening of February 25th the division had no contact with its neighbours, as they were so far behind. At 0430 the next day the division started off again, but shortage of fuel forced changes in the battle groups. After mine clearing and a short sharp battle Serafimovka was captured, and at once the tanks went on to capture Plachtejewska.

However, when the division tried to enter Plissovo it lost two tanks. The town was bitterly defended by Soviet replacements, including a tank and three heavy and five medium anti-tank guns. Divisional infantry held the defenders down while the armoured battle group outflanked the town and entered from the south behind the Soviet defences. The enemy was attacked from two sides and the town fell at 0930.

The divisional units kept up the momentum of the offensive. The villages of Sofievka and Plachtejewska were taken quickly and the German reconnaissance pushed ahead to the east. On the left 6.Panzer Division was attacking Nadeshino and 5-SS Panzer Grenadier Division "Wiking" was fighting its way into Afrikanovka.

At Bespalizevo the 17.Panzer Division split for flanking attacks. Tanks went westwards and the infantry east using a depression in the ground for cover. New half track lorries (Opel Maultier) gave good cross country performance, and the division was able to avoid roads that were under Soviet artillery fire. By 1230 the town was taken, and the rapid advance enabled the divisional units to take Krutaj Balka an hour later. As 17.Panzer Division was so far in front it could open fire on any columns sighted, as they were certain to be Soviet. This saved valuable time previously spent in friend or foe recognition.

That evening 17.Panzer Division tanks cautiously entered the day's objective, Metchepilovka. The enemy had fled to the east and north. Reconnaissance established the Soviets to be holding the surrounding villages, one of which (Fedorovka) was taken that evening. Metchepilovka made warm billets for the exhausted German soldiers. During the last twenty-four hours 17.Panzer Division had knocked out four enemy tanks, captured three tanks, two armoured cars, twenty-one heavy field guns, eight anti-tank guns, one anti-aircraft gun, one mortar, eight heavy machine guns, and several anti-tank rifles, light infantry weapons, and lorries. In addition 200 horses were taken. The Soviets lost many dead and 388 were taken prisoner. The Division's losses were one dead and eight wounded. Two operational Panzer III tanks and four self propelled guns were supplied as replacements.

The main body of 17.Panzer Division took Petrovsaya on 27 February while flanking units pursued the fleeing soviets. As the Division was not at this point equipped with armoured troop carriers (Sd Kfz. 251s), the initial assaults had to be carried out by dismounted infantry to find the enemy. Then artillery fire weakened the defensive line and finally a tank assault from the flank and rear to avoid anti-tank guns was carried out.

17.Panzer Division had proved the essence of pursuit tactics was not to stop because of strong points or threatened flanks. It always retained momentum and the initiative, and never let the enemy rest. This came at a cost though. The Division had only two operational tanks left after the recent hard fighting with six more coming from repair. The Pz.Jg.Abt. had ten self propelled anti-tank guns and the artillery regiment, Pz.Art.Rgt.27, had ten light (10.5 cm) and three heavy (15cm) field guns. Infantry strength was 1840 men, including the Pioneers (Pz.Pi.Btl.). On 27 February Divisional losses were seven dead and fourteen wounded.

The Division found itself to the south side of the Donets near Balakleya. Motorcyclists looked for a way for the Division to cross the river, but although the unit had access to the river at all points it could not be crossed. The closest German unit, 5.SS Panzer Division "Wiking," reported that it was fighting off heavy enemy assaults to the south of Margaritowka. On 27 February Divisional losses were seven dead and fourteen wounded. Soviet losses were three tanks, ten field guns, nine anti-tank guns, seven mortars, eight heavy machine guns, seventeen anti-tank rifles, and fifteen vehicles. Personnel losses were over 100 dead and 310 taken prisoner. That night an attack by a Soviet cavalry regiment on the Divisional staff was shot to pieces by the accompanying 2cm anti-aircraft guns (Flak 38).

Early the next day part of 17.Panzer Division, *Gruppe* von Heydebreck, met up with part of 5.SS Panzer Division "Wiking" in Petrowskaja before the latter moved on to Metschepilowka. The 17.Panzer Division *Kampfgruppes* attacked and repelled enemy infantry on the right flank of the Division area. Later in the day 17.Panzer Division repelled a Soviet assault in the area of Metschepilowka consisting of a column of 2,000 infantry supported by tanks and artillery. The Soviets lost one tank knocked out, three field guns, four anti-aircraft guns, thirteen anti-tank rifles, eight machine guns, and fifteen lorries. Two hundred and twenty-four prisoners were taken. 17.Panzer Division losses were six dead and twenty-four wounded.

On 4 March 17.Panzer Division was transferred from 48.Panzer Korps and tasked to hold the Donets river across from Balakleya.

At the time of the battle of Kharkov 17.Panzer Division was part of 4th *Panzerarmee* in reserve near Slavyansk. During the battle the reserve of *Heeresgruppe Süd* (Army group south) was made up of 17.Panzer Division, 23.Panzer Division, and SS Wiking Panzer Grenadier Division. This reserve force sounds impressive, but in reality consisted of three weak battalions of tanks, one for each of the Divisions. In total tank strength was 171 operational vehicles, of which only 77 were the long barrelled Panzer IV F or G that could outgun the Soviet T-34 at most ranges. 17.Panzer Division's only operational tank *Abteilung* was second battalion with four companies (3 light and 1 medium): II./Pz.Rgt 39, 3 lePz.Kp., and 1m.Pz.Kp. The division was not one that was proposed to receive the new Pz.V Panther tank armed with the deadly 7.5 cm KwK 42 L/70 gun. In March 1943 17 Pz.Div. reported operational armour:

9 Panzer III (kz) Short 5 cm. KwK 38 L/42 gun.
11 Panzer III (lg) Long 5 cm. KwK 39 L/60 gun.
1 Panzer IV (kz) short 7.5 cm. L/24 gun.
26 Panzer IV (lg) long 7.5cm. L/48 gun.
And 23 tanks in repair.

At the end of March the Division occupied defensive positions on the Donets River, and after 14 May was put into quarters near Izyum for refitting.

Stab/Pz.Rgt. 39 was re-designated Pz.Rgt.-Stab 39 of the *Heeres-Truppe* (Army Troops) on 20 April 1943 and left the division.

The motorcycle battalion, Kradsch.Btl. 17, was re-designated Pz. Aufk.Abt. 17, in line with Panzer Division regulations on 1 May 1943. On the same day 1 and 2 *Kompanies* Pz.Jg.Abt.27 were ordered to be issued with sPak (Sfl.) – self propelled anti-tank guns.

On 9 May *Heeres* Flak-Art.Abt 297 was attached to 17.Panzer Division, and later on 4 June the 4th (Flak) Company of Pz.Jg.Abt 27 was absorbed as 4./H.Flak-Art. Abt. 297. On 25 May I./Pz.Art.Rgt.27 was ordered to convert to self propelled guns (Art.Abt Sfl.).

On 20 May 1943 *Panzergrenader* regiments 40 and 63 were issued twelve self propelled 15 cm heavy infantry guns on the Pz.38(t) tank chassis (sIG(Sfl.), commonly known as the "Grille." These were under the command of the regimental staff and issued to 13 *Kompanie*, the infantry gun Company. The production of the sIG(Sfl.) had started in April 1943, and Hitler had ordered (3 May 1943) priority delivery of these weapons to Divisions fighting in the East.

General der Panzertruppen Frido von Senger und Etterlin left the Division (his "unpretentious, poorly equipped Bavarian-Swabian 17 Panzer Division") for high command in Italy; another example of the career success of 17.Panzer Division officers. *Generalleutnant* Walter Schilling replaced him on 16 June. Two days later 17.Panzer Division moved southeast of Izyum in the Slaviansk region.

17.Panzer Division was with the 1st *Panzerarmee* in the Donez basin and was involved south of the main battle of Kursk. In mid to late 1943 the Division was involved in heavy fighting on the Donez and the Dneiper bend, repulsing the Russian attacks after the German defeat at Kursk.

On 1 July the Division reported as operational: 4 Panzer II, 29 Panzer III, 32 Panzer IV, and 2 *PanzerBefehlswagen* (command tanks).

3./Pz.Aufk.Abt.17 was ordered to the Sennelager training area on 15 July 1943 to reorganise and be ready for operations by 5 September.

In July 1943 17.Panzer Division had only one operational Panzer *Abteilung* in Pz.Regt.39. Also it was not authorised to have a Pz.Gren.Btl.(gep), ie *Panzergrenadiers* in armoured half-tracks, the Sd.Kfz. 251 series, in Pz.Gren. Regts. 40 and 63. This greatly reduced the Division's strength in battle.

Parts of the 17.Panzer Division were immediately involved helping to repel a Soviet offensive around Izyum that started on 17 July 1943. For this I./Pz.Gr.Rgt 40 and a battery of Pz.Art.Rgt. 27 were seconded to 46.Infantry Division fighting south of Izyum near Tihotski. II./Pz.Gr. Rgt. 40 was also assigned this time to SS-Pz.Gren.Div. "Wiking." The Division's fighting skill and spirit greatly contributed to the blunting of the Soviet attacks, which were called off on 27 July.

The divisional commander *Generalleutnant* Schilling was killed in action on 21 July. The loss of such senior officers showed how the German Army was "led from the front," particularly the elite units, such as the Panzers. The next day *Generalleutnant* Karl-Friedrich von der Meden took over 17.Panzer Division command.

On 3 August 1943 a *Kampfgruppe* of 17.Panzer Division destroyed 23 enemy tanks in a bold thrust towards Golaja-Dolina, achieving total success in their mission. On the following day the *Kampfgruppe* attacked and took hill number 199.5 from the south.

August 8th saw 17.Panzer Division fighting with 23.Panzer Division and 16.Motorised Division, and up to 10 August 1943 17.Panzer Division was involved in heavy local fighting in the Izyum area. The Soviets started another strong offensive on 16 August, attacking 17.Panzer Division positions south of Izyum near Krasnopolie. The Division once again fought tenaciously and skilfully, giving little ground. This made a large contribution to stopping the Soviets, who called off their offensive on 28 August 1943.

The Soviets had meanwhile started a major offensive against the Germans on the River Mius starting on 18 August. This had surrounded the Greman XXIX *Armme* Korps by 27 August northwest of Taganrog. To be part of a relief force for this trapped unit 17.Panzer Division was moved southwest of Stalino near Staro-Beshovo during 28 and 29 August. The Soviets launched a powerful offensive to stop the relief effort on the 29th and the division was involved in fighting on the 30th. This time 17.Panzer Division was unable to contain the Soviets and was forced to the west, occupying positions at the River Kalmius near Staro-Beshovo.

The Division attacked a soviet bridgehead at Krynka, southeast of Stalino, on 1 September. This had threatened to open a gap between XXIX and XVII *Armee* Korps near Amvrosiyevka.

The heavy fighting over the summer had caused the Division heavy casualties. By 1 September 1943 II./Pz.Gr. Rgt.40, I./Pz.Gr.Rgt. 63, and 3./Pz.Jg.Abt.27 had been decimated and were not fit for battle (17 Panzer Division Order of Battle 1.9.1943).

In September 17.Panzer Division moved further west to positions southeast of Zaporozhe. Welcome news was the order of 19 September to transfer 3./Pz.Aufk.Abt.17 and Stab/Pz.Aufk.Abt.17 from Germany to rejoin the Division at Zaporozhe. The 3rd Company was likely to have been equipped with 31 leSPW (SdKfz 250 series).

II./Pz.Gr.Rgt.40 was attached to 3.Gebirg. Division (mountain troops), fighting with them from 28 September up to the beginning of November.

The fighting continued to take its toll. 17.Panzer Division OOB/1.10.1943 shows 5., 6., and 7./Pz.Rgt.39 and 2. and 3./Pz.Jg.Abt.27 were reduced to a level where they could not take the field. This means that 5 companies having the weapons to stop Soviet armoured advances existed solely on paper!

On 26 September the Soviets started another major offensive against the German lines between Zaporozhe and Melitopol. Despite its weakened state 17.Panzer Division fought extremely well and made a major contribution to slowing the Soviet advance. However, the German forces were in gradual retreat west. The division fought between Vasilievka and Michailovka, to the north of Melitopol, which was itself abandoned on 23 October. The Soviets followed this by a major assault west on 24 October which broke the German line. 17.Panzer Division retreated west to the Dnieper.

Every Panzer Division should have had one battalion mounted in armoured half-tracks, the Sd.Kfz. 251 series (SPW). Due to the shortage of such vehicles it had not been possible to create a Pz.Gren.Btl.(gep) in 17.Panzer Division. However, on 15 October 1943 German High Command ordered one company, 1./Pz.Gr.Rgt. 40, to be equipped with armoured half-tracks manned by trained convalescents and recruits. This was a normal practice to prevent combat veterans beng taken away from the front for traning. The company was to report to the Divison six weeks later, fully operational.

17.Panzer Division abandoned the "Wotan" line and retreated north of the Dneiper on 25 October. Later on 5 November I./Pz.Gr.Rgt 40 was ordered to activate a planned Pz.Gren.Btl.(gep) in Germany (Military District 7) to be ready for 10 December 1943.

17.Panzer Division also lost out on the planned armoured flame thrower platoon Flamm-Zug (gep) for Panzer Divisions. This was ordered for Stab.Kp./Pz.Gr.Rgt. 40, but was sent to 20.Panzer Division instead.

On the Dnieper 17.Panzer Division was much depleted. Joining Companies 5., 6., and 7./Pz.Rgt.39 and Companies 2. and 3./Pz.Jg.Abt. 27, the following units were down to minimal strength: I./Pz.Gr.Rgt. 63; 2., 4./H. Flak-Art.Abt.297; and 3./Pz.Pi.Btl.27 (OOB/1.11.1943). In view of this the Division was employed between Kherson and Berislav, on the north bank of the Dnieper, where it was given time to rest and refit. Some of the shattered units were withdrawn completely to quarters near Krivoi Rog and made up to strength.

By way of replacements, what was left of I./Pz.Rgt. 2 of 16.Panzer Division was assigned to 17.Panzer Division at the beginning of December. This *Abteilung* handed over all its equipment to II./Pz.Rgt. 39, including Panzer V Panthers. This at last gave the Division the new and powerful tanks. It is strange to see Panthers in the second Battalion of a Panzer regiment, as they were always assigned to the first Battalion (the second Battalion in a Panzer Regiment were issued Panzer IVs).

In a condition reprt of 5 December 1943 this period was used for intensive training of NCOs and replacement troops. Despite high morale of the Division there was a shortage of tanks and heavy weapons. The subunits of the Division lacked mortars, machine guns, and anti-tank guns (sPak.). There was a dire shortage of spare parts. All this would greatly reduce 17.Panzer Division's ability to resist the strong Soviet attacks.

Improvement came first on the 5 December when 5./Pz.Aufk.Abt. 17 was ordered to convert into a heavy armoured half-track company, sPz.Aufk.Kp.(gep), equipped with 27 mSPW (half-tracks of the Sd.Kfz. 251 series). This was carried out in the rear area of Army Group South (H.Gr. "Sud").

After the Soviets had launched a major offensive southeast of Kirovograd on 5 December the Division was sent to that area. The first divisional units arrived on the 10th and were committed to the fighting that day. II./Pz.Rgt.39 as Pz.Kpf.Gr. "Düwel" (Armoured battle group "Düwel") went into action assigned to 384.Inf.Div. southeast of Novgorodka near Kuzovka. The remainder of 17.Panzer Division fought south of Novgorodka.

On 7 December what was left of 2./Pz.Aufk.Abt. 17 was ordered to Mielau (Mlawa), where on 16 December it was restructured into a Pz.Sp.Kp. "c" at the Sennelager training area. This company structure consisted of:

Headquarters with two Sd.Kfz 251/3

Three platoons each with three Sd.Kfz. 251/1 and one Sd.Kfz. 251/17.

One heavy platoon with three Sd.Kfz. 251/17, two SdKfz. 251/2, and two SdKfz 251/9.

Authorised manpower was 183 men, two unarmoured vehicles, and four motorcycles.

Between 14 and 16 December II./Pz.Rgt. 39 and I./Pz.Gr.Rgt. 40 formed an armoured battle group (*Panzerkampfgruppe* Pz.Kpf.Gr.) and counterattacked south of Novgorodka. The Pz.Kpf.Gr. attacked the eastern flank of the Soviets and pushed west towards Novgorodka. The aggressive action of the Pz.Kpf.Gr. defeated the Soviets and made them retreat. On 21 December the Soviets called off their offensive. Parts of the division were still involved in fierce isolated actions east of Novgorodka near Bogdanovka. Once again 17.Panzer Division had triumphed over greater odds. This came with heavy losses, however, which caused Pz.Gren.Rgt. 40 and Pz.Gren.Rgt. 63 to be amalgamated into one temporary Pz.Gren.Rgt. under the command of Stab/ Pz.Gren.Rgt. 63.

The Soviets were never idle, and on 24 December 1943 they started a huge offensive in the Brusilov area which breached the Greman defensive lines. 17.Panzer Division was transferred to the area of Vinnitsa in the final days of 1943.

17.Panzer Division had given its all in battle once more, but again occurring heavy losses in men and equipment. OOB/1.1.1944 gives the following units as unfit for battle: 5./Pz.Rgt. 39; 6.,7., and 8./ Pz.Gren.Rgt. 40; Stab.Kp./ Pz.Gren.Rgt. 63; and I./ Pz.Gren.Rgt. 63. It must be remembered that 2. and 5./Pz.Aufk.Abt. 17 were still reforming away from the Division.

In January 1944 17.Panzer Division was part of the 4th *Panzerarmee* at Vinnitsa. At the beginning of January the Division counterattacked with *SS-Freiwilligen-Sturm-Brigade* "Wallonien" (the Belgian Walloon Division) against the Soviet 5th Guards Tank Army. 17.Panzer Division was on the left and the Walloons on the right. The area of the attack was southeast of Vinnitsa between Zozovka and Pogrebishtenskiy. The enemy advance was temporarily halted, but soon renewed with reinforcements. 17.Panzer Division was pushed back south to positions east of Vinnitsa near Lipovets (Gaisin) on 7 January.

On the same day an order was received to reorganise I./ Pz.Gren.Rgt. 40 as an armoured half-track battalion Pz.Gren.Btl.(gep). This would be achieved by amalgamating the new I.(gep)/ Pz.Gren.Rgt. 40 that was in Germany and the men from I./ Pz.Gren.Rgt. 40 in the division's positions. This would be carried out at the Mielau training area and be operational for 1 March 1944. This timescale was not considered possible, and on 22 February it was put back to 15 March. All of I./ Pz Gren.Rgt. 40 were withdrawn from the front back to Germany by 28 February.

Welcome tank resupply came in the form of 30 Panzer IVs delivered to II./Pz Rgt. 39 between 8 and 11 January 1944.

Kpf.Gr. "Brux" (reinforced II./Pz Gren.Rgt. 40) counterattacked northwest of Uman, near Monastyrishte, starting 10 January. This had surrounded the enemy south of Potach by 14 January and contained the Soviet offensive. The Soviet command called off the Zhitomer-Berdichev action the next day.

The armoured flame thrower platoon finally materialised with an order of 15 January 1944 which raised a Flamm-Zug (gep) in Stab.Kp./Pz.Gr.Rgt. 40. On 1 February this platoon was ordered to Mielau to join I.(gep)/Pz.Gren.Rgt. 40 and issued with six mSPW – SdKfz 251/16.

Kpf.Gr. "Brux" (Pz.Gren.Rgt. 40 and II./Pz.Gr.Rgt. 63) was fighting northeast of Monastyrishte from 15 January. On the 17th it was surrounded near Ostroshany but was relived by a German attack on 19 January.

17.Panzer Division was issued 25 *Leichter Schutzenpanzerwagen* (light half tracks) between 19 January and 19 March 1944. These consisted of Sd.Kfz. 250/9 armed with 2 cm canon in a fully rotating turret with a coaxial 7.92 mm MG 42 machine gun and the Sd.Kfz 250/5 *Leichter Beobachtungspanzerwagen*, an observation vehicle armed with a 7.92 mm MG 42 machine gun. This gave the Division a total of 38 of this class of vehicles. The Division should have had 98.

From 21 to 25 January, 17.Panzer Division carried out a series of attacks northwest of Uman between Vladislavchik and Medovata. Pz.Aufk.Abt.17 was meanwhile seconded to 101.Jg.Div. (*Jager* Division – Light Infantry). These units took part in Operation "Gaissin" in the vicinity of Lipovets, encircling and defeating the Soviets.

Although the battles had been successful, 17.Panzer Division had once again taken heavy losses. OOB/1.2.1944 listed the following units as unfit for battle: 5./Pz.Rgt. 39; 6., 7., 8., and 10./ Pz.Gren.Rgt. 40; Stab.Kp./ Pz.Gren. Rgt.63; 10./ Pz.Gren.Rgt. 63; I./ Pz.Gren.Rgt. 63; and 3./ Pz.Jg.Abt. 27. 2./Pz.Aufk.Abt. 17 was still in Germany.

17.Panzer Division took part in Operation "Watutin" from 26 January to 31 January. The Division attacked from Medovata, northwest of Uman. The Soviet forces were surrounded and defeated close to Balabanovka. 17.Panzer Division was also involved in the relief of the Cherkassy pocket in January/February 1944. Here the Soviets had cut off a bulge in the German front containing the German XI and XXXXII Army Corps.

The two German corps had been cut off completely by the Soviets. A second Stalingrad threatened. Instead of ordering the trapped German forces to breakout, the German High command considered the Soviet forces were exhausted and planned encirclement against them. In reality, the German forces were not strong enough to carry this out.

17.Panzer Division formed part of III Panzer-Korps with 16. Panzer Division, 1st SS-Panzer Division "Leibstandarte Adolf Hitler," and s.Pz.Rgt. "Bäke" with 34 Tiger tanks and 47 Panther tanks. The division was used as the southern pincer of the counter attack against the Russian encirclement.

The III Panzer-Korps would constitute the northern attack group. XXXXVII Panzer Korps, consisting of 3.Panzer Division, 11.Panzer Division, 13.Panzer Division, and 14.Panzer Division would form the southern attack group. The 24.Panzer Division was held in reserve.

At the end of January 17.Panzer Division was sent to the aid of *Gruppe* "Stemmermann," which was surrounded near Korsun-Shevchenkovski in the Cherkassy encirclement. The Division was teamed up with Pz.Kpf.Gr. "Bäke." (Stab/ Pz.Rgt.11 of 6.Panzer Division, II (Panther Battalion)/ Pz.Rgt. 23 of 23.Panzer Division, and Tiger Tanks of the sPz.Abt. 503.) The right flank would be formed by 17.Panzer Division. It was planned that *Leibstandarte* SS "Adolf Hitler" and 1.Panzer Division would assist as soon as possible.

On February 3rd only 16.Panzer Division and 17.Panzer Division were ready. Both divisions had received only two days rest from their last actions and were weary. The other two units had not arrived. On 4 February they attacked with sPz.Rgt. "Bäke" (commanded by *Oberstleutnant* Dr. Bäke).

17.Panzer Division started well by fighting its way into Votylevka on 4 February. The arrival of heavy fog the next day, which grounded *Luftwaffe* support, and the thick mud slowed the advance. A sudden thaw turned the frozen ground into the dreaded Rasputitsa mud. A double problem occurred when this froze solid at night, trapping the German vehicles. The Soviets tried to block the German units by deploying large numbers of tanks, which 17.Panzer Division engaged near Votylevka. After some heavy fighting the Division drove off the Soviet armoured assaults and consolidated their positions at the town. Despite this local success strong Soviet assaults came in from the north, east, and west on the advancing German units. The southern attack group XXXXVII Corps was pushed back on the defensive.

This pressure caused heavy casualties, and the decimated German units were withdrawn and prepared for a fresh assault eastwards. Despite all the strenuous efforts between 4 and 9 February the relief operation had been unsuccessful. The Soviets had now built a double ring around the Cherkassy pocket: one to contain the trapped forces and one to fend off the attempted relief. The German High Command's plan to encircle the Soviet forces had failed, and the task of freeing the encircled German units was made even more difficult.

The welcome arrival of *Leibstandarte* SS "Adolf Hitler" and 1.Panzer Division reinforced the offensive and gave real hope of success. *Gruppe* "Stemmermann" in the pocket shortened its lines and started attacking towards Shenderovka, moving towards III Panzer Korps. The relief forces had tremendous problems regrouping and advancing to their positions due to the thick mud, in which vehicles sank up to their axles. Only a maximum of 15 to 20 kilometres could be travelled in a day. Sometimes no movement at all was possible.

The Germans tried again on 11 February to relieve *Gruppe* "Stemmermann," with 17.Panzer Division attacking northeast from Rubannyi. The Division was advancing with 16.Panzer Division side by side as the spearhead of the offensive. 1.Panzer Division covered the right southern flank and *Leibstandarte* SS "Adolf Hitler" was on the left northern flank. 16.Panzer Division and 17.Panzer Division crossed the river Gniloy-Tikich and established small bridgeheads. 17.Panzer Division captured Stepok and went on to occupy Bosovka at 1700. Here it defended itself all night against several Soviet tank attacks. The Division had had a successful but exhausting day.

Thick fog hampered German air support. Many tanks got bogged down in thick mud, which also pulled the narrow tracks off the personnel carrier half-tracks (Sd. Kfz. 251). Only the heavy artillery tractors and tanks could drag the guns through the mud. Fuel supplies dried up, and the only fuel obtained was air dropped. Junkers 52/3m transport aircraft dropped 200 litre drums of fuel and canisters of ammunition and food from 30 to 40 metres. There was great wear and tear on all the vehicles. When the mud froze at night the vehicles had to be chipped free using pickaxes and blow torches in the morning.

The enemy had to struggle against the same difficulties. Capture of German supply and fuel dumps, along with their greater manpower to distribute the fuel and ammunition, greatly helped the Soviets.

On February 12th 17.Panzer Division was battling Soviet tanks. "Leibstandarte" and 16.Panzer Division were on the defensive and 1.Panzer Division was pushing ahead towards Lysyanka. 17.Panzer Division had to be diverted to help "Leibstandarte" against the furious Soviet assaults. The offensive by III Panzer Corps had beome a narrow corridor whose flanks had to be protected by "Leibstandarte" and 1.Panzer Division. The forward elements had only got to slightly less than 20 kilometres from the pocket. sPz.Regt. "Bäke" had got to 10 kilometres, but were forced back by relentless pressure from the Soviet Fifth Guards Tank Korps.

On 13 February 17.Panzer Division had consolidated in Bosovka and Buzhanka. It was then ordered to renew the assault and attack Lysyanka from the northwest in order to relieve the pressure on 1.Panzer Division. Meanwhile, 1.Panzer Division was to attack towards Zhurzhintsy via Hill 239, while 16.Panzer Division and Pz.Rgt. Bäke were to take Khizhitsy. 17.Panzer Division would protect the North flank, particularly to let 1.Panzer Division achieve its objective.

On the 14th 17.Panzer Division contacted 1.Panzer Division at Lysyanka and established defensive positions on the northwest side of the town on hill 216.7. The following two days saw heavy Soviet assaults on 17.Panzer Division positions.

During this time *Gruppe* "Stemmermann" made strenuous efforts to prepare a breakout area in the southwest, as it was clear that III Panzer Korps would not be able to break through to them in time. To this end Novo Buda, Komarovka, and Shenderovka were captured by 105.Infantry Regiment, SS-Brigade "Wallonie," and 5-SS Panzer Division "Wiking."

Finally, on 15 February the commander of Army Group South, *Feldmarschall* von Manstein, ordered *Gruppe* Stemmermann to breakout and link up with III Panzer Korps at Hill 239 near Dzhurzhentsy. The *Feldmarschall* did not check with *Führer* Headquarters to avoid any objections. However, it was assumed that Hill 239 was in German hands, which it was not. The armoured forces to take this hill were exhausted and bogged down in the thick mud.

Inside the pocket, the trapped divisions were fighting furiously to breakout. The attacks were lead by infantry with fixed bayonets followed by the heavier weapons, such as artillery, mortars, and anti-tank guns. By the evening of 15 February the pocket had been reduced to 3.5 kilometres in diameter.

On 16 February III Panzer Korps made a final effort to break through. 17.Panzer Division and 1.Panzer Division were to advance from Lysyanka toward Hill 239 south of Dzhurzhentsy. 16.Panzer Division was to guard their rear and north flank. sPz.Rgt. Bäke's mission was to advance in the direction of the pocket through Chishintsy towards Komarovka.

16.Panzer Division had considerable success and caused the Soviets heavy casualties in tanks, artillery, and men. However, the exhausted and understrength 1.Panzer Division and 17.Panzer Division made little progress. In the evening III Panzer Korps were held in a line through Lysyanka – Oktyabr – Chishintsy. There was 10 to 15 kilometres between them and the trapped German units in the pocket. At 1500 on 16 February the last radio message from III Panzer Korps, "Oktyabr taken!," gave encouragement to those breaking out from the pocket.

The relief force had given their all to help their countrymen but could not break through. The distance for the breakout had, however, been shortened considerably by III Panzer Korps' efforts and sacrifices. Unfortunately, the men trying to break out were not aware that the Tigers of Dr Bäke had reached Hill 239 south of Dzhurzhentsy, that Panzergrenadiers were holding Oktyabr, and that 1.Panzer Division had built a bridge at Lysyanka for them to cross the swollen river Gniloy Tikich.

The breakout went further south and took hundreds more casualties crossing the fast flowing river under enemy fire. Many weak swimmers drowned. About 30,000 men escaped from the pocket out of 56,000 trapped there. Two German Army Corps had ceased to exist and had lost all their armour, weapons, vehicles, and horses. Six divisions had been decimated. 10,000 German troops would not be fit for battle for a period of time. Shortly afterwards III Panzer Korps had to pull back from Lysyanka.

Once again, after the repeated heavy fighting 17.Panzer Division strength had been reduced considerably. OOB/1.3.1944 gave the following units as unfit for battle: 5., 6., 7./Pz.Abt.II./39; 10./Pz.Gr.Rgt.40; 10./Pz.Gr.Rgt.63; I./Pz.Gr.Rgt.63; 1., 3., 8., and 9./Pz.Art.Rgt.27; 2. and 3./Pz.Jg.Abt. 27; and 2./Pz.Pi.Btl. 27. Still absent were 2./Pz.Aufk.Abt. 17 and I.(gep)/Pz.Gr.Rgt. 40, who were still restructuring in Germany.

On 5 March 17.Panzer Division was in reserve southeast of Vinnitsa near Tulchin. This was not to last, as the Soviets launched a large attack between Shepetovka and Tarnopol. The Division moved to the front, and on 8 March counterattacked northwest of Proskurov near Nikolaiev. The gallant fighting of 17.Panzer Division had stopped the Soviets, and 20 March it was withdrawn for rest and moved southwest towards Kamenets-Podolski.

Later, on 26 March 17.Panzer Division and the entire 1.Panzer *Armee* were encircled by strong Soviet forces in the same area. On 27 March the division returned to combat near Glozkovo north of Kamenets-Podolski. The entire surrounded German forces (1.Panzer *Armee*) began a spirited breakout move to the west, gaining the nickname "Hube's Wandering Pocket."

On 31 March 17.Panzer Division established a bridgehead over the Zbrucz west of Kamenets-Podolski, and on 2 April made another bridgehead over the Secret twenty-two miles south of Chortkov. By the 4th the Division was approaching Ustsechko on the Dneister river, about twenty-five miles southeast of Buchach. It was at Buchach, northeast of Stanislav, where the pocket broke through to the German lines, meeting up with 10.SS-Panzer Division "Frundsberg" of 2. SS. Panzer Korps on 6 April.

Away from the front 2./Pz.Aufk.Abt. 17 was ordered from the Wildflecken training area to Mielau to join I./(gep)/Pz.Gren.Rgt. 40 on 16 April. This unit was equipped with twenty-five leSPW (Sd.Kfz. 250 series). The next day both I.(gep)/Pz.Gr.Rgt. 40 and 2./Pz.Aufk.Abt 17 were ordered from Mielau to Lwow to rejoin 17.Panzer Division. Ninety-eight mSPW (Sd.Kfz. 251 series) were issued to I.(gep)/Pz.Gr.Rgt. 40. This was to be completed by 25 April.

The Division formed part of the German defensive line along the Dnestr river on 12 April with 6.Panzer Division, 101.Le.Div. (light Division), and 365.Infantry Division. On 17 April, as part of a German offensive, 17.Panzer Division attacked the enemy southeast of Stanislav near Tlumasz. This broke through the Soviet lines and the Division advanced to the south. At this time (19 April) came welcome reinforcement to the tank strength in the form of II./Pz.Rgt.23 (less its 5.Kp.) being assigned to 17.Panzer Division. This became part of Pz.Kpf.Gr. "Knorr." The division also received the assignment of sPz. Abt.506, heavy Tiger tanks as well. The good news did not stop there, as the next day 17 Panzer IV were delivered to II./Pz.Rgt. 39.

The reinforced Division wasted no time. On 19 April it attacked near Jezierzany, divided into two *Kampfgruppe*: Kpf.Gr. "Brux"(the reinforced Pz.Gr.Rgt. 40) and Pz.Kpf.Gr. "Knorr" (including II./Pz.Rgt.23 and sPz.Abt.506). Despite taking some ground Soviet strength was too much and the attack was called off on 5 May. On 8 May most of the Division was withdrawn for welcome rest and refit near Buchach.

During this time, on 28 May II./Pz.Rgt.39 received another 17 Panzer IVs. Pz.Aufkl.Abt. 17 reported le SPW SdKfz 250 series in the 2.Kp. and 4.Kp. on 1 June 1944.

June 14, 1944, saw 17.Panzer Division transferred to H.Gr. "Südukraine," and on 16 June units began to depart for Rumania, where they were quartered north of Bacau. High command changed its mind on 2 July and the Division was transferred back to H.Gr. "Nordukraine" and deployed northeast of Lwow near Pervotyche.

Throughout May and June 1944 the Division, like all the other Panzer divisions, reorganised under the "Freie Gliederung," or "Panzer-Division 1944" regulations. On 1 July the Divisional commander, Karl-Friedrich von der Meden, was promoted to *Generalleutnant*.

Massive Soviet offensives had largely destroyed Army Group Centre and were preparing their next big offensive against Army Group South in the Ukraine. This was to be carried out by the First Ukrainian front under the command of Marshall Konev. He split his forces into two groups. The north was made up of two armies comprising 16 Rifle Divisions, two Cavalry Corps, twenty-nine Tank Brigades, and five Tank and Mechanised corps. The southern group consisted of four armies made up of twenty-nine Rifle Divisions, twenty-four Tank Brigades, and five Tank and Mechanised Corps. In addition was the huge Soviet Air Force.

Opposing this might, the German forces were well rested and confident, as they had already repelled Soviet assaults in this section. However, the German front consisted of only one Infantry Division next to each other in line. There was no defence in depth.

17.Panzer Division and 16.Panzer Division were the armoured reserves for 4 Panzer Army. 1.Panzer Division and 8.Panzer Division were the reserves for 1 Panzer Army. The Panzer Divisions were greatly under strength, and in reality were armoured battle groups. 17.Panzer Division, 16.Panzer Division, and 1.Panzer Division had been involved in the recent heavy fighting at Cherkassy and Tarnopol. They were too weak to resist the Soviet onslaught and were not a replacement for defence in depth.

On 1 July 1944 2nd Battalion Pz.Rgt 39 had 31 operational Panzer IV L/48 and 2 in short term repair. Pz.Jg.Abt. 27 had 7 operational Stug III and 2 in short term repair with 15 operational Marder III and 14 in short term repair. Panzer Artillery Regiment 27 had armoured self propelled guns Wespe (10.5 cm) and Hummel (15 cm).

The divisional command reported on 13 July 1944 that the Division's morale was good. Although its fighting capability had been improved with weapons it was short of tanks. Only one Zgkw/18t Famo tank recovery half-track was available. Pz.Nach.Abt.27 was short of signals equipment, lorries (LKW), and tires. II./Pz.Rgt.39 had only three incomplete companies: 5., 7., and 8. Additionally II./ Pz.Gr.Rgt.40 and 4./Pz.Gr.Rgt.63 had to travel on foot due to a complete shortage of motor transport.

On this day the Soviet offensive started at 0345 with a tremendous artillery and rocket barrage. This lasted until 0930 when the floods of Soviet tanks, aircraft, and infantry swarmed forward supported by huge barrages of artillery fire. The thin German infantry lines could not hold. The Soviets achieved deep penetrations near Horochow north of Brody and near Koltov south of Brody. On the second day they had isolated the German XIII Corps.

After local counterattacks had failed the Panzer Divisions were thrown in to close the gaps and push back the Soviets. 17.Panzer Division and 16.Panzer Division attacked in the north and 1.Panzer Division and 8.Panzer Division in the south.

17.Panzer Division's attack was southeast of Poryk near Gorohov. The German tanks and tank destroyers attacked the waves of Soviet T-34 and IS-2 tanks. Dismounted *Panzergrenadiers* fought the seemingly never ending masses of Soviet Infantry. The Panzer Divisions were strafed and bombed constantly by Soviet ground attack aircraft and heavy bombers, some supplied by the United States and Britain. The under strength Panzer Divisions could make no headway and their offensive ground to a halt.

After six days of fighting XIII Corps was totally encircled. On 17 July a relief attempt by 17.Panzer Division and 16.Panzer Division again failed, and the Soviets threw more reserves in further attacks on the dwindling pocket. This picture was repeated in the south, where 1.Panzer Division and 8.Panzer Division were trying to break through to the trapped XIII Corps. The armoured relief columns had, like Cherkassy and Stalingrad, got close to the pocket and almost broken through. This gave a false sense of hope and encouraged the pocket to stay and not to attempt a breakout until too late.

XIII Corps was destroyed, and the road was open to the Soviets to southern Poland. About 12,000 men eventually escaped from the pocket, but something like 30,000 were killed and 17,000 captured, including several Generals. With the other German forces 17.Panzer Division began to retreat to the west. By 18 July it occupied positions near Sokal, on the river Bug.

On 1 August 1944 17.Panzer Division was reduced to 9 operational Panzer IV L/48 and 5 in short term repair, no operational or short term repair Stug III, and only 4 operational Marder III tank destroyers with 2 Marders in short term repair. In the same month divisional personnel losses were 296 killed in action, 1359 wounded in action, and 411 missing in action. This was typical of the heavy losses that German front line units were experiencing on the Eastern Front.

On 20 July the Germans continued their westerly retreat, 17.Panzer Division in the direction of Zamosc, southeast of Lublin. On 22 July Kpf.Gr. "Brux," consisting of Pz.Gr.Rgt.40 reinforced with tanks, one Art.Abt.(Sf) self propelled artillery, one Pz.Pi.Kp.(gep) armoured engineers, and one Pz.Auf.Kp.(gep)-armoured reconnaissance company was detached from the Division and moved north towards Chelm.

The rest of 17.Panzer Division retreated towards the west and were ferried across the Vistula river. At the end of July the Division was ordered further south, crossing the Vistula again before moving southeast and taking up positions near Rzezow.

Another 17 Panzer IVs were delivered to II./Pz.Rgt.39 on 21 July. *Kampfgruppe* "Brux" had not been idle. On 23 July it had been fighting between Lublin and Chelm near Trawniki and Piaski. The *Kampfgruppe* slowed down the Soviet advance but could not stop it, and on 25 July it retreated west, crossing the Vistula near Annapol on the 28th. On 31 July the group rejoined 17.Panzer Division near Rzeszow.

This is where the Division was already in action, making a fierce defence and containing enemy attacks. On 31 July the Soviets attacked so strongly that the Division was forced to the west. By 6 August, however, having established strong positions east of Debica and Tarnow, it was able to stop the Soviet advance.

Now 17.Panzer Division was split up, part moving north to positions northwest of Radomysl near Szczucin and part fighting near Mielec. Due to heavy losses, by the end of July 10./Pz.Gr.Rgt.63 and 1.(Stug)/Pz.Jg.Abt.27 were disbanded. The Panzer Grenadier company was reformed in November and the Stug. company in September.

I.(gep)/Pz.Gr.Rgt.40 was assigned to Kpf.Gr. "Künzberg" on 6 August, with which it fought southwest of Rzeszow in the Krosno area. On 14 August it was assigned to 545.Infantry Division and then on 16 August to 8.Panzer Division. The Battalion finally rejoined the Division on 18 August at the Sandomierz bridgehead.

Meanwhile, on 14 August II./Pz.Rgt.39 was issued with 17 Panzer IV. On the same day the enemy launched a massive offensive near Sandomierz, which on 17 August surrounded the German forces to the West of the town. 17.Panzer Division was sent to attack north of the pocket near Ozarow and Ostrowiec. On the 19th the Division succeeded in breaking through to relieve the trapped German units. After this 17.Panzer Division took part in an attack with other units to push back the Sandomierz bridgehead. This had only limited success and was called off on 23 August.

The German High Command still wanted to encircle the enemy in this area. On 27 August a mobile group (*Bewegliche Gruppe*) "Huppert" was formed that was commanded by Stab/Pz.Aufk.Abt.17 and was made up of Pz.Aufk.Abt.1 (from 1.Panzer Division), Pz.Aufk.Abt.17, Pz.Aufk.Abt.23 (from 23.Panzer Division), and I.(Sf)/ Pz.Art.Rgt.27. This was attached to 17.Panzer Division, which attacked from the Lagow area eastwards. The Soviets resisted fiercely, and by the 28th had fought the Germans to a standstill. *Bewegliche Gruppe* "Huppert" was broken up on 30 August 1944.

A final attack against the Sandomierz bridgehead was started on 31 August. 17.Panzer Division again attacked near Lagow. The attack produced the same result, as the Soviets were too strong, and it was finally called off on 5 September.

On 9 September 17.Panzer Division was in positions west of Opatow. On 11 September 2./Aufk.Abt.17 restructured as a light half track Company (lePz.Aufk. Kp.(Gep)) equipped with 30 leSPW (SdKfz.250 series). On the same day II./Pz.Rgt.39 received another 17 Panzer IVs.

Due to the depleted and weak state of the Division the period of October 1944 to December 1944 was one of restructuring and reconstitution.

To start this programme Pz.Jg.Abt.27 (less 3.Kp.) was transferred to the Mielau training area on 15 October. The process had to be finished by 20 November. Pz.Jg.Abt. 27, the division's anti-tank troops, was ordered to reorganise into two self propelled companies and one towed anti-tank gun company following the "Frei Gliederung" organisation of Panzer Divisions.

The Division got a new commander on 20 September in *Oberst* (later *Generalmajor*) Rudolf Demme. Shortly after the Division was pulled out of the front to Chmielnik, south of Kielce, on 25 October. Here 17.Panzer Division received 17 of the powerful tank destroyers Pz.IV/70 (V) on 26 October. These were armed with the same potent KwK 42 L/70 gun as the Panther tank.

An order was received on 13 November to reinforce the Stab. and Stab.Kp./Pz.Rgt.39 with personnel from Stab. and Stab.Kp./Pz.Brig.108.

The German High Command ordered 27 November that XXIV.Pz.Kp. was to have a Stab., two Divisions (ie 16.Panzer Division and 17.Panzer Division), and various Corps units. This was done to reduce the personnel strengths of the two Divisions without affecting their fighting efficiency. To this end both divisions were stripped of their supply units and some fighting units. These were converted into Corps troops. II./Pz.Gr.Rgt.63 was reformed as the third battalion (III.Btl.) in Pz.Gren.Rgt. 40.

On 1 December 1944 Pz.Aufkl.Abt. 17 reported le. SPW Sd.Kfz. 250 series vehicles equipped the 1 *Kompanie* and 2 *Kompanie*. On 30 December there was a total of 43 of these vehicles, including seven Sd.Kfz. 250/5 *Leichter Beobachtungspanzerwagen*, two Sd.Kfz. 250/8 *Leichter Schutzenpanzerwagen* (7.5 cm), and sixteen Sd.Kfz. 250/9 (2 cm).

More change was implemented at the top on 2 December when *Generalmajor* Rudolf Demme was transferred to *Führer* reserve and replaced by *Oberst* Albert Brux.

More welcome was the order of 17 December to form a first Battalion with Panther tanks, ie I.(Panther)/Pz.Rgt.39. This was done using three companies from Pz.Abt.2103 of Pz.Brig.103, which had been disbanded. This was carried out in Bielefeld (Military District 6). The Division had a complete two Battalion Panzer regiment again from 20 January 1945, the first Battalion being fully equipped with the powerful Panther Tank. On 24 December Pz.Jg.Abt.27 got the Christmas present of twenty-one Pz.IV/70(V) tank destroyers and rejoined 17.Panzer Division This was short of the 28 that should have been delivered. The New Year found the division stationed north of Pinczow near Kielce.

January 12th saw the Soviets unleash a massive offensive, the Vistula-Oder operation. As part of this the Sandomierz bridgehead was attacked and the Soviets pressed westwards. The next day 17.Panzer Division was part of a counterattack south of Kielce and met the Soviets north of Chmielnik. The spearhead consisted of a Pz.Kpf. Gr. made up from II./Pz.Rgt.39 (tanks) and I.(gep)/Pz.Gr. Rgt.40 (armoured infantry). However, the Red Army was increasingly more powerful and the German attack was halted, and on 14 January 17.Panzer Division was surrounded. The Division had lost all its tanks in battle by 15 January, but despite this managed to break out of encirclement and move north from the Soviet's clutches.

Hitler now personally ordered I./Pz.Rgt.39 (the Panther Battalion) to step up fighting preparedness. It was to join the Division at Breslau and be ready for battle on 22 January 1945. It was to be issued with 42 Pz.V Panthers, 3 Befl.Pz.V Command Panthers, and 2 Berg.Pz.V recovery Panthers. Forty-five panthers were issued between 16 and 22 January.

However, at this time (17/18 January) the Division was in retreat. Its weakened remnants formed *Gruppe* "von Müller" with 16.Panzer Division and became the spearhead of the "Nehring moving pocket" of XXIV.Pz.Kp.

17.Panzer Division commander *Oberst* Albert Brux had been captured by the Soviets on 19 January. He was replaced by *Generalmajor* Theodor Kretschmer, who would be the last commander of 17.Panzer Division. Kretschmer was rewarded by receiving the Knight's Cross on 8 March 1945.

On 21 January the "Nehring moving pocket" reached the Dlutow south of Lodz and joined up with Pz.Kp. "Grossdeutschland" on the 22nd on the Warthe river at Sieradz. The groups amalgamated to form the "von Saucken moving pocket," which retreated towards the West. It reached the Oder river near Glogau on 27 January.

It was planned to form another company in the I. Battalion to be fully ready on the 28 February. After becoming part of Pz.Rgt. "Coburg" under the command of Stab/Pz.Brig.103, I./Pz.Rgt.39 rejoined 17.Panzer Division in the second half of March. No doubt this was most welcome.

In the retreat through Poland 17.Panzer Division (as other German units) had suffered very heavy losses and casualties. It was recorded on 26 January that the total strengths of both 16.Panzer Division and 17.Panzer Division consisted of sixteen SPW (armoured half tracks), two leFH (sfl) "Wespe" self propelled guns, and one leFH (mot Z) towed howitzer. Their fighting worth was valued as a lowly "IV" in the German scale of battle strength.

In view of this, what was left of the Division was gathered near Sagan and Sorau, southeast of Cottbus, for rest and refitting. Part of I.(gep)/Pz.Gr.Rgt.40 was assigned as a Battle Group, with 16.Panzer Division taking part in actions against the Soviet bridgehead on the Oder river northwest of Breslau at Steinau from 28 January.

This was joined by I./Pz.Rgt.39 as part of Pz.Brig.103. One company with 15 Panthers was encircled in Steinau and wiped out by 4 February. During the rest of February what was left of the Battalion fought with Pz.Brig.103 in lower Silesia. Other survivors of the 17.Panzer Division now fought as Kpf.Gr. "Lissa," consisting of 450 men, and Kpf.Gr. "2/17" with 370 men.

An order was issued on 6 February to restructure the Division as a battle group with the following composition:

Headquarters – Stab/17.Panzer Division with Div.Kdo., Pz.Sp.Kp. (armoured cars), Div.Kart.St.(mot) (Mapping section, motorised), and Feld.Gend.Trp(mot) (Military Police)

A Tank Battalion – Stab, Stab.Kp., two Pz.Kp.(Pz. IV/70) tank destroyer companies, one Pz.Kp.(Pz.IV) tank company armed with Panzer IV tanks, Pz.Werk.Kp. (less one platoon) workshop company, and Vers.Kp.(mot) supply company.

A Panzer Grenadier Regiment – Pz.Gren.Rgt.40 with headquarters and three Battalions - Stab., Stab.Kp.(mot), sIG.Kp.(motZ) motorised towed heavy infantry guns, and Pz.Gren.Pi.Kp.(mot) Engineers in armoured half-tracks (SdKfz 251/5 and Sd.Kfz 251/7).

I.Btl., II.Btl., and III.Btl. each consisting of Stab. three Pz.Gren.Kp.(mot), Panzer Grenadier Companies, MG.Kp.(mot) machine gun company, Gr.Werf.Kp.(mot) Rocket Launchers, and Vers.Kp.(mot) supply company. The exception was that in the third battalion, III.Btl., the three *Panzergrenadier* companies were not motorised, but mounted on bicycles, a common practice late in the war when motor transport was short.

An Artillery Battalion – Stab., Stab.Bttr.(mot), and three Bttr.leFH(mot Z) batteries of motor towed 10.5cm Howitzers.

A Tank Destroyer *Abteilung*– Stab, Stab.Kp., two Jg.Pz. Kp. tank destroyers based on Panzer IV chassis, one Pz.Jg. Kp./SPW anti-tank Pak 40 7.5 cm gun on the Sd.Kfz. 251 chassis (Sd.Kfz.251/22), and Vers.Kp.(mot) supply company.

Engineer Company – Pi.Kp.(mot)
Signals Company – Pz.Na.Kp.(Pz.Fu.Kp.)
Supply Forces

The men assigned to the reformed division came from two K.M.Btl. Combat Personnel Transfer Battalions (750 men) and convalescents. Armour provided was 16 Panzer IV Tanks (11 February), 28 Pz.IV/70 (V) Tank Destroyers (8 February), 3 Flak.Pz.IV/2cm Flak-Vierl. Quadruple 2 cm flak guns on the Panzer IV chassis (9 February), and 12 mSPW Sd.Kfz. 251/22. The latter was called the "Pakwagen" and consisted of a half-track mounting the potent 7.5cm Pak 40 anti-tank gun.

The divisional supply units were rebuilt using supply units of XXIV.Pz.Kp.

By 6 January 1945 17. Panzer Division, like most armoured units, could not be supplied with enough tanks and had to fight with tank destroyers, such as the Panzer IV/70 (V) (Sd Kfz 162/1) in the second Panzer Battalion and the *Mittlerer Schützenpanzerwagen* Ausf D (Sd Kfz 251/22) in the *Panzerjäger* Battalion, 4th Half-track Company. The former mounted the formidable 7.5 cm L/70 gun of the Panther tank and the latter the 7.5 cm Pak 40 L/48 anti-tank gun. Both weapons had limited traverse, but the vehicles were cheaper and easier to produce than tanks. In the desperate defensive battles at the close of the war they took a heavy toll on Soviet armour.

Also on 6 February Pz.Jg.Abt.27 (less 3.Kp.) was transferred to the Grafenwöehr training area for reconstruction. It turned over all its motor towed anti-tank guns sPak(mot Z) to 10.Panzer Grenadier Division. The *Abteilung*'s men had all arrived by 12 February.

Of the 28 Panzer IV/70(V) on 8 February 1945 that I./Pz.Rgt. 39 took possession of, one was knocked out in Chuchelna, Moravia, March 1945, by tankers of the 1st Czechoslovak Independent tank Brigade.

The division also received 20 Steyr trucks with 3cm Flak guns during February 1945. These provided much needed anti-aircraft cover.

The Soviets let loose the Lower-Silesian operation, a massive offensive between Glogau and Ohlau, on 8 February. All operational units of 17.Panzer Division were sent to Berndorf, southeast of Glogau, getting involved in combat on 9 February. The next day saw the division units split into two parts. A larger group was fighting west and northwest of Liegnitz, being pushed westwards to Naumberg and Bunzlau. The smaller part was an armoured battle group Pz.Kpf.Gr. fighting south of Liegnitz. Both groups had rejoined at the end of the month on the defensive near Görlitz.

The state of the Division can be glimpsed in a report that stated on 28 February Pz.Gren.Rgt.40 had fit for action: I.Btl.-280 men, II.Btl.-364 men, and III.Btl.- 392 men.

Reinforcements had arrived from G.E.Btl. 192 (404 men) and Fst.Inf.Btl. (Marine) 1458 (519 men). The latter was a Fortress Infantry Battalion made up of sailors who had little military training.

Artillery Regiment Pz.Art.Rgt. 27 was just as bad. I.Abt. had only twelve 10.5 cm. towed Howitzers, while II.Abt. had four heavy 15cm towed howitzers and three 10 cm. towed guns.

The Reconnaissance Battalion Pz.Aufk.Abt. 17 had only its HQ Stab, one alarm platoon of 42 men, and seven sections operational. The Engineer Pz.Pi.Btl. 27 had two Companies mounted on bicycles and one on foot. The Signals Pz.Nach.Abt. was desperately short of signals equipment.

Due to its weakened state 17.Panzer Division took only a supporting action in the German offensive near Lauban on the 2 March. It attacked from the Hennersdorf area northeast of Görlitz northwards towards Hochkirch, covering the western flank of the German troops. The offensive surrounded the Soviets on 4 March and destroyed them on 5 March. 17.Panzer Division continued fighting through Hochkirch to the northeast. I./Pz.Rgt.39 took part in the Lauban operation as part of Pz.Brig. 103, fighting north of Lauban.

Pz.Brig. 103 was then broken up, and I./Pz.Rgt. 39 was briefly assigned to the 20.Panzer Division before being reassigned to 17.Panzer Division on 15 March. Another welcome addition to the division on that day was the reconnaissance unit Pz.Aufk.Abt. "Hirschberg" from Pz.Brig. 103. This reinforced the under strength Pz.Aufk. Abt.17.

The division reported the following on 8 March 1945: nine Pz.IV tanks, twenty Pz.IV/70 tank destroyers, three Flak.Pz.IV/2-cm Flak-Vierl anti-aircraft tanks, one Befl.Pz III command tank, two Pz.II Ausf.L light tanks, four lePz. SPWg. light armoured cars, four sSPWg. heavy armoured cars, nine leSPW Sd.Kfz.250 series half-tracks, thirty-five mSPW SdKfz.251 series half-tracks, one sPak(Sfl) Sd.Kfz.138 self propelled anti-tank gun, eight sPak (mot Z) towed anti-tank guns, nineteen leFH (mot Z) towed 10.5 cm howitzers, nine sFH (mot Z) towed 15 cm howitzers, and three 10 cm sK (mot Z) towed 10 cm guns.

A welcome addition to the Division's strength was the assignment on 13 March of Pz.Jg.Kp. (Sf) 669 (H.Tr.), which was equipped with the powerful 8.8 cm sPak (Sfl), i.e. the dreaded 8.8cm. anti-tank gun on a Panzer IV chassis. This gave 17.Panzer Division much needed increased anti-tank capability against the Soviet armour onslaughts. On 15 March the Division could report that it had the following armour: fourteen Panzer IV, ten operational; nineteen Pz.IV/70, eighteen operational; and three Flak.Pz. anti-aircraft armour.

A serious situation occurred when a major Soviet offensive (Upper Silesian Operation) broke through the German lines in Upper Silesia on 15 March. On 18 and 19 March 17.Panzer Division moved to Leobschütz, northwest of Ratibor. The Division joined the fighting on 22 March and helped to stop the Soviet advance, and the enemy offensive was called off on 31 March. Between 29 and 30 March 17.Panzer Division was pulled out of the front line and moved to Opava (Troppau).

Meanwhile, Pz.Jg.Abt. 27 was still at the Grafenwöehr training area. It was reported to be at 100% strength in men but only 30% and 25% in materiel and motor vehicles, respectively. It still had no armour. Despite being planned for 15 March, reorganisation was never completed and the *Abteilung* never rejoined its parent Division.

The report from 17.Panzer Division on 1April 1945 tells us the Division consisted of:

Headquarters consisting of Stab and Div.Kdo., Div. Kart.St (mot), and Feld.Gend.Trp. (mot).

Panzer Regiment Pz.Rgt.39 consisting of Command Stab, Maintainance Pz.werk.Kp., and two Battalions.

I.Abt. – Stab, Stab.Kp., three companies of Panther tanks Pz.Kp. (Pz.V) and supply company Vers.Kp. (mot)

II.Abt. - Stab, Stab.Kp., three companies of tank destroyers Pz.Kp. (Pz.IV/70) and supply company Vers.Kp. (mot).

Panzer Grenadier Regiment Pz.Gren.Rgt. 40 - Headquarters company, Stab.Kp., heavy self propelled infantry gun company sIG.Kp. (Sfl), and motorised engineer company Pz.Gren.Pi.Kp. (mot).

I.Btl. made up from Command Stab, three motorised *Panzergrenadier* Companies (1., 3., 5.) Pz.Gren.Kp. (mot); an armoured (Sd.Kfz.251 half-track) Company (2.) Pz.Gren.

Kp. (gep); a motor borne heavy weapons company sPz. Gren.Kp. (mot); and a motorised supply company Vers. Kp. (mot).

II.Btl. made up from command Stab, four motorised *Panzergrenadier* companies Pz.Gren.Kp. (mot); a motor borne heavy weapons company sPz.Gren.Kp. (mot); and a motorised supply company Vers.Kp. (mot).

III.Btl. made up from Headquarters Stab, three motorised *Panzergrenadier* companies Pz.Gren.Kp. (mot); a motor borne heavy machine gun company MG.Kp. (mot); a motor towed rocket launcher company Gr.Werf.Kp. (mot); and a motorised supply company Vers.Kp. (mot).

Panzer Artillery Regiment 27 (Pz.Art.Rgt. 27), which was made up of:

Headquarters – Stab and Stab.Btrr. (mot)

I.Abt. consisting of command Stab, Stab Bttr., three batteries of motor towed 10.5 cm guns (1., 3., 5) Bttr.leFH (mot Z) and one battery of motor towed 15 cm Howitzers (9.) Bttr. sFH (mot Z).

II.Abt. consisting of command Stab, Stab Bttr., two batteries of motor towed 10.5 cm guns (2.,8.) Bttr.leFH (mot Z) and one battery of motor towed 15 cm Howitzers (9.) Bttr. sFH (mot Z).

Panzer Reconnaissance Pz.Aufk.Abt. 17 made up from command Stab, two companies of armoured half-tracks (Sd.Kfz. 250 series) Pz.Sp.Kp./SPW, two companies in VW *Kubelwagen* Pz.Aufk.Kp.(VW), one armoured half-track company (Sd.Kfz. 251 series) sPz.Sp.Kp. (gep), and a motorised supply Company Vers.Kp. (mot).

Anti-tank battalion Pz.Jg.Abt 27 made up of three companies of 7.5 cm Pak 40 anti-tank guns on the Sd.Kfz. 251 half-track (Sd.Kfz. 251/22) and a motorised Supply Section Vers.Stf. (mot).

Signals Battalion Pz.Nach.Abt. 27 made up from a telephone company Pz.Fsp.Kp., a radio company Pz.Fu. Kp., and a motorised Supply Section Vers.Stf. (mot).

The division could also call on various supply units.

This shows that 17.Panzer Division was ending the war in a reasonable state, at least on paper.

At 1000 hrs on 16 April 1945 two Panther Ausf. G of I./39 Pz. Rgt. were knocked out by two T34/85s of 2nd Battalion 1st Czechoslovak Independent Tank Brigade commanded by Sgt.Danca and Cpl. Penkert. The Czech tanks were then knocked out by two Panzer IV/70(V) of I./39 Pz. Rgt. Shortly after this one of the Panzer IV/70 (V) was knocked out by a T34/85 commanded by 2nd Ltn. Popovic, 3rd Battalion Czech Independent Tank Brigade, who had fired through an opened door and window of a house. The German panthers had no markings and the Panzer IV/70 (V)s were marked solely with a *Balkenkreuz* on the rear side plates.

At the end of the war the reconnaissance Stabs.Kp./ Pz.Aufk.Abt.17 operated a hybrid vehicle that was a turret of a Sd.Kfz.123 Luchs tank on a Sd.Kfz.234 eight wheel armoured car chassis. Pz.Aufk.Abt.17 listed two Pz.Sp. Luchs on 1 March 1945 and one of these vehicles on 1 April 1945. There is no record of delivery of this vehicle. In March 1945 Pz.Aufk.Abt. "Sternberg" from Pz. Brig.103 was incorporated into Pz.Aufk.Abt.17. This unit had been formed from 1./Pz. Aufk.Aufk.190 of 90.Pz.Gren.Div. in January 1945 after having received twelve s.Pz.Späh-Wg 234 between December 1944 and January 1945. It is possible that the mechanics of the workshop Pz.Werkst. Kp. combined two damaged vehicles, the turret of the tank "Luchs" and the chassis of the Sd.Kfz.234 armoured car, to form an operational hybrid.

The Germans were ahead of the Allies in night fighting capacity due to their lead in infrared technology. To this end it was planned to give every Panzer Division at least one Company of Panthers equipped with infrared night sights. One company of Pz.Rgt.39 (probably 4.) was ordered to Fallingbostel training area on 3 April 1945 to be outfitted and trained for night fighting. Ten Panzer V Panthers with the infrared night vision devices FG 1250 or BIWA were to be issued. Due to the war's end this was never completed and the company never rejoined the Division.

At the beginning of April 1945 17.Panzer Division was fighting hard in defence near Opava. The Division managed to repel all enemy attacks.

The last report on 10 April gave the Division's state in armour: one operational Panzer III, three Panzer IV (one operational), thirteen Pz.IV/70 (seven operational), sixteen Pz.V Panthers (six operational), and four Flak Panzers (two operational). In addition the Division had thirteen heavy anti-tank guns sPak (ten operational). Belatedly, the division was ordered to reorganise as a "Panzer-Division 1945" on 18 April. The reality was that the Division was simply a *Kampfgruppe* and no bigger than a regiment.

By 8 May the Division had begun to leave the front and retreat to the west. 17.Panzer Division crossed from Troppau to Tabor, west of Gorlitz, finally surrendering to the Soviets on the 10 May near Olomouc. Elements of the Division reached the American lines at Pisek, but were handed over to the Soviets a couple of days later.

Despite being a truly elite unit with a fine fighting record, not a lot has been written about 17.Panzer Division. Erich's diaries rectify this.

Appendix 1

Commanders of 17.Panzer Division

Generalleutnant von Arnim	1 Jan 1940 - 1 Nov. 1940.
Generalmajor Karl Ritter von Weber	1 Nov 1940 -17 July 1941.
General der Panzertruppen Wilhelm Ritter von Thoma	17 July 1941 – 15 Sept 1941.
Generaloberst Hans-Jurgen von Arnim	15 Sept 1941-11 Nov 1941.
Generalleutnant Rudolf-Eduard Licht	11 Nov 1941-10 Oct 1942.
General der Panzertruppen Fridolin von Senger und Etterlin	10 Oct 1942-16 June 1943.
Generalleutnant Walter Schilling	16 June 1943-21 July 1943.
Generalmajor Karl-Friedrich von der Meden	21 July 1943- 20 Sep 1944.
Generalmajor Rudolf Demme	20 Sep 1944-2 Dec 1944.
Oberst Albert Brux	2 Dec 1944-19 Jan 1945.
Generalmajor Theodor Kretschmer	1 Feb 1945- 8 May 1945.

Knights Cross Winners 17th Panzer Division

Hans-Juergen Arnim	04/09/1941
Ludwig Beckmann	26/10/1943
Kurt Boettcher	04/091941
Otto Buesing	21/11/1942
Gunther Corssen	08/02/1943
Kurt Cuno	18/01/1942
Johann Goettler	01/09/1943
Hans Gradl	15/11/1941
Josef Gretschmann	11/08/1941
Walter Henrich	08/02/1943
Erich Kaiser	26/02/1942
Max Kluever	12/10/1943
Wilhelm Lehner	15/06/1943
Freidrich Lindenberg	30/01/1943
Franz Mentz	22/09/1943
Werner Pietsch	16/11/1943
Karl Proell	30/01/1943
Konrad Rehnitz	12/08/1942
Josef Rueger	07/03/1944
Walter Schilling	28/07/1943
Friedrich-Ferdinand Schleswig-Holstein-Sonderburg-Gluecksbur	22/02/1945
Fridolin Senger und Etterlin	08/02/1943
Hans Troeger	04/05/1944
Helmut Vocke	26/03/1943
Lothar Zahn	02/10/1943

17 Panzer Division Service History

Date	Pz.Korps	*Armee*	*Heersgruppe*	Area
Jan 1940-March 1041	XXIV	2 *Armee* C	Germany	
April 1941		11 *Armee* C	Germany	
May 1941-June 1941	WK XIII	2 Pz.*Gruppe*	Germany	
July 1941-Oct 1941	XXXXVII	2 Pz.*Gruppe*	Mitte	Smolensk
Nov 1941-Dec1941	XXIV	2 Pz.*Armee*	Mitte	Tula
Jan 1942-Feb 1942	XXXXVII	2 Pz. *Armee*	Mitte	Orel
March 1942	LIII	2 Pz *Armee*	Mitte	Orel
April 1942	XXIV	2 Pz. *Armee*	Mitte	Orel
May 1942-July 1942	XXXXVII	2 Pz. *Armee*	Mitte	Orel
August 1942	Reserve	2 Pz. *Armee*	Mitte	Orel
Sept 1942	LIII	2 Pz. *Armee*	Mitte	Orel
Oct 1942-Nov 1942	XXXV	Pz. *Armee*	Mitte	Orel
Dec 1942	Reserve		Don	Kotelnikowo
Jan 1943-Feb 1943	LVII	4 Pz. *Armee*	Don	Rostow
March 1943	LVII	4 Pz. *Armee*	Sud	Kharkow
April 1943-June 1943	LVII	1 Pz. *Armee*	Süd	Donez(Isjum)
July 1943	XXIV	1 Pz. *Armee*	Süd	Donez(Isjum)
	Reserve	1.Pz.*Armee*		
August 1943	XXXXVII	4. Pz. *Armee*	Süd	Donez(Isjum)
Sept 1943	Reserve	4. Pz. *Armee*	Süd	Donez(Isjum)
Oct 1943	IV.A.Kp	8.*Armee*	A	Dnjepr
Nov 1943	XXIV.Pz.Kp.	8 *Armee*	A	Cherson
Dec 1943	XXXXIV	4 *Armee*	A	Cherson
Jan 1944	XXIV	4 Pz.*Armee*	Sud	Winniza
Feb 1944	XXXXVII	8 *Armee*	Sud	Tscherkassy
March 1944	Reserve	1 Pz. *Armee*	Sud	Kamenetz-Podolsk
April 1944	II SS-Pz.Kp.	1 Pz. *Armee*	Nordukraine	Stanislau
May 1944-June 1944	III	1 Pz. *Armee*	Nordukraine	Stanislau
July 1944	XXXXVI Pz.Kp.	4 Pz. *Armee*	Nordukraine	Lemberg
August 1944	XXXXVI Pz.Kp.	4 Pz. *Armee*	Nordukraine	Tarnow
Sept 1944	IV.SS-Pz.kp.	4 Pz. *Armee*	Nordukraine	Baranow
Oct 1944	IV.SS-Pz.Kp.	4 Pz. *Armee*	A	Baranow
Nov 1944-Jan 1945	Reserve H.Gr."A"		A	Baranow
Feb 1945	Friedrich	4 Pz. *Armee*	Mitte	Oder(Steinlau)
March 1945	LIX	17. *Armee*	Mitte	Jagerndorf
April 1945	Reserve	1. Pz.Armee		Mahren
May 1945	XXIV.Pz.Kp.	1. Pz. *Armee*		Mahren

Tank Strength 39 Panzer Regiment

22 June 1941, Eve of Barbarossa
I, II and III Battalions
Panzer I 12
Panzer II 44
Panzer III (5.0cm Kurtz) 106
Panzer IV (7.5cm Kurtz) 30
Befehlswagen 10

28 June 1942
71 total tank strength

I Battalion.
Panzer II 25
Panzer III (5.0cm Kurtz) 35
Panzer IV (7.5cm Kurtz) 10
Befehlswagen 5

II Battalion.
Panzer II 17
Panzer III (5.0cm Kurtz) 36
Panzer IV (7.5cm Kurtz) 16
Befehlswagen 2

December 1942. 39 Panzer Regiment Strength
Panzer II 4
Panzer III (5.0cm) 20
Panzer III (7.5cm Kurtz) 9
Panzer IV 32
Befehlswagen 2

July 1943 During the battle of Kursk. II/Panzer Regtiment 39 Strength
Panzer II 4
Panzer III (5.0 cm Kurtz) 1
Panzer III (5.0 cm lang) 19
Panzer III N (7.5 cm Kurtz) 9
Panzer IV (7.5 cm Kurtz) 1
Panzer IV (7.5 cm Lang) 31
Befehlswagen 2

September 1943 17. Pz. Div. Strength
Panzer III 12
Panzer IV 14

October 1943
Panzer III 1
Panzer IV 5

November 1943
Panzer III 3
Panzer IV 13

December 1943
Panzer III 5
Panzer IV 14

January 1944
Panzer III 2
Panzer IV 5

February 1944
Panzer III 2
Panzer IV 5

May 1944
Panzer III 1
Panzer IV 0

September 1944
Panzer III 0
Panzer IV 57
Panther 53

October 1944
Panzer IV 52
Panther 41

November 1944
Panzer IV 40
Panther 29

December 1944
Panzer IV 49
Panther 33

January 1945
Panzer IV 49
Panther 33

February 1945
Panzer IV 0
Panther 0

March 1945
Panzer IV 0
Panther 0

April 1945
Panzer IV 8
Panther 14

Main Combat Units 17th Panzer Division
Divisional Staff (Stabs)
Panzer Regiment 39
Panzer Grenadier Regiment 40
Panzer Grenadier Regiment 63
Aufklarungs *Abteilung* 17
Panzerjäger Battalion 27
Artillery Regiment 27
Army Flak battalion 297
Panzer Pioneer Battalion 27
Panzer Signals Battalion 82
Supply Troop 27
Truck Park 27
Bakery Company (mot) 27
Butcher company (mot) 27
Administration Platoon (mot) 27
Medical Company (mot) 1/27 and 2/27
Ambulance Company (mot) 1/27, 2/27, and 3/27
Miliatry Police Troop (mot) 27
Field Post Office (mot) 27

In 1942 the first battalion, ie I/39 of the Panzer Regiment, formed the 129th Panzer Battalion in the 29th Panzer Grenadier Division. Hence 17.Panzer Division had only one Panzer Battalion during 1942.
Total tanks available were:
Pz II 17
Pz III (50cm kz) 38
Pz IV (kz) 16
PzBefWg 2

After being merged with the 27th Reconnaissance Battalion the 17th Motorcycle Battalion became the 17th Panzer Reconnaissance Battalion in 1943. Also that year the Division gained Army Flak battalion 297. During 1943 the II/39 Panzer Regiment had three companies of Pz III and one company of Pz IV. The Panzer Grenadier regiments had no Flak Companies or any half-tracks (Sd.Kfz. 251 and Sd.Kfz. 250 series).

According to OKH records the division was organised thus:

Divisional Staff (Stabs)
27th Mapping Company

Panzer Regiment 39
Regimental Staff
1 Signals Platoon
Regimental Band
Second Battalion
Regimental staff and staff company
2 Panzer Companies of 22 Pz III each, changed to Pz IV by June.
1 Company of Pz IV with one added on 14th June.
1 Panzer Maintainance Company.

Panzer Grenadier Regiment 40
Regimental Staff
Regimental Band
1 (mot) Regimental Staff Company
1 signals Platoon
1 PanzerJager Platoon (three 5cm Pak 38 and three LMGs)
1 Motorcycle Platoon
1st and 2nd (mot) Battalions
Each consisting of:
3 (mot) Companies (four HMGs, eighteen LMGs, two 8cm Mortars and three PzBu 39 antitank rifles in each company)
1 (mot) Heavy Company consisting of:
1 Pioneer Platoon (four LMGs)
1 *Panzerjäger* Platoon (three 5cm Pak 38 and three LMGs)
1 Infantry Gun Platoon (four 7.5cm leIG)
1 Support Platoon (three LMGs and three PzBu 41 anti-tank rifles)
1 Self-Propelled Infantry Gun Company (six 15cm sIG and seven LMGs)

Panzer Grenadier Regiment 63
As for Pz Gren Regt 40

Aufklarungs *Abteilung* 17
1 Armoured Car Company (eighteen 2cm guns and twenty four LMGs)
3 Motorcycle Companies (two 8cm Mortars, four HMGs, eighteen LMGs and three PzBu 39 each)
1 (mot) Heavy Reconnaissance Company

Panzerjäger Battalion 27
3 Self-Propelled *Panzerjäger* Companies (fourteen 7.5cm Pak 40 and fourteen LMGs each)

Artillery Regiment 27
Regimental Staff
1st Battalion
1 Battalion staff
2 Self-Propelled Batteries each of six 10.5cm leFH Sd.Kfz. 124 "Wespe" and four LMGs
1 Self-Propelled Battery of six 15cm sFH Sd.Kfz. 165 "Hummel" and four LMGs.

2nd Battalion
1 Battalion Staff
3 (mot) Batteries each of three 10.5cm leFH and two LMGs.
3rd (mot) Battalion)
1 Battalion Staff
3 (mot) Batteries each of 15cm sFH and two LMGs
Observation Battery 27 (mot)

Army Flak battalion 297
Staff
1st and 2nd (mot) Heavy Flak Batteries (four 88mm, three 20mm and two LMGs each)
3rd (mot) Light Flak Battery (twelve 20mm and two LMGs each)

4th Self propelled Battery (eight 20mm and two quad 20mm flakvierling Half-Tracks and four LMGs)
1 (mot) Light (20 ton) Flak Supply Column.

Panzer Pionner Battalion 27
Staff
1 Half-track Pioneer Company (twenty-five LMGs, two 8cm Mortars, and three PzBu 39)
1 (mot) Pioneer Company (eighteen LMGs, two 8cm Mortars and three PzBu 39)
1 Bruko K Bridging Column (three LMGs)
1 (mot) Light Pioneer Supply Column (two LMGs)

Panzer Signals Battalion 82
1 Panzer Telephone Company (six LMGs)
1 Panzer Radio Company (sixteen LMGs)
1 (mot) Light Signals Supply Column (one LMG)

Supply Troop 27
Three (mot) (90 ton) Transportation Companies (three LMGs each)
Three (mot) Light Transportation Companies (two LMGs each)
27th (mot) Supply Column (six LMGs)

Truck Park 27
1.2.3./27 (mot) Maintenance Companies (four LMGs each)
Bakery Company (mot) 27
Butcher company (mot) 27
Administration Platoon (mot) 27
Medical Company (mot) 1./27 and 2./27 (two LMGs each)
Ambulance Company (mot) 1./27, 2./27, and 3./27
Military Police Troop (mot) 27 (two LMGs each)
Field Post Office (mot) 27

On 1 July 1943 the armoured part of the Division ie II/39 Panzer Regiment stood at:
1 Regimental Staff Signals Platoon
1 Regimental Staff Light Panzer Platoon
1 Battalion consisting of:
1 Panzer Staff Company
2 Light Panzer Companies
2 Medium Panzer Companies
Total Tanks available:
Pz. II 4
Pz. III (kz – short 5cm gun) 1
Pz. III (lang- long 5cm gun) 19
Pz. III (short 7.5cm gun) 9
Pz. IV (short 7.5 cm gun) 1
Pz. IV (long 7.5 cm gun) 31
Pz.Bef.Wg. 2

On 15 September 1943 two of the motorcycle companies received half-tracks (two armed with 8cm mortars, three with 3.7cm Pak, four HMGs, and fifty-six LMGs each).

By 7 October 1943 it was as the standard for reconnaissance Battalions:

1 Armoured Car Company (twenty four LMGs and eighteen 2cm guns)
1 Half-track Company (twenty five LMGs and sixteen 2cm guns)
1 Motorcycle Company (two 8cm mortars, four LMGs and three PzBu. 39s
1 (Half-track) Heavy reconnaissance Company consisting of:
1 Staff
1 Infantry Platoon (nine LMGs)
1 Pioneer Platoon (one 3.7cm Pak, six flamethrowers and thirteen LMGs)
1 *Panzerjäger* Platoon (three 7.5cm Pak 40 and four LMGs)
1 Infantry Gun Section (two 7.5cm leIG)
1 Half-track Gun Section (six 7.5cm guns and eight LMGs)
1 (mot) Light Reconnaissance Supply Column (three LMGs)

In August 1943 the (mot) Artillery Batteries were increased to four guns per Battery and the 15cm sFH Batteries re-equipped with F18 10cm guns.

The 297th Army Flak Battalion changed its (mot) Light Flak Battery to nine 20mm guns and two quad 20mm guns (*flakvierling*).

The 27th Supply Troop replaced the three Light (mot) supply columns with two (mot) (90 ton) transportation companies (three LMGs each).

Monthly Deliveries of Armour

1943
June - 2 lePz.Sp.Wg. (light armoured cars Sd.Kfz. 222 series.)
August – 8 Panzer IV tanks.
September – 18 Panzer IV tanks.
October – 21 mSPW (Sd.Kfz.251 series half-tracks) and 8 sPak (Sfl) Sd.Kfz. 138, 7.5cm "Marder" self propelled anti-tank guns.
December – 4 Panzer V Panther tanks (to I./Pz.Rgt.27) and 81 mSPW. The latter included 6 Sd.Kfz. 251/16 flamethowers.

1944
January – 5 mSPW. Sd.Kfz 251 half tracks.
February - 36 Panzer V Panther tanks (to I./Pz.Rgt.27)
March - 49 Panzer V Panther tanks (to I./Pz.Rgt.27) and 5 mSPW.
May – 6 mSPW all Sd.Kfz. 251/16
June – 40 Panzer IV tanks, 3 Befl.Pz.IV command tanks, 10 Jg.Pz.IV self propelled anti-tanks guns, 30 leSPW, 122 mSPW, 6 sIG (Sfl) Sd.Kfz. 138/1, 15cm self propelled Infanrty Guns.
July – 38 Panzer IV tanks, 14 Panzer V Panther tanks, 8 Flak.Pz.IV anti-aircraft tanks, 2 BeobPzIV artillery observation tanks, 11 Jg.Pz.IV 2 leSPW, 102 mSPW and 19 lePz.Sp.Wg.
August – 25 leSPW.
September – 2 Beob.Pz. IV.
October – 15 mSPW.
December – 20 mSPW, 1 sIG (Sfl)

1945
January – 4 mSPW, 1 sIG (Sfl) self propelled gun.
February – 20 Panzer IV tanks, 15 Panzer V tanks, 3 sIG (Sfl)
March – 3 Beob.Pz. IV, 2 leSPW.

Appendix 2

German Vehicles

Volkswagen Type 82 *Kübelwagen*
The *Kübelwagen* or *Kübelsitzwagen* (bucket seat car) was designed by Ferdinand Porsche and built by Volkswagen. It was used by all units in the *Whermacht* throughout World War II. Top speed was 80 kilometres per hour. Fuel capacity was 30 Litres.

Based heavily on the Volkswagen Beetle (VW Type 1 Kdf-Wagen), it could carry four fully equipped troops. Although only two wheels were driven the *Kübelwagen* had superb cross country performance due to its light weight, high ground clearance, independent suspension on all four wheels and self locking differential. The underbody was flat and smooth, which enabled the vehicle to slide over the ground surface if it needed to. The exceptional cross country performance of the *Kübelwagen* endeared it to troops on all fronts.

The first *Kübelwagens* had a 985cc (23 hp) air cooled engine, but after March 1943 this was replaced with the 1,131 cc (25 hp) engine designed for the *Schwimmwagen*. This gave more torque and power. The air cooled engine was not affected by the hot temperatures of the desert nor the extreme cold of the Eastern Front. The lack of a radiator prevented breakdown by damage caused from shrapnel or bullets. For winter conditions a small auxiliary fuel tank held volatile fuel for starting.

By the end of the war 50,435 *Kübelwagens* had been produced.

Volkswagen Type 166 Schwimmwagen
The *Schwimmwagen* was an amphibious four wheel drive vehicle used by all branches of the *Wehrmacht* in WWII. It still remains the most produced amphibious car in history and the most versatile offroad wheeled vehicle of WWII.

Based on the VW Type 86 four wheel drive prototype of the *Kübelwagen*, the *Schwimmwagen* had a bathtub lower chassis structure to move better in water. Four wheel drive was only possible in first and reverse gears. ZF self locking differentials were fitted on front and rear axles. The engine was a flat four cylinder 1,131 cc giving 25 hp. Fuel capacity was 50 litres.

In water a screw propeller was lowered down from the rear engine deck which had a mounting that was driven directly from the engine's crankshaft. Steering was carried out by turning the front wheels as on land.

From 1941 to 1944 a total of 15,584 *Schwimmwagens* were built. The vehicle was much appreciated by the troops for its cross country and river crossing abilities. Many were used by reconnaissance units, in which role they proved ideal.

Opel "Blitz" Truck. Kfz.305
With the build up to war in September 1939 the German *Wehrmacht* needed huge numbers of trucks. The excellent civilian Opel "Blitz" S (4 x 2) met army standard Kfz.305 and were drafted into military service. The truck served throughout the war and gained a reputation for toughness, cross country performance, and ease of repair which came close to legend. It also had superb load carrying capability.

Power was supplied by a 68 hp 6 cylinder 3,626 cc engine coupled to a 5 speed gearbox and transmission. Maximum speed was 85 kilometres per hour on road and 35 kilometres per hour off road. The 82 litre fuel tank gave a range of 320 km and 230 km on road and offroad respectively. The truck was rear wheel drive and weight was 3 tons.

The "Blitz," with its distinctive lightning emblem on the radiator front, was used on all fronts by all units of the *Wehrmacht*. Its low ground pressure gave it obstacle crossing ability that even some three axle trucks could not match.

The "Blitz's" popularity with the troops was even higher in the Panzer units, as the truck used gasoline fuel, the same as the tanks. Another advantage was that in very cold weather the engine could be started by pouring a bucket of boiling water over it. Diesel engines were much more difficult to start under similar conditions.

Between 1937 and 1944 a total of 14,122 Opel "Blitz" were built. The military made 140 different modifications on the basic load carrier chassis. This included radio vehicles, repair stations, fuel trucks, and troop carriers. The Soviets prized and used any that they captured in working order.

Junkers Ju 52/3m aircraft

The Junkers 52/3m was a three engined aircraft manufactured from 1932 to 1945 by the firm Junkers in Germany. It served as a civilian airliner and freight plane before the war. In military service with the *Luftwaffe* it was a troop and cargo carrier, as well as briefly a medium bomber. The troops nicknamed the Ju 52 the "Tante Ju" (Auntie Ju), or "Iron Annie."

The Ju 52 was covered by corrugated metal, which strengthened the airframe. The fuselage was rectangular, with windows along the sides. There was a door on the port side. The wings had a second part that ran along the trailing edge as a "double wing." This lowered the stall speed.

The main undercarriage was fixed and divided. Some aircraft were fitted with skis or floats instead of wheels. Engines were the BMW 770 hp 132.

Crew was three men, two pilots, and a radio operator. 18 troops or 12 stretcher patients could be carried. Top speed was 265 kilometres per hour and maximum range was 870 kilometres. Service ceiling was 5,490 metres. Armament consisted of one 13mm MG 131 machine gun in a dorsal position and two 7.92 mm MG 15 machine guns mounted in side windows.

Ju 52s were first used in military service during the Spanish Civil War. During World War II the aircraft was used in all theatres as a transport and for paratroop drops. Lightly armed and slow, the Ju 52 had to have fighter escort when flying in a combat zone. Many Ju 52s were shot down by ground fire while resupplying German units.

After the end of WWII the Ju 52 remained in military service with Portugal until the 1960s and Switzerland until 1982. Civilian operators used the Ju 52 in the late 1940s, including BEA on UK routes. In this time production was continued in France and Spain, where another 585 aircraft were produced. Total number built was 4,845.

Messerschmitt Bf 109 (Me 109)

The Messerschmitt Bf 109 fighter was a German fighter aircraft designed by Willy Messerschmitt in the early 1930s. The Me 109 was one of the first true modern fighters with its all metal construction, closed canopy, and retractable landing gear. It was produced in greater numbers than any other fighter aircraft; 33,984 were built up to April 1945.

The Me 109 was the principal fighter of the *Luftwaffe* in WWII. It was partially replaced by the Focke-Wulf Fw 190 from 1941. However, it remained the most successful fighter of WWII, shooting down more aircraft than any other fighter of any nation. The Me 109 was later developed to fill roles as a bomber escort, fighter bomber, night fighter, and ground attack aircraft.

Panzer I Sd. Kfz. 101

Built by Henschel, MAN, Krupp-Gruson, and Daimler-Benz, the Panzer I was originally known as the MG *Panzerwagen* (armoured Machine Gun tank). It was a light tank armed only with two 7.92 mm MG 13 machine guns in a small turret and was originally designed only as a training tank. Hitler's insistence on going to war in 1939 made the German army use the Panzer I in battle due to the shortage of more capable machines. The thin armour, proof against small arms and shell splinters only, and its puny armament limited the tank's use in battle.

The Panzer I was built in two versions, the original 5.4 ton Ausf A and the later 5.8 ton Ausf B, which was longer and had a more powerful engine. Both models were equipped with radio. They had the same armour, armament, and the crew of two: a commander/gunner in the turret and the driver in the right hull.

***Kleine Panzerbefehlswagen* (Sd. Kfz. 265)**

This was an armoured command vehicle based on the Panzer 1 that deleted the turret and in its place substituted an armoured superstructure containing map boards and FuG6 and FuG2 radios. A single 7.92 mm MG 13 or 34 machine gun in a ball mount in the front of the superstructure was the only armament. Some were converted to armoured ambulances.

***Munitionsschlepper auf Panzerkampfwagen I Ausf A* (Sd Kfz 111)**

This vehicle was a Panzer I Ausf A with the turret removed and a large hinged hatch substituted. This served as an armoured ammunition supply vehicle to front line tanks in Panzer regiments.

Panzerkampfwagen I Ausf A ohne Aufbau
Panzerkampfwagen I Ausf B ohne Aufbau

These were driver training vehicles with the superstructure and turret removed.

Panzer II Sd.Kfz. 121

Originally called the 2cm MG *Panzerwagen*, the Panzer II was designed to support the Panzer I with a weapon that could fire high explosive and armour piercing rounds. Armament was a 2cm KwK 30 L/55 cannon with a coaxial 7.92 mm MG 34 machine gun. Crew was three men: commander/gunner, loader, and driver.

The tank was produced in several variants: Ausf a, b, c, D, E, and F. Weight and armour increased from 7.6 tons in the a to 9.5 tons for the F. Engines were up-rated to cope with the heavier weight.

From the c version the road wheels were increased in size and independently sprung. The final F version had a proper commander's cupola with periscopes rather than a two piece hatch.

Armour thickness was 13mm on the early models to 30 mm on the F. This and the 2 cm armament relegated the tank to reconnaissance and liaison duties after the Polish campaign. In 1942 the chassis started being converted to carriages for self propelled guns and tank destroyers (*Panzerjager*).

7.5 cm Pak 40/2 *Fahrgestell Panzerkampfwagen* II (Sf) Marder II. Sd.Kfz. 131

This was a tank destroyer (*Panzerjager*) created by mounting the 7.5 cm PaK 40 anti-tank gun on the obsolete Panzer II chassis. The gun was mounted in an open topped fighting compartment protected by 30mm front armour and 10-15 mm armour on the sides. This made the vehicle quite vulnerable.

Power was supplied by a Maybach HL 62 TRM 140 hp engine giving a top speed of 40 km/h. Weight was 10.8 tonnes and operational range was 190 km. Thirty-seven rounds were carried for the main armament, and secondary armament was a 7.92 mm MG 34 or 42 machine gun. The crew consisted of three men.

Panzer III Sd.Kfz. 141

Built originally by Daimler-Benz, production was also undertaken by Henschel, FAMO, MAN, MIAG, and MNH. The Panzer III was originally designed to be the main tank of the *Panzerwaffe*, but it was soon obvious after the campaigns in the West and on meeting the superior Soviet T-34 and KW1 that it was under-gunned and under-armoured for this task.

The size of the turret ring did not allow for much needed heavier weapons to be installed, and the tank's role was taken over by the larger Panzer IV from 1942.

The Panzer III was crewed by five men: commander, gunner, loader, driver, and radio operator. Production started in 1937, and there were 12 versions: Ausf A to Ausf N, progressively being up-armoured and up-gunned. Weight increased from 15.4 tons to 23 tons in the final model, and more powerful engines were used in the later variants.

The main armament started as the 3.7cm KwK L/46.5, then the short 5 cm KwK L/42 in Ausf G, H, and J models. This was followed by the long 5 cm KwK 39 L/60 in the later J, L, and M tanks (designated Sd. Kfz. 141/1). Finally, the Ausf N (Sd.Kfz. 141/2) got the short 7.5 cm KwK L/24 made redundant from the Panzer IV. The Panzer III N was now purely a support tank, eg for Tiger tank units, a role originally designed for the later Panzer IV.

All models had secondary armament of two 7.92mm MG 34, one coaxial in the turret and one in the front left side fired by the radio operator. The Ausf M and N versions were fitted with additional armour plates hung over the turret sides and rear and over both sides of the superstructure (*Schurtzen*). This was introduced to combat the effective Soviet anti-tank rifles, although later it was found to be equally useful to defeat hollow charge rounds (HEAT).

Specialist versions of the Panzer III were produced:

"Flammpanzer" *Panzerkampfwagen* III (F1) Sd.Kfz. 141/3: a flamethrower tank designed for use at Stalingrad. It carried a 14mm flamethrower instead of the main armament. Based on the Ausf M, one hundred were built.

Panzerkampfwagen III als Tauchpanzer: Equipped with waterproofed fabric covers and snorkel devices for air intake and exhaust emission, these tanks were designed for Operation Sealion, the invasion of Britain. *Tauchpanzer*, or "diving tanks," could operate up to depths of 15 metres. After the cancellation of "Sealion" *Tauchpanzers* were adapted for river crossings and proved useful in the initial stages of the invasion of Russia.

Panzerbefehlswagen, or command tanks: Sd.Kfz. 266 to 268. These were based on the Ausf D, E, and H versions. Main armament was removed and replaced by map boards and additional radio sets. Both turret and superstructure had additional vision ports. A dummy gun was mounted, but the *Befehlswagen* could be easily recognised by the large frame aerial on the rear deck. Due to heavy losses a later version was produced that kept the 5 cm main armament but with fewer rounds carried.

Artillerie-Panzerbeobachtungswagen Sd.Kfz. 143: An artillery observation vehicle to keep up with the fully tracked self propelled artillery, such as the Wespe and Hummel vehicles. Main armament was again removed and a dummy gun fitted. One 7.92 mm MG34 was carried in the turret front. A periscopic sighting device was installed in the turret roof.

Bergpanzer III: These were armoured recovery tanks with the turret removed and a crane and other recovery equipment carried.

Panzer IV Sd.Kfz. 161

Built by Krupp BW and first issued to troops in 1938, the Panzer IV was originally designed as a support tank with the armament of a short 7.5cm gun. It was crewed by five men: commander, gunner, loader, driver, and radio operator.

Due to the large turret ring it could be up-gunned with longer and more powerful 7.5cm guns to cope with the T-34 and KW1 tanks fielded by the Soviets. In addition there were two MG34 7.92 mm machine guns, one co-axial in the turret and one fired by the radio operator in the front right hull. By 1943 it had overtaken the Panzer III as the tank to fight enemy armour. Panzer IIIs were relegated to support roles or the chassis were used for self propelled guns (Stug III).

Panzer IVs were built in nine main variants from the first Ausf A through to the final Ausf J. Armour protection and weight increased from 20 tons in early models to 25 tons in the final version.

Models Ausf A, B, C, D, E, and F1 used the short 7.5 cm KwK37 L/24, then models Ausf F2 and G were equipped with the long KwK40 L/43. Later Ausf G, H, and J benefited from the even more powerful KwK40 L/48.

Ausf G, H, and J were also equipped with the same sort of additional armour plates hung over the turret and the superstructure (*Schurtzen*) as the Panzer III.

The Panzer IV served throughout the war on all fronts, the only German tank to do so. Even with the introduction of the Panther, Panzer IVs were still produced and soldiered on in the second Battalion of Panzer regiments until the last shots were fired in WWII.

Specialist versions of the Panzer IV included:

Panzerkampfwagen IV als Tauchpanzer: "Diving tanks" based on the Panzer IV on similar lines to the *Tauchpanzer* III.

Panzerbefehlswagen mit 7.5cm KwK L/48: A command tank based on the Panzer IV. The main armament was retained due to the lager size of the vehicle. Extra radios and less conspicuous antennae were fitted. These were an aerial for the FuG5 radio on the turret roof and a star antenna on the rear right hand tail plate for the FuG7 or FuG8 radio.

Panzerbeobachtungswagen IV: An artillery observation vehicle retaining main armament, but had a rotating periscope on the left hand side of the turret roof.

Panzer VI Tiger Sd. Kfz. 181

The result of competition between Henschel and Porsche to develop a new heavy breakthrough tank, Henschel's design won and was put into production as the *Panzerkampfwagen* VI Ausf E, but was known as the Tiger.

The Tiger weighed 56 tons and had eight sets of interleaved road wheels. The suspension was provided by torsion bars. Armament was provided by a tank version of the famous 8.8cm gun, the KwK 36 L/56, and two 7.92 mm MG 34 Machine Guns, one coaxial and the other in the front left hand side.

The Tiger was thickly armoured - 100mm at the front and 80 mm at the sides and back. The turret was a horseshoe shaped piece of armour. Crew consisted of 5 men: the commander, gunner, loader in the turret, and driver and radio operator in the front hull.

Tigers were placed in special companies or Battalions and used to achieve certain missions where their powerful armament and thick armour would be an advantage. Later versions had all steel wheels, a better commander's cupola with periscopes, and Zimmerit anti-magnetic mine coating.

First used at Leningrad in August 1942, such a powerful, well armoured and armed tank instantly gave the Germans a technical advantage, but not enough could be produced to counter the Allies' greater numbers. Nevertheless, the Tiger took a heavy toll of Allied armour on all fronts.

Panzer VI Tiger Ausf B *Konigstiger* (Kingtiger) Sd.Kfz. 182

In January 1943 it was decided a new Tiger was required that could mount the 8.8cm KwK 43 L/71 gun and have frontal armour of 150 mm. Side armour remained at 80 mm. All the armour plate was sloped to give added protection, particularly the frontal armour.

The first fifty Kingtigers had a turret designed by Porsche, but the curved front plate deflected shots through the hull roof. Subsequent Kingtigers had an improved turret by Henschel. Suspension was torsion bars on nine sets of interleaved road wheels. Crew was five men: commander, gunner, loader (turret), driver, and radio operator (hull).

Secondary armament was two 7.92 mm MG 34 machine guns, one co-axial with the main armament and one in the front hull.

The first Kingtigers were delivered to fighting units in June 1944 serving in *schwere* Panzer *Abteilung*, the heavy tank detachments. A number of Kingtigers were converted to command tanks with additional radio sets replacing some of the main gun ammunition. These had the designation Pz. BefWg. mit 8.8cm KwK 43 L/71.

Panzer V Panther Sd.Kfz. 171

The Panther was classed as a medium tank despite weighing 43 tons. The design came from studying the Russian T-34, which came as a great shock to the Germans with its sloped armour and 7.6 cm gun. The Panther was first used in July 1943 at the battle of Kursk, and despite being introduced after the Tiger, the Panther was given the designation *Panzerkampfwagen* V.

The Panther had sloped armour 100 mm to 40 mm thick. The main gun was a powerful 7.5cm KwK 42 L/70 backed up by two 7.92 mm MG 34 Machine Guns, one coaxial and the other in the front left hull.

As with usual German practice the five man crew was retained: commander, gunner, loader (turret), driver, and radio operator (hull).

The Panther was produced in three main variants:

Ausf D: earliest production with a drum commander's cupola and no ball mount for the hull machine gun.

Ausf A: mid-production introduced a ball mounting for the hull machine gun, commander's cupola with periscopes, and an episcope for the loader on the turret right hand roof. The small ammunition loading hatch on the turret left hand side was eliminated.

Ausf G: Late production introduced single piece, thicker side armour, a driver's periscope in place of the hatch in the front plate, and the pivoting hatches for the driver and radio operator replaced with hinged ones. Final production Ausf Gs had a crew heater, flame damper exhausts, and a gun mantlet that had an armoured "chin" that stopped deflected shots going through the hull top armour.

The Panther is regarded as one of the best if not the best tank of WWII. The French used Panthers after the war. There was never enough produced to fully equip the German Panzer regiments. Panthers were issued to the 1st Battalion and the Panzer IV equipped the 2nd Battalion of the Panzer divisions. The Panther Variants included:

Panzerbefehlswagen mit 7.7 cm KwK 42 L/70: a command tank based on the Panther. The main gun was retained with fewer rounds to make space for an extra radio. A FuG 5 was carried in the turret and a FuG 7 or FuG 8 in the hull front over the gearbox. A star aerial was placed on the centre rear of the engine deck and a 1.4 m rod aerial on the turret roof right hand side.

Panzerbeobachtungswagen Panther: an artillery observation tank based on the Panther with a dummy main gun. A stereoscopic range finder was carried. Radio fittings and aerial configuration was as in the *Panzerbefehlswagen*.

***Panzerkampfwagen* 38(t) Sd.Kfz. 140**

When Germany took over Czechoslovakia they also took over its excellent tank production. The Panzer 38(t) was a Czechoslovakian tank, designation LTN. vz. 38, that was used by the Germans.

The 38(t) was of riveted construction. Non-sloped armour varied from 10mm to 25mm. This was increased later to 50mm. Weight was 9.5 tonnes. The tank had a crew of 4 men: commander/gunner and loader in the turret, and driver and radio operator in the hull.

Main armament was the 3.7cm Skoda A7 gun designated by the Germans as 3.7cm KwK 38(t) L/47.8 in the turret. Secondary armament consisted of two 7.92mm ZB53 machine guns. The radio operator manned one in the hull and the second was mounted beside the main armament in a ball mount. This meant it had to be trained on targets independently of the main armament.

As the turret could not take a bigger weapon production of the gun tank ceased in 1942. The reliable chassis and mechanics were used as the basis for several self propelled guns and tank hunters.

***Panzerjager* 38(t) mit 7.5cm PaK40/3 (Sd.Kfz. 138) Marder**

After the Czech 38(t) tank had become obsolete as a battle tank it was found that the chassis was able to be used as a gun carriage for anti-tank weapons. At first stocks of captured Russian 7.62cm PaK 36(r) were used and then the German 7.5cm PaK 40/3.

Early versions (Ausf H) retained the engine at the rear and the gun was mounted in the middle of the vehicle. Later the engine was moved to the middle and the gun mounting to the rear, which gave the crew more space and allowed them greater armour protection. This was designated Ausf M. Crew for all versions was four men and secondary armament consisted of one machine gun.

15cm *Schweres Infanteriegeschütz* 33 (Sf) *auf Panzerkampfwagen* 38(t) Ausf H (Sd. Kfz. 138/1). Grille
15cm *Schweres Infanteriegeschütz* 33 (Sf) *auf Selbstfahrlafette* 38(t) (Sf) Ausf K (Sd. Kfz. 138/1). Grille

These both used the Panzer 38(t) tank chassis to mount the heavy infantry gun sIG33. Secondary armament was one 7.92mm MG34 machine gun. The Ausf H mounted the gun in the middle and had a crew of five men. The later Ausf K had the engine in the middle and the gun moved to the rear. As with the "Marder," this arrangement gave more space for the crew to serve the weapon and allowed for better armour protection. Crew was reduced to four men.

A disadvantage of the Grille was the small amount of main gun ammunition it could carry, 15 in the Ausf H and 18 in the Ausf K. The gun elevated to +70 degrees to allow indirect fire. On high elevation the gun was protected by a heavy steel spring flap.

Grilles served in *schwere Infanteriegeschütz* (heavy infantry gun) companies of *Panzergrenadier* Regiments in Panzer divisions and *Panzergrenadier* Divisions from early 1943 to the end of the war. Both versions could be found in the same unit.

***Sturmgeschütz* III Sd.Kfz. 142 (Stug)**
***Gepanzerter Selbstfahrlafette für Sturmgeschütz* 7.5 cm Kanone**

This vehicle was based on WWI German assault guns that were pulled close to the enemy for the support of infantry attacks. This lead to heavy losses in the crews, so an armoured vehicle was selected to fulfil this role. The chassis was based on the Panzer III, with the turret removed and the gun fixed in an armoured superstructure. Traverse left and right was limited so the vehicle had to be moved to aim the gun.

Stug IIIs had seven versions Ausf A through Ausf G. The early models had a short 7.5 StuK 37 L/24 gun replaced from the Ausf F by the more powerful StuK 40 L/48. Later Ausf F and G Stugs also mounted a 7.92 mm MG 34 over the loader's hatch for close defence (Sd.Kfz. 142/1). Final production introduced a coaxial MG 34 with the main armament.

Armour and weight increased from 19.6 tons in the Ausf A to 23.9 tons in the Ausf G. Engines were up-rated to account for the heavier vehicles. Crew was four men: commander, gunner, loader, and driver.

Stugs were a great success. They were originally organised in Stug brigades that were allocated out for specific tasks. The longer gunned Stugs increasingly took on the role of tank destroyers. Being easier and cheaper to build Stugs replaced tanks in Panzer units towards the end of the war.

10.5cm *Sturmhaubitze* 42 (Sd.Kfz. 142/2)

This was a Stug where the main armament was replaced with a 10.5 cm howitzer to provide a heavier high explosive weapon for Stug units.

Sd.Kfz. 10 Half-track

This was a light half-track that saw widespread use with the German armed forces, mainly as a prime mover for lighter towed weapons. It could carry up to eight men in addition to towing the gun.

The vehicle was produced in several versions. The Sd.Kfz. 10/1 was the basic prime mover. The Sd.Kfz. 10/4 carried the 2 cm flak 30 or 38 on a self propelled mount and towed a trailer for the gun's ammunition.

Suspension was by torsion bars, and the engine was a petrol Maybach 6 cylinder water cooled HL42 TRKM giving 100 hp. Top speed was 75 km/h on road, and the range was 300 km on road and 150 km cross country. Fuel capacity was 110 litres. Approximately 14,000 were built by several manufacturers, including Demag, Alderwerke, and Büssing-NAG.

Sd.Kfz. 250 Half-track

The Sd.Kfz. 250 was a light armoured half-track built by Demag. The front wheels were not powered, but the length of track (more a three quarter track than a half-track) gave it good mobility.

The vehicle was based on the Sd.Kfz. 10 prime mover and adopted in service in 1939 to supplement the standard armoured half-track, the Sd.Kfz. 251. The Sd.Kfz. 250 was used in specialist roles. Twelve versions were produced to undertake various tasks in armoured units. The troop carrier version was used for reconnaissance and was armed with two 7.92 mm MG34 or MG42 machine guns. Other variants carried 2 cm, 3.7 cm, or 7.5 cm guns to support their role.

Weight was 5.5 tons. Power came from a Maybach HL 42TRKM six cylinder petrol engine giving 100 hp. Operational range was 300 km and top speed 60 km/h. Armour was a thin 8-15 mm but well sloped. This gave protection only against small arms fire and small shell splinters, however.

The early versions were made from multi-angled plates which made the vehicle expensive to build. Production was stopped in 1943 after 4,200 were built. A second design, the "neue art" or new version, replaced it. The second design was simpler and thus speeded up manufacture.

Sd.Kfz. 251

This vehicle was an armoured half-track based on the Sd.Kfz. 11 prime mover. It was designed and first built by the firm of Hanomag and produced throughout the war by several other manufacturers. The front wheels were not powered, but the long track length gave it better cross country mobility.

The vehicle was meant to carry a squad of infantry (*Panzergrenadiers*) to battle up with the tanks. The thin armour (6 to 12.5 mm) gave protection from small arms fire and shell splinters. The open top (like the Sd.Kfz. 250) meant it was more vulnerable than a fully closed vehicle like a tank.

The Sd.Kfz. 251 was built mainly in the standard infantry carrier armed with a 7.92 mm MG 34 or 42 machine gun at the front of the open topped compartment behind an armoured shield and a second at the rear for anti-aircraft defence. Twenty-three variants were produced for various roles with armament that varied for purpose.

There were never enough troop carriers built to equip all the *Panzergrenadier* Battalions. Many had to be transported in trucks. A second simpler production design was started in 1943 that speeded up production, the Sd.Kfz. 251D.

The Sd.Kfz. 251 was powered by a Maybach HL 42 six cylinder engine giving 100 hp. Weight was 7.8 tonnes. Range was 300 km, maximum speed was 52.5 km/h, and crew consisted of two men. Ten infantry could be carried.

After the war the Czechs built a version with a diesel engine and an armoured roof. This was called the OT-810.

Sd.Kfz. 251/16 – *Mittlerer Flammpanzerwagen*

A version of the SdKfz 251 half-track armed with two 14cm flamethrowers and two 7.92mm MG 34 or 42 machine guns. Crew was 5 men. 700 litres of flame fuel was carried that allowed 80 bursts of up to two seconds duration. 2,010 rounds of 7.92mm were carried for the machine guns.

The flamethrowers were fitted on either side of the vehicle with a traverse of 90 degrees and a maximum elevation of 40 degrees. Maximum range was about 35 metres.

Some versions were also armed with a portable 7mm *Flammwerfer* 42 with 10 metres of hose to the flame fuel tank.

SdKfz 251/17 – *Mittlerer Schützenpanzerwagen* (2cm) – *Auführung* D

Designed for fighting low flying aircraft or ground targets, the first production vehicles were delivered to the troops in November 1944.

A heavy pedestal mount fixed to the chassis was fitted with a 2 cm. Flak 38 gun. This had 360 degree traverse over the tall sides of the Sd.Kfz. 251. A small armoured shield protected the gunner and breech.

The Sd.Kfz. 251/17 had a crew of three: a driver in the hull, and a gunner and loader who were seated either side of the pedestal. The weight of the gun when elevated was balanced by the gunner's weight. Elevation was -10 to +60 degrees. Secondary armament was an MG 42 machine gun.

Slightly over 150 Sd.Kfz 251/17 were delivered from November 1944 to February 1945. Theoretical allocation was a 1 to 3 ratio with the troop carrying vehicles.

Sd.Kfz. 251/21 – *Mittlerer Schützenpanzerwagen* (1.5/2cm. Drilling) – *Ausführung* D

The role of this vehicle was the same as the Sd.Kfz. 251/17 but with different armament. The *Luftwaffe* had standardised on the 3cm cannon to equip its planes. This left many 1.5cm and 2cm cannon surplus to requirements. The *Heer* was keen to use these and mounted them on a triple pedestal mount designed for *Kriegsmarine* use. The gunner was protected by a three plate shield. On some vehicles the superstructure sides and front were heightened.

The gunner's weight balanced the guns when elevated. Angle of elevation varied from -5 to +49 degrees. Benches inside the vehicle were replaced by 3 single seats. Crew consisted of four or five men.

The outer two guns had 250 round feeds, but as the middle one was hard to reach it had a feed of 500 rounds and so needed resupply less often. Rounds consisted of ball and tracer, but armour piercing rounds could also be used.

The first fifty vehicles were armed with the 1.5cm MG 151/15. Later vehicles had the more powerful 2cm weapons. In total 387 Sd.Kfz. 251/21 were delivered to front line units between September 1944 and February 1945.

Sd.Kfz. 251/22 – *Mittlerer Schützenpanzer* (7.5cm Pak) – *Ausführung* D

The German military proposed to mount the 7.5cm Pak 40 L/46 on the Sd.Kfz. 251 on 27 November 1944. When Hitler read this he immediately ordered that all Sd.Kfz. 251/9 already armed with the short 7.5cm L/24 gun were to be armed with the more powerful weapon. This gave rise to the Sd.Kfz. 251/22. Conversion kits were supplied to convert other Sd.Kfz. 251/9 to the more powerful gun.

The Sd.Kfz. 251/22 had a powerful punch but was overweight, which strained the chassis and power plant.

Ammunition storage was 17 rounds in a floor rack and 5 in a ready rounds rack on the right hand side of the interior. Crew was four men. About 100 Sd.Kfz. 251/22 were factory built, being delivered up to February 1945.

Appendix 3

Soviet Tanks

T-34
The T-34 is regarded as the most effective and influential tank in WWII.

It was the main tank fielded by the Red Army and the most produced model of the war. The tank could be easily and quickly assembled in a variety of factories, being first produced at the KhPZ factory in Kharkov, Ukraine. Armament was a 7.62 cm gun and two 7.62 mm machine guns in the first models, up-arming to an 8.5 cm main gun in a larger three man turret in 1944.

Weight started at 34 tons, and the tank was powered by an effective 12 cylinder V-2 diesel engine giving 500 hp. The choice of diesel was an advantage over petrol in the war on the eastern front. Wide tracks also gave an edge when fighting in sub zero temperatures, crossing ice, snow, and mud in which the German tanks could not move. The use of Christie coil spring suspension gave excellent cross country performance. Top speed was 34 mph.

The crew consisted of 4 men: commander/gunner, loader, driver, and co-driver. This increased to 5 when the larger 3 man turrets were introduced allowing for a gunner. The larger turret allowed the commander to command the tank and the gunner and loader to operate the gun. Cleverly sloped armour gave protection against most German anti-tank weapons when first encountered and started an up-gunning of the German armoured forces. The German troops started calling their PaK 36 3.7cm anti-tank gun "the army's door knocker" due to its inability to penetrate the T-34's armour. The poor training of Soviet tankers and tactical ineptitude of commanders limited the tank's effectiveness and led to heavy losses.

Although weak transmission and clutch, lack of radios, poor tactics, and a two man turret in the initial models hampered its early effectiveness, the T-34 came as a great shock to the Germans. It greatly influenced the design of the Panther tank and was respected by the Germans, who used many captured examples often repainted in their own colours.

Greater production gave the T-34 a numerical advantage over the technical advantage of later German tanks like the Panther and the superior training of the German crews. It is some measure of the T-34's quality that modernised versions were in use from the end of WWII up to 1996 in various countries.

KV-1 (KW-1)
Named after the Soviet defence chief, the Kliment Voroshilov or KV-1 was a heavy tank weighing 45 tons, twice that of German tanks then in service. Armament consisted of a 7.62 cm main gun and three 7.62 mm machine guns. Crew was five men: driver, co-driver, commander/gunner, loader, and another co-driver who operated the turret rear machine gun.

The thick armour of 90 mm maximum and heavy armament gave the Germans considerable problems when they first encountered the KV-1. As the anti-tank weapons could not penetrate the armour, 8.8cm Flak guns or pioneer demolition teams had to be used to knock out any KV-1 encountered.

Despite good cross country performance the KV-1 was slow and difficult to steer. It also suffered from an unreliable transmission. Crew layout and visibility was poor. The improved German anti-tank guns coming into service could penetrate its armour and its slow speed caused it to be easily outflanked. The cheaper T-34 had as good armament and was much easier to produce. This led to the KV series of tanks being gradually phased out in favour of the improved T-34.

A variant was the KV-2, which was armed with a 15.2cm howitzer in a huge turret. It was designed as a "bunker buster" after Red Army experience in Finland. It was even less mobile than the KV-1, and the heavy turret could not be turned on sloping ground.

The Germans used limited numbers of KVs against their former owners.

Infantry Tank Mark III Valentine

This was a private design by Vickers-Armstrong based on the A10 Cruiser tank. It was intended to combine the weight of a cruiser tank with the thick armour of an Infantry tank. This made the size of the tank very small, particularly in the cramped two man turret and the crew compartment.

Despite being unpopular with the War Department, the grave losses at Dunkirk and its successful trials lead to the tank being rushed into production. The Valentine became the most numerous tank produced by Great Britain during WWII. 6,855 were made in Britain and another 1,420 in Canada. It was cheap and reliable, and remained in production until April 1944.

The Valentine was the main export to the Soviet Union under Lend-Lease. 2,394 of the British production and 1,388 of the Canadian built tanks made their way east. The Soviets used them from the battle of Moscow until the end of the war. Soviet tankers criticised the Valentine for its slow speed and weak main armament. However, they liked its small size, good armour, and reliability.

Crew was three men: commander, gunner, and driver. Weight was 17 tons and top speed 24 kph. The Mark III had a diesel engine and a range of 145 km. Armament consisted of a 2 pounder 4.0 cm gun and one 7.92 mm BESA machine gun.

M3 Lee

This was an American 28 ton medium tank that had been designed as an interim solution to a main tank design. The USA had been concerned by the success of the new German tank designs, such as the Panzer III and Panzer IV. The Lee's main armament was a 7.5 cm main gun in a sponson on the right hull front. This was backed up by a 3.7 cm gun in a small turret on top of the hull, and on top of this was a small commander's cupola with a M1919A4 .30 machine gun. Another M1919A4 was set co-axially with the 3.7cm and two more in the hull front alongside the driver.

The 7.5 cm gun could fire high explosive rounds and armour piercing shot. The 3.7 cm was only effective with anti-armour rounds.

By putting the main gun in the sponson the tank could be brought into production faster by not having to wait for a suitable turret to accept it.

The M3 Lee was crewed by 7 men: commander, 3.7cm gunner, 3.7cm loader, 7.5cm gunner, 7.5cm loader, radio operator, and driver. The tank had a range of 193 km and a top speed of 40 kmh on road and 26 kmh off road. It was powered by a 400 hp Wright (Continental) R975 EC2 engine.

The M3 was first used in action in the North African desert by the British, who adapted the turret to take a larger radio and called their tanks "Grants." They did not like the tall profile, which made it a good target and prevented the main gun being used in "hull down" positions. However, the tank brought much needed firepower to the British desert forces. It also outclassed the British designs in reliability and armour protection. Another problem identified was the tendency of the rivets used in construction to fly off if the tank was hit and cause damage and injuries inside the tank.

Under lend-lease arrangements over 1,300 Lees went to the Soviet Union in the years 1942 and '43. In the intense tank combat on the eastern front the Lee was even less popular than in the desert when its disadvantages were known. The Red Army tank crews nicknamed it a "coffin for seven brothers," and few were used after mid-1943, being replaced by better Soviet designs or lend-lease Shermans. The exception was the Arcic Litsa front in the direction of Kirkenes, where the Germans fielded no tanks. Here the Red Army's offensive of October 1944 was the eastern front's swan song for the M3.

M3 Stuart

The M3 Stuart was a 15 ton light tank developed from the earlier M2 series. It was armed with a 3.7 cm gun in the turret and up to five M1919A4 0.30 Browning machine guns: one co-axial, one in the hull front, two in the side sponsons, and an anti-aircraft mounted gun on the commander's hatch. The tank was powered by a 250 hp Continental-Wright air-cooled radial engine, giving it a range of 120 km and top speed of 58 kmh on road and 30 kmh off-road. Crew was four men: driver, co-driver, loader, and commander/gunner.

The British were again the first to use the American tank in action in North Africa. They liked the high speed and mechanical reliability, giving the tank the unofficial nickname "Honey." However, the British were concerned about the weak main armament, which was not as good as German tanks, and the poor layout involving the two man turret.

After the arrival of U.S. medium tanks the British used the Stuart mainly for reconnaissance.

The Red Army obtained the Stuart under lend-lease and was even less happy with it. They considered it under-gunned, poorly armoured, prone to catching fire if hit, and sensitive to fuel quality, as the Stuart used high octane aviation fuel. The Stuart was, however, superior to early soviet light tanks, such as the T-60. Stuarts remained in Red Army use until 1944.

Being cheap and reliable, Stuarts remained in use until 1996, particularly with armies that did not require heavy main battle tanks.

Bibliography

Neither Fear nor Hope. General Frido von Senger und Etterlin.

Panzers in Russia. A pictorial history of the German armoured divisions on the Eastern Front 1941-45. Horst Scheibert and Ulrich Elfrath.

Uniforms, Organisation and History of the Panzertruppe. Roger James Bender and Warren W. Odegard.

Fire Brigades. The Panzer Divisions 1943 – 45. Kamen Nevenkin. J.J. Fedorowitz 2008.

Panzerwrecks 2. Lee Archer and William Auerbach.

Panzerwrecks 4. Lee Archer and William Auerbach.

SS Armor on the Eastern Front 1943-45. Velimir Vuksic.

Thanks to all the members of the Track-Link and Schwerpunkt Forums who answered David's questions on German terms and abbreviations.

The authors would be grateful if readers can send in any information they have on 17.Panzer Division, particularly Panzer Regiment 39. This would be used in future publications.

Contact can be made through the publishers.